A TREATISE
ON THE MEDICAL
JURISPRUDENCE
OF INSANITY

THE HISTORICAL FOUNDATIONS OF FORENSIC PSYCHIATRY AND PSYCHOLOGY

A DA CAPO PRESS REPRINT SERIES

A TREATISE
ON THE MEDICAL
JURISPRUDENCE
OF INSANITY

BY
ISAAC RAY

DA CAPO PRESS • NEW YORK • 1983

Library of Congress Cataloging in Publication Data

Ray, Isaac, 1807–1881.
A treatise on the medical jurisprudence of insanity.

(The Historical foundations of forensic psychiatry and psychology)
Reprint. Originally published: Boston: C.C. Little and J. Brown,
1838.
    1. Insanity — Jurisprudence — United States.
I. Title. II. Series.
KF9242.R3 1983   614′.1   82-072289
ISBN 0-306-76181-1

This Da Capo Press reprint edition of *A Treatise on the Medical
Jurisprudence of Insanity* is an unabridged republication of the edition published in Boston in 1838.

Published by Da Capo Press, Inc.
A Subsidiary of Plenum Publishing Corporation
233 Spring Street, New York, N.Y. 10013

A

TREATISE

ON THE

MEDICAL JURISPRUDENCE

OF

INSANITY.

By I. RAY, M. D.

BOSTON:

CHARLES C. LITTLE AND JAMES BROWN.

M.DCCC.XXXVIII.

BOSTON:

PRINTED BY FREEMAN AND BOLLES,

WASHINGTON-STREET.

TO THE

Hon. HORACE MANN;

TO WHOSE PERSEVERING EXERTIONS,

OUR COUNTRY IS MAINLY INDEBTED

FOR ONE OF ITS NOBLEST INSTITUTIONS FOR AMELIORATING

THE CONDITION OF THE INSANE,

THIS WORK IS RESPECTFULLY INSCRIBED

AS A HUMBLE ACKNOWLEDGMENT OF ESTEEM,

BY

I. RAY.

PREFACE.

FEW, probably, whose attention has not been particularly directed to the subject, are aware, how far the condition of the law relative to insanity is behind the present state of our knowledge concerning that disease. While so much has been done, within a comparatively short period, to promote the comfort of the insane, and so much improvement has been effected in the methods of treating their disorder, as to have deprived it of half its terrors, it is both a curious and a melancholy fact, that so little has been accomplished towards regulating their personal and social rights, by more correct and enlightened principles of jurisprudence. While nations are vying with one another in the excellence of their public establishments for the accommodation of this unfortunate class of our fellow-men, and physicians are every year publishing some instance of an unexampled proportion of cures, we remain perfectly satisfied with the wisdom of our predecessors in every thing relative to their legal relations. This, no doubt, is mainly the fault of medical men themselves, who have neglected to obtain for the results of their researches, that influence on the law of insanity, which they have exerted on its pathology and therapeutics. In general treatises on legal medicine, this branch of it has always received a share of attention; but the space allotted to it is altogether too limited to admit of those details, which can alone be of any really useful service; and it is one of those branches on which the author is usually the least qualified by his own experience, to throw any additional light. Insanity itself is an affection so obscure and perplexing, and the occasions have now become so frequent and important when its legal relations should be properly understood, that an ampler field of illustration and discussion is required for this purpose, than is afforded by a solitary chapter in works of this description.

Notwithstanding the great prevalence of insanity in Great Britain, and the vast amount of property affected by legal regulations and decisions respecting it, yet the English language does not furnish a single work, in which the various forms and degrees of mental derangement are treated in reference to their effect on the rights and duties of man. Dr. Haslam's tract on *Medical Jurisprudence as it Relates to Insanity*, (1807), which was republished in this country in 1819 by Dr. Cooper, in a volume of tracts by various English writers on different subjects of medical jurisprudence, though abounding in valuable reflections, is altogether too brief and general, to be of much practical service as a book of reference. Among a few other works more or less directly concerned with this subject, or in which some points of it are particularly touched upon, the *Inquiry Concerning the Indications of Insanity*, (1830), by Dr. Conolly, late Professor in the London University, is worthy of especial notice in this connexion, for the remarkable ability and sound judgment with which all its views are conceived and supported. Though not entirely nor chiefly devoted to the legal relations of the insane, yet the medico-legal student will find his views of insanity enlarged and improved by a careful perusal of it; and every physician will do well to ponder the suggestions contained in the chapter on the "*Duties of medical men when consulted concerning the state of a patient's mind.*" In the JUDGMENTS of Sir John Nicholl, (contained in Haggard, Phillimore and Addams's Reports) in the Ecclesiastical Courts, which, in their jurisdiction of WILLS, have frequent occasion to inquire into the effect of mental diseases on the powers of the mind, are also to be found, not only some masterly analyses of heterogeneous and conflicting evidence, but an acquaintance with the phenomena of insanity in its various forms, that would be creditable to the practical physician, and an application of it to the case under consideration, that satisfies the most cautious with the correctness of the decision.

In Germany this branch of legal medicine has received a little more attention, and in a work entitled, *Die Psycologie in ihren Hauptanwendungen auf die Rechtspflege*, (*Psychology in its chief Applications to the Administration of Justice*) by J. C. Hoffbauer, a Doctor of Laws and Professor in the University of Halle, and published in 1809, we had, till quite recently, the only complete and methodical treatise on insanity in connexion with its legal relations. It bears the impress of a philosophical mind, accustomed to observe the mental operations when under the influence of disease; it contains a happy analysis of some states of mental impairment, and its doctrines are generally correct, and in many instances in advance of his own, and even our time. Hoffbauer, however, not being a practical physician, was less disposed to consider insanity in its pathological, than in its psychological relations, and consequently has attached too little importance to its connexion with physical causes, and to the classification and description of its different forms by means of which they may be recognised and distinguished from one another. It is also too deeply imbued with the peculiar metaphysical subtleties in which his countrymen are so fond of indulging, to suit the taste or convenience of the English reader. It has been translated into French by Dr. Chambeyron, with many valuable notes by Esquirol and Itard.

In France, M. Georget has cultivated this field of inquiry with a success proportioned to his indefatigable zeal and diligence; and his various writings will ever be resorted to by future inquirers, as they have been by the author of the present work, as to a fund of original and interesting information. Having long been devoted to the study of insanity, and especially to the observation of the manners and character of the insane, he was peculiarly well qualified to treat this subject in a spirit corresponding to the present condition of the science. His work entitled, *Des Maladies mentales, considérées dans leurs rapports avec la législation civile et criminelle,* (1827), is an admirable manual, and though but a humble brochure, it yet abounds with valuable information and is pervaded by sound and philosophical views. In his *Examen médical des procès criminels des nommés Léger, Feldtman, Lecouffe,* (1825), and his *Discussion médico-légale sur la Folie,* (1826), as well as a sequel to the last, entitled, *Nouvelle discussion médico-légale sur la Folie,* (1828), he has collected accounts of numerous criminal trials, in which insanity was pleaded in defence of the accused, and has taken the occasion to discuss the many important questions to which they give rise. In the course of these discussions there is scarcely a dark or disputed point in the whole range of the subject, which he has not examined with great ability; and if he has not always settled them satisfactorily to the unprejudiced inquirer, he has at least afforded him the means of forming more clear and definite views.

On becoming aware of the deficiency, in our medical literature, of works on insanity considered exclusively in

its legal relations, it was the author's first thought to make
a translation, either of Hoffbauer's or Georget's work, but
considering that the numerous notes which would be required in order to bring it up to the present state of the
science, and adapt it to our own laws, would prove incon-
venient and embarrassing to the reader, besides not fully
accomplishing the object, he was induced to abandon this
project, and, as the only means of fairly developing the
subject, to prepare an original work,—original strictly in
plan and in many of its general views only, for the materials
have been necessarily drawn, in a great degree, from other
sources than the author's own experience. The main
object which he proposed to himself, was to establish the
legal relations of the insane in conformity to the present
state of our knowledge respecting their disease. In furtherance of this object, he has given a succinct description
of the different species of insanity, and the characters by
which they are distinguished from one another, so that
the professional student may have some means of recognising them in practice, and thence deducing, in regard to
each, such legal consequences as seem warranted by a
humane and enlightened consideration of all the facts. He
is well aware that he has presented some views that will
not, at first sight, meet with the cordial assent of all his
readers. He can only say in justification, that they have
appeared to him to be founded on well-observed, well-
authenticated facts, and that as such, it was an imperative
duty required by the claims of humanity and truth, to
present them in the strongest possible aspect. Before
being condemned for substituting visionary and speculative
fancies, in the place of those maxims and practices which
have come down to us on the authority of our ancestors,
and been sanctioned by the approval of all succeeding
times, he hopes that the ground on which those alleged

fancies have been built, will be carefully, candidly, and dispassionately examined. Of the manifold imperfections of his work, no one can be more sensible than the author himself; but if it succeed in directing attention to the subject, and putting others on the track of inquiry, it will, at the very least, have been followed by one beneficial result.

Eastport, Me., March 20th, 1838.

CONTENTS.

MEDICAL JURISPRUDENCE

OF

INSANITY.

PRELIMINARY VIEWS.

STATUTES were framed and principles of law laid down, regulating the legal relations of the Insane, long before physicians had obtained any accurate notions respecting their malady; and, as might naturally be expected, error and injustice have been committed to an incalculable extent under the sacred name of law. The actual state of our knowledge of insanity, as well as of other diseases, so far from being what it has always heretofore been, is the accumulated result of the observations, which, with more or less accuracy and fidelity, have been prosecuted through many centuries, under the guidance of a more or less inductive philosophy. In addition to the obstacles to the progress of knowledge respecting other diseases, there has been this also in regard to insanity, that, being considered as resulting from a direct exercise of divine power, and not from the operation of the ordinary laws of nature, and thus associated with mysterious and .supernatural pheno-

mena confessedly above our comprehension, inquiry
has been discouraged at the very threshold, by the fear
of presumption, or, at least, of fruitless labor. To
this superstition, we may look as the parent of many
of the false and absurd notions, that have prevailed
relative to this disease, and especially of the reckless and inhuman treatment, once universally bestowed on its unfortunate subjects. Instead of the
kindness and care, so usually manifested towards the
sick, as if it were a natural right for them to receive
it ; instead of the untiring vigilance, the soothing attention, the lively solicitude of relatives and friends ;
the patient, afflicted with the severest of diseases,
and most of all dependent for the issue of his fate on
others, received nothing but looks of loathing, was
banished from all that was ever dear to him, and
suffered to remain in his seclusion uncared for and
forgotten. In those receptacles, where living beings,
bearing the image and superscription of men, were
cut off from all the sympathies of fellow-men, and
were rapidly completing the ruin of their immortal
nature, there were scenes of barbarity and moral
desolation, which no force of language can adequately
describe. The world owes an immense debt of
gratitude to the celebrated Pinel, who, with an ardor of philanthropy, that no discouragement could
quench, and a courage that no apprehension of danger could daunt, succeeded, at last, in removing
the chains of the maniac, and establishing his claims
to all the liberty and comfort, which his malady had
left him capable of enjoying. With the new aspect,
thus presented, of the moral and intellectual condition of this portion of our race, the medical jurispru-

dence of insanity became invested with an interest, that has led to its most important improvements.

§ 2. In all civilized communities, ancient or modern, insanity has been regarded as exempting from the punishment of crime, and vitiating the civil acts of those who are affected with it. The only difficulty, or diversity of opinion, consists in determining who are really insane, in the meaning of the law, which has been content with merely laying down some general principles, and leaving their application to the discretion of the judicial authorities. Inasmuch, as the greatest possible variety is presented by the mental phenomena in a state of health, it is obvious, that profound study and extensive observation of the moral and intellectual nature of man can alone prevent us, from sometimes confounding them with the effects of disease. It would seem, therefore, an almost self-evident proposition, that a certain knowledge of the mind in its healthy state is an essential preliminary, to the attainment of correct ideas concerning its diseased manifestations. If, in addition to this, it is considered, that opinions on the nature of insanity, viewed solely in the light of a disease—of a derangement of the physical structure, —have been constantly changing for the better, it follows of course, that its legal relations, which should be determined in some measure by our views of its nature, ought to be modified by the progress of our knowledge. That much of the jurisprudence of insanity, in times past, should bear marks of the crude and imperfect notions, that have been entertained of its pathological character, is not to be wondered at ; but, it is a matter of surprise, that it

should be adhered to, as if consecrated by age, long
after it has ceased to be supported by the results of
more extensive and better conducted inquiries. It
is to be feared, that the principles, laid down on this
subject by legal authorities, have received too much
of that reverence, which is naturally felt for the
opinions and practices of our ancestors; and that innovations have been too much regarded, rather as
the offspring of new-fangled theories, than of the
steady advancement of medical science. In their,
zeal to uphold the wisdom of the past, from the fancied desecrations of reformers and theorists, the
ministers of the law seem to have forgotten, that, in
respect to this subject, the real dignity and respect-
ability of their profession is better upheld, by yielding to the improvements of the times and thankfully
receiving the truth from whatever quarter it may
come, than by turning away with blind obstinacy,
from every thing that conflicts with long established
maxims and decisions. In the course of the review
proposed to be taken of the principles, that have
regulated the civil and criminal responsibilities of
the insane, the reader will have constant opportunity to witness the influence of the spirit above condemned ; and be inclined, perhaps, to consider it as
the source of that striking difference, presented by
the sciences of law and medicine, in the amount of
knowledge they respectively evince on the subject
of insanity.

§ 3. Legislators and jurists have done little more,
than merely to indicate some of the most obvious
divisions of insanity, without undertaking any thing
like a systematic classification of its various forms.

In the Roman law, the insane, or *dementes*, are divided into two classes ; those whose understanding is weak or null, *mente capti*, and those who are restless and furious, *furiosi*. The French and Prussian codes make use of the terms, *démence, fureur* and *imbécillité*, without pretending to define them. The English common law originally recognised but two kinds of insanity, *idiocy* and *lunacy*, the subjects of which were designated by the term, *non compotes mentis*, which was used in a generic sense and meant to embrace all, who, from defect of understanding, require the protection of the law. An occasional attempt has been made by jurists, to attach some definite ideas to these terms, and to point out the various descriptions of persons, to whom they may be applied. Lord Coke says, there are four kinds of men, who may be said to be *non compotes mentis :*—
1. An idiot, who, from his nativity, by a perpetual infirmity is *non compos;* 2. He that by sickness, grief or other accident, wholly loseth his memory and understanding ; 3. A lunatic that hath sometimes his understanding, and sometimes not, *aliquando gaudet lucidis intervallis;* and therefore he is called *non compos mentis*, so long as he hath not understanding; 4. He that by his own vicious act for a time depriveth himself of his memory and understanding, as he that is drunken.[1]

§ 4. That the above classification is exceedingly defective, is sufficiently proved, to go no farther, by the various attempts of law-writers to indicate the

---

[1] Coke's Littleton, 247 a.

precise characters by which they may be distinguished. An idiot is defined to be a person, who
cannot count or number twenty pence, or tell who
was his father or mother, or how old he is, so as it
may appear that he hath no understanding of reason, what shall be for his profit or what shall be for
his loss ; but if he have sufficient understanding to
know and understand his letters, and to read by
teaching or information, he is not an idiot.[1] Now
the truth is, that the proportion of idiots, capable
of attaining the kind of knowledge herein specified,
by means of the ordinary intercourse with men, or
of special teaching, is by no means small. The entire loss of memory and understanding, attributed to
the second class, is observed only as a sequel to
madness or some other disease, or as the result of
some powerful moral causes ; so that if this is to be
considered an essential character of madness, by
much the larger proportion of madmen will be altogether excluded from this classification ; for, instead
of wholly losing their understanding, they are for
the most part perfectly rational on some topics, and
in some relations of life; and a little effort is frequently necessary, in order to detect the fact of the
understanding being at all impaired. Judging from
the almost exclusive use of the term *lunacy*, and the
frequent reference to lucid intervals, the intermittent
character of madness was either more common,
some hundreds of years since, or, which is more
probable, in consequence of the general belief in its

---

[1] 1 Fitzherbert, Natura Brevium, 583, ed. 1652.

connexion with lunar influences, this intermission was imagined to occur far oftener than it really did. This certainly is a more reasonable explanation, than the idea that the course of nature has changed, so that lucid intervals, which were once of the most common occurrence in insanity, are now among its rarest phenomena.

§ 5. Common sense and a tolerable share of the intelligence of the time, if fairly exercised, would probably prevent, in practice, any grossly improper application of these theoretical principles ; but, in civil cases, the law, though not disposed to guage the exact measure of men's intellects, has sometimes insisted on technical distinctions, that have little foundation in nature or reason. Originally, commissions of lunacy were granted for the purpose of inquiring whether the individual were either an idiot *ex nativitate,* or a lunatic, in Coke's meaning of the term, and, in consequence thereof, incapable of governing himself and managing his worldly affairs. The injustice of leaving beyond the protection of the law, that larger class of insane, who, though neither *idiots,* nor *lunatics,* labor under more or less mental derangement, led to a change in the form of the writ, by which the phrase *unsound mind* was used for the purpose of embracing all others, who were considered proper objects of a commission. What is the precise meaning of this term, it is not easy to gather from the observations of various high legal authorities, who have attempted to fix its meaning. It seems to be agreed, that it is not idiocy, nor lunacy, nor imbecility, but beyond this all unanimity is at an end. Lord Hardwicke held, that unsoundness of mind did not mean mere weakness of mind, but a depravity of reason or a want of it.[1]   Lord Eldon once referred to the case of a person advanced in years, "whose mind was the mind of a child," and observed, that, "it was, therefore, in that sense, imbecility and inability to manage his affairs, which constituted unsoundness of mind."[2]   The same high authority had observed, on a previous occasion, that "the court had thought itself authorized to issue the commission *de lunatico inquirendo,* provided it is made out, that the party is unable to act with any proper and provident management ; liable to be robbed by any one; under that imbecility of mind, not strictly insanity, but as to the mischief, calling for as much protection as actual insanity."[3]   Mr. Amos, late professor of Medical Jurisprudence in the London University, has said, that "the term unsoundness of mind, in the legal sense, seems to involve the idea of a morbid condition of intellect, or loss of reason, coupled with an incompetency of the person to manage his own affairs."[4]   Whatever it may signify, it has always been insisted on, that the return of the commission must state the incapacity or inability of the party to manage his affairs, to be evidence of its existence, in order that the party may have the protection of the law.   If the jury are unwilling from what they see to infer the presence of a mental condition, to which the highest dignitaries of the law have declined fixing a precise, intelligible mean-

---

[1] *Ex parte* Barnsley, 3 Atkyns's Reports, 168.
[2] Haslam on the Medical Jurisprudence of Insanity, 336.
[3] 8 Vesey's Reports, 66.   [4] London Medical Gazette, Vol. 8, p. 19.

ing, then the inquisition is quashed. The feelings of dread and disgust, with which madness has been generally contemplated, have often deterred juries acting under a commission, from returning a verdict of unsound mind, which has become equivalent to insanity; either from a disinclination to embarrass the family with an odious distinction, or because the individual was not really unsound in the popular acceptation of the term, though his mental faculties might have been so far enfeebled by old age, or sickness, or congenital causes, as to render him absolutely incapable of conducting himself or his affairs,—a fact, which they have sometimes returned. These attempts to change the ordinary course have never succeeded, the court having in every case required the verdict to be in the words of the inquisition, or in equipollent words. "It is settled," says Lord Eldon, "that if the jury find merely the incapacity of the party to manage his affairs, and will not infer from that and other circumstances unsoundness of mind, though the party may live where he is exposed to ruin every instant, yet upon that finding the commission cannot go on." [1] The consequence is, that the afflicted party must either forego the protection of the law, or fix upon his family a sort of stigma of the most disagreeable and onerous description. When it is considered how many are the cases, where individuals are incapacitated from managing their affairs, simply from that impairment of the mind so common in old age, or mere defect of

---

[1] 19 Vesey's Reports, 286.

memory, the other powers remaining sound, it is a little surprising, that no effectual measures have been taken, to render the operation of the law less imperfect and unequal. It is not easy to see the ground of the extreme repugnance displayed by the English courts, towards any return that does not assert the mental unsoundness of the affected party, unless it may be some obstacle thereby thrown in the course of the subsequent proceedings. The object of the commission is, to ascertain whether or not the party in question is incapable, by reason of mental infirmities, of governing himself and managing his affairs; and if they so find him, it certainly is irrelevant to any useful purpose, to connect this inability as an effect with any particular kind of insanity, whether expressed in common or technical language. Indeed, to require a jury to infer explicitly unsoundness of mind from inability to manage affairs, which is of itself sufficient evidence of all the mental unsoundness, that is required for practical purposes, and reject their return if they do not, would seem exceedingly puerile, were it not strictly professional. In *ex parte* Cranmer,[1] where the jury pronounced the party in their verdict, "so far debilitated in his mind as to be incapable of the general management of his affairs," Lord Chancellor Erskine gives some reasons for finding fault with the terms of the verdict, and directing the inquisition to be quashed. "The verdict," he says, "does not state distinctly, that he is incapable ; but that he is so far debilitated in his

---

[1] 12 Vesey's Reports, 406.

mind, that he is not equal to the general management of his affairs." The very word *incapable*, it is true, is not used, but the words "not equal" are surely of equivalent meaning ; and it is not easy to conceive, how a clearer or stronger idea of a person's incapacity can be conveyed, than to pronounce him "not equal to the management of his affairs." "How can I tell," he asks, "what is '*so far* debilitated in his mind that he is not equal to the general management of his affairs ?'" He certainly could not tell the precise quantity of mind left, but even if the party had been returned *non compos* and *therefore* unequal to the management of his affairs, it is not quite obvious, how any more definite notion on this point would have been conveyed.[1]

§ 6. The business of the jury in these cases is, to ascertain whether the individual is mentally capable of managing his affairs; and this is a duty, which, generally speaking, they are able to perform with tolerable correctness. But what can be more irrelevant to the object in view, or more remote from the ordinary circle of their reflections, than the additional duty of deciding whether his mental impairment has gone far enough, to bear being designated by the technical phraseology, unsoundness of mind ? When it is recollected, too, that the members of these

---

[1] In a recent case, the inquisition was quashed by Lord Lyndhurst, because the verdict of the jury said too much, instead of too little, viz: "that the party was not a lunatic, but partly from paralysis and partly from old age, his memory was so much impaired as to render him incompetent to the management of his affairs, and consequently that he was of unsound mind, and had been so for two years." *In Re* Holmes, 4 Russel's Chancery Reports, 182.

juries are mostly uneducated men, and but few of them at all acquainted with the force of legal or medical distinctions, it cannot be supposed, that such a return is always the recorded opinion of un-biassed, understanding minds. Indeed, the inconvenience and injustice of these proceedings have been so strongly felt, as to have led to the repeated expression of a wish, that its defects were remedied by the action of the legislature. That it should still continue in a country, where it is linked in with a system, whose foundations are in the very constitution of the government, is perhaps not strange ; but, that it should be used in some of our own states, which are untrammelled by such considerations, is certainly an anomaly in legislation.

§ 7. This is not the only instance, where the principles of common sense and common justice, which ought to regulate the legal relations of the insane, have, with astonishing inconsistency, been strangely disregarded in the maxims of the common law. While it requires that contracts, to be valid, should spring from a free and deliberate consent, it refuses to suffer the party himself to avoid them on the plea of lunacy, in accordance with an ancient maxim, that no man of full age shall be allowed to disable or stultify himself ; though, at the same time, it does allow his heirs, or other persons interested, to avail themselves of this privilege.[1]   Thus, a person, who recovers from a temporary insanity, before the return of an inquisition, has no remedy at law

---

[1] Chitty on Contracts, 256.

or in equity for the most ruinous contracts, that he may have entered into while in that condition, except on the ground of fraud, though, after his death, his heirs may have them set aside by establishing the fact of lunacy alone. Well may a distinguished jurist exclaim, that, "it is matter of wonder and humiliation, how so absurd and mischievous a maxim could have found its way into any system of jurisprudence, professing to act on civilized beings."[1] It arose, no doubt, in part, from erroneous notions of the nature of insanity, and partly from apprehensions, not well founded, of the consequences, that might follow the admission of the plea of lunacy in avoidance of contracts. The ends of justice would have been better obtained, if no general rule at all had been adopted, and every case decided on its own merits. Where the insanity of one of the parties is perfectly well known to the other, or might have been so by the exercise of ordinary sagacity, a contract between them, except for the necessaries of life or comforts and luxuries suitable to his wealth or station, should obviously be held invalid, because the insane party is deprived by the act of providence of his natural share of discernment and foresight. It often happens, however, that a person's insanity is not generally known and is not very apparent, and, in such cases, if it can be proved, that the contract is a fair and reasonable one on the face of it, and was entered into in perfect honesty and good faith, he certainly should not be permitted to stultify him-

---

[1] 1 Story's Commentaries on Equity Jurisprudence, § 225.

self, in order to escape its performance.[1] Neither does his death or interdiction so change the case, as to render it proper for his heirs or guardians, to do that which he could not do for himself. Much as the law is bound to protect the interests of the insane, it is no less required to protect those who deal with them, unacquainted with their mental condition. It as often happens, that the sane party suffers from the avoidance of the contract, as that the insane or his heirs do from its validity ; and nothing can be more clearly unjust, than the application of a maxim or general rule, that favors only the interests of the unsound party.

§ 8. Though little of this pertinacious adherence to merely technical distinctions is observed, in the application of the law to criminal cases, yet there is much of the same respect for antiquated maxims, that have little else to recommend them but their antiquity, and are so much the more pernicious in their application, as the interests of property are of less importance than reputation and life. It by no means follows, that a person, declared to be *non compos* by due process of law, is to be considered, on that account, merely, to be irresponsible for his criminal acts. This is a question entirely distinct, and is determined upon very different views of the nature of insanity, and of its effects on the operations of the mind ; and, here it is, that the lawyer encroaches most on the domain of the physician. The first at-

---

[1] This principle has lately been adopted, where the contract was for articles suitable to the means and condition of the insane party. **Bagster v. Earl of Portsmouth. Chitty on Contracts, 256.**

tempt to point out precisely those conditions of insanity, in which the civil and criminal responsibilities are unequally affected, was made by Lord Hale. "There is a partial insanity," says he, "and a total insanity. The former is either in respect to things, *quoad hoc vel illud insanire.* Some persons that have a competent use of reason, in respect of some subjects, are yet under a particular *dementia,* in respect of some particular discourses, subjects, or applications : or else it is partial in respect of degrees ; and this is the condition of very many, especially melancholy persons, who for the most part discover their defect in excessive fears and griefs, and yet are not wholly destitute of the use of reason ; and this partial insanity seems not to excuse them, in the committing of any offence for its matter capital ; for, doubtless, most persons that are felons of themselves and others, are under a degree of partial insanity, when they commit these offences. It is very difficult to define the invisible line that divides perfect and partial insanity ; but it must rest upon circumstances duly to be weighed and considered both by judge and jury, lest on the one side there be a kind of inhumanity towards the defects of human nature ;—or, on the other side, too great an indulgence given to great crimes." [1]

§ 9. The doctrines, thus dogmatically laid down by Lord Hale, have exerted no inconsiderable influence on the judicial opinions of his successors ; and his high authority has always been invoked against

---

[1] Pleas of the Crown, 30.

the plea of insanity, whenever it has been urged by the voice of philanthropy and true science. If, too, in consequence of the common tendency of indulging in forced and unwarrantable constructions, whenever a point is to be gained, his principles have been made to mean far more than he ever designed, the fact impressively teaches the importance of clear and well-defined terms, in the expression of scientific truths, as well as of enlarged, practical information, relative to the subjects to which they belong. In the time of this eminent jurist, insanity was a much less frequent disease than it now is, and the popular notions concerning it were derived from the observation of those wretched inmates of the mad-houses, whom chains and stripes, cold and filth, had reduced to the stupidity of the idiot, or exasperated to the fury of a demon. Those nice shades of the disease, in which the mind, without being wholly driven from its propriety, pertinaciously clings to some absurd delusion, were either regarded as something very different from real madness, or were too few, too far removed from the common gaze, and too soon converted by bad management into the more active forms of the disease, to enter much into the general idea entertained of madness. Could Lord Hale have contemplated the scenes presented by the lunatic asylums of our own times, we should undoubtedly have received from him a very different doctrine, for the regulation of the decisions of after generations.

§ 10. Judging from the few cases that have been reported, the course of practice in the English criminal courts has been strictly conformatory to the prin-

ciples laid down by Hale. For instance, in the trial
of Arnold in 1723 for shooting at Lord Onslow, Mr.
Justice Tracy observed, "that it is not every kind
of frantic humor, or something unaccountable in a
man's actions, that points him out to be such a madman, as is exempted from punishment : it must be
a man, that is totally deprived of his understanding
and memory, and doth not know what he is doing,
no more than an infant, than a brute, or a wild beast,
such a one is never the object of punishment."[1]
This is but the echo of Lord Hale's doctrine, and
the circumstances of the case show how faithfully
the principles were applied. Arnold seems to have
been of weak understanding from his birth, and to
have led an idle, irregular, and disordered life,
sometimes unequivocally mad, and at all times considered exceedingly strange and different from other
people ; one witness describing him as a strange,
sullen boy at school, such as he had never seen
before. It was testified by his family and his neighbors, that for several years previous, they had considered and treated him as mad, occasionally if not
always, although so little disposed to mischief, that
he was suffered to be at large. Contrary to the
wishes of his friends, he persisted in living alone in
a house destitute of the ordinary conveniences ; was
in the habit of lying about in barns and under hay-
ricks ; would curse and swear to himself for hours
together ; laugh and throw things about the house
without any cause whatever, and was much dis-

---

[1] 8 Hargrave's State Trials, 322.

B

turbed in his sleep by fancied noises. Among other unfounded notions, he believed that Lord Onslow, who lived in his neighborhood, was the cause of all the tumults, disturbances, and wicked devices, that happened in the country, and his thoughts were greatly occupied with this person. He was in the habit of declaring, that Lord Onslow sent his devils and imps into his room at night to disturb his rest, and that he constantly plagued and bewitched him, by getting into his belly or bosom, so that he could neither eat, drink nor sleep, for him. He talked much of being plagued by the *Bollies* and *Bolleroys ;* he declared in prison it was better to die than live so miserably, and manifested no compunction for what he had done. Under the influence of these delusions, he shot at and wounded Lord Onslow. The proof of insanity was strong enough, but not that degree of it, which the jury considered sufficient to save him from the gallows, and he was accordingly sentenced to be hung. Lord Onslow himself, however, thought differently ; and, by means of his intercession, the sentence was not executed, and Arnold was continued in prison for life. It is clear, that the court recognised that class of madmen only, as exempted from the penal consequences of crime, whose reason is completely dethroned from her empire, and who are reduced to the condition of an infant, a brute, or a wild beast. If it be true, that such, as the court said, are never the objects of punishment, though it neglected to state that they are never the objects of prosecution, the converse must be equally true, that those not exactly in this condition can never avoid punishment on the plea of

insanity. It appears, then, that the law at that
time did not consider an insane person irresponsible
for crime, in whom there remained the slightest
vestige of rationality ; though, it did then and has
ever since deprived him of the management of himself and his affairs, and vitiates his civil acts, even
when they have no relation to the circumstances
that caused his madness. That the progress of
science and general enlightenment has produced no
improvement of the law on this subject, is abundantly shown in the strong declarations of Sir Vic-
ary Gibbs, when attorney-general of England, on
the trial of Bellingham, in 1812. " A man," says
he, " may be deranged in his mind,—his intellects
may be insufficient for enabling him to conduct the
common affairs of life, such as disposing of his property, or judging of the claims which his respective
relations have upon him ; and if he be so, the administration of the country will take his affairs into
their management, and appoint to him trustees ; but,
at the same time, such a man is not discharged from
his responsibility for criminal acts." [1] Lord Erskine
had previously given the same doctrine the sanction
of his authority, in his celebrated speech in defence
of Hadfield. " I am bound," he says, " to admit
that there is a wide distinction between civil and
criminal cases. If, in the former, a man appears,
upon the evidence, to be *non compos mentis*, the law
avoids his act, though it cannot be traced or connected with the morbid imagination which consti-

---

[1] Collinson on Lunacy, 657.

tutes his disease, and which may be extremely partial in its influence upon conduct ; but, to deliver a
man from responsibility for crimes, above all, for
crimes of great atrocity and wickedness, I am by
no means prepared to apply this rule, however well
established, when property only is concerned."

§ 11. That a person, whom the law prevents from
managing his own property, by reason of his mental
impairment, should, in respect to criminal acts, be
considered as possessing all the elements of responsibility, and placed on the same footing with men of
the soundest and strongest minds, is a proposition
so strange and startling, that few, uninfluenced by
professional biases, can yield to it unhesitating assent, or look upon it in any other light, than as
belonging to that class of doctrines, which, while
they may be the perfection of reason to the initiated,
appear to be the height of absurdity to every one
else.   Georget, an able French writer on the legal
relations of the insane, in commenting on the speech
of de Peyronnet, who, in the trial of Papavoine,
had adduced the passage above extracted from Lord
Hale, in support of his own views, expresses his
astonishment and indignation, that such sentiments
should ever have been uttered, least of all, quoted
with approbation, in a French court of justice, by
the chief law-officer of the government.   " Can we
help wondering," he exclaims, "at these sentiments
of Lord Hale, who seems to make more account of
property than life.   No excuse for the unfortunate
man, who, in a paroxysm of madness, commits a
criminal offence, while civil acts are to be annulled,
even when they have no relation to the insane im-

pressions, that might have influenced his conduct." [1]
The language of the law, virtually addressed to the
insane man, is, your reason is too much impaired to
manage your property ; you are unable to distinguish between those measures, which would conduce
to your profit and such as would end in your ruin,
and therefore it is wisely taken altogether from your
control ; but, if under the influence of one of those
insane delusions, that have rendered this step necessary, you should kill your neighbor, you will be
supposed to have acted under the guidance of a
sound reason ; you will be tried, convicted, and
executed like any common criminal, whose understanding has never been touched by madness. As
for any physiological or psychological ground, for this
distinction between the legal consequences of the
civil and criminal acts of an insane person, it is
in vain to look for it. That the mind, when medi-
tating a great crime, is less under the influence of
disease, and enjoys a more sound and vigorous exercise of its powers, than when making a contract, or
a will, few, probably, will be hardy enough to
affirm ; and yet the practice of the law virtually
admits it. The difference, if there be any, would
seem to be all the other way. In the disposal of
property, the mind is engaged in what has perhaps
often exercised its thoughts ; the conditions and consequences of the transaction require no great mental
exertion to be comprehended ; and there may be
nothing in it, to deprive the mind of all the calmness

---

[1] Discussion médico-légale sur la Folie, p. 8.

aud rationality of which it is capable. Now, criminal acts, though abstractly wrong, may under certain circumstances become right and meritorious ; and, if the strongest and acutest minds have sometimes been perplexed on this point, what shall we say of the crazy and distorted perceptions of him, whose reason shares a divided empire with the propensities and passions ? Most maniacs have a firm conviction, that all they feel and think, is true, just, and reasonable ; and nothing can shake their convictions. The contracts of the insane are, in many cases, declared to be invalid, and are set aside, in courts of law, as well as equity, on the ground of fraud ; in accordance with an established principle, that the parties to a contract must be capable of giving their deliberate and rational consent, the power of doing which is destroyed by mental derangement.[1] In point of mental soundness, they must be equal, and common justice requires, that the insane man, in his dealings with his fellow-men, should be protected from the effect of his disorder. Even in the simplest transaction, it is supposed that the insane party may not be able to discern all the circumstances, that may conduce to his advantage, and may not act as if his mind were perfectly sound. But, it remains to be proved, that, in the commission of a criminal offence, he has more clearly apprehended its abstract nature, its relations to the injured party, and its consequences to himself, than he would all the circumstances attending a contract ; if, therefore, he have not

---

[1] 1 Story's Commentaries on Equity Jurisprudence, § 227.

acted rationally, but under the influence of a disordered mind, he ought to be no more responsible for the former than for the latter.

§ 12. A distinction is also made between civil and criminal cases, in regard to evidence respecting the state of the party's mind. In the former, proof drawn from the nature of the act in question is paramount to all others, and, in the absence of others, admitted to be alone conclusive ; while, in the latter, to seek to prove the existence of insanity, from the character of the act, would be viewed as nothing less than a begging of the question. "If a lunatic person," says Swinburne,[1] "or one that is beside himself at sometimes but not continually, make his testament, and it is not known whether the same were made while he was of sound mind and memory or no, then in case the testament be so conceived, as thereby no argument of phrensy or folly can be gathered, it is to be presumed that the same was made during the time of his calm and clear intermissions, and so the testament shall be adjudged good, yea, although it cannot be proved that the testator useth to have any clear and quiet intermissions at all, yet nevertheless I suppose that if the testament be wisely and orderly framed, the same ought to be accepted for a lawful testament." Sir John Nicholl has observed, that where there is no direct evidence of the time, or, consequently, of the deceased's state of mind at the time, of the act done, recourse must be had to the usual mode of ascertaining it in such cases—which is by looking at the

---

[1] Of Testaments and Last Wills, Part II, Sec. 3.

act itself. "The agent is to be *inferred* rational, or
the contrary, in such cases, from the character
broadly taken of his act." [1]   So, on the other hand,
"in the case of a person who is sometimes sane and
sometimes insane, if there be in it a mixture of wisdom and folly, it is to be presumed that the same
was made during the testator's phrensy, even if
there be but one word sounding to folly." [2]   If, then,
testamentary dispositions that conflict with the natural distribution of property and the known and expressed intentions of the testator, yea, if they con-
tain but one word "sounding to folly," are to be
held as sufficient evidence of unsound mind, in
doubtful cases, why, when an atrocious crime is
shown to be motiveless, unnatural, in opposition to
the habits, feelings, and principles of the whole past
life, and unfollowed by any consciousness of guilt,
should not this act be considered as equally strong
proof of unsoundness of mind?   Why is it, that instead of being thus considered, it actually avails the
accused nothing; the character of the act, in the last
resort, being too often explained, on the supposition
of an inherent ferocity and thirst for blood, which no
considerations can restrain; even in the face of totally
different dispositions, indicated by the whole tenor of
his life.

§ 13. Notwithstanding that Lord Hale's doctrine was cited with approbation by de Peyronnet,
(§ 11), yet, by the French penal code, madness,

---

[1] 1 Addams's Ecclesiastical Reports, 74, Scruby and Finch *v.* Ford-
ham and others.   See also 1 Phillimore's Reports, 90; 1 Dow's Reports,
178, for a recognition of the same principle.
[2] Swinburne, Part II, § 3, pl. 16.

without limit or condition, exempts from the punishment of criminal acts. The language of the law is, that "there is no crime nor offence when the accused was in a state of madness at the time of the action." [1] The existence of insanity once established, the accused is, by the spirit of the law, acquitted. This intention has sometimes been near being defeated, in consequence of the great liberty allowed to French juries, in the construction of the phraseology of their verdict, in which they may declare, if they choose, not whether the accused was guilty or not guilty, sane or insane, but whether or not the act was committed *voluntarily.* [2] A verdict of this kind, in an instance mentioned by Georget, led to a curious result, in the hands of men who were not indoctrinated in the subtleties of metaphysics. The fact of insanity having been given to the jury for decision, they returned that the accused acted *voluntarily* and with *premeditation;* and, secondly, that he was insane at the time of committing the act. [3] This verdict, so consistent in reality, but so utterly contradictory in a legal sense, was received by the court and understood to mean, that the accused possessed the will of a madman, a merely animal will which excludes legal culpability. Had not the last question been raised, the accused, though mad, would have been condemned to death. [4] It seems evident,

---

[1] Il n'y a ni crime ni délit lorsque le prévenu était en état de démence au temps de l'action. Art. 64.

[2] Special verdicts in criminal cases are quite common in France.

[3] Des maladies mentales, 100.

[4] It is one of those metaphysical subtleties, so prevalent on the subject of insanity, that the acts of an insane mind are *involuntary.* It

that the legislator, in framing that law, was impressed with the difficulty of drawing the line between
general and partial insanity, and of estimating the
quantity of reason left after the invasion of this disease, and therefore determined to avoid it altogether
by recognising but one kind of insanity. Though not
prepared to acquiesce entirely in the dispositions of
this enactment, yet it is infinitely preferable, with
all its faults, to the English practice of requiring a
number of men, who may have had very little edu-

---

certainly can be of little practical consequence, what epithet is applied
to the acts of a mind admitted to be insane ; though it seems to be an
abuse of language, to call any act involuntary, which proceeds from a
person's own free will. The exercise of the will may be greatly influenced by the condition of the mind, even to such an extent as to deprive a person of all criminal responsibility. But this does not necessarily prove insanity, unless, for instance, every man, who commits a
criminal act under the influence of strong passions, is considered as insane. The objection to this distinction is, that it is used as a test in the
decision of doubtful cases, every one being left to decide, as he pleases,
what acts are voluntary, and what involuntary. A curious application
of the distinction is made by Mr. Shelford in his work on Lunatics,
(Introduction, p. xlix.) when speaking of suicide. " The art with
which the means are often prepared, and the time occupied in plan-
ning them, seem to mark it [suicide] as an act of deliberate volition ;
but the acts of an insane mind are involuntary, and not voluntary ;
therefore, the question must always revert to, what was the real condition of the mind when suicide was committed." If the preparation for
the suicidal act be so indicative of that volition which is exercised by
sound minds only, it is not very clear by what process of logic, from these
two propositions would be drawn the conclusion, that the " question
must always revert to what was the real condition of the mind when
suicide was committed." This calls to mind a character, commemorated in a work which appeared a few years since, called the " Clubs of
London," who was remarkably addicted in his discourse to that species
of reasoning, denominated by logicians the *non sequitur.* " The weather is uncommonly fine, this morning," he would say, " *therefore,* I
shall go home and not stir out of my house the whole day."

cation of any kind, and least of all, any very accurate notions of the influence of insanity on the opertions of the mind, to sit in judgment on the measure of a man's understanding, and decide whether or not he had enough of reason left to discern the nature of the act he committed. Mental unsoundness is not necessarily incompatible with crime, for we can conceive of cases, where the criminal act is beyond the sphere of the influence of the reigning delusion, and therefore, as far as that is concerned, the offspring of a sound mind, yet we must acknowledge the extreme difficulty of establishing this fact, and the caution with which we should proceed to a decision.

§ 14. On the trial of Hadfield, for shooting at the king in Drury Lane theatre, in 1800, there occurred for the first time, in an English criminal court, any thing like a thorough and enlightened discussion of insanity as connected with crime; and the result was, that a fatal blow was given to the doctrines of Lord Hale by Mr. Erskine, who brought all the energies of his great mind to bear upon the elucidation of this subject.[1] In accordance with these doctrines, the

---

[1] One reason, why the criminal law of insanity has undergone so little improvement in England, is, probably, that the accused, not being allowed counsel to speak in their defence, except in trials for high treason, the officers of government have always been at liberty to put their own construction on the law, and urge it on the jury as the only correct one, without fear of being contradicted or gainsayed. Thus, the old maxims have been repeated, year after year, and not being questioned, their correctness has remained undoubted, both in and out of the legal profession. Can any one doubt, that had those insane criminals, who have been condemned within the last half century, been defended by an Erskine, many of them would have been acquitted, and a great advance made in the law of insanity, that would have prevented

attorney-general had told the jury, that to protect a
person from criminal responsibility, there must be a
total deprivation of memory and understanding.   To
this Mr. Erskine very justly replied, that if these
expressions were meant to be taken in the literal
sense of the words—which however he did not deny
—"then no such madness ever existed in the world."
This condition of mind is observed only in idiocy and
fatuity, and its unhappy subjects are never made
accountable to the laws.   In proper madness, on the
contrary, so far was there from being a total deprivation of memory and understanding, that "in all
the cases that have filled Westminster Hall," said he,
"with the most complicated considerations, the lunatics and other insane persons, who have been the
subjects of them, have not only had memory *in my
sense of the expression*—they have not only had the
most perfect knowledge and recollection of all the
relations they stood in towards others, and of the
acts and circumstances of their lives, but have, in
general, been remarkable for subtlety and acuteness.
Defects in their reasonings have seldom been trace-
able—the disease consisting in the delusive sources
of thought:—all their deductions, within the scope
of their malady, being founded on the *immovable* assumptions of matters as *realities*, either without any
foundation whatever, or so distorted and disfigured
by fancy, as to be nearly the same thing as their
creation."   Instead therefore of making that kind of

---

some of those exhibitions of presumptuous ignorance, which will one
day be universally regarded with feelings of disgust and pity?

insanity which would exempt from punishment to consist in the absence of any of the intellectual faculties, he lays down *delusion* as its true character, of which the criminal act in question must be its immediate unqualified offspring.[1] Here was a great step made in this branch of medical jurisprudence, and it might have been expected, that the victory, thus gained over professional prejudices and time-honored errors, would be felt in all subsequent decisions. But, though the day has gone by, when such insanity only, as is attended by total deprivation of memory and understanding, can be admitted in excuse for crime, the test offered by Erskine was altogether too simple and too philosophical, to be readily adopted by minds that delighted in subtleties and technicalities.

§ 15. In the case of Bellingham, for instance,[2] tried for the murder of the Hon. Spencer Percival in 1812, it appeared from the history of the accused, from his own account of the transactions, that led to

---

[1] It is surprising and perfectly unaccountable, that Mr. Erskine, in adverting to the case of Arnold (§ 10), should have declared, "that his counsel could not show, that any morbid delusion had overshadowed his understanding."! If it were no delusion in Arnold to believe that Lord Onslow was the cause of all the turmoils and troubles in the country—that he bewitched him in particular by getting into his belly and bosom, and sending his devils and imps into his room to prevent his rest, it surely was none for Hadfield to imagine that he had constant intercourse with God—that the world was about to come to an end—and that he was to sacrifice himself for its salvation, by taking away the life of another. Either the able advocate, in his zeal for his client, must have egregiously deceived himself respecting the facts of Arnold's case, or have attached some ideas to *delusion*, which have never entered into the ordinary conceptions of that kind of belief.

[2] 1 Collinson on Lunacy, 650.

the fatal act, and from the testimony of several witnesses, that he labored under many of those strange
delusions, that find a place only in the brain of a
madman. His fixed belief, that his own private
grievances were national wrongs; that his country's diplomatic agents in a foreign land neglected
to hear his complaints and assist him in his troubles,
though they had in reality done more than could have
reasonably been expected of them; his conviction,
in which he was firm almost to the last, that his
losses would be made good by the government, even
after he had been repeatedly told, in consequence of
repeated applications in various quarters, that the
government would not interfere in his affairs; and
his determination, on the failure of all, other means
to bring his affairs before the country, to effect this
purpose by assasinating the head of the government,
by which he would have an opportunity of making a
public statement of his grievances and obtaining a
triumph, which he never doubted, over the attorney-general; these were all delusions, as wild and
strange, as those of seven eighths of the inmates of
any lunatic asylum in the land.   And so obvious were
they, that though he had not the aid of an Erskine
to press them upon the attention of the jury, and
though he himself denied the imputation of insanity,
the government, as if virtually acknowledging their
existence, contended for his responsibility on very
different grounds.   As the various tests of this condition, commonly urged on such occasions, were
dwelt upon with unusual earnestness and force, and
with strong expressions of confidence in their value,
it may be well to examine them critically, in order

to ascertain how much weight they are really entitled to, in settling the question of criminal responsibility.

§ 16. In the trial of Arnold, already noticed, (§ 10) the jury were directed to settle it in their own minds, whether the accused was capable of distinguishing right from wrong, good from evil, and if they concluded that he was, that they must return a verdict of guilty. In Bellingham's case, the attorney-general declared, " upon the authority of the first sages in the country, and upon the authority of the established law in all times, which law has never been questioned, that although a man may be incapable of conducting his own affairs, he may still be answerable for his criminal acts, if he possess a mind capable of distinguishing right from wrong." [1] Lord Chief Justice Mansfield, who tried the case, echoed the same doctrine in his charge to the jury. In speaking of a species of insanity, in which the patient fancies the existence of injury, and seeks an opportunity of gratifying revenge by some hostile act, he says, "if such a person were capable, in other respects, of distinguishing right from wrong, there was no excuse for any act of atrocity, which he might commit under this description of derangement." [2] Mr. Russell, in his work on criminal law, includes inability to distinguish right from wrong

---

[1] 1 Collinson on Lunacy, 657.

[2] This opinion was delived scarcely a dozen years after the absurdity of its principles had been so happily exposed in a few words, by Mr. Erskine, on the trial of Hadfield. What a comment on the progress of improvement in the medical jurisprudence of insanity!

among the characters of that grade of insanity, which exempts from the punishment of crime.[1]

§ 17. That the insane mind is not entirely deprived of this power of moral discernment, but on many subjects is perfectly rational, and displays the exercise of a sound and well balanced mind, is one of those facts now so well established, that to ques-it would only betray the height of ignorance and presumption. The first result, therefore, to which the doctrine leads, is, that no man can ever successfully plead insanity in defence of crime, because it can be said of no one, who would have occasion for such a defence, that he was unable in any case to distinguish right from wrong. To show the full merits of the question, however, it is necessary to examine more particularly, how far this moral sentiment is affected by, and what relation it bears to insanity. By that partial possession of the reasoning powers, which has been spoken of as being enjoyed by maniacs generally, is meant to be implied the undiminished power of the mind, to contemplate some objects or ideas in their customary relations, among which are those pertaining to their right or wrong, their good or evil, tendency ; and it must comprise the whole of these relations, else the individual is not sane on these points. A person may regard his child with the feelings natural to the paternal bosom, at the very moment he believes himself commanded by a voice from heaven to sacrifice this child, in order to secure its eternal happi-

---

[1] Russell, on Crimes and Misdemeanors, 12.

ness, than which, of course, he could not accomplish a greater good. The conviction of a maniac's soundness, on certain subjects, is based in part on the moral aspect, in which he views those subjects ; for, it would be folly to consider a person rational, in reference to his parents and children, while he labors under an idea, that it would be doing God's service to kill them ; though he may talk rationally of their characters, dispositions and habits of life, their chances of success in their occupations, their past circumstances, and of the feelings of affection, which he has always cherished towards them. Before, therefore, an individual can be accounted sane on a particular subject, it must appear that he regards it correctly, in all its relations to right and wrong. The slightest acquaintance with the insane will convince any one of the truth of this position. In no school of logic, in no assembly of the just, can we listen to closer and shrewder argumentation, to warmer exhortations to duty, to more glowing descriptions of the beauty of virtue, or more indignant denunciations of evil-doing, than in the hospitals and asylums for the insane. And yet many of these very people may make no secret of entertaining notions utterly subversive of all moral propriety ; and, perhaps, are only waiting a favorable opportunity, to execute some project of wild and cruel violence. The purest minds cannot express greater horror and loathing of various crimes, than madmen often do, and from precisely the same causes. Their abstract conceptions of crime, not being perverted by the influence of disease, present its hideous outlines as strongly defined, as they ever were in the

c

healthiest condition ; and the disapprobation they
express at the sight arises from sincere and honest
convictions. The *particular* criminal act, however,
becomes divorced in their minds from its relations to
crime in the *abstract;* and, being regarded only in
connexion with some favorite object, which it may
help to obtain, and which they see no reason to refrain from pursuing, is viewed, in fact, as of a highly
laudable and meritorious nature. Herein, then, consists their insanity, not in preferring vice to virtue,
in applauding crime and ridiculing justice, but in
being unable to discern the essential identity of
nature, between a particular crime and all other
crimes, whereby they are led to approve, what, in
general terms, they have already condemned. It is
a fact, not calculated to increase our faith in the
march of intellect, that the very trait peculiarly
characteristic of insanity has been seized upon as
conclusive proof of sanity, in doubtful cases ; and,
thus, the infirmity that entitles one to protection is
tortured into a good and sufficient reason for completing his ruin.

§ 18. If this power of distinguishing right from
wrong do really indicate soundness of mind, it may
be justly complained, that the question of its existence is never agitated in any but criminal cases,
while it certainly should be whenever the rights and
liberties of the insane are to be invaded. If it is
proper to make those who possess this power responsible for their criminal acts, how unjust and absurd
is it to deprive them of their liberty, and seclude
them from their customary scenes and enjoyments,
before they have violated a single human law.   Un-

doubtedly, this measure will be conducive to their good, by taking from them effectually the opportunity of injuring the persons or property of themselves or others ; and so it would be for every other unprincipled and reckless individual, who bids fair to be a pest to society. But if it is alleged, that the latter are morally free, and, therefore, are personally free, till the commission of some external act, it may be replied, that the former, on the hypothesis of the law, which makes moral freedom consist in the power of distinguishing right from wrong, have the same claim to immunity from personal constraint. This preposterous distinction, between civil and criminal cases, gives rise in practice, to one of the most curious and startling inconsistencies, that human legislation ever presented. While the mental impairment is yet slight, comparatively, and the patient is quiet and peaceable, the law considers him incapable of managing himself or his worldly affairs, and provides him with a guardian and a place in the wards of a hospital ; but, when the disorder has proceeded to such a height as to deprive the maniac of all moral restraint, and precipitate him on some deed of violence, he is to be considered as most capable of perceiving moral distinctions, and, consequently, most responsible for his actions !

§ 19. The qualifications, with which some of the latest writers have promulgated this test of responsibility, encourage the hope, that it will ere long be viewed in a very different aspect. A disposition to disregard the old landmarks on this point was manifested, not long since, by Lord Lyndhurst, in the case of the King v. Orford, when he directed the

jury to acquit the prisoner, if satisfied, "that he did
not know, when he committed the act, what the effect of it, if fatal, would be, with reference to the
crime of murder;" [1] in other words, they were to
satisfy themselves, before acquitting him, that he did
not know, that the act would be essentially murder,
that crime, which in the abstract is equally abhorred
by the sane and the insane. Still, however, this is
not sufficient, for he might, like many others, have
loathed the act and been perfectly conscious of its
consequences to himself, while he felt impelled to its
execution by a voice from heaven, or by a strong
conviction of certain great ends which it was to promote, and thus have acted the part, if the expression
may be allowed, of an insane Abraham or Brutus.
This principle, therefore, is far from being universally applicable, though if it had been admitted in the
case of Bellingham, it would have produced the acquittal of that unfortunate man. The criminal act
which he committed was not viewed by him at all as
one of murder, any more than the killing of a brute
for the same purpose, but merely as a disagreeable
though justifiable method of bringing his affairs be-

---

[1] 5 Carrington and Payne, 168.   The defendant, in this case, was
tried for murder.   It appeared, that he entertained the notion, that the
person whom he shot and many others were desirous of depriving him
of his liberty, and had accordingly conspired together, to accomplish
their purpose, and, under the influence of this delusion, he would
abuse people whom he met in the streets, though wholly unacquainted
with them.   In his pocket was found a paper purporting to be "a List
of Hadleigh Conspirators against my Life," in which he had enrolled
the names of the deceased and his family.   Several medical witnesses,
who heard the evidence, deposed that the prisoner was affected with
monomania.

fore the country, and obtaining redress for his manifold wrongs and sufferings. And yet Lord Lyndhurst, in this very case, expressed his approbation of
the doctrines laid down by Lord Chief Justice Mansfield on the trial of Bellingham,—doctrines which he
had found it necessary here to modify, in order that
they might afford to an innocent man the protection
to which he was entitled! Mr. Chitty seems inclined to proceed a step farther on this point. " The
substantial question presented to the jury," he observes, "is, whether, at the time the alleged criminal act was committed, the prisoner was incapable
of judging between right and wrong, and did not
then know he was committing an offence against the
law of God and of nature." [1] By some late Scotch
writers on criminal law, this test of responsibility
has been disapproved of, in still more explicit terms.
Baron Hume disposes of it in the following language :
"Would he have answered on the question, that it is
wrong to kill a fellow creature ? this is hardly to be
considered a just criterion of such a state of mind, as
ought to make him answer to the law for his acts.
Because a person may happen to answer in this way,
who is yet so absolutely insane as to have lost all
power of observation of facts, all discernment of the
good or bad intentions of those who are about him,
or even the knowledge of their persons. Besides,
the question is put in another and a more special
sense, as relative to the act done by the panel, and
his knowledge of the place in which he did it. Did

---

[1] Medical Jurisprudence, 354.

he at that moment understand the evil of what he did ? Was he impressed with the consciousness of guilt and fear of punishment ?—it is then a pertinent and a material question, but one which cannot be rightly answered, without taking into consideration the whole circumstances of the situation. Every judgment in the matter of right and wrong supposes a case, or state of facts to which it applies. And though the person may have that vestige of reason, which may enable him to answer in the general, that murder is a crime, yet if he cannot distinguish a friend from an enemy, or a benefit from an injury, but conceives every thing about him to be the reverse of what it really is, and mistakes the ideas of his fancy in that respect, for realities, those remains of intellect are of no sort of service to him in the government of his actions, in enabling him to form a judgment as to what is right or wrong on any particular occasion." [1]   From all this, Hume draws the broad conclusion, that the judgment of right and wrong has nothing to do with the question of responsibility. This view of the subject is certainly liberal enough, and increases our regret, that it should be contrasted in a subsequent stage of his remarks, by one of those vague and senseless notions, that seem to have obtained a prescriptive place in the books on criminal law. "It is not to be understood," he continues, "that there is any privilege of mere weakness of intellect, or of a strange and

---

[1] Commentaries on the Law of Scotland respecting Crimes, Vol. I, p. 36.

moody humor, or of a crazy and capricious, or irregular temper and habit. None of these things either are, or ought to be law." When all these traits are observed in an undividual, or any one of them in a remarkable degree, there is great reason to suspect the existence of insanity, and the most faithful means should be resorted to, in order to determine this fact. In the great majority of cases, the suspicion will prove to be well founded, and the judgment of right and wrong on "particular occasions" to be completely perverted. These traits of character must not be considered, as they too generally are, in and by themselves exclusively, and unconnected with the previous moral and intellectual habits of the individual, but as symptoms of a deviation from the normal condition—of pathological changes in the action of the cerebral organism. When viewed in this light, they will be examined with the patience and intelligence, necessary to establish, beyond doubt, the existence of that insanity, of which they are the almost certain signs, instead of being hastily dismissed, as only the words of an ill-governed, malicious, temper.

§ 20. Mr. Alison lays down the principle, that "to amount to a complete bar to punishment, the insanity, either at the time of committing the crime, or of the trial, must have been of such a kind as entirely deprived the accused of the use of reason, *as applied to the act in question,* and the knowledge that he was doing wrong in committing it." [1] This is all very clear and rational, but a subsequent remark

---

[1] Criminal Law of Scotland, p. 645.

shows, that in his struggle with the errors of the
law, he had not completely emancipated his mind
from their binding influence. " Any thing," he observes, "short of this complete alienation of reason,
will be no defence ; and mere oddity of manner, or
half-craziness of disposition, if unaccompanied by
such an obscuring of the conscience, will not avail
the prisoner." The idea that "any thing short of
complete alienation of reason will be no defence,"
is not only at variance with his previous qualification, that this loss of reason must be in reference
" to the act in question," but is identically the doctrine of the last century, the fallacy of which was
clearly exposed by Erskine in Hadfield's case.
What is precisely meant by such vague phraseology,
as "half-craziness of disposition," it would be hardly
worth while to inquire; it is enough to say, that,
taking the language in its most natural and obvious
signification, the mental condition expressed by it is
one utterly unknown in metaphysics or medicine.
Mr. Alison very justly disapproves of the law, as
laid down by Chief Justice Mansfield, in Bellingham's
case, viz. ; that the prisoner was accountable, because he could distinguish good from evil, and knew
that murder was a crime ; but his remark respecting
it betrays an ignorance of insanity, that would be
surprising were it not so common in discussions upon
this subject. "On this case," says he, "it may be
observed, that unquestionably the mere fancying a
series of injuries to have been received will not
serve as an excuse for murder, for this plain reason,
that, supposing it true, that such injuries had been
received, they would have furnished no excuse for

the shedding of blood ; but, on the other hand, such an illusion, as deprives the panel of the sense that what he did was wrong, amounts to legal insanity, though he was perfectly aware that murder in general was a crime; and, therefore, the law appears to have been more correctly laid down, in the cases of Hadfield and Bowler, than in this instance." If this be the law by which maniacs are to be tried, few will escape punishment for criminal acts; for, in by far the greater proportion, such acts have been committed in consequence of a fancying of injuries received. One man kills his neighbor, whom he fancies to have joined a conspiracy to defraud him of his property or his liberty ; or for having insulted and exposed him to scorn and derision ; or for standing in the way of his attaining certain honors or estates; yet the insanity is not to excuse him, unless it deprived him of the consciousness, that he was doing a wrong act. The existence of the illusion is obvious and cannot be mistaken ; but what may be the views of the maniac, respecting the moral character of the criminal acts which he commits under its influence, can never be exactly known; and, therefore, they ought not to be made the criterion of responsibility. But it is known, that one of the most striking and characteristic effects of insanity in the mental operations is, to destroy the relations between end and means—between the object in view and the course necessary to pursue in order to obtain it. It was in accordance with these views, that Lord Erskine pronounced *delusion* to be the true test of such insanity as exempts from punishment, and that the correctness of the principle was recognised by the Court.

It is impossible, therefore, to divine why Mr. Alison should say, that the law was more correctly laid down in Hadfield's case, when it is in direct conflict with his own opinions. Thus, as if frightened by their own temerity in overthrowing one ancient land-mark on the domain of error, it would seem as if these writers were anxious to compound with their fears, by adhering with unusual pertinacity to all the rest. The radical fault of this test of responsibility lies in the metaphysical error of always looking on right and wrong in the abstract,—as things having a positive and independent existence, and not as they really are, mere terms expressing the relations, that exist between actions and certain faculties of our moral nature. That they express the same relations in nearly all men, is because nearly all men possess the same faculties; but when these faculties are absent, as in idiots, or when their action is perverted by disease, as in the insane, the relations of right and wrong are widely different.

§ 21. Another trait, which has been greatly relied on as a criterion in doubtful cases, is the design, or contrivance, that has been manifested in the commission of the criminal act. That it should ever have been viewed in this light, is an additional proof, if more were wanting, of the deplorable igno-rance, that characterizes the jurisprudence of insan-ity; for the slightest practical acquaintance with the disease would have prevented this pernicious mis-take. The source of this error is probably to be found in the fact, " that, among the vulgar, some are for reckoning madmen, those only who are frantic, or violent to some degree ; " [1] the violence being supposed to preclude every attempt at design, or plan of operations. In the trial of Bellingham, the attorney-general declared, that, "if even insanity in all his other acts had been manifest, yet the *systematic correctness*, with which the prisoner contrived the murder, showed that he possessed a mind, at the time, capable of distinguishing right from wrong." [2] In Arnold's case (§ 10), great stress was laid on the circumstances of his having purchased shot of a much larger size, than he usually did when he went out to shoot, with the design then formed of committing the murder he afterwards attempted. Mr. Russell [3] recognises the correctness of the principle, and lays it down as part of the law of the land. If, however, the power of design is really not incompatible with the existence of insanity, this pretended test must be as fallacious as that already adverted to. What must be thought of the attainments of those learned authorities, in the study of madness, who see in the power of systematic design a disproof of the existence of insanity, when, from the humblest menial in the service of a lunatic asylum, they might have heard of the ingenuity of contrivance and adroitness of execution, that preëminently characterize the plans of the insane ? If the mind continues rational on some subjects, it is no more than might be expected, that this rationality should em-

---

[1] Sir John Nicholl, in Dew *v.* Clark, 3 Addams's Reports, 441.
[2] Collinson on Lunacy, 657.
[3] 1 Russell, on Crimes and Misdemeanors, 13.

brace the power of design, since a person could not properly be called rational on any point, in regard to which he had lost his customary ability to form his plans and designs for the future. These views are abundantly confirmed by every day's observation. The sentiment of cunning, too, which is necessary to the successful execution of one's projects, holds but a low place in the scale of the mental faculties—being a merely animal instinct—and is oftentimes observed to be rendered more active by insanity, so as to require the utmost vigilance to detect and defeat its wiles. One, who is not practically acquainted with the habits of the insane, can scarcely conceive of the cunning which they will practise, when bent on accomplishing a favorite object. Indeed, it may be said, without greatly distorting the truth, that the combined cunning of two maniacs, bent on accomplishing a certain object, is always a match for the sagacity of any sound individual. Those, for instance, whose madness takes a suicidal direction, are known to employ wonderful address, in procuring and concealing the means of self-destruction ; pretending to have seen the folly of their designs, and to have renounced them entirely, sending away their keepers after thus, lulling them into security, and, when least expected renewing their suicidal attempts. When desirous of leaving their confinement also, the consummate tact, with which they will set suspicion at rest, the forecast with which they make their preparations for escape, and the sagacity with which they choose the time and place of action, would do infinite credit to the conceptions of the most sound and

intelligent minds. Mr. Haslam has related a case
so strikingly illustrative of this trait, that it is well
worth extracting in this connexion. An Essex farmer,
after having so well counterfeited recovery as to
produce his liberation, and being sent back again,
immediately became tranquil, and remonstrated on
the injustice of his confinement. "Having once
deceived me, he wished much, that my opinion
should be taken respecting the state of his intellects,
and assured his friends that he would submit to my
determination. I had taken care to be well prepared
for this interview, by obtaining an accurate account of
the manner, in which he had conducted himself. At
this examination, he managed himself with admirable address. He spoke of the treatment he had
received, from the persons under whose care he was
then placed, as most kind and fatherly : he also expressed himself as particularly fortunate in being
under my care, and bestowed many handsome com-
pliments on my skill in treating this disorder, and
expatiated on my sagacity in perceiving the slightest
tinges of insanity. When I wished him to explain
certain parts of his conduct, and particularly some
extravagant opinions, respecting certain persons and
circumstances, he disclaimed all knowledge of such
circumstances, and felt himself hurt that my mind
should have been poisoned so much to his prejudice.
He displayed equal subtlety on three other occasions,
when I visited him ; although, by protracting the
conversation, he let fall sufficient to satisfy my mind
that he was a madman. In a short time he was removed to the hospital, where he expressed great
satisfaction in being under my inspection. The pri-

vate madhouse, which he had formerly so much commended, now became the subject of severe animadversion ; he said that he had there been treated with extreme cruelty ; that he had been nearly starved, and eaten up by vermin of various descriptions. On inquiring of some convalescent patients, I found (as I had suspected) that I was as much the subject of abuse, when absent, as any of his supposed enemies, although to my face, he was courteous and respectful. More than a month had elapsed since his admission into the hospital, before he pressed me for my opinion ; probably confiding in his address and hoping to deceive me. At length he appealed to my decision, and urged the correctness of his conduct during confinement, as an argument for his liberation. But, when I informed him of circumstances he supposed me unacquainted with, and assured him, that he was a proper subject for the asylum which he then inhabited, he suddenly poured forth a torrent of abuse ; talked in the most incoherent manner ; insisted on the truth of what he formerly denied ; breathed vengeance against his family and friends ; and became so outrageous that it was necessary to order him to be strictly confined. He continued in a state of unceasing fury for more than fifteen months." [1] But the purely intellectual power of combining a series of acts, that shall accomplish or eventuate in certain results, when properly carried into execution, seems to be not only less frequently involved in the mental derangement, but often to

---

[1] Observations on Madness, 53.

have received a preternatural degree of strength and activity. Pinel speaks of a maniac, who endeavored to discover the perpetual motion, and, in the course of his attempts, constructed some very curious machines. The plans, which the brain of a maniac, who imagines himself a monarch, is perpetually hatching for the management of his kingdom, will bear to be compared with the political schemes of some rulers, who are supposed to have the advantage of sanity on their side.

§ 22. If then, the knowledge of good and evil, of right and wrong, and the power of design, are to be considered as fallacious tests of responsibility, notwithstanding they have proved the death-warrant of many a wretched maniac, let us come back to that proposed by Erskine—*delusion*—and see if that will bear a more rigid scrutiny, when viewed by the light of modern discovery.[1] Now, if it were a fact, that the reason, or, to speak more definitely, the intellectual powers, are exclusively liable to derangement, this test would be unobjectionable, and would

---

[1] The use of this test of insanity has been sanctioned by the high authority of Sir John Nicholl, in the case of Dew v. Clark, 3 Addams, 79. "The true criterion," says he, "the true test, of the absence or presence of insanity, I take to be the absence or presence of what, used in a *certain* sense of it, is comprisable in a single term, namely—*delusion*." "In short I look upon delusion in this sense of it, and insanity to be, almost if not altogether, convertible terms." "On the contrary, in the absence of any such delusion, with whatever extravagances a supposed lunatic may be justly chargeable, and how like soever to a real madman he may either think or act on some one, or on all subjects; still, in the absence, I repeat, of any thing in the nature of *delusion*, so understood as above, the *supposed* lunatic is in my judgment, not properly, or essentially insane."

furnish an easy and satisfactory clew to the elucidation of doubtful cases.[1]   But it must not be forgotten,
that the author of our being has also endowed us
with certain moral faculties, comprising the various
sentiments, propensities and affections, which, like
the intellect, being connected with the brain, are
necessarily affected by pathological actions in that
organism.   The abnormal condition thus produced
may exert an astonishing influence on the conduct,
changing the peaceable and retiring individual into a
demon of fury, or, at the least, turning him from the
calm and quiet of his lawful and innocent occupations, into a career of shameless dissipation and debauchery, while the intellectual perceptions seem to
have lost none of their ordinary soundness and vigor.
The existence of this form of insanity is now too well

---

[1] Even Mr. Erskine himself has furnished an exception to his own
rule, in a case he has related of a young woman indicted for murder,
who was acquitted on the ground of insanity, though it was not pretended, that she labored under any delusion whatever.   " It must be a
consolation," he says, "to those who prosecuted her, that she was acquitted, as she is at this time in a most undoubted and deplorable state
of insanity ; but I confess, if I had been upon the jury who tried her,
I should have entertained great doubts and difficulties ; for, although
this unhappy woman had before exhibited strong marks of insanity
arising from grief and disappointment ; yet she acted upon facts and
circumstances, which had an *existence*, and which were calculated,
upon the ordinary principles of human action, to produce the most
violent resentment. Mr. Errington having just cast her off, and married
another woman, or taken her under his protection, her jealousy was
excited to such a pitch, as occasionally to overpower her understanding ; but when she went to Mr. Errington's house where she shot him,
she went with the express and deliberate purpose of shooting him."
"She did not act under a delusion, that he had deserted her when he
had not, but took revenge upon him for an actual desertion." Erskine's
Speeches.

established, to be questioned by those who have any scientific reputation to lose; and though the proofs of this will be furnished in their proper place, it will, for the present, be supposed that the assent of the reader has been obtained without them. In this, the most deplorable condition, to which a human being can be reduced, where the wretched patient finds himself urged, perhaps, to the commission of every outrage, and though perfectly conscious of what he is doing, unable to offer the slightest resistance to the overwhelming power that impels him, the responsibility is to be considered not affected, because no *delusion* is present to disturb and distort the mental vision! In short, the very character, that renders this mental disorder more terrible than all others, is also that which is made to steel the heart against the claims of humanity in behalf of its miserable victim.

§ 23. The doctrine of moral insanity has been as yet unfavorably received by judicial authorities, not certainly for want of sufficient facts to support it, but probably from that common tendency of the mind, to resist innovations upon old and generally received views. If, a quarter of a century ago, one of the highest law-officers of Great Britain pronounced the manifestation of "systematic correctness" of an action, a proof of sanity sufficient to render all others unnecessary, it is not surprising, that the idea of moral insanity has been considered by the legal profession, as having sprung from the teeming brains of medical theorists. In the fulness of this spirit, Mr. Chitty declares, that, "unless a jury should be satisfied that the *mental faculties* have been *perverted*, **or,** at least, the faculties of reason and judgment, it is believed, that the party subject to such a *moral* insanity, as it is termed, would not be protected from criminal punishment"; [1] and, in the trial of Howison for the murder of the widow Geddes at King's Cramond, Scotland, two or three years since, moral insanity, which was pleaded in his defence, was declared by the court to be a "groundless theory." [2] Such opinions, from quarters, where a modest teachableness would have been more becoming than an arrogant contempt for the results of other men's inquiries, involuntarily suggest to the mind a comparison of their authors with the saintly persecutors of Galileo, who resolved, by solemn statutes, that nature always had operated and always should operate in accordance with their views of propriety and truth.

§ 24. It appears, then, that, in cases of doubtful insanity, delusion is a test no better than those before mentioned; and, indeed, there is no single character which is not equally liable to objection. Jurists, who have been so anxious to obtain some definition of insanity, which shall embrace every possible case, should understand, that such a wish is chimerical, from the very nature of things.   Insanity is a disease, and, as is the case with all other diseases, the fact of its existence is never established by a single diagnostic symptom, but by the whole body of symptoms, no particular one of which is present in every case.   To distinguish the manifestations of

---

[1] 1 Chitty, Medical Jurisprudence, 352.

[2] Simpson on Homicidal Insanity, in a Treatise on Popular Education. Boston, 1834.

health from those of disease requires the exercise of
learning and judgment; and, if no one doubts this
proposition, when stated in reference to the bowels,
the lungs, the heart, the liver, the kidneys, &c.,
what sufficient or even plausible reason is there,
why it should be doubted when predicated of the
brain ? The functions of those organs proceed with
the regularity and sameness of clock-work, compared
with the ever-varying and unequal phenomena of
this; and yet there are persons, who assume a magis-
terial tone in writing or talking of the latter, who
would defer to a tyro's judgment, in whatever concerns the others. If, when anxious to know all we
can, respecting a disease of the lungs or stomach, we
repair to those who have a high and well-founded
reputation, in the pathology of these parts, why
adopt the converse of this rule in regard to diseases
of the brain ? No reasonable person would desire
to set up an insuperable barrier, between the domain
of professional knowledge, and that of common sense
and common information; but, it is not too much to
insist, that facts, established by men of undoubted
competence and good faith, should be rejected for better reasons, than the charge of "groundless theory."

§ 25. In the passage taken from Lord Hale (§ 8),
it will be observed, that he considers all crime to be
the offspring of partial insanity, and the inference he
meant should be drawn from it is, that partial insanity furnishes no excuse for crime. It is a curious
fact, that many benevolent people in their desire to
palliate the sins of criminals have inculcated the
same principle, for the purpose of drawing from it a
very different inference. The logic, by which such

opposite conclusions are arrived at, is certainly not unworthy the days of Duns Scotus or Thomas Aquinas. Says the former : crime must be punished ; but all crime proceeds from madness, therefore madness furnishes no exemption from punishment. Say the latter : madmen are not responsible for their criminal acts ; but madness is the source of all crime, therefore madmen and criminals are equally irresponsible and exempt from punishment. Which of these two precious specimens of human subtlety can claim the triumph of absurdity, it would not be easy to determine. Crime is not necessarily the result of madness, not even when perpetrated under the excitement of fierce and violent passions; in the true sense of the word, it is never so, but is always actuated by motives ; insufficient it may be, but still rational motives, having reference to definite and real objects. The misfortune which the criminal is going to avert, the interest which he is going to subserve, the revenge he is about to gratify, the insult or injury he is about to repay, are *real* injuries and insults and interests, however much they may be exaggerated, or however disproportionately small they may be to the crime they provoke; and, the ends, to be obtained by the criminal act, are real and have an appreciable value. In the most violent transports of passion, he never loses his knowledge of the true relations of things. The person whom he considers his enemy, or the author of the insult, is really such, or at least, he has some ground for believing him such; and, with the absence of the object of his passion, disappears the intention to offend. Violent passions may weaken the judgment, and diminish its power of control, but they do not vitiate the perceptions, nor deprive the mind of its powers of comparison. All this is very different in mental derangement. The causes, which urge the insane to deeds of violence, are generally illusory—the hallucinations of a diseased brain—or they may act from no motive at all, solely in obedience to a blind impulse, with no end to obtain, nor wish to gratify. Madness too is more or less independent of the exciting causes, that have given rise to it, and exists long after those causes have been removed, and after the paramount wish or object has been obtained. In short, madness is the result of a certain pathological condition of the brain, while the criminal effects of violent passions merely indicate unusual strength of those passions, or a deficient education of those higher and nobler faculties, that furnish the necessary restraint upon their power. It is admitted, that strong passions do deprive the individual of the power of calmly deliberating, and perceiving the terrible consequences of his fury; and legislators have wisely distinguished it from deliberate, premeditated mischief, by uniting it with a minor degree of punishment. In drunkenness the same effect is produced to such a degree as to amount to temporary insanity; but neither does this any more than strong passions exempt from all punishment; for the plain reason, that, in each case, the impairment of moral liberty is the voluntary act of the individual himself. The fact of mental unsoundness admitted, it always remains to be determined, whether it is of the person's own immediate procuring, or is the result of circumstances, over which he had no control. If the remarks on this point may seem to be unnecessarily prolix, it can only be observed, by way of excuse, that, where opinions are handed down, as they are in law, from one generation to another, they attain much the same kind of value, that is possessed by established facts in natural science, and exert an influence that demands for them a degree of consideration, which their intrinsic merits do not deserve.

§ 26. Enough has been said, it is believed, to convince every unprejudiced reader, that, in Great Britain, the law of insanity, especially that relative to criminal cases, is still loose, vacillating, and greatly behind the present state of the knowledge of that disease. That it is no better in this country, may be readily inferred, when it is considered, that, in the absence of any provisions by statute, the practice of our courts is completely regulated by that of England. Criminal trials, in which insanity is pleaded in defence, are generally so little known, beyond the place of their occurrence, that it is difficult to ascertain on what particular principles of the common law, the decisions of the courts have been founded, though from all that can be gathered, their practice, like that of the British, has been diverse and fluctuating. In one or two instances, the jury have been permitted to found their verdict on the principles laid down in Hadfield's case ; in some others, they have imitated the conduct of the English courts, which, as if blinded by the little light struck out in the discussions connected with that trial, turned back to the old maxims and again rejoiced in the wisdom of their ancestors. The frequency with which insanity is pleaded in defence of crime, the magnitude of its consequences to the parties concerned, and the perplexity in which the discussions it occasions involve the minds of judges and· jurors, are ample reasons why the law relative to insanity should be simple and easily understood— a result that can only be obtained by direct legislative enactments. It is time for the legislature to determine, what, amid the mass of conflicting opinions on this subject, shall be the law of the land; and thus no longer permit the lives and liberties of our citizens to be suspended on the dicta of men, whose knowledge of insanity was exceedingly imperfect, and which have not even the merit of uniformity and consistency. It may be doubted, whether a less general provision, than that of the French penal code would better promote the purposes of justice. Under this law, when strictly applied, if the existence of insanity is once established, the responsibility of the party is taken away; and all nice discussions concerning the effect of this or that kind or degree of mental derangement, and the exact measure of reason that has been left or taken away, are thus effectually precluded. It is not certain, that insanity, under every form or circumstance whatever, ought to annul a person's criminal or civil liabilities; and, to allow the court or jury any latitude on this point, would be equivalent to having no law at all on the subject. If the mental unsoundness, necessary to exempt from punishment, were required by the law to have embraced the criminal act within the sphere of its influence, as much perhaps would then be accomplished as is practicable in a specific enactment. True, the fact of insanity would be left, as it now is, with the jury to decide ; but, as they would no longer be puzzled with metaphysical distinctions between total and partial insanity, and engaged in nice estimates of the knowledge of good and evil, of right and wrong, and of the power of design possessed by the accused, their inquiries would be narrowed down to the single fact of mental impairment on a certain point—a duty much less remote from the train of their ordinary habits and pursuits.   Thus a great object would be gained, for the more that is provided by statute and the less that is left to judicial discretion, the greater is the benefit afforded by law.[1]

§ 27. As the conclusions of the jury, relative to the existence of insanity, must necessarily be based on the testimony offered by the parties, it is a subject of the utmost importance, by whom and in what manner, this testimony shall be given. If the decision of this point were purely a matter of facts, the only duty of the jury would be to see that they were sufficient for the purpose and proceeded from authentic sources ; but, on the contrary, it is a matter of inference to be drawn from certain data, and this is a duty for which our juries, as at present constituted, are manifestly unfit. That a body of men, taken promiscuously from the common walks of life, should be required to decide, whether or not certain opin-

---

[1] The state of New York has adopted the principle of the French law, in reference to this point. "No act done by a person in a state of insanity can be punished as an offence, and no insane person can be tried, sentenced to any punishment, or punished, for any crime or offence which he commits in that state." 2 Revised Statutes, 697.

ions and facts in evidence prove derangement of
mind, or, in other words, to decide a professional
question of a most delicate nature and involving
some of the highest interests of man, is an idea so
preposterous, that one finds it difficult, at first sight,
to believe that it ever was seriously entertained.
Such, however, is made their business, and, in the
performance of it, there is but one alternative for
them to follow ;—either to receive with the utmost
deference the opinions of those, who have a professional acquaintance with the subject, or to slight
them altogether, and rely solely on their own judgment of the facts. The latter course has sometimes
been adopted, though no one, probably, personally
concerned in the issue of the case, would congratu-
late himself on their choice, unless specially anxious
to become a victim of ignorance and obstinacy. But,
in the larger proportion of cases, the medical testimony, which is given in the shape of opinions, though
rather an anomaly in evidence, that courts have been
sorely puzzled at times whether to admit or reject,
is mostly relied on, and determines the verdict of the
jury. It is, perhaps, of little consequence, who
testifies to a simple fact, that it requires only eyes
to see, or ears to hear ; but it is all very different
with the delivery of opinions, that are to shape the
final decision. As this requires an exercise of judgment as well as observation, there ought to be some
kind of qualification, on the part of those who render
such opinions, not required of one who testifies to
mere facts. The understanding certainly is, that
their habits, pursuits, and talents, have rendered
them peculiarly competent for this high duty, for in

the absence of the power of cross-examination, these constitute the only pledge that can be had of its correct and faithful performance. But as the law makes no exclusion, and the witnesses' stand is open to any one, whom the parties may choose to call, it frequently happens, that the witness has nothing but his professional character to rely on, to give his opinions the authority they ought to possess. And even when he may have been preceded by the shadow of a great reputation, the jury may not know, nor be able to discover, how much of that reputation is a factitious one; and, in consequence, may be induced to confide in opinions, which, from a different quarter, they would have listened to with feelings of doubt and distrust.

§ 23. It is not enough, that the standing of the medical witness is deservedly high in his profession, unless it is founded on extraordinary knowledge and skill relative to the particular disease, insanity. Lunatic asylums and retreats for the insane have so multiplied in our country, that patients of this class are almost entirely taken away from the management of the private physician, and consigned to the more skilful conductors of these institutions; so that many a medical man may spend a life of full practice, without having been intrusted with the care of a dozen insane persons. To such, therefore, a practical knowledge of the disease is out of the question, and thus the principal inducement is wanting, to become acquainted with the labors of those, who have enjoyed better opportunities. If a particular class of men only are thought capable of managing the treatment of the insane, it would seem to follow, as a matter of course, that such only are capable of giving opinions in judicial proceedings relative to insanity. True, in important cases, the testimony of one or more of this class is generally given ; but it may be contradicted by that of others utterly guiltless of any knowledge of the subject, on which they tender their opinions with arrogant confidence—for ignorance is always confident—and the jury is seldom a proper tribunal for distinguishing the true from the false, and fixing on each its rightful value. An enlightened and conscientious jury, when required to decide in a case of doubtful insanity, which is to determine the weal or woe of a fellow-being, fully alive to the delicacy and responsibility of their situation, and of their own incompetence unaided by the counsels of others, will be satisfied with nothing less than the opinions of those, who have possessed unusual opportunities for studying the character and conduct of the insane, and have the qualities of mind necessary to enable them to profit by their observations. If they are obliged to decide on professional subjects, it would seem but just and the dictate of common sense, that they should have the benefit of the best professional advice. This, however, they do not always have ; and, consequently, the ends of justice are too often defeated by the high-sounding assumptions of ignorance and vanity.

§ 29. It may at first sight be thought impossible to remedy this defect, without what would seem to be an engraftment upon our judicial system, of practices not in perfect harmony with it; but the difficulty, after all, may not be found utterly intractable, if names are not allowed to usurp in our minds the place of things. Instead of the unqualified and irresponsible witnesses, now too often brought forward to enlighten the minds of jurymen on medical subjects, it would be far better, if we had a class of men, more or less like that of the *experts* [1] of the French, peculiarly fitted for the duty by a course of studies expressly directed to this end. They might be appointed by the government, in numbers adapted to the wants and circumstances of the population, and should be always ready at the call of courts, to examine the health of criminals, draw up reports touching the same, and deliver opinions. When the

---

[1] The term *experts* is used in the French law, to designate certain persons, appointed in the course of a judicial proceeding, either by the court or by the agreement of the parties, to make inquiry under oath, in reference to certain facts and to report thereon to the court. They are not examined as witnesses; nor have they the power of deciding the cause, like arbitrators; their functions are more analogous to those of a master in chancery, according to our laws. The following extract from Pothier's Treatise on Civil Procedure (Part I, chap. III, art III, § I,) will give an idea of the functions of these officers.

"The decision of a cause frequently depends on some fact, contested between the parties, which can only be established by a visit to the thing, which makes the object of the contestation; for example, the buyer of a horse brings a *redhibitory* action against the seller, to compel the latter to take back the horse, on account of some pretended defect, which the former alleges entitles him to a return; if the seller denies the existence of the defect, this fact, upon which the decision of the cause depends, can only be ascertained by an examination of the horse by *experts*; and the judge, therefore, before rendering a definitive judgment, must order the animal to be examined by *experts*, who shall report whether he labors under the said defect or not. In like manner, if I make a bargain with a workman, to do certain work upon a house, and when the latter demands the agreed price of me, I object that the work is badly done and therefore not receivable, there must be an order for an examination by experts."

courts see the minds of jurors perplexed and confounded by the contradictory opinions of medical
witnesses, and with no means of satisfying themselves
as to what is really true, it should be their duty to
submit the accused to the examination of *experts*, who
should report at a subsequent period. Something
like this is often done in France, which is much before our own country, or even England, in every
thing relative to the judicial relations of medical
men.[1] Thus, in the case of Henriette Cornier, in Paris,
for murdering a neighbor's child, November 4, 1825,
the court, at the request of the prisoner's counsel,
made shortly before the trial, which was ordered to
take place February 27, 1826, appointed a committee
of three distinguished physicians, to report, after due
examination, whether or not she was a fit subject for
trial. Their reports not being satisfactory to the
avocat-general (attorney-general), the trial, at his
request, was postponed to another session, and the
prisoner was again subjected to the examination of
the committee, who reported three months after-

---

[1] Foderè (De medicine legale, Tome I, Introd. p. xlii.) relates with
the most naïve astonishment, that, in a question of survivorship, arising out of the accouchement of Mrs. Fischer in England, the opinion
of the celebrated Denman was rejected by a jury, that yielded implicit
belief in the testimony of one Dallas who was not a physician, and of
two ignorant women, who spoke only from memory, after the expira-
tion of fourteen years. Many readers may recollect, that, in the case of
Donellan, tried in 1781 (see 2 Beck's Medical Jurisprudence, fifth
edition, page 563), for the murder of Sir Theodosius Boughton, by
poisoning, the opinions of three or four physicians, as unknown to
fame, as the science they professed to understand seems to have been
unknown to them, far outweighed with the court, that of John Hunter,
though illustrated by his various learning, and supported by his reputation for unrivalled talents and original research.

wards.[1] What a contrast, does this calm and deliberate inquiry present to the indecent haste, with
which the legal proceedings were precipitated against
Bellingham, who committed his offence, was indicted,
tried and hung, all within the space of eight days.
In this case, there was a strong disinclination manifested by the court, to listen to the plea of insanity;
as if it were a fiction set up by counsel, in the absence of any other ground of defence; and the earn-
est request of his counsel for a little delay, that he
might obtain witnesses from the part of the country,
where the accused had lived and was well-known,
who would substantiate the fact of his insanity, of
which there was already more than suspicion, was
disregarded. Few, it is believed, at this period,
unbiassed by the political prejudices of the times,
and examining the event as a point of history, will
read the report of Bellingham's trial, without being
forced to the conclusion, that he was really mad, or,
at the very least, that the little evidence, which did
appear relative to his state of mind, was strong
enough to have entitled him to a deliberate and
thorough investigation of his case. Mr. Simpson,[2]
after mentioning the case of Howison, who was tried
and executed for the murder of the widow Geddes,
in which the evidence of his insanity was so strong,
that it is almost impossible to conceive what additional evidence could make it stronger, states, that
"application was made without success to the secre-

---

[1] Georget, Discussion médico-légale sur la Folie, p. 71.
[2] Homicidal Insanity, p. 222.

tary of state, by Howison's law-agent, for time to obtain further evidence of his insanity. To this that gentleman was emboldened, by receiving the concurring opinions of some of the first medical men in Edinburgh, who had not been cited, that even the evidence adduced on the trial was sufficient; but, that, when several post-judicial facts were added, there could be no doubt that the unhappy man was not a fit subject for punishment." Cases like these ought to convince us, that the feelings of horror and vengeance, excited by the bloody deeds of the insane, completely unfit the popular mind for a careful and impartial investigation of the plea of insanity, and that the mental condition of the accused should be examined by men, who have become fitted for such duties, by a peculiar course of study and experience. Is it necessary, to go into a labored argument to prove, that this method of determining the grave and delicate question of insanity must be infinitely more satisfactory, than that of summoning medical witnesses to the trial—most of whom have but very imperfect notions of the disease, and probably have not had the least communication with the accused,—and forcing out their evidence, amid the embarrassment produced by the queries of ingenious counsel, bent on puzzling and distracting their minds? If a physician, after listening to divers vague and rambling details, concerning a person's ill-health, and looking at him across the apartment, without being permitted to address to him a single word, or lay a finger on his person, should then be required to say on his oath, whether or not the individual in question were laboring under inflammation of the lungs, bowels, or kidneys, he would scarcely restrain a smile at the stupidity, which should expect a satisfactory answer. And yet, absurd and foolish as such a course would be considered, in the abstract, it is the only one recognised by our laws, when the disease, whose existence is to be established, happens to be insanity. Besides, where mental derangement is suspected, there are many physical symptoms and numerous other circumstances, that cannot be investigated in an hour or a day, but require a course of diligent observation, that may occupy weeks or months, before the suspicion can be confirmed or disproved. From these considerations, the general conclusion is, that, in criminal cases, where insanity is pleaded in defence, the ends of justice will be best promoted, by the appointment of a special commission, consisting of men who possess a well-earned reputation in the knowledge and management of mental derangement, who shall proceed to the examination of the accused, with the coolness and impartiality proper to scientific inquiries.

§ 30. If the above hasty review of the judicial opinions and practices, that have hitherto prevailed relative to insanity, have left the impression, that this disease is as yet but imperfectly understood, as well in the medical profession as out of it, an explanation of this fact may perhaps be demanded; but, as it would be hardly relevant to the present purpose, to enter largely into a discussion of this point, nothing more will be attempted than merely to indicate what seems to have had the principal share in producing it. To explain the little progress, comparatively speaking, that has been made by medical men in the knowledge

of insanity, it is too much the fashion to allege, that
they have neglected the study of mental philosophy,
or that of mind in the healthy state, which is indispensable to correct notions on the disordered condition of mind. So far, however, is the fact here indicated from being true, generally, that one can
not hesitate to say, that the result in question has
been owing to the undue account, that physicians
have made of the popular philosophy of mind, in
explaining the phenomena of insanity, and that they
have failed, in consequence of studying metaphysics
too much instead of too little. While it is admitted,
that the knowledge of healthy structure and functions is necessary to a thorough understanding of
diseased structure and functions, there is every reason to believe that the converse of the proposition
is equally true ; neither can be successfully studied
independently of the other. In the prosecution of
psychological science, this latter truth has been almost entirely disregarded, and therefore it is, that
we see the metaphysician looking for his facts and
his theories in the healthy manifestations of the
mind, and directed in his course solely by his own
self-consciousness, while the student of insanity,
after collecting his facts with commendable diligence
and discrimination, amid the disorder and irregularity of disease, resorts to the theories of the former,
for the purpose of generalizing his results, instead of
building upon them a philosophy of his own. Metaphysics, in its present condition, is utterly incompetent to furnish a satisfactory explanation of the phenomena of insanity, and a more deplorable waste of
ingenuity can hardly be imagined, than is witnessed

in the modern attempts to reconcile the facts of the one with the speculations of the other. In proof of the truth of these assertions, it is enough barely to mention, that the existence of monomania, as a distinct form of mental derangement, was denied, and declared to be a fiction of medical men, long after it had taken its place among the established truths of science ; because, probably, it was a condition of mind not described by metaphysical writers. All this, however, is in accordance with a well-known law of the human mind, which resists important innovations upon the common modes of thinking, till long after they shall have been required by the general progress of knowledge. The dominant philosophy has prevailed so long and so extensively, and has become so firmly rooted in men's minds, that they who refuse to take it on trust and seriously inquire into its foundations, and after finding them too narrow and imperfect, are bold enough to endeavor to remedy its defects by laying foundations of their own, are stigmatized as visionaries and overwhelmed with ridicule and censure. The only metaphysical system of modern times, which professes to be founded on the observation of nature, and which really does explain the phenomena of insanity, with a clearness and verisimilitude, that strongly corroborate its proofs, was so far from being joyfully welcomed, that it is still confined to a sect, and is regarded by the world at large, as one of those strange vagaries, in which the human mind has sometimes loved to indulge. So true it is, that, in theory, all mankind are agreed in encouraging and applauding the humblest attempt to enlarge the sphere of our ideas, while, in practice, it often seems, as if they were no less agreed to crush them, by means of every weapon, that wit, argument, and calumny, can furnish. In the course of this work, the reader will have frequent occasions to see how the popular misconceptions,—which are too much adopted by professional men—of the nature of various forms of mental derangement, have been produced and fostered by the current metaphysical doctrines, and thus may have some means of judging for himself, how far the imperfect notions of insanity, that are yet prevalent, may be attributed to the cause above assigned.

CHAPTER I.

MENTAL DISEASES IN GENERAL.

§ 31. CORRECT ideas of the pathology of insanity are not unessential to the progress of enlightened views respecting its legal relations. If it be considered as withdrawn from the influence of the common laws of nature, in the production of disease, and attributed to the direct visitation of God; if the existence of physical changes be overlooked or denied, and we are referred exclusively to some mysterious affection of the immaterial spirit, for its cause; then is it in vain to hope, that such a condition can ever be the object of discriminating, salutary legislation. In the prevalence of such views in past times, however, we may look for the cause of much of the error and absurdity, that pervade the law of insanity, and that are equally at variance with the principles of science and the dictates of humanity. It is an undoubted truth, that the manifestations of the intellect, and those of the sentiments, propensities and passions, or generally, of the intellectual and affective powers, are connected with and dependent upon the brain. It follows, then, as a corollary, that abnormal conditions of these powers are equally connected with abnormal conditions of the brain; but this is not merely a matter of inference. The dissections of many eminent observers, among whom it is enough to mention the names of Greding, Gall and Spurzheim, Calmet, Foville, Fabret, Bayle, Esquirol, and Georget, have placed it beyond a doubt; and no pathological fact is better established—though its correctness was for a long while doubted—than that deviations from the healthy structure are generally presented in the brains of insane subjects. In the few cases, where such appearances have not been observed, it is justly concluded that death took place before the deviation was sufficiently great to be perceptible,—a phenomenon, not rare in affections of other organs.

§ 32. These pathological changes are not sufficiently definite to admit of classification, or of practical application in the treatment of the various kinds of insanity. To us they are chiefly valuable, as showing the frequent liability to disease, either from excessive exertion or disuse of its own powers, or from its proneness to be affected by morbid irritations, that radiate from other parts of the body. We learn from them, also, that changes of structure may proceed in the brain, as in other organs, to an incurable degree, without giving rise to much, if any, very perceptible disturbance of its functions, until some striking and unexpected act leads the enlightened physician to suspect its existence, and draws down upon the unfortunate subject the restraints and penalties of the law.

§ 33. A natural classification of the various forms of insanity, though of secondary importance in regard to its medical treatment, will be of eminent service to the legal inquirer, by enlarging his notions of its phenomena, and enabling him to discriminate.

where discrimination is necessary to the attainment
of important ends.   The deplorable consequences of
knowing but one kind of insanity, and of erecting
that into a standard, whereby every other is to be
compared and tested, are too common in the records
of criminal jurisprudence; and it is time that it were
well understood, that the philosophy of such a method
is no better than would be that of the physician, who
should recognise no diseases of the stomach, for instance, but such as proceed from inflammation, and
reject all others as anomalous and unworthy of attention.   The various diseases, included in the general term insanity, or mental derangement, may be
conveniently arranged under two divisions, founded
on two very different conditions of the brain; the
first being a want of its ordinary developement, and
the second, some lesion of its structure subsequent
to its developement.   In the former of these divisions, we have IDIOCY and IMBECILITY, differing from
each other only in degree.   The various affections,
embraced in the latter general division, may be arranged under two subdivisions, MANIA and DEMENTIA,
distinguished by the contrast they present in the
energy and tone of the mental manifestations.   Mania
is characterized by an exaltation of the faculties, and
may be confined to the intellectual, or to the affective powers, or it may involve them both, and these
powers may be generally or partially deranged.
Dementia depends on a more or less complete enfeeblement of the faculties, and may be consecutive
to injury of the brain, to mania, or to some other
disease; or it may be connected with the decay of

old age.   These divisions will be more conveniently exhibited in the following tabular view.

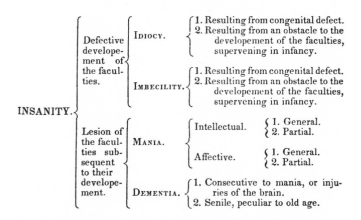

INSANITY.	Defective developement of the faculties.	IDIOCY.	1. Resulting from congenital defect. 2. Resulting from an obstacle to the developement of the faculties, supervening in infancy.
		IMBECILITY.	1. Resulting from congenital defect. 2. Resulting from an obstacle to the developement of the faculties, supervening in infancy.
	Lesion of the faculties subsequent to their developement.	MANIA.	Intellectual. { 1. General. 2. Partial. } Affective. { 1. General. 2. Partial. }
		DEMENTIA.	1. Consecutive to mania, or injuries of the brain. 2. Senile, peculiar to old age.

§ 34. It is not pretended, that any classification can be rigorously correct; for such divisions have not been made by nature, and cannot be observed in practice.   Diseases are naturally associated into some general groups only; but if these be ascertained and brought into view, the great end of classification is accomplished.   We shall often find them running into one another, and be puzzled to assign to a particular disease its proper place; but since such is the order of nature, we must make the most of the good it presents, and remedy its evils in the best manner we can.   The above arrangement, with the exception of some slight modifications, is that adopted by Esquirol, and has this advantage over some others, that it preserves the divisions made by nature, and will thus be serviceable to our present purpose, by dissipating some of the false notions, that prevail relative to the nature of insanity.

CHAPTER II.

IDIOCY.

§ 35. IDIOCY is that condition of mind, in which the reflective, and all or a part of the affective powers, are either entirely wanting, or are manifested to the slightest possible extent. As the organic defects, on which idiocy depends, are various in kind and degree, and also as it regards the parts of the brain affected, we should be led to expect, what observation shows is actually the case, considerable variety in the manifestations of this condition. The individual may hardly rise to the level of some of the brutes, his movements being confined to the necessities of the automatic life; or he may be capable of performing some useful services, of exercising some talent, or of displaying some of the higher moral sentiments. In short, there is even more diversity, in the characters of the idiotic and imbecile, than in those of the sound, and this truth must not be forgotten, if we would avoid the flagrant error of regulating judicial decisions by rules, which, though perfectly correct in regard to one case or set of cases, may be wholly incorrect in regard to others.

The most striking physical trait of idiocy, and one seldom wanting, is the diminutive size of the head, particularly of the anterior-superior portions, indicating a deficiency of the anterior lobes of the brain.

Its circumference, measured immediately over the orbitar arch and the most prominent part of the occipital bone, is fixed by Gall, whose observations on this subject are entitled to great confidence, at between 11⅓ and 14½ inches.[1] The brain consequently equals that of a new-born infant ; that is, about one fourth, one fifth, or one sixth of the cerebral mass of an adult's, in the full enjoyment of his faculties. The above is the only constant character observed in the heads of idiots;—their forms are as various as those of heads of the ordinary size. When idiocy supervenes in early infancy, the head is sometimes as remarkable for immense size, as in the former case, it is for its diminutiveness. The cause of this enlargement is some kind of morbid action, preventing the developement of the cerebral mass and producing serous cysts, immense dropsical effusions, &c. In idiocy the features are irregular; the forehead low, retreating and narrowed to a point; the eyes are unsteady and often squint; the lips are thick, and the mouth being kept open, the saliva is suffered to escape, and their spongy gums and defective teeth are displayed; the limbs are crooked, and feeble and limited in their motions. The senses are very imperfect at best, and often entirely wanting. Many are deaf and dumb, or blind. Many are incapable of perceiving odors, and have so little taste as to show no discrimination in their choice of food, swallowing whatever comes to hand. Their movements are constrained and awkward; they walk badly,

---

[1] Sur les Fonctions, p. 329.

easily falling down; and are constantly dropping whatever is placed in their hands. None are able to articulate more than a few words, to which they seem to attach no meaning; while the most of them utter only cries or muttered sounds. Some make known their most important wants by means of signs or sounds, that are intelligible to those who have the care of them. Idiots are generally affected with rickets, epilepsy, scrofula, or paralysis, and their whole physical economy indicates a depraved and defective constitution. Idiocy, as above described, is congenital, or begins at a very early period, and is incurable. Its wretched subjects seldom live beyond their twenty-fifth year, continuing all their lives in the same brutish condition, utterly unchanged by external circumstances, and scarcely indicating the species to which they belong, in their stupid, brute-like countenance, in their dull or glaring eyes, gaping mouth, their wild and hideous laugh, their inarticulate sounds, their obtuse sensations, and utter unconsciousness of social and domestic relations.

§ 36. In reasoning power, idiots are below the brute. Unable to compare two ideas together, nothing leads them to act but the faint impressions of the moment, and these are often insufficient to induce them to gratify even their instinctive wants. It frequently happens, however, that some one or more of the intellectual faculties, always excepting the reflective, are manifested in more or less perfection. Among the moral sentiments, it is not uncommon to find self-esteem, love of approbation, religious veneration, and benevolence, bearing a prominent part, if not constituting the entire character, and thus producing a slight approximation to humanity. Rush [1] speaks of one who was remarkable for kindness and affection, and spent his life in acts of benevolence, though he showed no one mark of reason. Dr. Combe [2] saw two, who, though differing much, in other respects, agreed in evincing a strong predilection for religious worship, and for listening to sermons and prayers. Some can recollect names, numbers, or historical facts; some are capable of repeating what they have frequently heard; others are able to sing a few airs, and even to play on musical instruments. Gall [3] saw one at Hamburgh, sixteen years old, who learned names, dates, numbers, history, and repeated them all mechanically, but was destitute of all power of combining and comparing his ideas, and was incapable of being engaged in any employment. Various propensities, such as the sexual feelings, cunning, and destructiveness, they often manifest in an inordinate degree of vigor and activity.

§ 37. In that form of idiocy, called cretinism, which is endemic in the Alps and some other mountainous countries, opportunities of observing its phenomena are offered on a grand scale. The difference in the degrees of this affection has led to its division into three classes, viz., cretinism, semi-cretinism, and cretinism of the third degree. In the first, life seems to be almost entirely automatic; most of its subjects are unable to speak, their senses are dull,

---

[1] Medical Inquiries.
[2] Observations on Mental Derangement, 243.
[3] Sur les Fonctions I, p. 193.

if not altogether wanting, and nothing but the most urgent calls of nature excite their attention. The semi-cretins show some glimmering of a higher nature ; they note what passes around; they remember simple events ; and make use of language to express their wants. They are capable of little else, however, for they have no idea of numbers, and, though taught to repeat certain passages, they learn nothing of their meaning. The actions of those of the third kind indicate a still higher degree of intellect ; they have a stronger memory of events, and they learn to read and write, though with scarcely any conception of the purposes of either. Particular talents are often displayed by them in a very respectable degree. Music, drawing, painting, machinery, &c., have each had its followers, in a humble way, among these cretins. In the construction of some parts of a watch, they are often employed in Geneva, and their work is characterized by neatness. Others have executed drawings of some merit, and some have even studied several languages, in which their acquisitions were by no means insignificant ; while others have even attempted poetry, though succeeding in nothing but the rhyme. Though, in all degrees of idiocy, the intellectual powers are so deficient as hardly to be recognised, and therefore these distinctions can be of little practical importance, yet they may serve to teach us how independent of one another are the various moral and intellectual faculties, and lead us to be cautious how we infer the soundness or capacity of the whole mind, from the perfection manifested by one or two of its faculties.

CHAPTER III.

IMBECILITY.

§ 38. By imbecility is meant an abnormal deficiency either in those faculties that acquaint us with
the qualities and ordinary relations of things, or in
those which furnish us with the moral motives that
regulate our relations and conduct towards our
fellow-men ; and frequently attended with excessive
activity of one or more of the animal propensities.
In imbecility the developement of the moral and intellectual powers is arrested at an early period of
existence. It differs from idiocy, in the circumstance,
that while in the latter, there is an utter destitution
of every thing like reason, the subjects of the former possess some intellectual capacity, though infinitely less than is possessed by the great mass of
mankind. Imbeciles can never attain that degree of
knowledge which is common among people of their
own rank and opportunities, though it is very certain
that they are not entirely unsusceptible of the influences of education. They are capable of forming a
few simple ideas and of expressing them in language ; they have some memory and a sense of the
conveniences and proprieties of life. Many of them
learn to read, write, and count, and make some
progress in music, though for the most part, they

are untaught and employed in the coarsest and
rudest labors.   Their moral and intellectual character presents the same infinite variety that is witnessed in the normal state of the mind.   While some
are changing their plans and resolutions with the
fickleness of the winds, others have some favorite
project which they are bent on accomplishing; while
nothing can arrest the attention of some for a moment, others pertinaciously retain some crotchet
that occupies nearly all their thoughts.   Some engage
in certain occupations, and manage to take care of
themselves and their property, though frequently
obliged to resort to others for advice and assistance.
They talk but little, and will answer questions correctly, provided they are not without the circle of
their customary thoughts and habits, and are not
required to follow a conversation.   They are particularly deficient in forethought, and in strong and
durable affections, and they generally labor under a
certain uneasiness and restlessness of disposition
that unfit them for steady employment.   It is also
worthy of notice that the same physical imperfections and a tendency to the same diseases which accompany idiocy, are generally observed, though in a
less degree, in imbecility.

§ 39. Much as the moral and intellectual powers
vary in the different cases, but little has been done
towards distinguishing the various degrees of imbecility, by a system of classification, though it must
be obvious at first sight, that something of this kind
is absolutely necessary before its legal relations can
be determined with much correctness, or consis-

tency. Hoffbauer [1] alone has made an attempt to supply this want, and though perhaps not perfectly satisfactory, as might have been expected from the nature of the subject, yet it evinces such a correct appreciation of mental diversities, and so much ability in the analysis of deficient understandings, that it would be doing injustice to the subject, to neglect giving some account of his views, in this place.

§ 40. Mental deficiency is manifested under two different forms, which Hoffbauer designates by the terms imbecility *(blödsinn)*, and stupidity *(dummheit)*. The former consists in a defect of the *intensity*, the latter, in a defect of the *extensity*, necessary to a sound and healthy mind. By intensity is meant the power of the mind to examine the data presented to it by the senses and therefrom to deduce correct judgments; by its extensity, the mind perceives and embraces these data, and suffers none to escape,— one, it may be added, is the *reflective;* the other, the *perceptive* power.

"In reference to the faculty of judgment, it may be observed, that the stupid person is more liable than the imbecile to form erroneous decisions; the latter experiences great difficulty in bringing himself to any conclusion. Secondly, the stupid person sometimes judges very correctly on subjects to which his attention has been strongly applied; occasionally he surpasses, in this respect, those of superior intelligence. When he judges wrongly, it is through

---

[1] Die psychologie in ihren hauptanwendungen auf die rechtspflege, §§ 26—46.

neglect of some of the considerations which ought to
have formed the groundwork of his judgment, and
he will say, in order to excuse himself, that 'he
never should have dreamt of this or that circumstance.' To the imbecile, on the contrary, the most
simple act of judgment is difficult. A lady, for instance, who said she was twenty-five years of age,
and had been married six years, could not, after
many efforts, tell how old she was at the period of
her wedding; at one time, calling it twenty, at another, twenty-two. Thirdly, the stupid man may
often be induced to correct his mistake; some simple
reason, or particular circumstance being suggested
to him which leads to its detection. The imbecile
man can scarcely rectify his errors, being unable
sufficiently to concentrate his attention on any particular subject. Fourthly, the stupid man, in recovering from his error, frequently falls into the opposite extreme, passing from the blindest confidence to
the most jealous distrust, because he views every
subject on one side only, and is embarrassed by
every complex idea.

§ 41. "In relation also to memory, there is a decided difference between the stupid and the imbecile.
The latter appear to be almost entirely deficient in
this faculty, while the former recollect after a long
interval of time, and with tolerable accuracy, some
insulated circumstances.

§ 42. "Weakness of intellect is displayed in both
these classes, when their defect is excessive, by a
propensity to talk to themselves. This is mostly
observable when the individual is alone, or supposes
himself alone. In reality, we employ words, not

merely for purposes of intercourse, but as an instrument of thought; and when the mind is morbidly enfeebled, the silent and unperceived, or mental employment of words is insufficient; they must be repeated more or less audibly. This practice is not uncommon with imbecile and stupid people, but when in company, they generally perceive its incongruity and abstain from it. If, however, such individuals talk to themselves, knowing that they are in the presence of company, it is a proof of greater deficiency.

§ 43. "Another distinction between the imbecile and the stupid person is, that the latter imagines himself equal, if not superior, to other men in intelligence; whereas the former is sensible of his defect, and even exaggerates it. Hence results another difference between the stupid and the imbecile person. The former acts precipitately and without reflection; the latter never can make up his mind, even on the simplest affair, from the fear that there may be consequences which he is incapable of foreseeing. The imbecile is frequently timid, and even misanthropic; not only because he is conscious of his deficiency, but because he has had a disagreeable experience of the superiority of others. When this is the cause of his jealous distrust, we observe, first, that he reposes unlimited confidence in those whose benevolence he has experienced; secondly, that when his condition in society places him beyond the reach of injury, he has none of this misanthropy of which we speak, and is at peace with all the world. The pusillanimity and misanthropy of the imbecile lead them to a species of devotion, if such it may be called; for it is natural that, on seeing themselves repulsed, or ill-treated by men, they should apply to the deity for support. The stupid, more confident in themselves, fancy that they acquire merit by their devotions, or confer an honor on the divinity."

§ 44. Hoffbauer, while he acknowledges the various and almost imperceptible shades of difference between one case of imbecility and another, has reduced its numberless gradations to five degrees, and those of stupidity to three. To these as described and explained by him, he looks for the means of a consistent and rational application of the legal principles that should regulate their civil and criminal relations.

"The *first* degree of imbecility manifests itself in the inability to form a judgment respecting any new object, even when the necessary data are furnished, and the question is one which in itself, presents no difficulties. In this degree of the affection, the individual can very well judge respecting objects to which he is daily accustomed, and in familiarity with which he may be said to have grown up. In the pursuit of his daily concerns, he often shews a minute exactness that appears to him a matter of absolute necessity. His memory is very limited; not that he loses absolutely the remembrance of things, but because he cannot apply his recollections according to his wishes. He scrupulously observes whatever he thinks becoming in his situation, because he fears to offend by neglecting it. When he gives himself up to avarice, there is observed in him rather an apprehension of losing than a desire of accumulating. The propensity to talk to himself, and the species of devotion to which we have alluded, is seldom to be met with in this instance; the former, because the routine of daily occupations, above which the individual seldom raises himself, makes but small demands on his intelligence; the latter, because his infirmity is not so remarkable in ordinary society as to render it a subject of general observation, and entail upon him frequent annoyance, and thus make him feel the necessity of seeking support elsewhere. He is very subject to gusts of passion, which nevertheless are as easily appeased as they are excited."

The description of the *second* degree of imbecility applies to the subjects of dementia, which will be considered in another place; and it may therefore be omitted here.

§ 45. "A person affected with imbecility in the *third* degree, is unfitted for all matters that require more than a mechanical mode of action; but he preserves sufficient intelligence to be aware of his weakness and of the intellectual superiority of others. We may likewise remark in him that propensity to devotion and misanthropy of which we have spoken above. His mind is not completely inactive, although it cannot raise itself to any elevated views; hence he has the propensity to talk to himself. He has not the power of seizing an idea so clearly as to impress it on his mind; hence a very marked defect of memory and a great propensity to pass rapidly from one topic to another. He is very irritable and suspicious, fancies a design to insult him where it is impossible, because his state yet permits him to feel and resent injuries —of which susceptibility those about him often take advantage in order to annoy him.

§ 46. "The *fourth* degree of imbecility is marked by a clouded state of the understanding and memory, with a great insensibility, which nevertheless leaves the patient a confused idea of his weakness. He eagerly seeks excitement by various stimuli."

§ 47. The *fifth* degree of imbecility as described by Hoffbauer, corresponds to the last stage of dementia, or the fatuity which results from some cerebral diseases, and therefore does not belong to this condition of mind according to the arrangement above adopted.

§ 48. Stupidity, generally speaking, is a defect less severe than imbecility, according to the definition given of each. The slightest degree of imbecility, however, indicates an imperfection of the intellectual powers, less severe than the greatest degree of stupidity.

"In the *first* degree of stupidity, the individual is only incapable of judging, and deciding, when it is necessary to weigh opposing motives. Then he feels his incapacity, and resorts to the intelligence of others, unless too proud, which often happens. If he acts absurdly, it is often because he applies to his actions a rule good in itself, but the application of which requires other considerations.

§ 49. "The subject of the *second* degree of stupidity judges accurately and sometimes even promptly, respecting things by which he is habitually surrounded; but he commits serious errors whenever it is necessary to exert a certain vigor of judgment. He is embarrassed in any train of reasoning however simple it may be. His memory is perhaps faithful, but it is slow; he cannot, without great difficulty, express a complex idea, if it is the result of his own reflections, and has not been received from another. When his faculties have been somewhat developed by education, he is an obstinate partisan of any thing which is, as we say, good in theory but useless in practice; because he cannot observe the circumstances that distinguish particular cases, and appreciate them according to their just value. These two conditions are indispensable, however, to the proper application of general rules.

§ 50. "In the *highest* degree of stupidity the individual cannot go beyond one single idea; and he must completely lose that one before he can pass to another. Hence he is less capable of judging than the imbecile, because the comparison of several ideas is necessary to form a judgment. Individuals who are affected with stupidity in the third degree, often express themselves in half-uttered words, return incessantly to the same subject, make known their ideas by sentences, short, incoherent, and unfinished, like children who can retain words but do not know how to connect them together; they often express the subject and the attribute without connecting the one to the other by the affirmative or negative. If they wish to say, 'the rose is beautiful,' they will say, 'rose beautiful,' or only 'rose,' or 'beautiful,' according as the subject or attribute strikes them most. Often they reverse the natural order of words, and say, for example, 'rose beautiful is;' and when they perceive an omission which they wish to repair, they become still more perplexed."

§ 51. It does not need the high authority of Esquirol to convince us, that these distinctions are drawn with a minuteness and show of accuracy that savor more of the labors of the closet than of the rigid and faithful observation of nature. This objection, however, which might not have been unsuspected by the author himself, does not entirely destroy the utility of his attempt, so long as it is admitted to be an approximation to the truth; for, with all its defects, it establishes the important fact that mental deficiency is distinguished by various grades of intensity, instead of being invariably the same condition, and therefore that it is properly subject to precisely the same legal regulations. It is a material defect in the above descriptions, that the state of the moral faculties is seldom adverted to, though their deviations from the normal condition are no less striking than those which the intellectual powers exhibit. Whatever may be their character, it is obvious that their ordinary relations to the intellect must be affected, and thus the idea is forced upon us, that as accountable beings, the subjects of mental deficiency must be viewed in a very different light from that in which we are accustomed to regard those of sound and well-developed minds. The observations of Georget on the moral faculties of imbeciles, partially supply this defect in Hoffbauer's descriptions, and therefore are worthy of notice in this connexion.

§ 52. "In hospitals for the insane," says he, "there is always a certain number of imbeciles who do the coarser work of the house, or serve as domestics and assistants to the regular officers. They become sufficiently intelligent at last, to perform their duties well, to sweep the courts, carry burdens, move machines, execute simple commissions, know the use of money, and procure various enjoyments. But they have no idea, or a very imperfect one, of society, laws, morality, courts and trials; and though they may have the idea of property, they have no conception of the consequences of theft. They may have been taught to refrain from injuring others, but they are ignorant of what would be done to them if guilty of incendiarism or murder. Indeed, it is well known how common theft is among imbeciles and idiots, and for a very obvious reason. Some of them have no conception of property, nor of the distinctions of *meum* and *tuum;* their conduct is actuated solely by the fear of punishment when capable of experiencing this sentiment, and by their own desires. Others have some notions of property, but neither a sense of morality, nor a fear of punishment furnish motives sufficiently powerful to prevent them from stealing. The sentiment of cunning, too, may be very much developed, while the other faculties are more or less deficient. Among the lower orders of society, are many imbeciles a little more intelligent than these, and not considered as utterly devoid of understanding, who, nevertheless have but vague and imperfect notions of social duties and of justice. They engage in occupations that require no great extent of intellect, and even in the simplest of the mechanic arts. If they do not pass among their acquaintances for imbeciles, they are at least, regarded as singular beings, with feeble understandings, and are teazed and tormented in innumerable ways. Many of them, for want of some powerfully restraining motive, indulge in drinking, and become lazy, drunken, and dissipated, and finally fall into the hands of justice in greater numbers than is generally suspected. They steal adroitly, and hence are considered as very intelligent; they recommence their offences the moment they. are released from confinement, and thus are believed to be obstinately perverse; they are violent and passionate, and the slightest motive is sufficient to plunge them into deeds of incendiarism and murder. Those who have strong sexual propensities, soon become guilty of outrages on female chastity. I have had occasion to see many examples of this class in prisons, who had been judicially decided to be rational, but whose demi-imbecility was manifest enough to me." [1]

If this is a correct representation of the moral character of the lesser grades of imbecility—and the ability and good-faith of Georget are not to be doubted—it may be easily imagined, without the help of further description, what it must be in the higher degrees.

§ 53. The prevalent error of looking at mind in the abstract, as a unique principle endowed with a certain appreciable measure of strength and activity, has been the cause of much dispute and discrepancy of opinion, in cases where the acts of persons affected with Hoffbauer's first degree of imbecility, have been made the object of judicial investigation. One witness has observed a range and tenacity of memory which he could not square with his notions of mental weakness; another, perhaps, has seen the

---

[1] Discussion médico-légale sur la Folie, p. 140; and Des maladies mentales, considérées dans leurs rapports avec la legislation civile et criminelle, p. 8.

party whose acts are in question conducting himself with the utmost propriety, and observing the social usages proper to his station, and this he has deemed incompatible with imbecility of mind; and another has heard him replying to questions on common-place subjects, readily and appropriately, and he also draws similar conclusions. On the other hand, he is seen engaging in occupations and amusements, and associating with company seemingly below the dignity of his age, or station, by one who desires no further proof of an imbecile mind; or he may be so extravagantly vain of some personal accomplishments, as to impress another with the idea, that his understanding has scarcely the strength of a child's. And it is worthy of notice that oftentimes the very fact which furnishes undoubted proof of imbecility to one observer, conveys an unshaken conviction of mental soundness, to another. Few, indeed, are capable of sounding the depths of another's intelligence, because few are aware of the necessity, or have the ability if they were, of scrutinizing, not one act or trait of character alone, but every intellectual manifestation as it appears in the conduct, conversation and manners, as the only means of obtaining an insight into his real, mental capacity. Scarcely a case comes up in which the understanding of an imbecile is judicially investigated, that does not furnish striking illustrations of this fact, as might be shown by numerous instances in point. The following, however, which occured in 1832, may serve as examples.

§ 54. " Miss Bagster was a young lady of fortune, and perpetrated a runaway-match with Mr. Newton. An application was made by her family to dissolve

the marriage, on the ground that she was of unsound
mind.   The facts urged against her before the commissioners, were, that she had been a violent, self-
willed, and passionate child ; that this continued till
she grew up ; that she was totally ignorant of arithmetic, and therefore incapable of taking care of her
property; that she had evinced a great fondness for
matrimony, having engaged herself to several persons ; and that, in many respects, she evinced little
of the delicacy becoming her sex.   Dr. Sutherland
had visited her four times, and came to the conclusion that she was incapable of taking care of herself
or of her property.   She had memory, but neither
judgment nor reasoning power.   Dr. Gordon did not
consider her capacity to exceed that of a child of
seven years of age.   Several non-medical witnesses
who had known her from infancy, spoke of her extremely passionate, and occasionally indelicate conduct.   On her examination, however, before the
commissioners, her answers were pertinent and in a
proper manner.   No indelicate remark escaped from
her.   Drs. Morrison and Haslam had both visited
her, and were not disposed to consider her imbecile
or idiotic.   She confessed and lamented her ignorance of arithmetic, but said that her grandfather
sent excuses when she was at school, and begged
that she might not be pressed.   Her conversation
generally impressed these gentlemen in a favorable
manner as to her sanity.   The jury brought in a
verdict, that Miss Bagster had been of unsound mind
since November 1, 1830, and the marriage was consequently dissolved." [1]

---

[1] 1 Beck, Medical Jurisprudence, 579.

§ 55. There would seem to have been no doubt as to the existence of some degree of mental deficiency in this young lady; the question was, whether it was constitutional, or merely the result of a neglected education and misplaced indulgences. In proof of its constitutional nature, we have the opinion of a respectable physician, that she was incapable of taking care of herself or of her property; and of another, that her capacity did not exceed that of a child seven years old, which opinion is corroborated by the facts in evidence, that she was extremely passionate, and often indelicate in her conduct; that her mind ran greatly upon matrimony; and that she had not made the most ordinary attainments in knowledge. On the other hand, it appears that her education was unquestionably neglected; that, before the commissioners, her answers were pertinent and in a proper manner; and that two eminent physicians were not disposed to consider her idiotic or imbecile. It is obvious, that in cases like this, the opinions of the medical witnesses will depend, very much, if not altogether, on the extent of their previous acquaintance with the manifestations of the mind, both in its normal and abnormal conditions. Hence it is that a trait by no means incompatible with imbecility was considered, in this case, as indicative of a proper soundness of mind. Persons laboring under far more imbecility than Miss Bagster are capable, on occasions, of controlling themselves and concealing their more prominent faults, to such a degree that a stranger finds it difficult to believe, that in point of understanding, they are much below the level of ordinary people.

It should be recollected that imbecility is manifested in the conduct and manners, as well as the thoughts and language ; and when it is considered, that persons like Miss Bagster, are confessedly of narrow understandings, and often of defective education, it could not be expected that strong indications of imbecility would be observed in their conversation alone.   Her answers, it seems, were pertinent, and properly delivered, as they might well have been, if they related to things, in which she was particularly interested and were not beyond her powers of comprehension, and she still have been imbecile or stupid.   In the description of the first degree of imbecility, already quoted (§ 44), Hoffbauer expressly says that " the individual can very well judge respecting objects to which he is daily accustomed, and in familiarity with which he may be said to have grown up."   It may be also added, that their answers are sometimes not only pertinent, but characterized by considerable pith and shrewdness.

Miss Bagster's education was, no doubt, grossly neglected, but this circumstance could not have produced so much mental deficiency as to have impressed a careful and intelligent observer, with the conviction that her capacity did not exceed that of a child seven years old.   Neglected or vicious education is a cause of ignorance, but can never degrade the mind into a state of imbecility or stupidity, which are always congenital, or the effect of disease.   Dr. Morrison indeed stated under oath, that he would undertake to teach her, in six months, arithmetic and the use of money, but his success would have been far from disproving the existence of imbecility.

It is not doubted that in this condition of mind, there
is some susceptibility of education, and the cases are
not unfrequent, where, in regard to one or two particular powers, the individual is quite on a level with
his more happily-endowed fellow-men.

§ 56. In the case of Portsmouth v. Portsmouth,
which was a suit of nullity of marriage, on the ground
of the mental unsoundness (which was, in fact, imbecility in the first degree) of the husband, the earl
of Portsmouth, numerous facts were deposed to by
witnesses, in proof that he possessed a capacity and
understanding fully equal to the ordinary transactions of life. It appeared that when at school, he
evinced a very good memory, and made a respectable proficiency in arithmetic and the languages ; and
that, after coming of age, he settled accounts with
his agents,—attended public meetings and commit-
tees,—prosecuted an offender and was examined as a
witness,—and that his friends had failed in making
him the object of a commission of lunacy. In regard
to these circumstances, the court, Sir John Nicholl,
observed in substance, that the capacity for instruction and improvement is possessed even by the brute
creation, and therefore did not of itself disprove the
fact of imbecility ; that when he appeared as a witness in a court of justice, it was only a simple fact
he had to state, requiring little, if any thing, more
than memory, and that his cross-examination could
require nothing more than the recollection of facts—
not any considerable exercise of the understanding
and of the reasoning powers; that his behavior in
company, and his few observations on the state of

the weather, horses, and farming, were not incompatible with great imbecility of mind, because, under the restraint produced by formal company and by the sense of being observed, the more prominent features of imbecility would be shaded, and the individual might pass as possessing a considerable degree of understanding. On the contrary, it was satisfactorily proved that he had always been treated by his family as one of feeble capacity, and by a family-arrangement, he was married, when thirty-two years of age, to a lady of forty-seven, evidently for the purpose of saving him from improper connexions, and obtaining for him suitable care and protection. It appeared that his servants were his play-fellows, and that he played all sorts of tricks with them ; that he was fond of driving a team, and that his wife so far indulged him, as to have a team of horses kept for his amusement as a toy and a plaything, with which he carted dung, timber, and hay ; that he had a propensity for bell-ringing, was fond of slaughtering cattle, and indulged in wanton cruelty towards man and beast, never expressing regret, but merely observing, "serves him right," on his own acts of cruelty. It also appeared that a medical man was taken into the family, to assist in superintending the earl, and that he obtained complete ascendancy over him, the mention of his name being sufficient to intimidate him and exact his obedience. This gentleman at last thought prudent to deliver up his charge to the earl's trustees in London, one of whom, within one week after, married him to his own daughter. This marriage was

declared by the court null and void.[1]   In the above
statement a few facts only have been selected from
a mass of evidence given by one hundred and twenty-
four witnesses ; but this is sufficient to illustrate the
general principle that proof of imbecility is not to be
found in a few insulated facts, but in an investigation
of the whole character and conduct of the party.

---

[1] 1 Haggard, 359.   The reader who wishes to extend his inquiries
farther, will find in the judgment of Sir John Nicholl, in Ingraham *v.*
Wyatt, 1 Haggard, 384, some excellent observations on the characters
of imbecility, besides a masterly analysis of evidence relative to this
condition, ranging through a life of seventy-four years.

CHAPTER IV.

LEGAL CONSEQUENCES OF MENTAL DEFICIENCY.

§ 57. The general principles that determine the legal relations of idiocy are so obvious, and the fact of its existence so easily established that little occasion has been afforded for doubt or diversity of opinion. The maxims of the law have sprung from the suggestions of common sense, and its provisions have equal reference to the best interests of its wretched subjects and of those who are about them. It may be mentioned as a curious fact however, that while the idiot is denied the enjoyment of most of the civil rights, he is quietly left by the constitutions of the several states of the union, in possession of one of those political rights, that of suffrage, the very essence of which is the deliberate and unbiassed exercise of a rational will. How this anomaly has arisen, it is not easy to conceive. A natural jealousy of any attempt to encroach upon the popular right, might apprehend evils to this institution in allowing the mental qualifications of voters to be too closely scrutinized, but such fears could hardly have been expected in view of the unlimited control maintained by the law over the property and personal liberty of idiots.

§ 58. The little indulgence shown to imbecility in criminal courts, sufficiently indicate that either the psychological nature of this condition of mind is very imperfectly understood, or the true ground on which the idea of responsibility reposes is not clearly perceived. Whichever it may be, it may no doubt be attributed to the prevalent habit of studying the moral and intellectual phenomena in sound and healthy minds only, without a suspicion, apparently, of the great modifications they present, when the developement of the cerebral organism is interrupted by disease. It will be necessary, therefore, before coming to any positive conclusions relative to the legal accountability of imbeciles, to bring into view some considerations on this point, which have been too much, if not altogether, overlooked.

§ 59. Our moral and intellectual constitution is constructed in harmony with the external world on which it acts and by which it is acted upon; the result of this mutual action being the happiness and spiritual advancement of an immortal being. Thus endowed with the powers of performing the part allotted us, and placed in a situation suitable for exercising and developing them, we become accountable for the manner in which they are used,—to our Maker, under all circumstances, to our fellow-men, when the institutions of society are injured. All legal responsibility, therefore, is founded on this principle of adaptation and ceases whenever either of its elements is taken away. The intellect must not only be sufficiently developed, to acquaint the individual with the existence of external objects, and with some of their relations to him, but the moral powers must be sound enough and strong enough to furnish, each its specific incentives, to pursue that course of conduct which the intellect has already approved. It is nothing that the mind is competent to discern some of the most ordinary relations of things, and is sensible of the impropriety of certain actions;—so long as the individual is incapable by defect of constitution of feeling the influence of those hopes and fears and of all those sentiments and affections that man naturally possesses, an essential element of legal responsibility is wanting, and he is not fully accountable for his actions.

§ 60. In the normal mind the idea of crime is associated with those of injury and wrong; can we then impute crime where there is neither intention nor consciousness of injury? For want of the higher and nobler faculties, the actions of the imbecile are contemplated by him solely in relation to himself; not a thought enters his mind respecting their consequences to others. For the same reason that he puts to death a brute, that of mere personal gratification, he murders a fellow-being, and is constitutionally unable to appreciate any difference in the moral character of the two actions. In the latter case, as in the former, he has a selfish object in view, and is restrained from pursuing his purpose by none of the considerations that actuate the sound and well-developed mind. The natural right of every one to the undisturbed possession of his own life, and the sentiment of wrong awakened by the infliction of injury, are things as far beyond the sphere of his contemplations, as the most difficult problem in mathematics, and he merely feels the animal impulse—which to him has the strength of a natural right,—to appropriate to himself whatever will conduce to his momentary gratification. The thought of the wounds inflicted on the friends and connexions of his victim by his decease, could not restrain him, because the feelings of benevolence and sympathy which they suppose, are utter strangers to his own bosom; and it would be preposterous to expect him to be influenced by a regard to feelings which he never experienced himself. The sense of future accountability could not restrain him, for the idea of an Almighty, All-seeing Being, ever witnessing his actions, is too confused and too limited in his mind, to present the slightest check to the indulgence of his caprices and passions. The fear of punishment could not restrain him, because his intellect can discern no necessary connexion between his crime and the penalty attached to it. To make such a person responsible for his actions to the same degree as one enjoying the full vigor and soundness of the higher faculties, is therefore manifestly unjust; because an essential element of responsibility is a power to refrain from evil-doing, which power is furnished by the exercise of those faculties, that are but imperfectly, if at all, developed in the imbecile. The law looks only to the intention, not to the amount of injury committed; and since there can be no criminal intention where there is no consciousness of wrong, it consequently cannot reach those wretched objects, who, to use the expression of one of them, whose case will be shortly noticed, "can see no difference between killing an ox, and killing a man."

§ 61. Many, it is true, find it hard to be convinced that one who labors under no delusion, and enjoys a certain degree, at least, of moral liberty, may still not be responsible for his criminal acts. They see perhaps that he has intelligence enough to perform the inferior kinds of employment, and feel assured that observation must have made him acquainted with the consequences of such acts, even though a stranger to that high moral power which instinctively teaches the distinctions of right and wrong. "He *knew* better," is their language, "and therefore justice requires his punishment." The error of this reasoning arises in the vulgar habit of estimating the strength and extent of the moral faculties by the ability to go through certain mechanical duties, and provide for the wants and exigencies of the present moment. Not only has this ability no connexion with the moral sentiments, but it is not even an index of the measure of intelligence; any more than the skill of the bee or beaver in erecting their structures, is indicative of great intellectual resources. These degraded specimens of our race are not without the capacity of being educated in a limited degree; and thus like those inferior animals which man has made conducive to his comfort, they are trained to perform some kinds of service with tolerable merit. This, however, no more proceeds from the kind of intelligence that discerns moral truth, than the isolated talent for music or construction not unfrequently met with in the complete idiot.

§ 62. For the purpose of illustrating and confirming the above views, some account will now be given of a few criminal trials, the subjects of which seem to have been affected with mental imbecility, stating very briefly the facts as they are found recorded, and accompanying them with such reflections as the par-

ticular circumstances of the case require.   They are
well worth the consideration of every honest and unprejudiced inquirer, for he will find in them a kind
of information which he can obtain from no other
quarter, and will be able to see for himself, how little of true philosophy has presided over the department of criminal jurisprudence.

§ 63. I. In November, 1821, John Schmidt, aged
17, was tried at Metz for parricide. He had manifested from an early age, a proneness to mischief and
even cruelty.   As soon as he was old enough to run
in the streets, he would amuse himself by throwing
stones into the rivulet, that ran through the village,
in order to spatter and hurt the people who were
passing by, many of whom were injured by him.
They contented themselves, however, with charging
his parents to take care of him, for he was even considered to be mad.

The first count in the indictment charged him with
wounding on the head his sister-in-law, in one of
their domestic quarrels.   The second charged him
with an attempt on the life of one of his cousins, whom
he pushed into the water while fishing by the side of
a pond, and then laughed at his struggles to extri-
cate himself.   When he finally succeeded, Schmidt
approached him and asked if he were wet, and if the
water had reached his skin; the boy, to show that it
had, opened his shirt when Schmidt plunged a knife
in his bosom. Happily, the wound was not severe.

On the night of the parricide, the father was boil-
ing potashes.   At four o'clock in the morning he
called to his wife to come and assist him in lifting
the kettle from the fire, but she refused and ordered

John to go.   John went in his shirt, and set the kettle on the floor, and while his father was bending
over to stir the potashes, he struck him a blow with
a hatchet lying near, that felled him senseless to the
ground.   He then ascended to the garret, where
his brother and sister were sleeping, and severely
wounded the latter with the hatchet.   On being
seized by his brother soon after, he asked to see his
father, who had just expired; and when gratified in
this wish, he uttered these remarkable words :—
"Ah, my dear father, where are you now ?   What
will become of me ?   You and my mother are the
cause of my misfortunes.   I predicted it long ago,
and if you had brought me up better, this would not
have happened."   When asked what had induced
him to commit such an atrocious crime, he replied
that the devil undoubtedly instigated him.   He also
declared that the itch which he had taken from his
sister-in-law, was repelled, and, in consequence,
frequently occasioned a mental derangement and fits
of fury which impelled him to sacrifice every thing.
Several witnesses testified that he had always been
remarkable for profound piety and religious habits.
He confessed to his counsel that whenever he saw a
cutting instrument, such as a hatchet, a knife, &c.,
he felt the strongest desire to seize it, and wound
the first person that came in his way.   His counsel
unsuccessfully pleaded in his defence mental derangement, though Schmidt interrupted him by declaring
that he was not mad.   Shortly before the fatal hour,
food was brought to him, but observing it to be meat,
he refused to eat it, saying that in a few minutes it
would be Friday.   As he walked barefooted to the

place of execution, his confessor asked him if the pavement did not hurt him? "I wish," he replied, "they had made me walk on thorns." When he arrived at the scaffold, they cut off his hand, but he uttered not a word or a cry, and remained firm to the last.

§ 64. Dr. Marechal, of Metz, who communicated this case, observes that he was struck with the smallness of the head, and its singular shape, and that on carefully examining his skull, he found the forehead very narrow and retreating, the sinciput tolerably high, and a marked prominence over the ears. He said it had the same shape as those of all the idiots mentioned by Pinel.

In Schmidt we have ample confirmation of the other indications of imbecility, in the physical structure, which speaks a language that cannot deceive. If his cranium were shaped like those of the idiots described by Pinel, what better manifestations of mind or morals could have been expected from one thus stamped by nature with the impress of inferiority ? This furnishes an explanation of his early indulgence in brutal propensities, to such a degree, as to be regarded mad ; and gives us a clew to the cause of his attempts on life, solely for the momentary gratification they afforded ; of the motiveless and cold-blooded murder of his father ; and of that regard of religious observances which had no better foundation than the merest superstition. His inclination to kill on seeing a cutting instrument, shows some morbid action in the brain not uncommon in imbecility, which is also indicated by the paroxysms of fury in which he felt himself urged on to indis-

criminate slaughter. These vehement impulses,
even the slight consciousness of wrong, denoted by
his exclamation on seeing the corpse of his father,
was totally unable to restrain ; and, by a process
unknown to himself, and which he could only explain on the popular notion of the instigation of the
devil, they would burst forth with fatal violence.
His extraordinary proneness to mischief and cruelty,
and the early age at which it began to appear, point
distinctly to an original defect of constitution, which,
though not attended by what is properly called
mania, furnishes no controlling influence over the
purely animal propensities. Ferocity of disposition
in imbeciles no more implies responsibility for criminal acts, than it does in the brutes; and affords but
an indifferent reason for ridding the world of their
presence. To conclude then, we cannot hesitate to
believe with Dr. Marechal and Georget, that Schmidt
was one of those wretched beings who are disgraced
by nature from their very birth, and whose vicious
propensities are counterbalanced neither by a sense
of justice and morality, nor a fear of punishment.

§ 65. II. Pierre Joseph Delepine, aged sixteen,
was tried at Paris for eight different incendiary acts,
committed in the Faubourg St. Antoine, in 1825.
The first time, a bird with burning tow dipped in
spirits attached to its tail, was let loose in a garden
adjoining that of the accused. At another time,
August 17th, a fire broke out in the adjoining garden, two heaps of straw being burnt and a part of
the wall destroyed. Three days afterwards, a grange
belonging to Delepine's garden was burned, and
three days after this, a cousin of his was awakened

by a dense smoke, and soon discovered that a chest containing his effects was on fire. The next night, a person passing through the street, observed a heap of straw in flames at the farther end of the garden which laid on the street. He sprang over into the garden to render assistance, when Delepine and his family rose and finally extinguished the fire. While this was being done, a bucket-full of burning charcoal was discovered in the garret, in time however to be extinguished. In the morning of the 7th September, a piece of burning canvass was found in a wood-closet under the stair-case ; and Delepine, who expressed his astonishment, helped to extinguish the flames. Soon after, there was found under the two mattresses in his sister's room, a handful of burning flax by which the bed-furniture had been already set on fire, and some was also discovered in his own chamber, placed under his pillow, and an hour or two afterwards, a heap of straw in a neighboring garden was observed to be on fire. He was also charged with having committed several thefts.

§ 66. On the trial, his father stated that the prisoner's intellectual faculties were not what might have been expected from one of his age ; and, in support of his assertion, he adduced the nature of the criminal acts themselves, and the absence of sufficient motives to excite him to so many attempts, both against his own family and people who were indifferent to him. He also produced a certificate signed by nine of his neighbors, which purported that Delepine's thoughts and feelings were frequently in a disordered condition ; that he would often wander in his conduct and conversation ; that he would sometimes strip himself naked and run like a madman through his father's garden ; that they heard his parents say that in the January previous, he attempted to hang himself, and sometime after, to jump into a well. It appears from the evidence that he led an irregular life, was jealous of his brothers and sisters, and caused his father much uneasiness. At various times he had stolen from his parents, and it was for having stolen a horse that he met in the street, without its owner, that he was first arrested by the police.

§ 67. On his trial, Delepine replied to the questions put to him with calmness ; his countenance was devoid of expression and presented a picture of stupidity. He denied the facts charged in the indictment, and could not conceive how they happened. The newspapers described him as having a low forehead ; and all the witnesses who had an opportunity of knowing, agreed in believing that there was some singular defect in his mental organization. His mother testified that for sometime previous, his parents had had occasion to reprove him for his conduct, and that they had intended to seclude him. She said he was odd, addicted to the strangest tricks, and, in short, showed that " there was something wrong about his head," though he was nòt mad nor idiotic. This testimony of the mother was confirmed by that of eight or nine other witnesses, who agreed in representing him as having been always very odd and strange in his conduct, and addicted to mischief, though not mad, nor properly speaking, idiotic. He was, notwithstanding,

convicted, and condemned to death ; but he heard
the sentence as unmoved as he had continued to be
during the trial.

§ 68. In a memoir addressed to the king by his
counsel, M. Claveau, he is described as being " weak
in body, his face pale, his eye dull, and his mind
infirm ; as manifesting no disposition for employment, wrapped in silence, and subject to convulsive
agitations.   He was in the habit of shunning his
companions, and when he did incline to join them,
he proposed only the most frightful sports.   Once,
in the middle of the night, he placed baskets on his
head, wrapped himself in the bed-clothes, and ran
through the garden, uttering the most fearful howl-
ings.   On one occasion he kindled a fire in a stove
with thirty crackers, and though covered with the
ruins, he was not astonished at the result.   After
the trial, while in prison and in irons, and under the
eyes of his keepers, he contrived to place burning
coals in his bed, and then laid down upon it while
actually on fire.   It cannot be doubted that he is
enslaved by a passion for conflagrations, incessantly
haunted by images of flames, cinders, and ruins, and
would not mind perishing himself, provided he could
enjoy the sight of them, in the act.   He belongs to
that class of wretched beings who are doomed from
the cradle ; who live without motives, and are cut
off without understanding why."   In consequence
of this memorial, his punishment was commuted for
that of imprisonment for life.

§ 69. While in prison he amused himself with
scribbling his name in every variety of form on the
copy of the indictment that was left with him; by

writing on it unmeaning or disconnected words, or
words formed by letters put together at random; by
drawing on it grotesque figures, and changing the
letters in such a manner that some parts of it could
scarcely be read.   Thus, the words, "Acte d'accusation contre Joseph Delepine," were changed in
the following manner ;—*Dacte deaccusationiss contre
Josephu Delapine;* and the first page is filled with
ink-spots, and detached and insignificant words, such
as, *Marieux, meche, a mosire non, dacculer, mosieur
je dit, bonjour a monsieur leru,"* &c.   "Can it be
conceived," says Georget, "that a person who is
conscious of the enormity of his crime, and who cannot be without some anxiety respecting the result of
his trial, should be absorbed in such puerilities ?
that he should read such grave charges, not only
without a single emotion of horror, but even with
the most perfect indifference, and use the paper containing them for his amusement ?   Such conduct not
only displays insensibility, which is not rare in hardened criminals, but betokens the mind of a child ;
and in a lad of sixteen, indicates stupidity, silliness
and imbecility."   The physical characters attributed
to Delepine, and his manners as described by those
who were in the habit of frequently seeing him,
clearly indicate a natural deficiency of his moral
powers; but though his crimes were the acts of a
child five or six years old, his imbecility alone may
not be sufficient to account for the particular form
his offences assumed.   It must be borne in mind,
that in imbecility, as in other abnormal conditions,
there is not only deficiency and irregularity, but also
a great tendency to diseased cerebral action, mani-

festing itself in excessive, uncontrollable indulgence of some one or more propensities. In Delepine, it assumed the form of that monomania which consists in a morbid impulse, which the higher powers cannot restrain, to acts of incendiarism. That the incendiary acts of Delepine arose from diseased action in the brain, and not from mere love of mischief, is abundantly proved by the slightest examination of their nature. To let loose a bird with burning tow attached to it, without knowing or caring where it would alight, is what, perhaps, might have been expected from a low and simple, though sound mind, deliberately bent on mischief; but certainly, nothing less than genuine, unequivocal insanity, can account for his setting his own bed on fire, and then calmly lying down upon it. If too he had been actuated by malice or a pure love of mischief, it is absurd to suppose that he would have chosen his own home for its objects, and thus deliberately endeavored to deprive himself of a shelter, as well as those on whom he depended. In short, the fact of imbecility, combined with mania, is so plainly written on the history of this singular case, that it would be hopeless, to attempt, by any additional comments, to make it more clear to those who cannot read it for themselves.[1]

§ 70. III. Abraham Prescott was tried at Concord, New Hampshire, in September 1834, for the

---

[1] The facts in the above cases are taken from Georget's work, already referred to, entitled, Discussion medico-legale sur la Folie, pp. 130, 144.

murder of Mrs. Sally Cochran.[1]   On the morning of
June 23, 1833, he left home with the deceased, who
was the wife of his employer, for the purpose of picking strawberries in a neighboring pasture.   An hour
and a half afterwards, the family heard a whining,
moaning sound in the barn, which was found to proceed from Prescott, who, on being asked what was
the matter with him, said that " he had struck Sally
[Mrs. Cochran] with a stake and killed her."   He
then went with them and showed them the body,
which they found had been dragged a little distance
from the place where the murder was committed
and concealed among some bushes.   On his way
thither he asked the husband if he would hang him ;
he showed no disposition to escape, though not arrested till several hours afterwards, and slept soundly
the succeeding night.   He was eighteen years old,
had lived three years in Mr. Cochran's family, by
which he had been always kindly treated, and his
conduct had been uniformly correct and satisfactory.
No misunderstanding had occurred between him and
any other member of the family, and they reposed
unlimited confidence in his fidelity and attachment,
though on one occasion it was strongly tried.   On
the 6th of January 1833, that is, about six months
previously, he arose in the night, procured an axe
from the shed, went to the bed where Mr. and Mrs.
Cochran were sleeping and struck each of them some
severe blows on the side of the head which left them

---

[1] The facts of this case are derived from the report of the trial, published at Concord, in 1834, and from an article in the Boston States-
man of January 9th, 1836, entitled " Execution of Abraham Prescott."

senseless.   He then went to an adjoining room
where Mr. Cochran's mother slept, and told her, he
"believed he had killed Mr. and Mrs. Cochran."
They recovered however, and warmly repelled every
suspicion of the truth of his own statement that he
committed the act in his sleep, unconsciously, though
he had never been known to walk in his sleep before.
For several months after the murder, he continued
to explain his conduct in regard to it, by saying that
while in the pasture he had the toothache, that he
sat down on a stump, and fell asleep, and that was
the last he knew, until he found he had killed Mrs.
Cochran.   On being much pressed by the coroner
and warden to confess the whole truth, for they did
not believe that he acted without a motive, and assured by them that he would stand a better chance
of being pardoned if he confessed, he told these officers, that he made an insulting proposal to Mrs.
Cochran which she resented, and threatened to tell
her husband of and get him punished ; that he supposed he should have to go to prison, and thinking
he would rather be hung than go there, he caught
up a stake and killed her.   Subsequently, he stated
that he did not make such proposals to Mrs. Cochran, and uniformly denied that he had ever so confessed; but declared that the coroner and warden
had troubled him so much that he did not know what
he told them.   To the keeper of the jail, and the
clergymen who visited him, he invariably stated,
"that he attempted to kill Mr. Cochran and his wife,
in January, 1833, in order to get possession of their
property; and that when he found he had not despatched them, he feigned that he had been asleep

when he did it.   In June, he said, that his intentions were, first to kill Mrs. Cochran in the hollow, and then call down Mr. Cochran and kill him."

§ 71. His counsel set up in defence the plea of homicidal insanity, which they supported by quoting numerous cases of this disorder, and citing the opinions of high medical authorities and witnesses; and in short, nothing was omitted by them that could help to render the defence satisfactory to the jury. Chief Justice Richardson, in his charge, strongly inclined to the belief of his insanity, and observed that if the prisoner "had been all the time sane, his conduct had certainly been most extraordinary. And on the other hand, if he had been otherwise than sane, it was a most extraordinary case of insanity."

§ 72. There certainly are strong reasons for believing that Prescott was utterly unconscious of what he was doing when he murdered Mrs. Cochran, but, on the contrary, a careful examination of all the circumstances of the case presents us with still stronger reasons for thinking that he did know well enough what he was doing. It appears perfectly evident that he belonged to that wretched class of men, in whom mental imbecility is accompanied by more or less perversion of the moral faculties. Upon any other than this view of his mental condition, it is impossible to furnish a satisfactory explanation of his conduct and the circumstances attending it. His original statement that he was unconscious when he committed the murder, is opposed by his subsequent confessions that he was actuated by motives; so that we are presented in the outset, with the very unusual case of a criminal defended on the ground of insanity, who denies that he was insane, and furnishes rational motives for his conduct. There is good ground for believing that his last confession was the true one, first, because he could have had no reason *then* for inculpating himself falsely, while, on the other hand, the hope of escaping punishment was a sufficient reason for his fabricating the story which he told at first; and secondly, because it furnished the same motive for the attempt to kill in January, and this establishes a consistent and satisfactory relation between these two acts. To remove as he did the only doubt in his favor founded on the suspicion of his madness, and confess a rational motive for his conduct, when none really existed, strikingly indicates—not mania, for such a trait is never witnessed in mania, or at least, not in the partial form of that disease—but imbecility. We are obliged therefore to believe that he was actuated by a motive and that this motive was a desire of gain; and nothing can more strongly show the imbecility of his mind than the means which he took to obtain his object. It seems that the idea haunted his mind that the death of the Cochrans would put him in possession of their property; and with this view, "he thought," as he said, "a thousand times of killing them along through the fall before the attempt on their lives in January." When asked if he did not know that the property would descend to the children, he replied "that he knew it would so descend, but he did not think of it at that moment." In fact he was not even the most distantly related to the Cochrans, and had no reason whatever for supposing that they had made testamentary dispositions in his

favor.   His imbecility is also strikingly manifested
in the feebleness of spirit and want of resolution
which characterized his criminal attempts.   He kills
both husband and wife in their bed, as he supposes;
but when he returns to their room and finds them
still living, instead of completing his work by an additional blow, as the cool assassin would have done,
he goes and arouses the rest of the family and the
neighbors, and tells them what he has done.   Again,
instead of taking an opportunity when both his victims might be finished together, with some shade
of secrecy, he despatches one in open day, almost
within call of help, intending to trust to his chance
of overpowering the other under similar circumstances.   The latter part of this plan—that of calling
Mr. Cochran and killing him—he abandons the moment he has murdered the wife; and seems then for
the first time to have thought of concealing the body
and his own share in the bloody act.   This purpose
too, he but half performs, and finally goes and dis-
closes the whole transaction to the very person most
interested in knowing it.   Such conduct is perfectly
inexplicable on the supposition of his possessing a
soundly-acting mind; but it is a fair specimen of that
vacillation of purpose, feebleness of resolution, and
capriciousness of design, which are among the most
common features of imbecility.   Had he belonged to the class of ordinary criminals, he certainly,
after obtaining the object he had in view in committing the murder, would either have fled, or taken
some means of turning suspicion from himself and
provided for his escape in this last resort.   But he
was an imbecile, and because he was an imbecile, he

immediately proclaims his own agency in the act, relying for his safety on the very suspicious excuse of being unconscious of what he was doing,—an excuse which at best, would not have saved him from much tedious, perhaps perpetual confinement, and the ineffaceable stigma of having murdered a fellow being. Even the motive he assigned to the coroner and warden and on which the attorney-general rested the burden of his argument against him, supposing it were actually the true one, would only strengthen this view of his mental condition ; for none but an imbecile or an idiot would ever have imagined that he would be sent to jail for offering an insulting proposal to a woman, or would have preferred hanging to temporary imprisonment, and then added murder to insult for the purpose of obtaining his preference. Nothing that appears in what is said of him during his confinement gives any higher idea of his moral and intellectual powers. The utmost efforts of zealous and judicious clergymen failed to impress him with a sense of his awful situation, or inspire him, in the least degree, with those cheering hopes which even the most abandoned criminals often entertain. This did not arise from a spirit of bravado, nor from the utter recklessness sometimes manifested by the hardened victims of the law ; but from stupid indifference, or sheer inability to comprehend the simple truths of religion, or imagine any thing beyond the present worse than the annoyances to which he was subjected. In short, so obvious was his imbecility, that the writer, from whose statement the foregoing account is in part taken, observes that ''no one who has had any intercourse with Prescott has come to the conclusion that he is or has been insane, but they all consider him to have been deficient in intellect or common sense.[1] The signs of imbecility were not wanting even in his physical constitution. A medical witness who had been physician of a private asylum for the insane, for fifteen years, speaking of his appearance at the bar, said, "the motion of his eye is idiotic, dull, lazy, indifferent ; no appearance of fear or anxiety in his countenance. I noticed no agitation, nor anxiety in the prisoner during the examination of the first two government witnesses." It is also worthy of notice, that insanity had been a common disease in the Prescott family ; that his mother was fifty-six years old when he was born and his father but one year younger ; and that the prisoner, when a child, had a scrofulous or rickety affection, for which they used cold bathing and some external remedies. Stronger predisposing causes of imbecility than these when combined, do not exist.[2]

---

[1] It is true, that one witness with whom the accused lived a year and a half previous to living with the Cochrans, described him as "intelligent," and another who had been acquainted with him from a child said, "he was as intelligent as boys in general ;" but when we bear in mind how ill-qualified most persons are to estimate the intellectual capacity of others, and that with them intelligence generally means only manual skill, or a tolerable aptness in performing the coarser labors of the farm and the work-shop, we shall place little reliance on these representations, more especially too, as they are not sustained by other testimony. The keeper of the jail and his wife who seem to have been particularly interested in him and to have had considerable intercourse with him, both testified that they considered him "*not* as intelligent as boys in general."

[2] Before dismissing this case, it is gratifying to be able to add, that the knowledge of the phenomena of insanity in its various forms,

Such are the reasons that induce the belief, that Prescott was a subject of imbecility, not mania—that he belonged to that unfortunate class described by Georget (§ 52) who know no other incentive than the gratification of animal passion ; and who are restrained from evil doing by no higher sentiment than the fear of punishment. This consequence he certainly should have been made to suffer in a limited degree ; but to mete it out to him in the same measure that is bestowed on ordinary criminals, was manifestly contrary to the principles of natural justice.

§ 73. IV. On the 14th of May, 1833, a young man, John Barclay, was executed at Glasgow, for the murder of Samuel Neilson, for whom he had previously showed some affection. He took from him three one pound notes and a watch, to obtain possession of which seems to have been the cause of the murder. So little sense had he of having done wrong, or of his own situation, that he hovered about almost without disguise, and, while going to spend part of the money with the first person he spoke to, he dropped first one and then another note at his feet, as a child would have done. When questioned, he could see no difference between killing a man and killing an ox, except that he "would never hear him fiddle again ; " and so little did he know of the nature of the watch, that he regarded it as an ani-

---

evinced by the court and by the counsel for the prisoner, and the general correctness of their notions, were exceedingly creditable to them, and furnish a remarkable contrast to the crude and narrow views so commonly taken by men in similar situations, who yet have had far ampler means of obtaining information on this branch of medical jurisprudence.

mal, and when it stopped from not having been wound up, believed it had died of cold from the glass being broken. So obvious was Barclay's mental deficiency, that the court of justiciary, before whom he was brought, declined proceeding to his trial till it was decided by medical evidence, that he was a fit subject for trial. In his parish, he was familiarly known as "daft Jock Barclay ; " and the clergyman who knew him well, "always regarded him as imbecile, and had never been able to give him any religious instruction, and did not consider him a responsible being." Notwithstanding the fact that Barclay's weakness of mind was recognised by all parties from the judge downwards, and that the jury strongly recommended him to mercy on that account, he was condemned and executed. It appears that much stress was laid on Barclay's *knowing* right from wrong, as affording indisputable proof of his being a moral agent. The reader is left to judge for himself, how extensive and accurate must have been the notions on this point, of one who thought a watch was a live creature, and could see no difference between killing an ox, and killing a man.

In the above cases the imbecility was congenital, and resulted from an imperfect developement of the cerebral organism. In the following, it was the effect of disease, by means of which the normal action of the brain was perverted.

§ 74. V. Louis Lecouffe aged twenty-four years, was tried at Paris, 11th December, 1823, for the murder of a woman, whom he robbed of a quantity of plate. It appears that he was an epileptic from infancy ; and those who were in the habit of associating with him always regarded him as an idiot or fool. He had some disease of the head when very young. At fifteen, he showed manifest signs of insanity ; and affirmed that God, from time to time, came to visit him. His mother, whom he strongly accused, and seriously compromised by his disclosures, declared, even while she stigmatised him as a monster and a villain, that he had always been in bad health, and hardly ever in possession of his senses. At his first examination he denied the charge, but subsequently he confessed, for the following reason. He stated that on the preceding night, while still awake, the spirit of his father appeared to him, with an angel at his right hand, and commanded him to confess his crime ; that God immediately after, placed his hand upon his heart, and said to him, "I pardon thee," and ordered him to confess every thing within three days. It appears that his mother, of whom he stood greatly in awe, had refused her consent to a marriage he was anxious to contract ; that she refused him again on another occasion, and, according to his confession, she long teased him to commit the murder and robbery, and decided his resolution by promising no longer to oppose his marriage. The plate was pawned for two hundred and thirty francs, of which his mother gave him only forty to defray the expenses of his marriage. He declared that his victim was fond of him, and that he deserved her good will by having rendered her many little services. On being confronted with his mother, he did not retract his assertions, but only showed some hesitation, saying he was not himself, and experienced a violent

nervous attack. He said, next day, that if placed
again in the presence of his mother, he would be
unable to answer for himself; that she would give
him the lie, and he would not have firmness enough
to maintain the truth. Her unbounded influence and
authority over him, which were deposed to by several witnesses, were such, that he did whatever she
ordered him, and absolutely deprived himself of
every thing to support her, giving her all his earnings without daring to retain a single sous. The
keeper of the prison testified that he talked incoherently, and that he seemed idiotical and weak-
minded. The chief keeper said, that he had often
seen the accused with haggard looks, and eyes filled
with tears, complaining of headache, but without
manifesting any true derangement of mind. During
the trial he had very frequent violent attacks of convulsions, and he stated that when he felt vexed, a
kind of flame or flash passed before his eyes.

§ 75. The facts here related may seem to some,
to establish the imbecility, or mania, or both, of
Lecouffe, beyond a reasonable doubt; but not so
thought the court or jury, and, accordingly, he was
condemned and executed with his mother. Certainly, nothing short of great weakness of mind can
account for the entire submission of a man twenty-
four years old to the despotic rule of his mother, to
whom he yielded the last sous of his earnings, sacrificed his matrimonial schemes, on which he was
strongly bent, and from whom he received only forty
of the two hundred and thirty francs, for which, at
her instigation, he had murdered his benefactress.
That this mental weakness amounted to imbecility,

is satisfactorily proved by the fear and convulsive agitations which he experienced when brought into her presence ; by the common opinion of those who were in the habit of associating with him ; and by the well-known effects of his disease on the understanding of its subjects. Epilepsy, the seat of which is in the head, seldom continues for any length of time without destroying the natural tone and soundness of the mind, rendering the patient listless and forgetful, indisposed and unable to think for himself, yielding without any will of his own, to every external influence, and finally sinking into hopeless fatuity, or becoming incurably mad. It appears from a table published by Esquirol, that out of three hundred and thirty-nine epileptics in the Salpetriere of Paris, in 1822, two were monomaniacs ; sixty-four maniacs, of whom thirty-four were furious; one hundred and forty-five were imbecile, of whom one hundred and twenty-nine were so only immediately after the attack ; eight were idiots ; fifty were habitually rational, but with loss of memory, exaltation of the ideas, sometimes a temporary delirium and a tendency to idiocy ; sixty were without any derangement of intellect, but very irritable, irascible, obstinate, capricious, and eccentric.[1] In these cases, the disease probably occurred at various periods of life ; when it appears in infancy, as it did in Lecouffe, the proportion of those, whose minds are affected, is still greater. If now, Lecouffe, after suffering the disease his whole life, had still possessed a sound mind, it

---

[1] Dictionnaire de Médecine, Art. Epilepsie.

would have been a fact almost, if not altogether, without a parallel ; but that he did not escape its deteriorating effects, is abundantly proved by the evidence adduced. Occasionally, his mental affection took the form of proper mania, as was indicated by the wildness and disorder of his looks, by talking incoherently to himself, by his groanings and mournful cries in the night, observed by one of the witnesses, by his nocturnal apparitions, and by the testimony of his own mother, that he was almost never in possession of his senses.

§ 76. Against all this array of evidence, the advocate-general had nothing to offer but the idle declamation usually resorted to on such occasions. The attempts of the prisoner's counsel to establish the existence of imbecility and mania, he reprobated in the severest terms, as dangerous to society, subversive of social order, destructive of morality and religion, and affording a direct encouragement to crime. It forms no part of the plan of this work, to show the utter groundlessness of these assertions ; and they are mentioned here, merely that the reader may see what powerful considerations succeeded in invalidating the evidence in favor of Lecouffe, and consigning him to an ignominious end.

§ 77. By imbecility is ordinarily understood a deficiency of intellect; but it has been seen above (§ 56) that its signification is here extended, in order to include that class of subjects in whom the mental defect consists in a great deficiency, if not utter destitution of the higher *moral* faculties, the intellectual, perhaps, not being sensibly affected. The following case will illustrate this form of the disorder.

VI. E. S., aged thirty-four, who had been ten years an inmate of the Richmond Lunatic Asylum, in Dublin, was brought before Mr. George Combe, during a visit to that institution, on the 20th of April, 1829, to be subjected with several others, to a phrenological examination. A few months after, Dr. Crawford, the physician of the asylum, addressed a letter to Mr. Combe respecting this patient, from which the following description is taken. "You observe in your notes, I am surprised he was not executed before he became insane." This would lead to the supposition that he had been afflicted with some form of insanity, in addition to a naturally depraved character. Such, however, is by no means the case; he never was different from what he now is; he has never evinced the slightest mental incoherence on any one point, nor any kind of hallucination. It is one of those cases where there is great difficulty in drawing the line between extreme moral depravity and insanity, and in deciding at what point an individual should cease to be considered as a responsible moral agent, and amenable to the laws. The governors and medical gentlemen of the asylum have often had doubts whether they were justified in keeping E. S, as a *lunatic*, thinking him a more fit subject for a Bridewell. He appears, however, so totally callous with regard to every moral principle and feeling—so thoroughly unconscious of ever having done any thing wrong—so completely destitute of all sense of shame or remorse when reproved for his vices or crimes—and has proved himself utterly incorrigible throughout life, that it is almost certain that any jury before whom he might be brought would satisfy their doubts by returning him *insane,* which, in such a case, is the most humane line to pursue. He was dismissed several times from the asylum, and sent there the last time for attempting to poison his father ; and it seems fit he should be kept there for life as a *moral lunatic;* but there has never been the least symptom of *diseased* action of the brain, which is the general concomitant of what is usually understood as *insanity.*" [1]

§ 78. Nothing can be more certain than that this individual was denied by nature the possession of those moral faculties, the due developement and exercise of which constitute an essential element of responsibility. By the aid of kind and intelligent friends, he was secluded from scenes, in which he was unfitted to mingle ; but if on the contrary, he had been suffered to go at large, with his animal propensities uncontrolled by the higher powers of our moral nature, and constantly meeting with opportunities for indulgence, what else could have been expected but some deed of violence, that would have brought upon him the tender mercies of the law ? Dr. Crawford, is altogether too sanguine, in believing that a jury would have pronounced E. S. insane; for the melancholy termination of the cases above given, teaches how little we can here rely on the intelligence of courts and juries. Had he committed a capital crime, he would probably have been

---

[1] The particulars of the last three cases are taken respectively from the Edinburgh Phrenological Journal, No. 49 ; from Georget's Examen des procès criminels, &c. ; and from the Edinburgh Phrenological Journal, vol. 6, p. 147.

condemned and executed, while the intelligent and the educated, the philosopher and the man of the world, would, for the most part, have joined the unthinking populace, in thanking God, that a monster of wickedness had fallen beneath the arm of the law.

§ 79. This form of insanity which is above denominated moral imbecility, in order to distinguish it from that in which the intellect is affected, is not very rare in receptacles for the insane, and is more common in society than is generally suspected. Dr. Rush says that in the course of his life, he had been consulted in three cases of it; and nothing can better express the true characters of their physiology, than his remark respecting them. "In all these cases," he observes, "there is probably an original defective organization in those parts of the body which are occupied by the moral faculties of the mind,"[1]—an explanation that will receive but little countenance in an age, that derives its ideas of the mental phenomena from the exclusive observation of mind in a state of acknowledged health and vigor. To understand these cases properly, requires a knowledge of our moral and intellectual constitution, to be obtained only by a practical acquaintance with the innumerable phases of the mind, as presented in its various degrees of strength and weakness, of health and disease, amid all its transitions from brutish idiocy to the most commanding intellect.

---

[1] Diseases of the Mind, p. 357.

§ 80. If the principles above laid down (§§ 55, 56, 57,) are not entirely incorrect, it follows that the persons whose cases have been related, were not fit subjects for criminal punishment—at least, not that of death. The usual treatment of such offenders, it is to be feared, is prompted more by prejudice and excited feelings than by enlarged views of human nature and of the objects of criminal jurisprudence. While the public feeling has become too refined to tolerate the infliction of blows and stripes on the imbecile and the mad in the institutions where they are confined, and is inclined to discountenance altogether the idea of punishment as applied to the insane, it can still be gratified by gazing on the dying agonies of a being unable to comprehend the connexion between his crime and the penalty attached to it, and utterly insensible of the nature of his awful situation. The voice of reason and humanity which speaks successfully in the first instance is in the last drowned by the more imperious tones of prejudice and passion. When imbeciles are convicted on a charge of great criminal offences, the only rational course to be pursued with them, is that of perpetual confinement, which at once secures society from their future aggressions, and is most conducive to their mental and bodily welfare.

§ 81. It has been already mentioned (§ 51), as an essential defect in Hoffbauer's descripton of the various grades of imbecility and stupidity, that he has almost entirely left out of view the state of the moral faculties—an omission that is fatal to the value of the principles which he lays down relative to the legal consequences of this mental condition in connexion

with crime.   The ground above taken (§§ 55, 56)
leads to the view, that the principle he has adopted, of
graduating criminal responsibility by the strength
and extent of the intellect alone, is exceedingly partial and unjust in its operation.   The only conditions of culpability which he recognises, are, first, a
knowledge that the act is contrary to law ; and
secondly, that the act is precisely the one prohibited
by the law.   In the first degree of imbecility—for in
the third, all legal culpability is annulled—the absence of these conditions may be alleged in excuse ;
but only, first, when the violated law neither forms
a part of those general relations which concern himself in common with other members of society, nor
belongs to his own particular condition or circumstances ; and secondly, when the action forbidden
by the law is not contrary to the law of nature.
Accordingly, he considers "that inattention or absence of mind, want of foresight, &c. are not to be
received in excuse when they have regard to objects
universally known, as to fire, or to those which are
familiarly used by the imbecile, as the tools &c. of
his profession.   In all other instances his fault loses
the degree of culpability that belongs to it, according
to the expression of jurists, *in abstracto*.   This is
also the case when the act is the result of sudden
anger or fear, to which weak persons are prone." [1]

§ 82. In settling the civil responsibilities and relations of the imbecile, Hoffbauer's descriptions are
not so unsuitable for practical application ; as these

---

[1] Op. cit. sup. § 55.

must be chiefly dètermined by the condition of the intellect alone. As his observations, however, have reference in a great measure, to the legal regulations of his own country, they will be noticed no farther than merely to state his opinion that when imbecility reaches, or approaches the third degree, the party can no longer be considered capable of taking care of his property, or of bequeathing it by will.

§ 83. No cases subjected to legal inquiry are more calculated to puzzle the understandings of courts and juries, to mock the wisdom of the learned, and baffle the acuteness of the shrewd, than those connected with questions of imbecility. Much of the difficulty consists, no doubt, in a want of that practical tact which is obtained by experience, in unravelling their intricacies, and of that knowledge of the psychological nature of this condition of mind, which directs the attention exclusively to the real question at issue, and abstracts whatever is extraneous, or without any direct bearing on its merits. It is impossible to specify any particular rules for ascertaining the mental capacity of imbecile persons; for circumstances always proper to be taken into the account, are constantly varying with each individual case. The education of the party, the sphere of life in which he has moved, his capacity of acquirement, his exposure to improper influences, and especially the nature of the act in question,—are points which require a close and thorough consideration. In questions of interdiction which present the greatest difficulty, some overt acts of extravagance, or indiscretion generally appear in evidence, when the party is really incapable of managing his affairs, which will remove the doubts that a direct investigation of his intelligence and capacity may have left behind. It ought to be considered as a general rule, that when no acts of this kind have been committed, notwithstanding the management of his property has been entirely in his own hands, beyond the control of others, the party cannot be interdicted on the score of imbecility. In all cases it will be indispensably necessary, as Mr. Haslam advises, to investigate his comprehension of numbers, without which the nature of property cannot be understood. But the assertion of this writer, that "if a person were capable of enumerating progressively to the number ten, and knew the force and value of the separate units, he would be fully competent to the management of property,"[1] is by no means to be admitted as true ; for it is very certain that a large proportion of those whose mental capacity is unquestionably inadequate to the management of property, have nevertheless these arithmetical acquirements. Cases, even, are occasionally met with of imbeciles who possess surprising powers of calculation, but have not the competency of children to manage pecuniary affairs of any extent. No doubt, the converse of the proposition, in reference to people of doubtful capacity, comes nearer the truth. When there exists this inability of comprehending the value of numbers, the individual ought to be considered as legally *non compos mentis,* notwithstanding we might hesitate to adopt this conclusion, after an investigation of his

---

[1] Medical Jurisprudence, as it relates to Insanity, 347.

intellectual capacity in regard to the general nature and relations of property and business transactions.

§ 84. Imbeciles in the third degree are evidently incapable of making wills ; but not necessarily so, Hoffbauer thinks,[1] are imbeciles in the first degree, even when subjected to a curator. The purpose of this guardianship is to protect them from the damage they might do themselves if left with the administration of their affairs, and to prevent them from entering into engagements which they would find it impossible to perform. But as testamentary dispositions depend on a single arrangement and one which the testator may have taken time to think upon and mature, they do not require the same degree of intelligence as the administration of property, and therefore the validity of a will ought not to be incompatible with the guardianship or interdiction of the testator. As a general principle, its correctness may be admitted, because it places no arbitrary restriction on the exercise of a natural right, the abuse of which can be sufficiently prevented by judicial interference ; and because, if it be rejected, we may have the curious spectacle of a person debarred from having any voice in the final disposition of his property—in an act which really comes within the reach of his understanding,—while in the continued management of his property, a judicious committee is paying all the deference to his wishes and suggestions which their reasonableness deserves. It cannot be denied that the nature and consequences of a

---

[1] Op. cit. sup. § 73.

testament may be sufficiently understood by many an imbecile who is utterly incapable of discerning the complicated relations that are involved in the management of property. Nothing can be more natural than that he should be attached to those who have rendered him important services, and perhaps have well-founded claims on his bounty ; and if anxious to leave some substantial token of his regard, no legal impediment ought to prevent him from bequeathing them a reasonable portion of his property. The danger anticipated from such an exercise of the testamentary power, is probably more imaginary than real ; for it can hardly be conceived that testamentary dispositions which turn the descent of property altogether from its natural channels, to heap it up in the lap of a stranger or a favorite, would not be attended by appearances of fraud or circumvention, that would inevitably destroy their validity. All that is required to establish the wills of people of weak understandings is that they should have been capable of comprehending their nature and effect [1]—a point entirely independent of the accidental circumstance of interdiction. The propriety of the practice here advocated was recognised on the 14th of February, 1808, by the Royal Court of Aix who confirmed the will of the Sieur Beauquaire, a person of weak understanding (though at the time of making it he was under the surveillance of a curator); for the reasons that the dispositions of the will were rational, and that the mind of the testator was capa-

---

[1] Shelford on Lunacy, 275.

ble of understanding them, though too weak to be intrusted with the management of his property.[1] The French tribunals, according to Georget, have ever shown themselves the protectors of the right of making wills, taking into consideration the mental condition of the testator and the dispositions of the will itself. Much injustice, therefore, might be committed by depriving all interdicted imbeciles of the testamentary power, compared with which the temporary inconvenience that would arise from the absence of any statutory provisions on the subject, is hardly to be mentioned. Of course, the slightest appearance of interference, or improper influence should be closely scrutinized, and as much less evidence required to substantiate its existence, as the party is more likely to have been affected by it.

§ 85. Imbeciles in the third degree, and others of whatever grade under interdiction, are legally incapable of contracting marriage, for since they are presumed to be incapable of transacting business of the smallest amount, they must be equally so, of becoming a party to a contract which is not only to

---

[1] Sirey, Recueil gen. des lois et des arrêts. Tome 8, p. 315. In coming to this decision, the Court considered the testator to be one of those persons whose case is contemplated in the following article (499) of the Civil Code, in which the power of making a will is not mentioned among the civil acts, which they are rendered unable to perform. " In rejecting a petition for interdiction, the court may, nevertheless, if circumstances require, decree that the defendant is henceforth incapable of appearing in suits, of making contracts, of borrowing, receiving payment for debts or giving a discharge, alienating or pledging his property, without the aid of a council which shall be appointed in the same judgment."

affect their pecuniary interests, but their whole future happiness and comfort.   When, however, the mental deficiency has not been sufficient to provoke inter-diction, though plain enough to be generally recog-nised, it, very properly, constitutes no legal impedi-ment to marriage, but on proof of fraud or circum-vention the marriage has been pronounced by the courts, null and void.[1]   It is obvious that no general rule can be applied to all such cases, for while mar-riage might conduce to the interests of each party in one case ; in another, it might be equally ruinous to the interests of one or both parties.   Every case should be judged on its own merits, and only annulled when the mind of either party is proved to have been operated on by improper influences.

---

[1] 1 Haggard Ecc. Rep. 355.   Portsmouth v. Portsmouth ; Miss Bag-ster's case, Ante, § 54.

CHAPTER V.

PATHOLOGY AND SYMPTOMS OF MANIA.

§ 86. WHILE medical literature is far from being deficient in works on Insanity considered as one of the most serious maladies to which man is liable, the popular notions respecting it are peculiarly loose and incorrect. As these, however, are the source of many of the faults in the jurisprudence relating to this affection, it is necessary to enter somewhat into its medical history, and to discuss points which might seem, at first sight, to be of an exclusively professional nature, but a proper understanding of which is absolutely necessary to save us from gross mistakes on this subject. Certainly no greater absurdity can be imagined than that of fixing the legal relations of persons in a particular state of mind, while entertaining the most imperfect notions of what that state really is,—unless it may be that of pertinaciously clinging to those notions and discouraging every attempt to correct them, after the progress of scientific knowledge has shown them to be erroneous. Before describing the phenomena of mania, it should be distinctly understood that it is, first, a disease of the brain; and secondly, that in its various grades and forms, it observes the same laws as diseases of other organs. The importance of these propositions makes it proper to state the grounds on which they rest ; for until they are clearly recognised and appreciated, it will be in vain to expect any improvements in the medical jurisprudence of insanity.

§ 87. I. *Mania arises from a morbid affection of the brain.* The progress of pathological anatomy during the present century, has established this fact beyond the reach of a reasonable doubt. It can hardly be necessary at the present time, to prove the fact of the dependence of the mind on the brain for its external manifestations—that, in short, the brain is the material organ of the intellectual and affective powers. Whatever opinion may be entertained of the nature of the mind, it is generally admitted—at least by all enlightened physiologists— that it must of necessity be put in connexion with matter, and that the brain is the part of the body by means of which this connexion is effected. Little as we know beyond this single fact, it is enough to warrant the inference that derangement of the structure, or of the vital actions of the brain, must be followed by abnormal manifestations of the mind ; and consequently, that the presence of the effect indicates the existence of the cause. If it be an organic law, that derangement of structure is followed and indicated by derangement of function, it cannot for an instant be doubted that insanity is the result of cerebral derangement, since the manifestation of the mind may be considered as one of the functions of the brain. Whether the morbid action arises in the digestive, or some other system, and is reflected thence to the brain by means of the nervous sympathies, or arises primarily in the brain, the soundness of the above principle is equally un-

touched.   This leads us to the source of the hesitation that has been evinced by pathologists to consider
the brain as the seat of insanity.

§ 88.   From the fact that organic lesions are not
always discoverable after death in the brains of the
subjects of insanity, it has been inferred that the
brain is not the seat of this disease ; though, if this
fact were true—it being also true that no other organ
in the body invariably presents marks of organic
derangement in insanity—the only legitimate inference would have been, that, in some cases, it is
impossible to discover such lesions by any means in
our power.   Besides, if insanity is produced by some
obscure affection of the nervous influence, or vital
principle, as has been seriously imagined, with what
consistency could the believers in this speculation
look for change of structure any where ?   But
the strangest theoretical error which this apparent
soundness of the brain in some cases, has occasioned,
is that of denying the existence of any material affection at all, and attributing the disease entirely to an
affection of the immaterial principle.   If the same
pathological principles had guided men's reasoning
respecting this disease, that they have applied to the
investigation of others, these errors would never
have been committed.   It will scarcely be contended,
at the present day at least, that the structural changes, found after death from any disease, are the primary cause of the disturbances manifested by symptoms during life ; or that if the interior could be
inspected at the beginning of the disease, any of
these structural changes would be discovered.   It is
now a well-recognised principle, that such changes

must be preceded by some change in the vital actions of the part where they occur. This vital change is now generally expressed by the term *irritation*, and nothing is implied by it relative to the nature of this change, more than an exaltation of action. Irritation then is the initial stage of disease,—the first in the chain of events, of which disorganization is the last—and, of course, nothing can be more unphilosophical than to attribute disturbances of function, exclusively to any structural changes that may take place during the progress of these successive stages. The departure from the normal course of vital action, which is probably as unexceptionable a definition of irritation as can be given, is sufficient to derange the functions of the part in which it occurs, without producing any visible change in its appearance; and hence, we may oftentimes explore the dead body with the utmost minuteness and skill, without being enabled to infer from any thing we find, an adequate cause of death. Before this can be found, the initial stage must have continued more or less time; and though it always tends to pass into the subsequent stages, yet death may take place from various causes, before they are developed and before a trace of their existence can be detected.

§ 89. There is this peculiarity in the pathology of insanity, that while the irritation deranges the mental functions so as to be manifest to every observer, its sympathetic effects upon the rest of the system are so slight that they contribute but little comparatively, by their reaction, to develope the stage of inflammation. The consequence is, that cerebral irritation, sufficient to produce insanity, may endure for years, and death occur at last from other causes, without our being able to discover any morbid appearances. Thus their existence, instead of being essential to the disease, is entirely the result of accidental circumstances. The probability of finding inflammation or any of its products, will depend on the duration of the disease, and the share which it had in causing the death of the patient. If it have existed for a short time only, or death have been occasioned by some other cause, examination will be likely to disclose no traces of morbid action ; but on the contrary, if it have been of long standing and have killed the patient by the constitutional disturbances it has produced, they will generally be found more or less abundantly. From not properly attending to these considerations, pathologists have been led into an egregious error by the absence of morbid changes,—no less a one than that of denying the disease to be an affection of matter, and jumping at the absurd conclusion, that it is the spiritual principle alone that suffers.

§ 90. It has never been denied, however, that the traces of disease, when they do occur, are oftener found in the brain than in any other organ ; nor that, in a very large proportion of the whole number of cases, the brain actually does show evident marks of having been diseased. And when we bear in mind the limited knowledge of the cerebral structure which pathologists have possessed till quite lately, and consequently, the difficulty they must have experienced, in detecting changes from the healthy condition, it may well be concluded that the absence of these changes might be attributed, in not a few instances, to the fault of the inquirer rather than to the nature of the disease. Certain it is, that as we have become better acquainted with the anatomy of the brain and with its sensible qualities, and been more thorough and persevering in our examinations, the rarer it has become to find a case of insanity presenting no organic changes after death. The very same observers who once could find nothing satisfactory in their pathological researches in the brains of the insane, have changed their views, as their field of observation has enlarged, and their acquaintance with the whole subject has been increased with time and practice, so that some have examined hundreds of subjects without finding one entirely free from some appreciable change.

§ 91. II. *Insanity observes the same pathological laws as other diseases.* Notwithstanding the air of mystery which ignorance and superstition have thrown around this disease, it cannot be said to present any thing very strange or peculiar; nor are the discussions concerning it involved in the obscurity which is generally imagined. It arises from a morbid affection of organic matter, and is just as much, and no more, an event of special providence, as other diseases ; and to attribute it to the visitation of God in a peculiar sense, is a questionable proof of true piety as well as of sound philosophy. It follows the same course of incubation, developement, and termination in cure or death, as other diseases ; sometimes lying dormant for months or even years, obscure to others, and perhaps unsuspected by the patient himself; at others, suddenly breaking out with no premonition of its approach; and again,

after being repeatedly warded off by precautions and
remedies, finally establishing itself in its clearest
forms; just as consumption, for instance, sometimes
begins its ravages so slowly and insidiously as to be
perceptible only to the most practised observer, for
years together, while in another class of patients,
it proceeds from the beginning with a progress as
rapid as it is painfully manifest. But its presence no
one thinks of denying in the former case, merely
because its victim enjoys a certain degree of health
and activity, though it would be no greater error
than to deny the existence of insanity while the
operations of the mind are not so deeply disturbed
as to be perceptible to the casual observer. When
fully developed too, it may, like other diseases, give
rise to severe constitutional disturbance, or it may
scarcely affect the system at large ; as inflammation of
the digestive organs may occasion fever and intolerable pain, or lead its victim slowly to the grave,
hardly aware of its presence, and in the enjoyment
of comparative health. Like other diseases, insanity
is made the object of remedial treatment and often
yields to judicious administration of medicines,—a
sufficient proof of its material origin, for though the
rationale of the operation of bathing, bleeding, and
digitalis, is perfectly obvious in cerebral disease, it
is not so clear how they restore the spiritual principle to its natural vigor. It may proceed through its
successive stages with a severity ever increasing to
the end, or like many other affections of the nervous
system, its progress may be interrupted by periods
more or less long, of relaxation of its ordinary force,
—from a mere abatement of the constitutional ex-

citement and mental extravagance, to complete intermission of the disease, when the patient is apparently restored to all his original soundness. In its
causes also, insanity is under the dominion of no
extraordinary pathological laws. It never arises in
a mysterious way, as if abstracted from the ordinary
relations of cause and effect, as it would do, were it
an affection of an immaterial principle ; but its origin
may be readily accounted for in the same way as
that of other diseases. Whether proceeding from
hereditary predisposition, or maternal influences
during gestation; from the cerebral irritation produced by disease in other parts, or by external injuries ; from excessive or deficient exercise of the
mind ; from great predominance or indulgence of
some faculties with a small endowment or neglect of
the rest ; from improper or insufficient nourishment
or air; from the unbridled license of the passions; or
the habitual use of intoxicating drinks ; we see the
influence of causes precisely analogous to those which
give rise to other diseases. Mania also furnishes an
illustration of a well known pathological law, in its
tendency to be confirmed and influenced by remedies,
in proportion to the length of its continuance—a
fact which is totally inexplicable on the supposition
of the mind itself being idiopathically diseased. In
common with other diseases it evinces the remedial
powers, of proper air and exercise, of cheerful conversation, of friendly sympathy and attention, and
of employments which furnish a healthful play to the
actions of the whole system, and abstract the patient
from the contemplation of his own condition. In
short, throughout the whole history of mania, in its

various forms, we clearly discover the evidence of a
bodily disease—of a suffering organ; and in not a
fact respecting it can we discover any thing anomalous or at variance with the principles of diseased
action. If this truth be steadily borne in mind, it
will be a faithful light to our steps; and no one at
all acquainted with the subject, can question the importance of the influence, which it will exert on judicial investigations.

§ 92. Mania then being a disease and governed
by the same pathological laws as other diseases, it
will be incumbent on us to give some account of its
symptoms; and, since we consider a well-settled
conviction of the above views as having an important bearing on the course of legal decisions, no
farther reason will be necessary for going more fully
into this part of the subject, than at first blush,
might seem proper for our purpose. So closely are
soundness and unsoundness of mind allied, that we
are met at the outset by the difficulty already hinted
at, of discriminating in some cases between mental
functions modified by disease, and those that are peculiar though natural to the individual. Madness is
not indicated so much by any particular extravagance
of thought or feeling, as by a well-marked change of
character, or departure from the ordinary habits of
thinking, feeling and acting, without any adequate
external cause. To lay down, therefore, any particular definition of mania founded on symptoms, and
to consider every person mad who may happen to
come within the range of its application, would induce the ridiculous consequence of making a large
portion of mankind of unsound mind. Some men's

ordinary habits so closely resemble the behavior of the mad, that a stranger would be easily deceived ; as in the opposite case, where the confirmed mono-maniac by carefully abstaining from the mention of his hallucinations, has the semblance of a perfectly rational man. Hence, when the sanity of an individ-ual is in question, instead of comparing him with a fancied standard of mental soundness, as is too com-monly the custom, his natural character should be diligently investigated, in order to determine whether the apparent indication of madness, is not merely the result of the ordinary and healthy constitution of the faculties. In a word, he is to be compared with himself, not with others, and if there have been no departure from his ordinary manifestations, he is to be judged sane ; although it cannot be denied that striking peculiarities of character, such as amount to *eccentricity*, furnish strong ground of suspicion of pre-disposition to madness.

§ 93. For the first announcement of this great principle, that, in doubtful cases, the mind of the supposed lunatic should be compared with his own when in its natural, habitual state, we are indebted, to the late Dr. Gooch,[1] though it has been since developed and illustrated with an ability worthy of its importance, by Dr. Combe in his *Observations on Mental Derangement.* If the truths contained in the following extract are faithfully considered by the medical student, he may be spared many an awkward mistake which he might otherwise have committed,

---

[1] London Quarterly Review, v. 42, p. 355.

and may save many a sound and worthy individual from incalculable pain and annoyance. "In investigating the nature of insanity, the first caution to be observed is not to confound disorders of mental functions with natural qualities which sometimes strongly resemble them. Many men in the full enjoyment of health are remarkable for peculiarities and idiosyncrasies of thought and feeling, which contrast strongly with the general tone and usages of society ; but they are not on that account to be held as insane, because the singularity for which they are distinguished is with them a natural quality, and not the product of disease ; and, from the very unlikeness of their manifestations to the modes of feeling and acting of other men, such persons are, in common language, said to be eccentric. It is true that, on the principle already explained, of excess in size of some organs over the rest being favorable to the production of insanity, eccentricity involves, all other things being equal, a greater than usual susceptibility to mental derangement ; but still it is not mere strangeness of conduct or singularity of mind which constitutes its presence. *It is the prolonged departure, without an adequate external cause, from the state of feeling and modes of thinking usual to the individual when in health, that is the true feature of disorder in mind ;* and the degree at which this disorder ought to be held as constituting insanity, is a question of another kind, on which we can scarcely hope for unanimity of sentiment and opinion. Let the disorder, however, be ascertained to be morbid in its nature, and the chief point is secured, viz. a firm basis for an accurate diagnosis ; because it is impossible

that such derangement can occur unless in consequence of, or in connexion with, a morbid condition
of the organ of mind ; and thus the abstract mental
states, which are justly held to indicate lunacy in
one, may, in another, speaking relatively to health,
be the strongest proofs of perfect soundness of mind.
A brusque, rough manner, which is natural to one
person, indicates nothing but mental health in him ;
but if another individual who has always been remarkable for a deferential deportment and habitual
politeness, lays these qualities aside, and without
provocation or other adequate cause, assumes the
unpolished forwardness of the former, we may justly
infer, that his mind is either already deranged, or on
the point of becoming so.   Or, if a person who has
been noted all his life, for prudence, steadiness, regularity and sobriety, suddenly becomes, without any
adequate change in his external situation, rash, un-
settled, and dissipated in his habits, or *vice versa*,
every one recognises at once these changes, accompanied as they then are by bodily symptoms, as evidences of the presence of disease affecting the mind,
through the instrumentality of its organs.   It is
therefore, I repeat, not the abstract act or feeling
which constitutes a *symptom ;* it is *the departure from
the natural and healthy character, temper and habits,
that gives it this meaning ;* and in judging of a man's
sanity, it is consequently as essential to know what
his habitual manifestations were, as what his present
symptoms are."

§ 94. Mania, under whatever form it may appear,
is generally preceded, except when produced by
injuries or moral shocks, by a change in the natural

conditions designated by writers as the period of *incubation*. In the following paragraphs by Georget, we have a most accurate and graphic description of this state. "Sometimes," says he, "the action of the cause is strong and rapid ; at other times, more moderate and slow. In the first case, madness breaks out at the end of some hours or some days, after a state of anxiety and uneasiness, with headache, sleeplessness, agitation or depression, and threatening of cerebral congestion ; the patient begins to babble, cry, sing, and becomes agitated and wild. He is then often taken for a person in a state of intoxication, and the mistake becomes apparent only after examining the previous circumstances and the duration of the malady. In the other case, thought only becomes affected gradually, and often very slowly ; the patient is generally conscious of some disorder in his intellectual faculties ; he is beset by new and odd notions, and by unusual inclinations ; he feels himself changing in his affections ; but, at the same time, he preserves a consciousness of his condition, is vexed at it, and tries to conceal it ; he continues his occupations as much as he can ; and lastly, as many people do in the first stage of intoxication, he makes every effort to appear reasonable. Meantime, his health continues to give way, and he either sleeps less or loses sleep altogether ; the appetite diminishes or disappears ; sometimes digestion is difficult, and constipation supervenes ; *embonpoint* decreases, the features alter, the monthly discharge becomes irregular, weak, and at last is suspended. At the same time, there is observed something unusual and even extraordinary, in the tastes of the patient, in his habits, his affections, his character and aptitude for business ; if he was gay and communicative, he becomes sad, morose, and averse to society ; if he was orderly and economical, he becomes confused and prodigal ; if he had long abstained from the pleasures of love, he becomes the victim of insatiable desires, and either seeks to associate with the other sex, or has recourse to disgraceful practices ; if he was moderate in his political and religious opinions, he passes to an extreme exaggeration in both ; if he was open and candid, he becomes suspicious and jealous ; if a wife, she regards her husband and children with indifference ; the merchant neglects his business ; tears and laughter succeed each other without apparent motive ; the exterior of candor and modesty gives place to an air of conceit and assurance, which, especially in women, astonishes us.   But all these phenomena are less prominent than they may appear to be here, and unless the individual have been insane before, no one may suspect the nature of the ailment which torments him ; all the questions put to him lead to no results, except that of fatiguing and giving him pain, for the ignorance that prevails relative to madness leads the friends to indulge in offensive insinuations, and to charge him with frivolous accusations, from not perceiving that he is under the influence of disease and not of reason.   Sometimes the appetite either remains entire, or is speedily recovered, as well as digestion, nutrition, &c. and it is in these circumstances that the conduct of the patient gives rise to a host of interpretations on the part of his relatives and the public."

§ 95. " This period of incubation of mental alienation, during which the true state of the patient is
generally misunderstood, or not appreciated, may
last a long time.   Pinel relates, that a man who believed his wife to have been ill only six months, the
period of the invasion of furious delirium, admitted,
after a multiplicity of questions, that the disease
must have been going on fifteen years.   The same
author mentions elsewhere, that in several instances
the maniacal or melancholic state, has begun four,
six, ten, or even fifteen or twenty years previously.
It is often easy to go back months, or years, in this
way ; and we finally discover that circumstances
taken for causes by the friends, are frequently only
the consequences of unobserved disease.   In fact, it
often happens at that period of the malady, that a
slight contradiction, or paroxysm of anger, or some
cause equally insignificant to a person in good health,
provokes the immediate and complete subversion of
reason, and gives rise to mistakes as to its true cause
and duration." [1]

§ 96. Sooner or later this disorder of the cerebral
functions becomes of a more obvious and positive
character.   The struggle between the convictions of
his sounder reason, and the impulses of this new condition, ceases, and the patient, instead of contending
any longer against the approaches of disease, or of
concealing his thoughts, now believes in their reality
and openly and strenuously avows them, except when
induced by powerful reasons to pursue a contrary

---

[1] Dictionnaire de Médecine, art. Folie.

course.   The symptoms of physical derangement are
also more striking and numerous.   A febrile excitement pervades the system.   The pulse is acceler-
ated, the eye has a wild and glassy look, the sensations have become either more acute or more obscure, and the patient complains of pain in the head,
sense of weight, giddiness, ringing in the ears.   A
singular insensibility to external impressions is often
witnessed in this stage of mania, by means of which,
exposure to intense cold, heat, hunger and thirst, is
borne to a wonderful degree, without producing
uneasiness, or even consciousness of the fact.   The
muscular power is sometimes inordinately developed,
the waking moments being a scene of almost constant restlessness and agitation ; while at others,
there is an equally unnatural sluggishness and indisposition to move about.   Hunger and thirst are seldom unaffected, the patient either taking immense
quantities of food, or scarcely sufficient to supply the
wants of nature.   The maniacal patient sleeps less,
and his slumbers are disturbed by frightful dreams.
Such are the more prominent symptoms of physical
disorder which in various degrees of intensity and
forms of combination, mark the invasion of mania.
The mental disorders are of course as numerous and
various as the mental constitutions of the insane
themselves ; and to consider any particular association of them as characteristic of the state of mind
called mania, would be only to blend things together
that have no uniform nor necessary relations to one
another ; and would convey no more really valuable
information, than it would to marshal forth every
symptom that has at any time been observed in the

countless disorders of digestion, as *the* symptoms of diseased stomach. The only use which the physician makes of the latter is to refer them as they occur, to some particular derangement of that organ, and thus establish the ground for an appropriate and efficient treatment. There is no reason, why the same process should not be pursued in mania ; and it is because a different one has been followed, that the common notions of this disease are so loose and incorrect, as not only to be of little service in judicial discussions, but absolutely in the way of arriving at just and philosophical conclusions. To furnish any light on the subject, it would be our duty to analyze the various phenomena of mania, associate them by some natural relations, and refer them, as far as our knowledge will permit, to particular faculties. It is proposed therefore, following this idea as closely as possible, to consider mania as affecting either the *intellectual*, or the *affective* faculties ; meaning by the former, those which make us acquainted with the existence and qualities of external objects and the relations of cause and effect, and conduct us to the knowledge of general truths ; and by the latter, those sentiments, propensities and passions necessary to man as a social and accountable being. It is not intended to convey the idea that mania is invariably confined to one or the other of these two divisions of our faculties ; for though they may sometimes be separately affected, the one presenting a chaos of tumult and disorder, while the other apparently retains its wonted soundness and vigor, yet more frequently, they are both involved in the general derangement. But unless we study these disorders separately, and recognise their independent exist-ence—and this effect it is the tendency of the above classification to produce,—we never shall be able to refer them to their true source, nor discover their respective influence over the mental manifestations.

CHAPTER VI.

INTELLECTUAL MANIA.

§ 97. INTELLECTUAL MANIA is characterized by certain hallucinations, in which the patient is impressed with the reality of facts or events that have never occurred, and acts more or less in accordance with such belief; or having adopted some notion not altogether unfounded, carries it to an extravagant and absurd extent. It may be *general*, involving all or the most of the operations of the understanding ; or *partial*, being confined to a particular idea, or train of ideas.

SECTION I.

General Intellectual Mania.

§ 98. This form of the disease not only presents the most chaotic confusion into which it is possible for the mind to be involved, but it is also attended by greater disturbance of the rest of the functions of the body, then any other. " The patient sometimes keeps his head elevated and his looks fixed on high ; he speaks in a low voice, or utters cries and vociferations without any apparent motive ; he walks to and fro, and sometimes arrests his steps as if excited by the sentiment of admiration, or wrapt up in profound reverie.   Some insane persons display wild excesses of merriment, with immoderate bursts of laughter. Sometimes also, as if nature delighted in contrasts, gloom and taciturnity prevail, with involuntary showers of tears, or the anguish of deep sorrow, with all the external signs of acute mental suffering. In certain cases a sudden reddening of the eyes and excessive loquacity give presage of a speedy explosion of violent madness and the urgent necessity of a strict confinement.   One lunatic, after long intervals of calmness, spoke at first with volubility, uttered frequent shouts of laughter, and then shed a torrent of tears ; experience had taught the necessity of shutting him up immediately, for his paroxysms were at such times of the greatest violence." [1] It must not be understood that no glimpse of natural soundness can be discerned amid all this intellectual disorder.   Questions on indifferent subjects may be appropriately answered ; many of the patient's relations to surrounding circumstances may still be perceived ; and no little acuteness and ingenuity are often manifested in accommodating the real and true to the delusions under which he labors.   The difficulty is to fix the attention on a particular point, the mind constantly running from one idea to another, or absorbed in the thoughts which happen, for the moment, to predominate over every other.

§ 99. In the present state of our knowledge of the mental constitution, it is not strange to find consid-

---

[1] Pinel, Traité de alienation mentale, p. 63.

erable diversity of opinion respecting the nature or cause of maniacal hallucinations; yet in a medicolegal point of view it is important that they should be correctly understood. Hoffbauer [1] says that they consist in a vicious relation between the imagination and the senses by which the patient mistakes the creations of the one for objects really perceived by the others. Esquirol, not entirely satisfied with this explanation, divides them into two classes, termed by him, *illusive sensations*, and *hallucinations*.[2] The first arise in the senses, as when a maniac mistakes a window for a door, passes through it and is precipitated to the ground; or takes the clouds which he sees in the sky for contending armies; or believes his legs are made of glass; or his head turned round. In all these instances, the error refers to the real impression which is ill-perceived; there is an error of sensation, a vicious relation between the sense which actually perceives and the intellect which judges falsely of the external object. In the second, on the contrary, the senses have no share; the imagination alone is exalted; the brain is exclusively the seat of the disturbance; the patient mistaking the creations of his imagination, for objects actually present to his senses. He sees images and apparitions amid the thickest darkness; hears sounds and voices in the most perfect silence; and smells odors in the absence of all odorous bodies. This distinction does not seem to be well supported. That the functions of the senses are sometimes greatly per-

---

[1] Op. cit. sup., § 84.   [2] Idem, § 82, note.

verted, there can be no question ; but it needs more
evidence than we yet have, to prove that such per-
versions bear any part in producing these illusions ;
more especially as Esquirol admits, that, in what
he terms hallucinations, an exalted imagination is
sufficient of itself to produce a very similar effect.
In senile dementia where, in consequence of the
decay of the senses, wrong impressions are being
constantly received, they nevertheless give rise to
none of these delusions.   When the hero of Cervan-
tes did battle with the sheep and the windmills, it will
not be contended that he was laboring under any
special optical infirmity which conveyed false impressions of outward objects, because on most occasions,
the action of his senses was unequivocally sound.
Ready as he was to mistake a company of peaceable
shepherds for the creations of his disordered intellect, he never imagined Sancho to be any other than
his faithful squire, for the reason that his reflective
faculties were not so far subverted as to be incapable
of any healthy action.   Besides, if erroneous sensation has any thing to do with producing these illusions, we must go the length of asserting, that at such
times all the senses are disordered, or deny that the
errors of one may be corrected by the others.   It is
not so strange that vision should sometimes be so
affected as to deceive a person with the idea that his
legs are made of glass or butter, but it certainly is
very strange, that on such occasions, the other senses
should all return equally false impressions;   the
touch being unable to distinguish the feel of flesh
and blood, and the hearing the sound produced by
striking them, while they retain this power in regard

to every other part of the body. These illusions appear to result from a morbid excitement of the perceptive faculties, whereby they are stimulated to involuntary and irresistible activity, reproducing their former impressions with unwonted rapidity and distinctness, while a coexistent impairment of the reflective faculties prevents them from being considered as illusions and not outward realities. The physician will not unfrequently hear a patient complaining of seeing colors of the utmost beauty and variety of combination passing and repassing before his eyes, or forms of objects of every possible description, whether his eyes be open or shut, the room dark or light. His understanding being sound, he is not deceived, but believes them to be what they actually are, merely illusions; but, if, on the contrary, it were unsound, then these illusions would be taken for realities, and he would conduct accordingly. Ben Johnson would keep awake an entire night, gazing at armies of Turks and Tartars, Carthaginians and Romans contending around his great toe; in which amusement there is no evidence of mania, but merely of a morbid activity of the internal perceptive organs. The apparitions of Nicolai of Berlin, and others of a similar kind, arose, no doubt, from the same cause. Indeed unnatural excitement of these organs in insanity is sometimes so obvious and well-marked, as to be immediately recognised and properly understood. Rush gives the case of a young woman who delighted her visiters with her efforts in singing and poetry, though previously she had never manifested any talent for either; and the author once attended an insane patient of feeble intellect and defective education, who occupied much of her time in making verses, though she had not shown the slightest trace of such a power before the invasion of her disease. The faculty of construction too is occasionally heightened to a wonderful degree. Pinel speaks of a maniac who believed he had discovered the perpetual motion ; and in the course of his researches, he constructed some very ingenious machines. The only real difference, then, between *hallucinations* and *illusions of the senses*, is, that in the latter, the morbid activity of the perceptive faculties, which is a common element in the production of both, requires to be excited by outward impressions, while in the former, this effect is produced by the remembrance of past impressions,—a distinction that can be of but little if any importance, in judicial investigations. We have been thus particular in showing the true origin of hallucinations, that any mistake arising from wrong views of their nature might be avoided,—an event not altogether beyond the limits of possibility, for one instance has come to our own knowledge, where it was attempted in a court of justice, in a neighboring state, to measure the extent of the insanity by the comparative number of the senses supposed to be deranged in the hallucination.

§ 100. To determine exactly what mental impairment it is which is essential to insanity, metaphysicians and physiologists have long and anxiously labored with hardly the shadow of success. The various definitions and explanations to which their inquiries have given rise, display some ingenuity, but would scarcely be worth considering in this place, were they not capable of an injurious application in judicial investigations.   It has been said that insanity consists essentially in diseased perception ; that this is the common attribute of its various kinds and degrees.   We have seen above, however, that in a state of perfect mental soundness, the perceptions may be deeply disordered, insomuch as to give rise to strange and most extraordinary impressions, while many a madman may be found who evinces no one single error of perception.   The doctrine that insanity consists in false judgments, conveys no more satisfactory notion of its essential characters, for though there most certainly is false judgment in every case of insanity, it is far from being confined to this condition of the mind.   Every one is occasionally guilty of some gross error of judgment on which he may reason accurately and arrive at specious conclusions, without being considered at the time madder than his neighbors.   Locke, as if strongly impressed with the curious fact of the coexistence of absurd fancies with the power of reasoning smartly and pertinently to a certain extent, which is occasionally observed in the insane, remarked that they did not seem to have lost the faculty of reasoning, "but having joined together some ideas very wrongly, they mistake them for truths, and they err as men do that argue right from wrong principles." [1] If Locke had possessed any practical acquaintance with insanity, if he had even spent an hour in a well-managed hospital for the insane, he never would have adopted this opinion, for nothing can be farther

---

[1] On the Human Understanding, Book II. ch. xi. § 13.

from the truth, than the idea that generally madmen reason correctly from wrong premises. The lady who imagined that a tooth which a dentist had removed, had slipped from his fingers and stuck in her throat, and insisted that she could not swallow a morsel, while she ate and drank heartily, was as wrong in her conclusion as she was in her premises; and the man who, like Bellingham, imagines that the government has been culpably negligent of his private interests, and thence proceeds to take the life of a person whom he believes to be perfectly innocent, in order that he may have an opportunity of bringing his affairs before the country, errs in every stage of his reasoning. Indeed, it is matter of common observation, that maniacs display their insanity, not more in the delusions which they entertain, than in the course they pursue in order to accomplish their objects. The last and most ably-supported speculation on this subject is that of Dr. Conolly, who makes insanity to consist in "the impairment of any one or more of the faculties of the mind, accompanied with, or inducing, a defect in the comparing faculty." [1] There can be no doubt that this power of comparison is often, perhaps, generally, affected in insanity ; but it may be questioned whether this author has not referred many phenomena to this faculty of the mind, which more properly belong to some other. And even when the mental disturbance does unquestionably flow from defect in the comparing power, it would seem as if this defect

---

[1] Indications of Insanity, p. 300.

were but the consequence of one affecting more deeply the secret springs of thought. It is said that the celebrated Pascal sometimes believed that he was near the brink of a fearful precipice, and that his attendants, to allay his apprehension of falling down it, were accustomed to place a chair near him, in the direction of the supposed precipice. "He then compared what was done with what appeared to him," says Dr. Conolly, "and drew the just conclusion, that a chair could not stand upon air, beyond the brink of a precipice, and that he was not therefore in real danger." "Whenever the comparison could not be made," he adds, "the delusion yet remaining, he was not sane on the subject of the precipice."[1] Now it cannot be denied that in both instances, Pascal saw the chair, and was sensible that it was in the direction of the precipice, and that the real difference between them was, that in the former, he could, in the latter, he could not, *draw the just conclusion* that a chair could not stand upon air. It is evident that, in this case at least, and there is much reason to believe the fact is a general one—the faculty of the mind primitively affected was that which recognises the relations of cause and effect. We might multiply examples of this fondness for definitions, but enough has been said on this point, to convince the student of legal medicine how barren of all practical benefit, such speculations are, and to place him on his guard against their admission in judicial investigations, as tests, or criteria of insanity.

---

[1] Idem, p. 316.

§ 101. It is not to be understood that, in this form of mania, the derangement is confined to the intellectual faculties, the moral continuing to be exercised with their ordinary soundness. On the contrary, the moral faculties seldom escape its influence; and one of the earliest symptoms of the disease is an unaccountable change in the patient's social and domestic feelings. He becomes indifferent to those whom he loved the most; the mother thinks no longer of her children, or regards them with loathing; the child forgets his parents; the husband is insensible to the endearments of his wife; and love, attachment and friendship are replaced by hatred, jealousy and indifference. These traits, however, are not so prominent as the intellectual disorders, (except in the earliest stage of the disease) and besides, are very different from those which characterize that form of mental derangement to be presently described under the title of moral mania.

Section II.

Partial Intellectual Mania.

§ 102. By the ancients this form of the disease was called MELANCHOLIA on the supposition that it was always attended by dejection of mind and gloomy ideas. This term was used and so understood by modern writers, till Esquirol proved its improper application by showing that the ideas are not always gloomy, but frequently of a gay and cheerful nature. He substituted the term MONOMANIA, which is now in general use; and though possessing a more correct and definite signification, it embraces, besides the cases which come under the present division, a class that will be treated of under a different head. Still, for convenience's sake, the use of the term will be continued, with the understanding that it always refers to that form of insanity which is the immediate subject of discussion.

§ 103. Monomania is often described as a derangement of one or a few of the intellectual faculties, but incorrectly, upon our views of the constitution of those faculties, many of which may be simultaneously deranged by the action of disease, without necessarily producing insanity. This point has been already established, when speaking of those affections of the perceptive faculties which give rise to apparitions, and change, to appearance, the outward qualities of objects. A multitude of cases are recorded, in which the faculty of language too has been wholly or partially lost, while the soundness of the reasoning powers remained unimpaired; indeed there is not a single perceptive faculty, whose functions have not been sometimes obliterated or diminished, without being accompanied by insane delusion. It is evident that before a person can be insane, partially or generally, the mental faculty or faculties must be deranged, by which we discern the relations of things, and arrive at the knowledge of general truths.

§ 104. The most simple form of this disorder is that in which the patient has imbibed some single notion contradictory to common sense and to his own experience, and which seems, and sometimes no doubt really is, dependent on errors of sensation. Thus, thousands have believed their legs were made of glass, or that snakes, fish, or eels had taken up their abode in their stomach or bowels. In many such cases the hallucination is excited and maintained by impressions propagated from diseased parts, the presence of which has been revealed by dissection after death. Esquirol, in a memoir read before the institute,[1] a few years since, has related numerous cases in proof of this proposition, among which is that of a woman who insisted she was pregnant with the devil, in whose womb, there was found after death, a mass of hydatids ; of another, in the Salpetrière, who imagined that a regiment of soldiers lay concealed in her belly, and that she could feel them struggling and fighting with each other ; and of another, who believed that the apostles and evangelists had taken up their abode in her bowels and were occasionally visited by the pope and the patriarchs of the old testament, in both of whom, the intestines were found agglutinated together in consequence of chronic peritonitis. That these hallucinations are not always connected with corporeal impressions of this kind, seems to be proved by the fact, that they are sometimes dissipated by the skilful application of arguments, or manœuvres, by which the patients are made to believe themselves cured of their complaint. The story of the " Turned Head," in the " Diary of a Physician," ludicrous as it is, is scarcely a caricature of the truth ; and one of M.

---

[1] **Medico-Chirurgical Review,** N. S. vol. 21, p. 524.

Manry's patients, who, after thinking himself cured of a serpent in his bowels by means of a pretended surgical operation, suddenly took up the idea, that the creature had left its ova behind ready to be hatched into a brood of young ones, was again restored by the dexterous reply of his physician, that the snake was a male.[1] In this class of cases, the mind is not observed to have lost any of its original vigor, and its soundness on every other topic remains unimpaired, though there unquestionably does exist some derangement in the reflective faculties.

§ 105. In another class of cases, the monomania takes a little wider range, involving a train of morbid ideas, instead of being limited to a single point. The patient imbibes some notion connected with the various relations of persons, events, time, space, resistance &c. of the most absurd and unfounded nature, and endeavors, in some measure, to regulate his conduct accordingly ; though, in most respects, it is grossly inconsistent with his delusion. It is certainly not one of the least curious phenomena of our mental constitution, that these hallucinations will sometimes continue for years together, unaffected by time, and proceeding parallel, as it were, with the most sound and healthy operations of the mind, though more often, the predominant idea instead of enduring in this manner is frequently changing, one insane notion disappearing to give place to another and another. Rush says that he knew one clergyman and had heard of another, who were deranged at all

---

[1] Medico-Chirurgical Review, N. S. vol. 21, p. 524.

times, except when they ascended the pulpit, where they discovered, in their prayers and sermons, all the usual marks of a sound and correct mind ; and he speaks of a judge who was rational and sensible upon the bench, but constantly insane when off it.[1] The celebrated case of the Rev. Simon Browne is another remarkable instance of this kind. For many years before his death, he entertained the belief that "he had lost his rational soul," though during that time he evinced great ability both in his ordinary conversation and in his writings. Having discontinued all public or private worship, he explained to his friends, that " he had fallen under the sensible displeasure of God, who had caused his rational soul gradually to perish, and left him only an animal life in common with brutes ; that it was therefore profane in him to pray, and incongruous to be present at the prayers of others." In a book of some merit which he dedicated to the queen he speaks of himself as "once a man ; and of some little name ; but of no worth, as his present unparalleled case makes but too manifest ; for by the immediate hand of an avenging God, his very thinking substance has for more than seventeen years been wasting away, till it is wholly perished out of him, if it be not utterly come to nothing."[2]

§ 106. The operations of the understanding, even on subjects connected with the insane belief, are sometimes not impaired in an appreciable degree ;

---

[1] On Diseases of the Mind, p. 204.
[2] An account of this case may be found in the Gentleman's Magazine, 1762.

on the contrary, we are occasionally struck with the acuteness of the reasoning power displayed by mono-maniacs. Muratori relates the case of a jesuit, named Sgambari who believed himself a cardinal, and claimed to be addressed by the title of eminence. A friend was anxious to convince him of his error, and obtained a patient hearing to his remarks. When he had finished, the madman replied ; "either you consider me insane or rational ; on the latter sup-position, you do me injustice by your remonstrances ; on the former, I hardly know which is most mad, I, for believing myself a cardinal, or you, for thinking to cure a madman by such reasonings." [1]

§ 107. Though monomaniacs are generally ready enough to declare their predominant idea, yet when sufficient inducement exists, such as interest, fear of ridicule &c. they will occasionally conceal it ; and this too without the occurrence of a lucid interval, and while they believe in its reality as firmly as ever. Chambeyron, the French translator of Hoffbauer's treatise, speaks of "a woman who on her admission to the Salpetrière told one of the overseers, 'that she was an apostle, and that Louis XVIII. had re-membered her in his will.' "The next day," says he, "at my visit, I asked her reasons for entering the hospital. 'If I tell you,' said she, 'you will think me mad.' On my protesting to the contrary how-ever, she replied, 'well I am remembered in the will of Louis XVIII.' Of the other notion whose absurdity was more palpable, she said not a word.

---

[1] Hoffbauer, Op. cit. sup. § 86, note.

Now [a few days after] she denies that she ever entertained either notion, though her conduct and conversation prove that she still believes them both." Some cases of a similar kind are also related in Erskine's speech in the defence of Hadfield.

§ 108. In the simplest form of monomania, the understanding appears to be, and probably is, perfectly sound, on all subjects but those connected with the hallucination. When, however, the disorder is more complicated, involving a longer train of morbid ideas, we have the high authority of Georget for believing, that though the patient may reason on many subjects unconnected with the particular illusion on which the insanity turns, the understanding is more extensively deranged, than is generally suspected. If we could follow these people to the privacy of their own dwellings, narrowly observe their intercourse with their friends and neighbors, and converse with them on the subjects nearest to their thoughts, we should generally detect some perversity of feeling or action, altogether foreign to their ordinary character. Cases illustrative of this remark will frequently occur to the reader in the course of this work; and it is not necessary to insist on the importance of this fact in estimating the degree of criminal responsibility remaining in monomaniacs. It is a fact that must never be forgotten, that the phenomena of insanity do not lie on the surface, any more than those of other diseases, but can be discovered only by means of close and patient examination.

CHAPTER VII.

MORAL MANIA.

§ 109. Thus far mania has been considered as affecting the intellectual faculties only; but a more serious error on this subject can scarcely be committed, than that of limiting its influence to them. It will not be denied that the propensities and sentiments are also integral portions of our mental constitution ; and no enlightened physiologist can doubt that their manifestations are dependent on the cerebral organism.   Here then we have the only essential conditions of insanity,—a material structure connected with mental manifestations; and until it is satisfactorily proved that this structure enjoys a perfect immunity from morbid action, we are bound to believe that it is liable to disease, and consequently, that the *affective*, as well as *intellectual* faculties are subject to derangement. To moral mania, as a distinct form of the disease, the attention of the profession was first directed by the celebrated Pinel in the beginning of the present century.   Previously to that time it was a matter of universal belief, that insanity is always accompanied by derangement of the reasoning powers, and a recognition of this fact entered into every definition of the disease. Participating in the common belief, he found, to his great surprise, on resuming his researches at the Bicetrè,

that there were many maniacs who betrayed no
lesion whatever of the understanding, but were
under the dominion of instinctive and abstract fury,
as if the affective faculties alone had sustained injury.
This form of mental disorder, he designated as *manie
sans délire*. The examples which he gives, being
chiefly characterized by violent anger and unbounded
fury, by no means furnish suitable illustrations of the
affection now styled moral insanity, though they do
illustrate a particular form of that disorder. This
defect however has been amply supplied by the researches of others, which have made us acquainted
with a great number and variety of cases, in which
the affective faculties, either singly or collectively,
were deranged, independently of any appreciable
lesion of the intellect. The reality and importance
of this distinction which thus establishes two classes
of mania, is now generally acknowledged by practical observers, among whom it is sufficient to mention
Esquirol, Georget, Gall, Marc, Rush, Reil, Andrew
Combe, Conolly and Pritchard, though some of them
are inclined to doubt whether the integrity of the
understanding is so fully preserved in moral mania,
as Pinel believed. Still, the apparent soundness, and
the difficulty, at least, of establishing the existence
of any intellectual derangement, while the intellectual powers are unequivocally and deeply deranged,
render it no less important in its legal relations, than
if the understanding were wholly and absolutely
unaffected. It is defined by Pritchard, who has
strongly insisted on the necessity of assigning it a
more distinct and conspicuous place, than it has
hitherto received, as " consisting in a morbid per-

version of the natural feelings, affections, inclinations, temper, habits, and moral dispositions, without
any notable lesion of the intellect or knowing and
reasoning faculties, and particularly without any
maniacal hallucination." [1] We shall distinguish it
into, first, *general*, where the whole moral nature
presents a scene of chaotic disturbance ; secondly,
partial, where one or two only of the moral powers
are perverted.

Section I.

General Moral Mania.

§ 110. This condition is thus vividly described by
Pritchard. " There are many individuals living at
large, and not entirely separated from society, who
are affected in a certain degree by this modification
of insanity. They are reputed persons of singular,
wayward, and eccentric character. An attentive
observer may often recognise something remarkable
in their manner of existence, which leads him to
entertain doubts of their entire sanity, and circumstances are sometimes discovered on inquiry which
assist in determining his opinion. In many instances
it is found that there is an hereditary tendency to
madness in the family, or that several relatives of
the person affected have labored under diseases of
the brain. The individual himself is discovered in

---

[1] Cyclopædia of Practical Medicine, art. Insanity, p. 825.

a former period of life to have sustained an attack of madness of a decided character. His temper and dispositions are found on inquiry to have undergone a change ; to be not what they were previously to a certain time ; he has become an altered man ; and this difference has perhaps been noted from the period when he sustained some reverse of fortune, which deeply affected him, or since the loss of some beloved relative. In other instances, the alteration in his character has ensued immediately on some severe shock which his bodily constitution has undergone. This has either been a disorder affecting the head, a slight attack of paralysis, a fit of epilepsy, or some fever or inflammatory disorder, which has produced a perceptible change in the habitual state of the constitution. In some cases the alteration in temper and habits has been gradual and imperceptible, and it seems only to have consisted in an exaltation or increase of peculiarities which were always more or less natural or habitual." "Individuals laboring under this disorder are capable of reasoning or supporting an argument, on any subject within their sphere of knowledge that may be presented to them, and they often display great ingenuity in giving reasons for their eccentric conduct, and in accounting for and justifying the state of moral feeling, under which they appear to exist. In one sense indeed, their intellectual faculties may be termed unsound, but it is the same sense in which persons under the influence of strong passions may be generally said to have their judgment warped, and the sane or healthy exercise of their understandings impeded. They think and act under the influence of strongly

excited feelings and a person sane is under such circumstances proverbially liable to error both in judgment and conduct." [1]   It was this class of persons
undoubtedly, that suggested the following description in a work published in the beginning of the
present century.   " Among the varieties of maniacs
met with in medical pactice, there is one, which,
though, by no means rare, has been little noticed by
writers on this subject : I refer to those cases in
which the individuals perform most of the common
duties of life with propriety, and some of them, indeed, with scrupulous exactness, who exhibit no
strongly marked features of either temperament, no
traits of superior or defective mental endowment,
but yet take violent antipathies, harbor unjust suspicions, indulge strong propensities, affect singularity
in dress, gait, and phraseology ; are proud, conceited and ostentatious ; easily excited and with
difficulty appeased ; dead to sensibility, delicacy,
and refinement ; obstinately riveted to the most absurd opinions ; prone to controversy, and yet incapable of reasoning ; always the hero of their own
tale, using hyperbolic, high-flown language to express the most simple ideas, accompanied by unnatural gesticulation, inordinate action, and frequently
by the most alarming expression of countenance.
On some occasions they suspect sinister intentions
on the most trivial grounds ; on others are a prey to
fear and dread from the most ridiculous and imaginary sources ; now embracing every opportunity of

---

[1] Op. cit. sup., p. 826.

exhibiting romantic courage and feats of hardihood, then indulging themselves in all manner of excesses. Persons of this description, to the casual observer, might appear actuated by a bad heart, but the experienced physician knows it is the head which is defective. They seem as if constantly affected by a greater or less degree of stimulation from intoxicating liquors, while the expression of countenance furnishes an infallible proof of mental disease. If subjected to moral restraint, or a medical regimen, they yield with reluctance to the means proposed, and generally refuse and resist, on the ground that such means are unnecessary where no disease exists; and when, by the system adopted, they are so far recovered, as to be enabled to suppress the exhibition of the former peculiarities, and are again fit to be restored to society, the physician, and those friends who put them under the physician's care, are generally ever after objects of enmity and frequently of revenge." [1]

§ 111. There is unquestionably a great tendency in this affection to pass into intellectual mania, which we have seen is no less strongly characterized by moral perversities than by hallucinations; and Esquirol and Georget actually describe it as belonging to the initiatory stage or *incubation* of the latter disorder. Without discussing the point whether any *stage* of a disease should under any circumstances be erected into a distinct affection, the fact that it may continue for an indefinite length of time and become

---

[1] Cox, J. M., Practical Observations on Insanity. London, 1804.

the object of judicial investigation, gives it incalculable importance in a medico-legal point of view, and entitles it to a prominent place in a work like the present. Heinroth and Hoffbauer both recognise a form of mental alienation consisting exclusively of morbid excitement of the passions and feelings. "It is clear, says the latter, that mania may exist uncomplicated with mental delusion ; it is in fact only a kind of mental exaltation, (*tollheit*) a state in which the reason has lost its empire over the passions and the actions by which they are manifested, to such a degree that the individual can neither repass the former, nor abstain from the latter. It does not follow that he may not be in possession of his senses and even his usual intelligence, since, in order to resist the impulses of the passions, it is not sufficient that the reason should impart its counsels ; we must have the necessary power to obey them. The maniac may judge correctly of his actions without being in a condition to repress his passions, and to abstain from the acts of violence to which they impel him."[1] Subsequently he observes, that when mania proceeds from inordinate passions, "its more immediate cause lies in the physical temperament, or in certain moral affections which induce frequent occasions of anger. In every other respect, the maniac may be master of his propensities and the actions to which they lead ; he may judge and act rationally. He is irrational only in his paroxysms of fury, and then his errors of judgment are rather the effect than the cause of his furious transports."[2]

---

[1] Op. cit. sup. § 122.   [2] Ibid. § 126.

§ 112. The form of mental disorder which we are now considering, has been so little noticed by writers, while an ample knowledge of its phenomena is essential to the correct administration of justice, that no farther apology is needed for illustrating it with several examples collected from the observations of others. The first is related by Pinel as belonging to his *manie sans délire.* "An only son of a weak and indulgent mother was encouraged in the gratification of every caprice and passion of which an untutored and violent temper was susceptible. The impetuosity of his disposition increased with his years. The money with which he was lavishly supplied removed every obstacle to the indulgence of his wild desires. Every instance of opposition or resistance roused him to acts of fury. He assaulted his adversaries with the audacity of a savage ; sought to reign by force and was perpetually embroiled in disputes and quarrels. If a dog, a horse, or any other animal offended him, he instantly put it to death. If ever he went to a fête or any other public meeting, he was sure to excite such tumults and quarrels as terminated in actual pugilistic encounters, and he generally left the scene with a bloody nose. This wayward youth, however, when unmoved by passions, possessed a perfectly sound judgment. When he became of age, he succeeded to the possession of an extensive domain. He proved himself fully competent to the management of his estate, as well as to the discharge of his relative duties, and he even distinguished himself by acts of beneficence and compassion. Wounds, law-suits, and pecuniary compensations were generally the consequences of his

unhappy propensity to quarrel.   But an act of noto-
riety put an end to his career of violence.   Enraged
with a woman who had used offensive language to
him, he precipitated her into a well.   Prosecution
was commenced against him ; and on the deposition
of a great many witnesses who gave evidence to his
furious deportment, he was condemned to perpetual
confinement in the Bicêtre." [1]   In this instance there
was something more than the unrestrained indulgence of strong passions, though, no doubt, the passions of this person were naturally remarkably
strong and active ; the understanding, though sound,
was incapable of restraining their impulses, for the
reason that they were excited by disease and therefore beyond its control.   The constant excitement of
passions already too much developed by means of a
vicious education, led to that condition of mind in
which the healthy balance of the affective and intellectual faculties, is destroyed,—in other words, to
moral mania.   A case of a very similar character to
this, and to which the rank of the person and the
disastrous results of the affection have given a melancholy preëminence over all others in the medico-
legal history of the disease, is that of earl Ferrers,
who was executed in 1760, for the murder of his
steward.   It differs from the above in exhibiting a
more advanced stage of the disease, and in more
distinctly revealing its approximation to intellectual
mania by the unfounded notions which the patient
had imbibed.   Though his reasoning powers were

---

[1] Sur l'Alienation Mentale, p. 156, § 159.

sound and his conversation rational, he imagined that his relatives had formed a conspiracy against him in which his victim was an accomplice ; and his conduct in many respects was so wild and strange, as to excite in those who were in the habit of meeting him, a suspicion, and even conviction of his insanity.[1]

§ 113. The following case from Metzger is cited by Hoffbauer, who observes that the patient labored under no delusion, properly speaking, but was only not master of his actions.

A Russian colonel came to Königsberg to receive an inheritance, and committed there so many acts of violence, that he was summoned before the tribunal of justice. His conduct before the magistrates was equally unreasonable. He had become so much an object of dread at Königsberg, that nobody would execute any commission for him—the very chimney-sweepers required a guard if sent to sweep his chimneys. At last, after several complaints made against him, he was arrested because he had threatened to stab his landlord with a pitchfork for demanding his rent, and pursued him with that intent. "In going into the prison," says Metzger, "I saw an old man with white hair, of a respectable appearance, who

---

[1] A report of Earl Ferrers's trial may be found in Hargrave's State Trials, and it is noticed at considerable length in Smollet's Continuation of Hume's History of England. Some valuable comments on this case, are contained in Combe's *Observations on Mental Derangement*, p. 204, to which every reader is referred, who is more anxious to enlighten his mind by correct facts and philosophical views, than to confirm his errors and gratify his prejudices by obstinately shutting his eyes against the progress of scientific improvement.

received me politely. I first inquired concerning his health. 'I am ill, through old age,' he replied, 'and tormented with gout, with the stone, and with the scurvy, evils for which I can have no remedy.' He desired to know who had sent me to see him; I told him it was the tribunal. 'I ought to be judged,' he replied, 'by a French tribunal,' and he pretended that I should find proof of what he said in a writing which he forced me to take. At last I informed him of the reason of his arrest. His eyes then sparkled, and he said in French, with much volubility, that M. M. —— and —— were his mortal enemies; that they had several times tried to ruin him; that he had experienced much injustice and oppression on the part of the tribunal; and that they had disposed, as they pleased of his brother's inheritance. Being asked what were his occupations, he replied, 'that he was, as every honest man should be, free and content, even in prison; that he amused himself with poetry, and copied verses relating to his situation.' "[1]

§ 114. The following cases are taken from Pritchard. "I. K., a farmer, several of whose relatives had been the subjects of mental derangement, was a man of sober and domestic habits, and frugal and steady in his conduct, until about his forty-fifth year, when his disposition appeared to have become suddenly changed in a manner which excited the surprise of his friends and neighbors, and occasioned grief and vexation in his family. He became wild,

---

[1] Op. cit. sup. § 126.

excitable, thoughtless, full of schemes and absurd projects. He would set out and make long journeys into distant parts of the country to purchase cattle and farming-stock, of which he had no means of disposing ; he bought a number of carriages, hired an expensive house ready furnished, which had been inhabited by a person much above his rank, and was unsuitable to his condition ; he was irascible and impetuous, quarreled with his neighbors, and committed an assault upon the clergyman of the parish, for which he was indicted and bound to take his trial. At length his wife became convinced that he was mad, and made application for his confinement in a lunatic asylum, which was consequently effected. The medical practitioners who examined him were convinced of his insanity, by comparing his late wild habits and unaccountable conduct with the former tenor of his life, taking into consideration the tendency to disease which was known to prevail in his family. The change in his character alone had produced a full conviction of his madness in his friends and relatives. When questioned as to the motives which had induced him to some of his late proceedings, he gave clear and distinct replies, and assigned with great ingenuity some plausible reason for almost every part of his conduct."

§ 115. " Abraham B., a working tradesman of industrious and sober habits, conducted himself with propriety until about forty-six years of age, and had accumulated a considerable property from the fruits of his exertions. About that period he lost his wife, and after her death became more and more penurious. At length, he denied himself the comforts, and in a great measure, the necessaries of life, and became half-starved and diseased ; his body was emaciated and beset with scaly eruptions.   Mr. S., a gentleman who had long known him, hearing of the condition into which he had sunk, sent a medical practitioner to visit him, by whose advice B. was removed from a miserable dirty lodging to a lunatic asylum.   Mr. S., who was present on the occasion, observed that Abraham B., previously to his quitting the room in which he had immured himself, kept his eyes fixed on an old trunk in the corner of the apartment. This was afterwards emptied of its contents, and in it were found, in the midst of various articles, dirty bank-notes, which had been thrown into it apparently at different times, to the value of more than a thousand pounds.   Abraham B., after his removal to an asylum where he had wholesome food and exercise, soon began to recover from his bodily infirmities, and at length became anxious to be at large.   The writer of this article visited him and conversed with him for some time, in order to ascertain his mental condition. He betrayed no sign of intellectual delusion, nor did it appear that any thing of that description had ever been a part of his complaint.   His replies to questions were rational according to the extent of his natural capacity.   He was determined to go and manage his property, and get a wife who should take care of him.   In a few days after his release he was married to a servant belonging to the lunatic asylum where he had been confined.   His new wife found after some months that it was impossible to endure the strange conduct of her husband, and after various expedients, brought him back to the asylum,

with a certificate from a medical man, who had examined him and declared him to be insane.   He still
remains in confinement, and his derangement is now
more complete than formerly, as it plainly involves
his intellect." [1]

§ 116. These are no uncommon instances of that
condition of mind so often mistaken for any thing
rather than what it really is—mental derangement.
Its true nature was here recognised by intelligent
practitioners who looked beyond the circle of a definition, and might have been recognised, perhaps, by
others of narrower views, in a calm investigation for
therapeutical purposes ; but, amid the excitement
produced by great criminal acts, and the struggles
between knowledge and ignorance, truth and prejudice, that spring up in judicial investigations, how
seldom, alas, has it been discerned.   The following
cases, in which this perversion of the moral faculties
was accompanied by a single insane belief, will serve
to complete our proofs of the intimate connexion of
moral with intellectual mania.

117. "Mr. H. P. had been for many years confined in a lunatic asylum, when, an estate having
devolved upon him by inheritance, it became necessary to subject him anew to an investigation.   He
was examined by several physicians who were unani-
mous in the opinion that he was a lunatic ; but a
jury considered him to be of sound understanding,
attributing his peculiarities to eccentricity, and he
was consequently set at liberty.

---

[1] Op. cit. sup. p. 831.

"The conduct of this individual was the most eccentric that can be imagined: he scarcely performed any action in the same manner as other men; and some of his habits, in which he obstinately persisted, were singularly filthy and disgusting. For every peculiar custom he had a quaint and often ludicrous reason to allege, which indicated a strange mixture of shrewdness and absurdity. It might have been barely possible to attribute all these peculiarities, as well as the morbid state of temper and affections, to singularity in natural character and to the peculiar circumstances under which this person had been placed. But there was one conviction deeply fixed on his mind, which, though it might likewise be explained by the circumstances of his previous history, seemed to constitute an instance of maniacal delusion. Whenever any person whom he understood to be a physician attempted to feel his pulse, he recoiled with an expression of horror, and exclaimed, 'If you were to feel my pulse, you would be lord paramount over me for the rest of my life.' The result has proved that confinement is not always necessary in cases of this description. Mr. H. P. has remained at liberty for many years, and his conduct, though extremely singular, has been without injury to himself or others." [1]

§ 118. A very common feature of moral mania is a deep perversion of the social affections, whereby the feelings of kindness and attachment that flow from the relations of father, husband, and child

---

[1] Pritchard, Op. cit. sup. p. 834.

are replaced by a perpetual inclination to tease, worry and embitter the existence of others. The ordinary scene of its manifestations is the patient's own domestic circle, the peace and happiness of which are effectually destroyed by the outbreakings of his ungovernable temper, and even by acts of brutal ferocity. Frederic William of Prussia, father of Frederic the Great, undoubtedly labored under this form of moral mania ; and it furnishes a satisfactory explanation of his brutal treatment of his son and his utter disregard of the feelings or comfort of any other member of his family. About a dozen years before his death, his health gave way under his constant debauches in drunkenness, he became hypochondriacal, and redoubled his usual religious austerities. He forbade his family to talk of any subject but religion, read them daily sermons, and compelled them to sing, punishing with the utmost severity any inattention to these exercises. The prince and his eldest sister soon began to attract a disproportionate share of his hostility. He obliged them to eat and drink unwholesome or nauseous articles, and would even spit in their dishes, addressing them only in the language of invective, and at times endeavoring to strike them with his crutch. About this time he attempted to strangle himself and would have accomplished his design, had not the queen come to his assistance. His brutality towards the prince at last arrived to such a pitch, that he, one morning, seized him by the collar as he entered his bed-chamber, and began beating him with a cane in the cruelest manner, till obliged to desist from pure exhaustion. On another occasion, shortly after, he seized his son by the hair and threw him on the ground, beating him till he was tired, when he dragged him to a window apparently for the purpose of throwing him out. A servant hearing the cries of the prince, came to his assistance, and delivered him from his hands. Not satisfied with treating him in this barbarous manner, he endeavored, though unsuccessfully, by a similar course of conduct, to make him sign an act renouncing his claim to the succession of the Prussian throne, in favor of his brother. To obtain this end, though in a different manner, he connived at the prince's attempts to escape from his tyranny, in order that he might procure from a court-martial, a sentence of death, and this even he was anxious to anticipate, by endeavoring to run him through the body with his sword. Not succeeding in procuring his death by judicial proceedings, he kept him in confinement, and turned all his thoughts towards converting him to Christianity. At this time, we first find mention of any delusion connected with his son, though it probably existed before. In his correspondence with the chaplain to whom he had entrusted the charge of converting the prince, he speaks of him as one who had committed many and heinous sins against God and the king, as having a heardened heart and being in the fangs of Satan. Even after he became satisfied with the repentance of the prince, he showed no disposition to relax the severities of his confinement. He was kept in a miserable room, deprived of all the comforts and many of the necessaries of life, denied the use of pens, ink, and paper, and allowed scarcely food enough to prevent starvation. His treatment of the princess was no less barbarous. She was also confined, and every effort used to make her situation thoroughly wretched,—and though, after a few years, he relaxed his persecution of his children, the general tenor of his conduct towards his family and others, evinced little improvement in his disorder, till the day of his death.[1]

§. 119. There can be little doubt that the affection above described, is far more common in the ordinary walks of society, than is generally imagined. It is so imperfectly understood, however, that those singular freaks of conduct and whimsical notions which would unquestionably subject a person to the imputation of insanity, were there the slightest aberration of reason, are set down to eccentricity of temper, or inherently vicious dispositions. The suspicion that they spring from insanity, is immediately dispelled by calling to mind the general correctness of his views, and the steadiness and sagacity with which he pursues his daily avocations. And so intimately connected are the ideas of insanity and delusion in the common mind, that it requires no little courage and confidence on the part of the practitioner who ventures, in a given case, to declare the existence of the former, independently of the latter. The consequences of these erroneous views are often strikingly and painfully exhibited, when a person thus affected becomes the object of a legal procedure. While he may be described by one, as acute and

---

[1] Lord Dover's Life of Frederic II. King of Prussia, vol. 1. B. 1. chap. 2, 3, 4, 5, 6, 7.

methodical in his business, and rational in his discourse, and believed to be perfectly sane ; another will testify to the strangest freaks that ever a madman played, and thence deduce the conviction of his insanity ; while one represents him as social and kindly in his disposition, ready to assist and oblige, and to accommodate himself to the varying humors of those about him, it will be testified by another, that in his domestic relations, his former cheerfulness has given way to gloom and moroseness, that equanimity of temper has been replaced by frequent gusts of passion, and that the warm affections, which spring from the relations of parent and child, husband and wife, have been transformed into indifference or hate. These are the cases that confound the wise and defy the scrutiny of the skilful, while they tempt the superficial and conceited to betray their ignorance, under the delusion of superior penetration ; which tarnish many a professional reputation, and expose even the pretentions of true science to popular mockery and derision.

Section II.

Partial Moral Mania.

§ 120. In this form of insanity, the derangement is confined to one or a few of the affective faculties, the rest of the moral and intellectual constitution preserving its ordinary integrity. An exaltation of the vital forces in any part of the cerebral organism, must necessarily be followed by increased activity

and energy in the manifestations of the faculty connected with it, and which may even be carried to
such a pitch as to be beyond the control of any other
power, like the working of a blind, instinctive impulse. Accordingly, we see the faculty thus affected, prompting the individual to action by a kind of
instinctive irresistibility, and while he retains the
most perfect consciousness of the impropriety and
even enormity of his conduct, he deliberately and
perseveringly pursues it. With no extraordinary
temptations to sin, but on the contrary, with every
inducement to refrain from it, and apparently in the
full possession of his reason, he commits a crime
whose motives are equally inexplicable to himself
and to others. The ends of justice require that this
class of cases should be viewed in their true light ;
and while it is not denied that their similarity to
other cases in which mental unsoundness is never
supposed to have existed, renders such a view difficult, yet this very difficulty is a fresh reason for extending our inquiries and increasing our information.
In the account now about to be given of partial
moral mania, those forms of it only will be noticed
which have the most important legal relations.

§ 121. Instances of an irresistible propensity to
steal, unaccompanied by any intellectual alienation,
are related on good authority and are by no means
rare. "There are persons," says Dr. Rush, " who
are moral to the highest degree as to certain duties,
but who, nevertheless, live under the influence of
some one vice. In one instance, a woman was exemplary in her obedience to every command of the
moral law except one,—she could not refrain from

stealing. What made this vice more remarkable was, that she was in easy circumstances, and not addicted to extravagance in any thing. Such was the propensity to this vice, that when she could lay her hands on nothing more valuable, she would often at the table of a friend, fill her pockets secretly with bread. She both confessed and lamented her crime." [1] Cases like this are so common, that they must have come within the personal knowledge of every reader who has seen much of the world, so that it will be unnecessary to mention them more particularly.[2] It would be difficult to prove directly, that this propensity, continuing as it does during a whole life, and in a state of apparently perfect health, is, notwithstanding, a consequence of diseased or abnormal action in the brain, but the presumptive evidence in favor of this explanation is certainly strong. First, it is very often observed in abnormal conformations of the head, and accompanied by an imbecile condition of the understanding. Gall and Spurzheim saw in the prison of Berne a boy twelve years old, who could never refrain from stealing. He is described as "ill-organized and rickety." At Haina they were shown an obstinate robber, whom no corporal punishment could correct. He appeared about sixteen years of age, though he was in fact twenty-six ; his head was round, and about the size of a child's one year old. He was also deaf and dumb, a common accompani-

---

[1] Medical Inquiries and Observations, v. 1.
[2] In Gall's great work, *On the Functions of the Brain*, Vol. 4, p. 131, Boston edition, the reader will find a considerable number of these cases related.

ment of mental imbecility. Secondly, this propensity to steal is not unfrequently observed in undoubted mania. Pinel says it is a matter of common observation, that persons who, in their lucid intervals, are justly considered models of probity, cannot refrain from stealing and cheating during the paroxysm. Gall mentions the case of two citizens of Vienna, who, on becoming insane, were distinguished in the hospital, for an extraordinary propensity to steal, though previously they had lived irreproachable lives. They wandered over the house from morning to night, picking up whatever they could lay their hands upon,—straw, rags, clothes, wood &c. which they carefully concealed in their room.[1] A propensity to theft is recognised by Pritchard, as being often a feature of moral mania, and sometimes, the leading if not the sole character of the disease, and he mentions a lunatic who would never eat his food, unless he had previously stolen it, and accordingly his keeper was obliged to put it into some corner within his reach, in order that he might discover and take it furtively.[2] Thirdly, it has been known to follow diseases or injuries of the brain, and therefore to be dependent on morbid action. Acrel mentions the case of a young man, who after receiving a severe wound on the temple for which he was trepanned, manifested an invincible propensity to steal, which was quite contrary to his ordinary disposition. After committing several larcenies, he was imprisoned and would have been punished according

---

[1] Op. cit. sup. vol. 4, p. 131.   [2] Op. cit. sup. p. 829.

to law, had not Acrel declared him insane, and attributed his unfortunate propensity to a disorder of the brain. In the *Journal de Paris*, March 29th, 1816, appeared the following paragraph : " An ex-commissary of police, at Toulouse, Beau-Conseil, has just been condemned to eight years confinement and hard labor, and to the pillory, for having while in office, stolen some pieces of plate from an inn. The accused persisted to the last in an odd kind of defence ; he did not deny the crime, but attributed it to mental derangement produced by wounds he had received at Marseilles in 1815." [1]　The late Dr. Smith of New Haven, Connecticut, once observed a similar effect consecutive to an attack of typhus fever. "One patient in particular, who had been extremely sick with this disease, after his recovery, had a strong propensity to steal, and did in effect take some articles of clothing from a young man to whom he was under great obligations for the care which he had taken of him during his sickness. He at length stole a horse and some money, was detected and punished. I took some pains to inquire into the young man's former character, and found it good, and that his family were respectable." [2]　Fourthly, this propensity to steal is sometimes followed by general mania. Foderè relates the case of a female servant in his own family, who could not help stealing secretly from himself and others, articles, even of trifling value ; though she was intelligent, modest and reli-

---

[1] Quoted by Gall in Op. cit. sup. vol. 4, p. 141.
[2] Medical and Surgical Memoirs, p. 62.

gious, and was all the while conscious of and admitted the turpitude of her actions. He placed her in a hospital, considering her insane, and after apparent restoration and a long trial, he again took her into his service. Gradually, in spite of herself, the instinct again mastered her, and in the midst of an incessant struggle between her vicious propensity on the one hand and a conscientious horror of her condition on the other, she was suddenly attacked with mania, and died in one of its paroxysms.[1] Fifthly, this propensity is sometimes produced by certain physiological changes in the animal economy. Gall met with four examples of women who, when pregnant, were violently impelled to steal, though perfectly upright at other times.

§ 122. An inordinate propensity to lying is also of no uncommon occurrence in society ; and most of the readers of this work have probably met with instances of it in people, whose morals in other respects were irreproachable, and whose education had not been neglected. The maxim of Jeremy Bentham, that it is natural for men to speak the truth, and therefore easier to do so than to utter falsehood, seems, in them, to be completely reversed, for they find nothing more difficult than to tell the truth. In repeating a story which they have heard from others, they are sure to embellish it with exaggerations and additions, till it can scarcely be recognised, and are never known to tell the same story twice alike. Not even is the slightest groundwork of truth necessary,

---

[1] Traitè de medicine legale, T. 1, p. 237.

in order to call forth the inventions of their perverted minds ; for they as often flow spontaneously and in the greatest profusion as when based on some little foundation in fact. This propensity seems to result from an inability to tell the truth, rather than from any other cause ; as it can be traced to no adequate motive, and is often indulged when truth would serve the interests of the individual better. Like that last mentioned, it is liable to degenerate into unequivocal mania, and is also quite a common feature in this disease—a circumstance which Rush considers as proof of its physical origin.

§ 123. We are not prepared to go the length of referring all the instances of these two propensities thus manifested, to the influence of disease, but they cannot all be attributed to faults of education, to evil example, or to innate depravity, without doing violence to the testimony of every day's experience. It may be difficult no doubt, in many cases, to distinguish them in respect to their physical or moral origin, but the distinction is no less real on that account ; the same principles are to guide us that regulate our decision in questions touching any other form of insanity ; and if common sense and professional intelligence preside over our deliberations, the final judgment will not often be wrong.

§ 124. Morbid activity of the sexual propensity is unfortunately of such common occurrence, that it has been generally noticed by medical writers, though its medico-legal importance has never been so strongly felt as it deserves. This affection, in a state of the most unbridled excitement, filling the mind with a crowd of voluptuous images, and ever hurrying its victim to acts of the grossest licentiousness, in the absence of any lesion of the intellectual powers, is now universally known and described by the name of EROTIC MANIA. We cannot convey a better notion of the phenomena of this disorder, than by referring to a few examples mentioned by Gall, by whom it was first extensively observed and its true nature discovered. Its milder forms and early stages, when not beyond the control of medical and moral treatment, are illustrated in the following cases. "A robust and plethoric young man came to reside in Vienna. Having no *liaisons*, he was unusually continent, and was soon attacked with erotic mania." Gall pursuing the treatment indicated by his peculiar views of the origin of the disease, succeeded in restoring him in a few days to perfect health.

§ 125. "A well-educated, clever young man, who, from his infancy almost, had felt strong erotic impulses, succeeded in controlling them to a certain extent, by means of equally strong devotional feelings. After his situation permitted him to indulge without constraint in the pleasures of love, he soon made the fearful discovery, that it was often difficult for him to withdraw his mind from the voluptuous images that haunted it, and fix it on the important and even urgent concerns of his business. His whole being was absorbed in sensuality." He obtained relief by an assiduous pursuit of scientific objects, and by finding out new occupations.

§ 126. "A very intelligent lady was tormented, like the subject of the last-mentioned case, from infancy, with the most inordinate desires. Her excellent education alone saved her from the rash indul-

gences to which her temperament so violently urged
her. Arrived at maturity, she abandoned herself to
the gratification of her desires, but this only increased their intensity. Frequently, she saw herself
on the verge of madness, and in despair, she left her
house and the city, and took refuge with her mother
who resided in the country, where the absence of
objects to excite desire, the greater severity of manners and the culture of a garden, prevented the explosion of the disease. After having changed her
residence for that of a large city, she was, after a
while, threatened with a relapse, and again she took
refuge with her mother. On her return to Paris,
she came to me, and complained like a woman in
perfect despair. 'Every where,' she exclaimed,
'I see nothing but the most lascivious images ; the
demon of lust unremittedly pursues me, at the table,
and even in my sleep. I am an object of disgust to
myself, and feel that I can no longer escape either
madness or death.' "

§ 127. In the following cases, the mind was finally
overwhelmed by the force of this frightful propensity,
and sunk into complete and violent madness. " A
man had lived many years in a happy and fruitful
union, and had acquired by his industry a respectable fortune. After having retired from business and
led an idle life, his predominant propensity gradually obtained the mastery over him, and he yielded
to his desires, to such a degree, that, though still in
possession of his reason, he looked on every woman
as a victim destined to gratify his sensual appetite.
The moment he perceived a female from his window,
he announced to his wife and daughters, with an air

of the utmost delight, the bliss that awaited him. Finally, this partial mania degenerated into general mania, and shortly after, he died in an insane hospital at Vienna."[1]

§ 128. Pinel has related a very similar case. "A man had creditably filled his place in society till his fiftieth year. He was then smitten with an immoderate passion for venereal pleasures ; he frequented places of debauchery, where he gave himself up to the utmost excesses ; and then returned to the society of his friends, to paint the charms of pure and spotless love." His disorder gradually increased ; his seclusion became necessary; and he soon became a victim of furious mania.

Many more cases like these might be quoted, but the above are sufficient to illustrate a truth as generally recognised as any other in pathology, and to convince the most skeptical mind, that if insanity— or, in more explicit terms, if morbid action in the brain inducing a deprivation of moral liberty—ever exists, it does in what is called erotic mania.

§ 129. A morbid propensity to incendiarism, where the mind though otherwise sound, is borne on by an invisible power, to the commission of this crime has been so frequently observed, that it is now generally recognised as a distinct form of insanity. A few cases, taken from a multitude at hand, will give the reader a better idea of it than a general description. Gall has quoted from a German journal an account of Maria Franck, who was executed for

---

[1] Sur les Fonctions du cerveau, T. 3, p. 318.

house-burning. Within five years, she fired twelve houses, and was arrested on the thirteenth attempt. She was a peasant's daughter of little education, and in consequence of an unhappy marriage, had abandoned herself to habits of intemperance. In this state, a fire occurred in which she had no share. "From the moment she witnessed this fearful sight, she felt a desire to fire houses, which, whenever she had drank a few coppers' worth of spirit, was converted into an irresistible impulse. She could give no other reason, nor show any other motive, for firing so many houses, than this impulse which drove her to it. Notwithstanding the fear, the terror, and the repentance she felt, in every instance, she went and did it afresh." In other respects her mind was sound.[1]

§ 130. Several German medical jurists have lately noticed this form of moral mania, and related numerous cases, among which are the following. "A young girl of a quiet, inoffensive disposition, and whose character had been hitherto exemplary, made seven different attempts at incendiarism in a village near Cologne. When interrogated as to the motives which had prompted her to act so wickedly, she burst into tears, confessing that, at certain periods, she felt her reason forsake her, and that then she was irresistibly impelled to the commission of a deed of which, when done, she bitterly repented. She was acquitted by a jury of all criminal intentions."[2]

---

[1] On the Functions of the Brain, vol. iv. p. 104.
[2] Medico-Chirurgical Review, July, 1836, p. 216.

§ 131. " A girl seventeen years of age became a servant to a Mr. Becker on the seventh of February. Strange to say, her master's house was discovered to be on fire several times in the course of a few days after she began to reside there. The girl was dismissed, in consequence of her master supposing that she was bewitched. Soon afterwards she got a place in another family, and it was not long before she again resorted to her incendiary practices. When charged with the offence, she at once confessed it, and bitterly grieved at the damage and distress she had caused. The judge before whom she was tried, very properly decided that she was the victim of an instinctive monomania." [1]

§ 132. One case has already been related (§ 61), in which this propensity was connected with mental deficiency. Gall says that such a conjunction is not very uncommon.[2] In the prison at Freyburg, in Brisgau, there was a half-imbecile youth, fifteen years old, who had set fire to nine houses in succession. When the fire was over he thought no more of it; which proves that he was governed solely by an animal instinct.

§ 133. The last and most important form of moral mania that will be noticed consists in a morbid activity of the *propensity to destroy;* where the individual without provocation or any other rational motive, apparently in the full possession of his reason, and oftentimes, in spite of his most strenuous efforts to resist, imbrues his hands in the blood of

---

[1] Medico-Chirurgical Review, July 1836, p. 216.
[2] Op. cit. sup. vol. 4, p. 104.

others ; oftener than otherwise, of the partner of his bosom, of the children of his affections, of those, in short, who are most dear and cherished around him. The facts here alluded to are of painful frequency, and the gross misunderstanding of their true nature almost universally prevalent, excepting among a few in the higher walks of the professions, leads to equally painful results. In the absence of any pathological explanation of this horrid phenomenon, the mind seeks in vain, among secondary causes, for a rational mode of accounting for it, and is content to resort to that time-honored solution, of all the mysteries of human delinquency, the instigation of the devil. Of the double homicide to which this affection gives rise, there can be no question which is most to be deplored, for shocking as it is, for one bearing the image of his Maker to take the life of a fellow-being with brutal ferocity, how shall we characterize the deliberate perpetration of the same deed, under the sanction of law and of the popular approbation ? We trust, however, that the ample researches of writers of unquestionable veracity and ability, which are now just reaching the attention of the legal profession, will be soon followed by a conviction of past errors, and a more rational administration of the criminal law. For the purpose of contributing to this object, it will be necessary to bring fully before the reader the results of these researches, and, in view of the importance of the subject, to risk the charge of prolixity by the number and length of the quotations.

§ 134. The form of disease now under consideration was first distinctly described by Pinel; and

though its existence as a distinct form of monomania
was for a long time after doubted, it has subsequently been admitted by the principal writers on
insanity ; by Gall and Spurzheim, Esquirol,[1] Georget,
Marc, Andral, Orfila, and Broussais in France ; by
Burrows, Conolly, Combe and Pritchard in England;
by Hoffbauer, Platner, Ethmuller, and Henke in
Germany; by Otto of Copenhagen ; and by Rush
in this country. It has received the various appella-
tions of *monomanie-homicide, monomanie-meurtriere,
melancholie-homicide, homicidal insanity, instinctive
monomanie.* Esquirol,. in his valuable memoir published in the shape of a note in the French translation of Hoffbauer's work, observers that homicidal
insanity, or *monomanie-homicide,* as he terms it,
presents two distinct forms, in the former of which
the monomaniac is always influenced by avowed
motives more or less irrational, and is generally regarded as mad; in the latter, there are no motives
acknowledged, nor to be discerned, the individual
being impelled by a blind, irresistible impulse. It
is with the latter only that we are concerned, for the
other is clearly a form of partial intellectual mania ;
but as this division has not been strictly made by
nature, cases often occurring that do not clearly
come under either category, the subject will be
better elucidated by noticing all the forms of this

---

[1] It is worthy of mention that though Esquirol, in his article *Manie*
in the Dict. Med. Sci. expressed his disbelief in the existence of homicidal insanity unconnected with other mental alienation, he has since
not only retracted his opinion, but has published the very best contri-
bution to our knowledge of the subject.

affection, and seeing how intimately they are connected together.

§ 135. In the following cases we have the simplest form of homicidal insanity,—that in which the desire to destroy life is prompted by no motive whatever, but solely by an irresistible impulse, without any appreciable disorder of mind or body.

" In a respectable house in Germany, the mother of the family returning home one day, met a servant, against whom she had no cause of complaint, in the greatest agitation ; she begged to speak with her mistress alone, threw herself upon her knees, and entreated that she might be sent out of the house. Her mistress astonished, inquired the reason, and learned that whenever this unhappy servant undressed the lady's child, she was struck by the whiteness of its flesh and experienced the almost irresistible desire to tear it in pieces. She felt afraid that she could not resist the impulse, and preferred to leave the house." " This circumstance," says the narrator, " occurred in the family of Baron Humboldt, and this illustrious person permitted me to add his testimony."

§ 136. " A young lady who had been placed in a *maison de santè*, experienced homicidal desires, for which she could assign no motive. She was rational on every subject and whenever she felt the approach of this dreadful propensity, she shed tears, entreated to have the straight-waistcoat put on and to be carefully guarded, till the paroxysm, which sometimes lasted several days, had passed." [1]

---

[1] Marc, consultation medico-légale.

§ 137. "Mr. R., a distinguished chemist and a poet, of a naturally mild and sociable disposition, committed himself a prisoner in one of the *maisons de santè* of the faubourg St. Antoine. Tormented by the desire of killing, he prostrated himself at the foot of the altar, and implored the divine assistance to deliver him from such an atrocious propensity, of the cause of which he could give no account. When he felt that he was likely to yield to the violence of this inclination, he hastened to the head of the establishment, and requested him to tie his thumbs together with a ribbon. This slight ligature was sufficient to calm the unhappy R.; who subsequently endeavored to kill one of his friends and finally perished in a fit of maniacal fury."[1]

§ 138. The following case is recorded by Gall, who derived it from a German .paper of April 13th, 1820. " A carrier belonging to the bailiwick of Frendenstadt, who had quitted his family in perfect health, was suddenly attacked by a paroxysm of furious madness, on the route between Aalen and Gemunde. His first insane act was to shut himself up in the stable with his three horses to which he gave no fodder; and when departing he harnessed only two of his horses, accompanying the carriage mounted on the other. At Moglengen he abused a woman; at Unterbobingen, he alighted, and walked before his horses with a hatchet in his hand. On the route between the last place and Hussenhofen, the first person he met with was a woman whom he

---

[1] Marc, op. cit.

struck several times with his hatchet, and left her lying in a ditch by the road-side. Next, he encountered a lad thirteen years old whose head he split open ; and shortly after, he split the skull of a man, thirty years old, and scattered his brains in the road; and after hacking the body, he left his hatchet and carriage, and thus unarmed proceeded towards Hussenhofen.   He met two Jews on the road, whom he attacked, but who, after a short struggle, escaped him.   Near Hussenhofen, he assaulted a peasant, who screamed till several persons came to his aid, who secured the maniac and carried him to Gemunde. They afterwards led him to the bodies of his victims, when he observed, ' It is not I, but my bad spirit, that has committed these murders.' " [1]

§ 139. William Brown was executed at Maidstone, England, in 1812, for strangling a child whom he accidentally met one morning while walking in the country. On the trial, he said he had never seen the child before, had no malice against it, and could assign no motive for the dreadful act.   He took up the body and laid it on some steps, and then went and told what he had done, requesting to be taken into custody.   He bore an exemplary character, and had never been suspected of being insane.[2]

140. A country gentleman enjoying good health and easy circumstances, consulted Esquirol in regard to his singular and unhappy condition.   He related that he had read the indictment of Henriette Cor-

---

[1] Sur les Fonctions, &c., vol. 4, p. 103.
[2] Newgate Calendar, vol. 4, p. 80.

nier, which however did not very strongly excite his attention. In the course of the night he suddenly awoke with the thought of killing his wife who was lying beside him. He left his wife's bed for a time, but within three weeks the same idea seized upon his mind three times, and always in the night. During the day, considerable exercise and occupation preserved him from this fearful inclination. He evinced not the slightest mental disorder ; his business was prosperous ; he had never experienced any domestic chagrins ; and he had no cause of complaint or jealousy in regard to his wife whom he loved and with whom he never had had the least disagreement. With the exception of a light headache occasionally, he had always been well and free from pain. He is sad and troubled about his condition, and has quitted his wife for fear lest he might yield to the force of his desire.[1]

§ 141. In most cases of homicidal insanity the presence of some physical or moral disorder may be detected ; and though none is mentioned in those above related, there is reason to suppose that it might have been ascertained by proper examination. In the following group of cases the homicidal fit was accompanied or preceded by disease or physical disorder of some kind.

§ 142. The following case is related by Gall, who obtained it from Dr. Zimmermann of Krumback. "A peasant, born at Krumback, Swabia, who never enjoyed very good health, twenty-seven years old,

---

[1] Note in Hoffbauer, p. 346.

and unmarried, had been subject from his ninth year to frequent epileptic fits. Two years ago, his disease changed its character without any apparent cause, and ever since, this man, instead of a fit of epilepsy, has been attacked with an irresistible inclination to commit murder. He felt the approach of the fit many hours, and sometimes a whole day, before its invasion, and from the commencement of this pre-sentiment, he begged to be secured and chained that he might not commit some dreadful deed. 'When the fit comes on,' says he, 'I feel under a necessity to kill, even it were a child.' His parents whom he tenderly loved, would be the first victims of this murderous propensity. 'My mother,' he cries out with a frightful voice, 'save yourself, or I must kill you.' Before the fit he complains of being exceed-ingly sleepy, without being able to sleep; he feels depressed, and experiences slight twitchings of the limbs. During the fit, he preserves his conscious-ness, and knows perfectly well that in committing a murder, he is guilty of an atrocious crime. When he is disabled from doing injury, he makes the most frightful contortions and grimaces, singing or talking in rhyme. The fit lasts from one to two days. When it is over, he cries out, 'Now unbind me. Alas! I have cruelly suffered, but I rejoice that I have killed nobody." [1]

§ 143. On the 15th February, 1826, Jacques Mounin, after many acts of violence and fury,

---

[1] Gall, op. cit. T. 4, p. 104.

escaped from his family who wished to restrain him, scaled the walls of several adjoining properties, and took to the fields without shoes, hat, or weapons of any kind. His flight having excited considerable alarm, as after some epileptic attacks he had formerly given many signs of a blind fury, the local authorities were informed, and several persons despatched after him as quickly as possible. On arriving at a field where many laborers were at work at a distance from one another, Mounin first threatened a man who was driving a cart, and immediately after pursued Joseph Faucher and pelted him with stones. The latter having escaped, he then made up to an old man almost blind, named Mayet, whom he knocked down and killed by beating him on the head with a large stone. He next attacked a man who was digging at a little distance, and killed him with a spade. A few minutes afterwards he met Propheti on horseback, whom he struck down with stones, but was obliged to leave him in consequence of the cries of his victim. He then chased some children, who saved themselves by hard running, but he overtook a man at work and slew him. On being questioned during his confinement, Mounin said he well recollected having killed the three men, and especially one, a relative of his own, whom he greatly regretted; he added that in his paroxysms of phrensy he saw nothing but flames, and that blood was then most delightful to his sight. At the end of a few days' imprisonment, he seemed to have entirely recovered his reason, but subsequently he relapsed. The court declined trying him, under the conviction that he was insane while committing the murders above mentioned.[1]

§ 144. "Frederick Jensen, a workman, thirty-seven years old, had for some time suffered from fits of giddiness which always obliged him to seize hold of the nearest objects. In the spring of 1828, he lost a beloved daughter, which afflicted him very much. The state of his health was nevertheless perfect in mind as well as in body, when he one day (Sunday 28th September, 1828) after dinner, told his wife that he would take a walk with his son, a boy ten years old. He did so, and went with him to the green which encircles the citadel. When he came there,—he now relates, 'a strange confusion came over me;' it appeared like a matter of absolute necessity to him to drown his son and himself in the waters at the citadel. Quite unconscious of what he was doing, he ran towards the water with the boy in his hand. A man surprised at his behavior, stopped him there, took the boy from him, and tried to persuade him to leave the water; but he became angry, and answered that he intended to take a walk, and asked, 'whether any body had a right to forbid him to do so?' The man left him, but took the boy along with him. An hour afterwards he was taken out of the water into which he had thrown himself, and taken to prison. As he still showed symptoms of insanity, he was bled and purged, and two days after, was brought into the hospital, and committed to the care of my friend Dr. Wendt who has per-

---

[1] Georget, Discussion medico-légale, &c. p. 153.

fectly cured him, and who kindly afforded me the opportunity to see and to speak with him. He now very quietly tells the whole event himself, but is not able to explain the cause of the suddenly rising desire to kill himself and the boy whom he loved heartily. This cause is only to be sought in congestion of blood to the brain, the same which before had caused his giddiness ; and whether we adopt an organ of destructiveness in the brain or not, it is to be assumed that the propensity to kill himself and the son arose from a morbid excitation of a certain part of the brain. The disposition to congestion originated from a fall he suffered on the head in 1820." [1]

§ 145. Another curious form of homicidal insanity occurs in women, and seems to be connected with those changes in the system produced by parturition, menstruation and lactation. It is a little remarkable that with scarcely an exception, the victim selected by the patient is always her own, or some other young child. Among several cases which Esquirol has related at length, are the two following which are abridged from his memoir.

§ 146. Madam N., whom Esquirol received into his hospital, and whom he describes as being perfectly rational in her conversation and conduct, and of a mild, affable and industrious disposition, very calmly related to him the circumstances connected with a strong inclination she felt to kill her child. After her last accouchement, fourteen months before,

---

[1] Dr. Otto, in the Edinburgh Phrenological Journal, vol. 6, p. 611.

she had several hysterical fits and was much troubled
with pains in the head, stomach and bowels ; with
vertigo and ringing in the ears. These mostly disappeared, but she then became exceedingly capricious in her temper and affections, being alternately
gay and sad, confiding and jealous, resolute and
weak. In this condition, she heard of the murder
committed by Henriette Cornier, when she was immediately seized with the idea of killing her infant,
and one day when her child entered the room, she
felt the most violent desire to assassinate it. ' I repelled the idea, said she, and coolly inquired of myself, why I should conceive such cruel designs—what
could put them into my imagination ? I could find
no answer. The same desire returned ; I feebly
resisted it, was overcome, and proceeded to consummate the crime. A new effort arrested my steps, I
raised the knife to my own throat, saying to myself,
better perish yourself, bad woman.' When asked
the cause of these evil thoughts, she replied, that
something behind her back urged her on. During
the first fortnight of her stay in the hospital, she was
afflicted by a return of the physical disturbances with
which she was first attacked, but at the end of six
weeks was so much better, in consequence of a proper
medical treatment, that she received her husband and
child with joy, and lavished on the latter the ten-
derest caresses. Suddenly she perceived a cutting
instrument, and was seized with the desire of snatch-
ing it up and committing two murders at once,—a
thought which she suppressed only by flying from
the room. The symptoms of physical disturbance
now again made their appearance, during which she

was informed that her child was sick, and while extremely distressed and weeping at the news, 'she felt a violent desire,' to use her own expression, 'to stab or stifle it in her arms.' After about three months residence at the hospital, she went away restored, and continued well.

§ 147. A girl fourteen years old, of strong constitution and difficult temper, enjoyed apparently good health, though she had not menstruated. Once a month she complained of pain in the head, her eyes were red, she was irascible, gloomy and restless; every thing went wrong with her and she was particularly inclined to dispute with her mother, who was always the object of her threats and abuse; and finally she became most violently angry, sometimes attempting her own life and sometimes her mother's. When the fit arrived to this degree, the blood escaped from her mouth, nose or eyes; she wept and trembled; the extremities became cold and affected with convulsive pains; and her mind was filled with distress. The fit which altogether continued one or two days, being over, she recovered her affection for her mother, and asked her forgiveness. She did not recollect all the circumstances of these fits, and denied with feelings of surprise and regret some of the particulars which were related to her. At the age of sixteen years, these fits of anger were often replaced by hysteric convulsions; the disease diminished progressively, but did not cease till she was seventeen years old, when her courses appeared. She afterwards married and became an excellent mother.

§ 148. Esquirol relates another case communicated to him by Dr. Barbier of Amiens, which will be briefly noticed. This lady, Marguerite Molliens, twenty-four years old, had suffered for three years past pains in the epigastrium, and right side of the abdomen; headache, vertigo, noise in the ears, disturbance of vision, palpitation of the heart, constrictions of the throat and trembling of the limbs. Her first child, which lived but three months, she loved and deeply regretted. Nine months ago she had another child. On the fifth day of her confinement she heard of Cornier's case, and was so deeply impressed with the story that her thoughts dwelt upon it, and from that moment she feared lest she also might be similarly tempted. In spite of all her efforts, she gradually familiarized herself with the idea of killing her child. One day while dressing it, the thought of murdering it seized upon her mind and became a violent desire. She turned around, and perceiving a kitchen-knife on a table near her, her arm was involuntarily carried towards it. She saw that she could no longer control herself, and cried out for assistance. The neighbors came in and she soon became calm. Shortly after she was separated from her child and sent to a hospital where she finally recovered. It is worthy of note that when the pains in the head and epigastrium, from which she suffered greatly in the hospital, were worst, then the bad thoughts appeared to be most imperious.

§ 149. Dr. Otto, of Copenhagen, relates that a female, who was received into a lying-in-hospital of which he was physician, requested a private conference with him previously to her accouchement. She appeared to be in great agitation and embarrassment, and earnestly begged of him that she might not be left in the same chamber with other women and their infants, as it would be utterly impossible for her to resist the propensity she felt to destroy the latter. Her request was granted and she was carefully watched. Her delivery was easy, and the child was kept from her and afterwards sent to her mother. The young woman on leaving the hospital went into service, and would not return to her mother's, lest she might be tempted to destroy her infant. She declared that the sight of a very young infant kindled up an irresistible propensity to destroy its life. This woman was a peasant who had been seduced, but had never led a dissolute life nor was in any way of corrupt manners. She had not been reproached, nor ill-treated by her parents, during pregnancy, nor was there the least cause for anxiety on account of the child, as her mother had engaged to provide for it. She entered into the service of a clergyman, and enjoyed good health. Sometime afterwards she informed the doctor that she had lost nearly all propensity to infanticide.[1]

§ 150. The next case is recorded by Dr. Michu in his *Memoire sur la monomanie-homicide.* " A country woman, twenty-four years of age, of a bilious sanguine temperament, of simple and regular habits, but reserved and sullen manners, had been ten days confined with her first child, when suddenly, having her eyes fixed upon it, she was seized with the desire

---

[1] Medico-Chirurgical Review, O. S. Vol. 13, p. 441.

of strangling it.   This idea made her shudder ; she
carried the infant to its cradle, and went out in order
to get rid of so horrid a thought.   The cries of the
little being who required nourishment, recalled her
to the house ; she experienced still more strongly the
impulse to destroy it.   She hastened away again,
haunted by the dread of committing a crime so horrible ; she raised her eyes to heaven, went to the
church and prayed.   The whole day was passed by
this unhappy mother in a constant struggle between
the desire of taking away the life of her infant and
the dread of yielding to the impulse.   She concealed
her agitations, until evening, when her confessor, a
respectable old man, was the first to receive her confidence.   He soothed her feelings, and counselled
her to have medical assistance.   ' When we arrived
at her house,' says Michu, ' she appeared gloomy
and depressed, and ashamed of her situation.'   Being
reminded of the tenderness due from a mother to her
child, she replied ; ' I know how much a mother
ought to love her child ; but if I do not love mine,
it does not depend upon me.'   She soon after recovered, the infant, in the meantime, having been
removed from her sight."

§ 151. Gall says he knew a woman, then twenty-
six years old, who experienced, especially at the
menstrual periods, inexpressible torture, and the
fearful temptation to destroy herself, and to kill her
husband and children, who were exceedingly dear to
her.   She shuddered with terror, as she described
the struggle that took place within her between her
sense of duty and of religion, and the impulse that
urged her to this atrocious act.   For a long time,

she dared not bathe her youngest child, because an internal voice constantly said to her, 'let him slip, let him slip.' Frequently she had hardly the strength and time to throw away a knife which she was tempted to plunge into her own breast and her children's. Whenever she entered the chamber of her children, or husband, and found them asleep, she was instantly possessed with the desire of killing them. Sometimes she precipitately shut behind her the door of their chamber and threw away the key, to remove the possibility of returning to them during the night, if she should fail to resist this infernal temptation." [1]

§ 152. In another class of cases, the exciting cause of the homicidal propensity is of a moral nature, operating upon some peculiar physical predisposition, and sometimes followed by more or less physical disturbance. Instead of being urged on by a blind, imperious impulse to kill, the subjects of this form of the affection, after suffering for a certain period much gloom of mind and depression of spirits, feel as if bound by a sense of necessity to destroy life ; and proceed to the fulfilment of their destiny with the utmost calmness and deliberation. So reluctant have courts and juries usually been to receive the plea of insanity in defence of crime, deliberately planned and executed by a mind in which no derangement of intellect has ever been perceived, that it is of the greatest importance that the nature of these cases should not be misunderstood. They are of not un-

---

[1] Op. cit. sup. T. 4, p. 110.

frequent occurrence, and are often attended by such horrid, heart-rending circumstances, that nothing but the plainest and strongest conviction of their true character can ever save their subjects from the last penalty of the law. The near affinity of this form of the affection to those already described will be manifest, upon a careful consideration of the few cases that will now be given.

§ 153. The following is related by Dr. Otto of a surgeon who had served in several campaigns against the French. "He always appeared of a lively and cheerful disposition, till certain pecuniary matters ruffled his temper and made him thoughtful and melancholy. He was now frequently observed to be studying the scriptures, and reciting passages from the bible. He was happily married and had four children. One morning he summoned his wife and children into the court of the house, and there informed them that it was his intention to kill them all, and afterwards himself. He descanted coolly on the propriety of homicide, and told his wife she must first be a spectator of the destruction of her children, and then her own turn would come. The woman appears to have possessed great presence of mind, and acted with great prudence on such a trying occasion. She entirely coincided in the justness of her husband's sentiments, and cheerfully agreed to the proposed tragedy. But she appeared suddenly to recollect that it would be proper for herself as well as the children, to confess and take the sacrament previous to their appearing before their final judge,—a ceremony which would necessarily require several days' preparation. The monomaniac replied

that this was a reasonable and proper procedure ;
but, in the meantime, it would be absolutely necessary that he took some person's life that day.   With
this purpose in view, he instantly set off for Salz-
bourg.   His wife having placed the children in security, made the best of her way to the above-mentioned town, and went directly to professor O., the
friend of her husband, for advice.   The monomaniac
had already been there, and not finding the professor at home, had gone away.   The woman now
recollected and told the professor, that her husband
had threatened *his* life for some imaginary slight ;
but at that time she thought he was in jest.   About
mid-day the monomaniac came back to the professor's residence, and appeared quite calm and peaceable.   The professor invited him to go and see the
hospital of the town, where he had a curious dissection to make, and they sat down to eat some refresh-
ments before proceeding thither.   At this repast, the
monomaniac informed his host that he had lately
been most immoderately disposed to commit homicide, and that he had actually murdered a peasant
that morning on his way to town.   He confessed
also that he had entered a coffee-house for the purpose of committing a second act of this kind, but had
been diverted from his purpose.   The murder of the
peasant was a fiction, as was afterwards proved.
The professor now turned the discourse to other subjects, and on all other topics the monomaniac was
perfectly rational.   They now set off for the hospital
and in their way thither the monomaniac met with
an old acquaintance and fellow-campaigner.   While
they were greeting each other, the monomaniac sud-

denly struck his friend a violent blow on the pit of the stomach, exclaiming in a burst of laughter, that he had done it for him, as he had hit the cœliac plexus. The professor reprimanded him in strong terms for this dishonorable and cruel act, at which the monomaniac was much surprised, and informed his preceptor that he was irresistibly led to commit homicide, and cared not who was the victim of this propensity. The professor now asked him somewhat tauntingly, if he had not a design against *his* life. The monomaniac acknowledged it ; but added that he had sufficient control over himself to prevent the destruction of his benefactor. The professor took his arm and they proceeded to the hospital, where the monomaniac was immediately confined. He almost instantly became furiously maniacal, and in a few months after died." [1]

Gall quotes from the Psychological Magazine, vol. iii., an account of Catherine Hansterin, who, in consequence of being detected in a petty theft which was reported to her husband, a man of harsh and austere manners, of whom she stood greatly in fear on account of his cruel treatment of her, became exceedingly melancholy and depressed. After suffering much and long from her cruel husband, she determined to leave him, and accordingly departed, taking her infant two and a half months old, and her little girl who had declared she would rather die than be left behind with her father. " The thought which this reply brought to her mind, the distress

---

that afflicted her, the fear of what would happen to her children in case of her death, and at the same time, her ardent desire to terminate her own existence;—all these united, gave rise to the barbarous design of drowning her two children. Having arrived at the bank of the Danube, she made her little girl kneel down and pray God for a good death. She then placed the infant in the hands of her sister, blessed them both, and making the sign of the cross, pushed them into the river. This done, she returned to the village and told what had passed." [1]

§ 154. Dr. Otto has published the case of Peter Nielsen, a joiner, aged forty-seven years, who drowned four of his seven children. He appears to have experienced some misfortunes, but was not in positive want of the necessaries of life at the moment when he committed the horrid deed. Many persons, who conversed with him on the same day both before and after the transaction, testified that he was not intoxicated, nor the least agitated in mind. He was, on the contrary, placid and tranquil. No domestic altercations, of any moment, had occurred, but he was disconcerted at not readily getting a new lodging on being turned out of that which he previously occupied. His love to his children was testified to by all. He confessed that the idea of killing his children came into his head on the morning of the day that he put the idea into execution, and that the impulse was quite irresistible. He determined to drown the three younger boys and spare the daugh-

---

[1] Op. cit. T. 4, p. 152.

ter who was older. But she insisted on accompanying her father and brothers in the walk he proposed, and though he endeavored to persuade her to return, she would not. He averred that his motive for destroying the boys was the fear of not being able to maintain them; whereas he would have spared the girl, not because he loved her more, but because she was better able to maintain herself. Having arrived at a turf-pit, he first embraced his children, and then pushed them all into the water. He stood by unmoved and saw them struggle and sink. He then returned quietly to the town and told what he had done. He was led back to the turf-pit, and beheld the dead bodies of his children without evincing any emotion. For a moment he wept, when he saw the bodies opened (for the purpose of medico-legal proof of the kind of death), but soon regained his tranquillity. He affirmed that he did not destroy his offspring in order to procure happiness for them in heaven, nor from any desire to be put to death himself, as he wished to live.[1]

§ 155. The case of Henriette Cornier, which occurred in Paris a few years since, in consequence of the imposing weight of medical opinions that were delivered on her trial, and of the discussions to which it gave rise in the various shapes of reports, newspaper criticisms, and elaborate treatises from some of the most distinguished physicians of that capital, has contributed, more than any other single event, to advance our knowledge of homicidal in-

---

[1] Edinburgh Phrenological Journal, vol. 5, p. 87.

sanity. A case so celebrated deserves a particular notice here. The facts as they will now be related are contained in the indictment (*acte d'accusation*), which is given at length by Georget in his account of the trial.[1]

Henriette Cornier, a female servant aged twenty-seven years, was of a mild and lively disposition, full of gaiety, and remarkably fond of children. In the month of June, 1825, a singular change was observed in her character ; she became silent, melancholy, absorbed in reverie, and finally sank into a kind of stupor. She was dismissed from her place, but her friends could obtain from her no account of the causes of her mental dejection. In the month of September she made an attempt to commit suicide, but was prevented. In the following October she entered into the service of dame Fournier, but there she still presented the melancholic and desponding disposition. Dame Fournier observed her peculiar dejection and endeavored in vain to ascertain its cause ; the girl would talk only of her misfortunes in losing her parents at an early age, and of the bad treatment she received from her guardian. On the 4th of November, her conduct not having been previously different from what it usually was, she suddenly conceived and immediately executed the act for which she was committed.

About noon her mistress went out to walk, having told Cornier to prepare dinner at the usual hour, and to go to a neighboring shop kept by dame Belon,

---

[1] Discussion medico-légale, p. 70.

to buy some cheese. She had frequently gone to this shop and had always manifested great fondness for Belon's little girl, a beautiful child nineteen months old. On this day she displayed her usual fondness for it, and persuaded its mother, who at first was rather unwilling, to let her take it out for a walk. Cornier then hastened back to her mistress's house with the child, and laying it across her own bed, severed its head from its body with a large kitchen knife. She subsequently declared that while executing this horrid deed, she felt no particular emotion—neither of pleasure, nor of pain. Shortly after, she said, the sight of the horrible spectacle before her eyes brought her to herself, and she experienced some emotions of fear, but they were of short duration. At the end of two hours, during which time, she had remained chiefly in her own chamber, dame Belon came and inquired for her child, from the bottom of the staircase. "Your child is dead," said Henriette. The mother, who at first thought she was only in jest, soon became alarmed, and pushed forward into the chamber, where she witnessed the bloody sight of the mutilated fragments of her child. At that moment, Cornier snatched up the head of the murdered child, and threw it into the street, from the open window. The mother rushed out of the house, struck with horror. An alarm was raised ; the father of the child and the officers of justice with a crowd of persons entered the room. Henriette was found sitting on a chair near the body of the child, gazing at it, with the bloody knife by her, her hands and clothes covered with blood. She made no attempt to escape, nor to deny the crime ; she confessed all the circumstances, even her premeditated design and the perfidy of her caresses, which had persuaded the unhappy mother to entrust her with the child. It was found impossible to excite in her the slightest emotion of remorse or grief ; to all that was said, she replied, with indifference, "I intended to kill the child." When closely and earnestly interrogated, as to her motives for committing this dreadful act, she replied that she had no particular reason for it ; that the idea had taken possession of her mind, and that she was destined to do it. When asked why she threw the head into the street, she answered that it was for the purpose of attracting public attention, so that people might come up to her chamber and see that she alone was guilty. The nature of her extraordinary replies, the want of motives for such an atrocious deed, the absence of every kind of emotion, and the state of stupor in which she remained, fixed the attention of the medical men who were called in, and impressed them with the belief that she was mad. On the examination before the magistrate she confirmed the above statements respecting her mental condition, adding, among other things, that she had been unhappily married seven years before; that she attempted to drown herself "because she was ennuied at changing her place of service so often;" that she knew her crime deserved death and she desired it.

She was tried for the first time, on the 27th of February, 1826. She then appeared to be in a state of great nervous irritation ; her limbs trembled ; her eyes were fixed ; and her understanding was dull and stupid. A few days previously, the court, at the request of her counsel, appointed a medical commission consisting of Adelon, Esquirol, and Léveillé, to examine the accused and all the documents of the case, and report on her " actual moral state." Accordingly they reported that they were unable to detect any sign or proof of mental derangement; but added that it is extremely difficult in some cases, to establish the existence of insanity, it requiring a long intimacy with the individual and numerous opportunities of watching him under every variety of circumstance, none of which they had possessed in this case. In fine, they reported that though they could not adduce any positive proof of her insanity, yet they were equally unable to pronounce her sane.

This report not being satisfactory, the trial was postponed to another session, and the prisoner was sent to the Salpêtrière to be observed by the above-named physicians. After recapitulating their observations which were continued three months, they came to the following conclusions : " first, that during the whole time Cornier was under examination, from the 25th of February to the 3d of June, they had observed in regard to her moral state great mental dejection, extreme dullness of mind, and profound chagrin ; secondly, that the actual situation of Cornier sufficiently explains her moral state, and thus does not of itself indicate mental alienation either general or partial." They also added that it was due to the cause of justice and to their own conscience, to declare that their judgment of her actual moral condition could not be considered final, if it were proved, as stated in the *acte d'accusation*, that long before the 4th of November, the character and habits had changed; that she had become sad, gloomy, silent and restless; for then that which might be attributed to her present situation, could be only the continuation of a melancholic state that had existed for a year.[1]

Cornier was again brought to trial on the 24th of June, and the jury returned a verdict of guilty of "committing homicide voluntarily but not with premeditation;"[2] and accordingly she was sentenced to hard labor for life.

§ 156. Sometimes, the individual confesses a motive for the homicidal act which is rational and well founded, but altogether inadequate to lead to such an action in a sound mind. There are seldom wanting other circumstances in the previous conduct, conversation, or bodily health, to confirm and establish beyond a reasonable doubt the presence of insanity, the suspicion of which is thus excited. All doubt of the correctness of this conclusion is removed in the first

---

[1] Georget justly observes that the meaning of the committee would have been better expressed in the following language. "The actual moral state of Henriette Cornier is doubtful. It may be the result either of a painful moral affection, or of melancholy; which it really is, the nature of the prior circumstances must decide. If, several months before the 4th of November, her character had changed; if she became sad and gloomy without cause; if she had a motiveless propensity to suicide; and finally, if the homicide she committed was without cause, and under the circumstances related in the *acte d'accusation*, it is certain that she has been and still is laboring under a kind of mental alienation."

[2] This verdict is very properly censured by Georget, who says, that if the accused was mad she ought to have been acquitted; and that if not mad she acted from premeditation, and should have suffered the punishment of death.

of the following cases, which is introduced to illustrate this form of the disorder, by the pathological changes discovered after death, and in the second by the previous existence of insanity.

§ 157. At Rouen, in 1820, a young man named Trestel, seventeen or eighteen years old, whose family was respectable and in easy circumstances, obtained an almost complete meeting of its various members to the number of thirteen, and endeavored to poison them all by putting arsenic into the soup. The severe vomiting which it produced, however, was the means of saving all their lives. It appeared in evidence, that Trestel was so imbecile at fifteen years of age, that he was incapable of executing the slightest commissions ; that he had strange and incoherent ideas ; that he was sad, taciturn and incapable of being instructed ; that he was in the habit of addressing letters to an imaginary female whom he was in love with. On the trial as well as on the previous examination, Trestel alleged as his motive for committing the crime, that his father had frequently threatened to send him to ´sea. Notwithstanding these strong indications of mental deficiency and alienation he was convicted and sentenced to be executed, but on the day appointed for the execution he killed himself by taking poison. His body was examined by Dr. Vingtrinier, surgeon of the prisons, in the presence of three other medical men, and there was found inflammation of the arachnoid membrane of the brain, characterized by thickening, induration and redness, and by its almost entire adhesion to the pia mater. In short not one of the four physicians had the least doubt of the existence of arachnoid inflammation of very long standing. However uncertain other symptoms and tests of insanity may be this at least is sure ; and we are left with the comfortable reflection, that an unfortunate youth paid the last penalty of the law for the consequences of bodily disease.[1]

§ 158. "A Portuguese, by the name of Rabello, was employed by a mechanic in the western part of Litchfield county, Connecticut, to assist him as a shoemaker. He had been in the neighboring towns, and his conduct appeared singular, but usually inoffensive. In the family of the mechanic he had appeared pleasant, and grateful for the kindness which had been extended to him. One day a little son of his new employer accidentally stepped upon his toes. The lad was twelve years old only. Rabello was exceedingly angry and in the moment of his rage threatened the boy's life. The next day he appeared sullen, refused his food, and looked wild and malicious. The following morning, he went to the barnyard with the boy, seized an axe, and killed him on the spot, mangling him in the most shocking manner. He went deliberately away from the house, but was soon overtaken by those in pursuit. He acknowledged that he killed the boy, and gave as a reason that he stepped on his toes. It was found, from the evidence produced at his trial, that this was an offence considered most heinous and not to be forgiven. Many instances were given in which the same accident had produced the same excitement of temper

---

[1] Georget, Discussion Medico-legale sur la Folie, 65, 165.

often accompanied with threats. One of the physicians who visited him in jail, stepped, apparently by accident, upon his toes while counting his pulse. The pulse, he declared, rose immediately forty strokes in a minute, his countenance flushed up, and he appeared instantly in a rage." [1] Insanity was pleaded in defence on his trial, and on this ground he was acquitted by the jury. It appeared in evidence that his life and conduct had been marked by much singularity during his residence in this country ; and after the trial it was ascertained from the Portuguese consul at New York that he had been previously deranged. He had been employed as a clerk in a mercantile house at Madeira, to which place he had returned a "little deranged" after having been to Brazil. From Madeira he went to Philadelphia, where he got employment as a clerk in the house of some merchants, natives of Madeira, who knew he had been a little deranged, but supposed he had recovered. One day one of the house came in and asked him if any body had called, when Rabello told him he would break his head, if he asked him any such questions.

§ 159. In the last phasis of the murderous propensity that will be noticed, though it is not properly homicidal mania, there exists some hallucination, and the individual acts from motives—absurd and unfounded it is true—but still, motives to him. In consequence of the universal prevalence, in some

---

[1] Dr. Woodward's Reports and other documents relating to the State Lunatic Hospital at Worcester, Mass. p. 177.

shape or other of religious fanaticism, and of the excitement of the religious sentiments thereby produced, a perversion of these sentiments is one of the most common exciting causes of the murderous propensity in this class of cases.   When thus excited its fury knows no restraints, and whole families are slaughtered in a single paroxysm.   Pinel gives the case of a vine-dresser, who thought himself commissioned to procure the eternal salvation of his family by killing them, or by the baptism of blood, as he called it ; and accordingly executed his commission so far as to kill two of his children, when he was arrested and confined.   Fourteen years after, when he was thought to be convalescent, he conceived the project of offering up an expiatory sacrifice, by killing all who might come within his reach, and he succeeded in wounding the keeper and cutting the throats of two other lunatics before he was arrested.[1]

§ 160. Sometimes the individual, even when in easy circumstances, imagines that he is coming to want, and to avoid this calamity, he kills his family and generally himself. The following case presents an illustration of this very common manifestation of mental disorder.

Captain James Purington, of Augusta, Maine, a rich, independent farmer, of steady, domestic habits, dark complexion, grave countenance, reserved in company, never looking in the face of persons he addressed, obstinate in his opinions, though he frequently changed his religious notions voluntarily,

---

[1] Alienation Mentale, § 130.

died a decided believer in universal salvation, often
expressed anticipation of the moment when his family would be happy, and sometimes how happy he
should be if they should die at once.   He was very
avaricious, and elated or depressed, as his affairs
were prosperous or adverse.   In August, 1805, he
moved to a new farm which he rapidly improved.
He seemed happy till within a few weeks of his death.
The uncommon drought depressed him greatly, lest
his family should suffer for want of bread, and his
cattle starve.   On Sunday, the 6th of July 1806,
Mrs. Purington and the eldest daughter being at
church, the second daughter saw her father writing
a letter which he, perceiving that he had been overlooked, attempted to hide.   She asked him what he
had been writing.   He said 'nothing,' and asked
for his butcher-knife, saying he wanted to sharpen
it.   Having made it very sharp, he stood before the
glass, and *seemed preparing to cut his throat.*   His
daughter, terrified, cried 'what are you doing ?'
He calmly said, 'nothing ;' and laid the knife away.
This was told to his wife ; she searched for the letter and found it.   [It was addressed to his brother,
and stated that he was about going a long journey,
and directed him to take charge of his children].
On the 7th of July, at dinner-time, he found his wife
sitting in the barn weeping ; she disclosed the cause ;
he said he did not intend suicide ; but he had a pre-
sentiment his death was near.   Towards the close
of the following day, he ground the axe ; when the
family went to bed, he was reading the bible ; it
was found open on the table at Ezekiel, chap. ix.
On the 9th of July, at two o'clock in the morning,

his eldest son alarmed the neighbors ; they found capt. Purington lying on his face, his two sons aged five and eight in bed, with their throats cut ; the razor on the table by his side, the axe near ; in the next room, Mrs. Purington aged forty-four, in bed, her head almost severed from the body ; near her on the floor, a daughter murdered, ten years old ; in the other room in bed, a daughter aged nineteen, most dreadfully butchered ; the second, aged fifteen most desperately wounded, reclining her head on the infant, eighteen months old, whose throat was cut. The eldest son was wounded, when capt. Purington attacked and dreadfully mangled the second, twelve years old, who attempted to escape ; capt. Purington did not speak a word." [1]

§ 161. The various forms of homicidal insanity have thus been illustrated, by selecting a few cases only, from a mass that would fill a considerable volume. Now, however these cases may differ from one another, whether the individual has succumbed to the propensity to kill, after a long struggle with his better nature, or has yielded to it at once and instantaneously ; whether harassed by previous disease of body or despondency of mind, or apparently in sound health and with a cheerful disposition ; whether his passions have been tamed by the discipline of a good education, or allowed to seek their gratification without restraint ; they all possess one feature in common, the *irresistible, motiveless impulse to destroy life*. Before entering upon any discussion

---

[1] Parkman : Illustrations of Insanity.

relative to the nature of these forms of insanity, it may be well to consider the following analysis of their most important features.

§ 162. I. In nearly all, the criminal act has been preceded, either by some well-marked disturbance of the health, originating in the head, digestive system, or uterus, or by an irritable, gloomy, dejected or melancholic state, in short by many of the symptoms of the incubation of mania. The absence of particulars in some of the cases we find recorded, leaves us in doubt how general this change really is; but a careful examination would, no doubt, show, often, if not always its existence where, *apparently* it has never taken place.

II. The impulse to destroy is powerfully excited by the sight of murderous weapons, by favorable opportunities of accomplishing the act, by contradiction, disgust, or some other equally trivial and even imaginary circumstance.

III. The victims of the homicidal monomaniac are mostly, either entirely unknown or indifferent to him, or they are among his most loved and cherished objects; and it is remarkable how often they are children, and especially his own offspring.

IV. While the greater number deplore the terrible propensity by which they are controlled and beg to be subjected to restraint, a few diligently conceal it, or if they avow it, declare their murderous designs, and form divers schemes for putting them in execution, testifying no sentiment of remorse or grief.

V. The most of them having gratified their propensity to kill, voluntarily confess the act and quietly give themselves up to the proper authorities; a very few only—and these, to an intelligent observer, show the strongest indications of insanity—fly, and persist in denying the act.

VI. While the criminal act itself is, in some instances, the only indication of insanity, the individual appearing rational, as far as can be learned, both before and after the act; in others, it is followed or preceded, or both, by strange behavior, if not open and decided insanity.

VII. Some plead insanity in defence of their conduct, or an entire ignorance of what they did; others deny that they labored under any such condition, and at most acknowledge only a perturbation of mind.

§ 163. Apart from the obvious similarity of all these cases to those where the murderous propensity coexists with hallucinations, as in the last two, the circumstances under which the homicidal act is perpetrated furnish strong ground for believing, that they depend on mental alienation in some form or other; so different are these circumstances from those which attend the commission of crime. In homicidal insanity, murder is committed without any motive whatever strictly deserving the name; or at most, with one totally inadequate to produce the act in a sane mind. On the contrary, murder is never criminally committed without some motive adequate to the purpose in the mind that is actuated by it, and with an obvious reference to the ill-fated victim. Thus, the motive may be theft, or the advancement of any personal interest, in which case it will be found that the victim had or was supposed to have property, or was an obstacle to the designs or ex-

pectations of another. Or it may be revenge, and
then the injury real or imaginary will be found to
have been received by the murderer from the object
of his wrath. In short, with the criminal, murder is
always a means for accomplishing some selfish object,
and is frequently accompanied by some other crime;
whereas, with the homicidal monomaniac, murder is
the only object in view, and is never accompanied
by any other improper act.

§ 164. The homicidal monomaniac, after gratifying his bloody desires, testifies neither remorse, nor
repentance, nor satisfaction, and if judicially condemned, perhaps acknowledges the justice of the
sentence. The criminal either denies or confesses
his guilt ; if the latter, he either humbly sues for
mercy, or glories in his crimes, and leaves the world
cursing his judges and with his last breath exclaiming against the injustice of his fate.

The criminal never sheds more blood than is
necessary for the attainment of his object ; the homicidal monomaniac often sacrifices all within his reach
to the cravings of his murderous propensity.

The criminal lays plans for the execution of his
designs ; time, place, and weapons are all suited to
his purpose; and when successful, he either flies from
the scene of his enormities, or makes every effort to
avoid discovery. The homicidal monomaniac, on
the contrary, for the most part, consults none of the
usual conveniences of crime ; he falls upon the object of his fury, oftentimes without the most proper
means for accomplishing his purpose ; and perhaps
in the presence of a multitude, as if expressly to
court observation ; and then voluntarily surrenders

himself to the constituted authorities. When, as is sometimes the case, he does prepare the means, and calmly and deliberately executes his project, his subsequent conduct is still the same as in the former instance.

The criminal often has accomplices, and always vicious associates; the homicidal monomaniac has neither.

The acts of homicidal insanity are generally, perhaps always, preceded by some striking peculiarities in the conduct or character of the individual, strongly contrasting with his natural manifestations; while those of the criminal are in correspondence with the tenor of his past history or character.

In homicidal insanity, a man murders his wife, children, or others to whom he is tenderly attached; this the criminal never does, unless to gratify some evil passion, or gain some other selfish end, too obvious to be overlooked in the slightest investigation.

§ 165. A stronger contrast than is presented, in every respect, between the homicidal act of the real criminal and that of the monomaniac, can hardly be imagined; and yet we are obliged to acknowledge that men of learning and intelligence have often refused to acknowledge it, though, undoubtedly, the number of such is fast diminishing. Much of the unwillingness manifested by juries to abide by the result, to which the above distinctions would necessarily lead them, arises from those feelings of horror and indignation excited by the perpetration of cold-blooded murders, which incapacitate them from discriminating with their usual acuteness between the various causes and motives of human action. Besides, notwithstanding the great similarity, for the most part, between these cases, one will occasionally occur, where, from defect of information, no little knowledge of insanity and of human nature is required to find one's way through the mists of doubt and obscurity in which it is involved. When, therefore, as in the case of jurors generally, the mind is not fitted by any of this preparation so necessary to a successful investigation of difficult cases, it seizes only on some of the most obvious though perhaps least important points which they present, and of course the verdict will often be deplorably at variance with the dictates of true science.

CHAPTER VIII.

LEGAL CONSEQUENCES OF MANIA.

§ 166. MAN, being destined for the social condition, has received from the author of his being the faculties necessary for discovering and understanding his relations to his fellow-men, and possesses the liberty, to a certain extent, of regulating his conduct agreeably or directly opposed to their suggestions. For the manner in which this power is used he is *morally* responsible, the elements of responsibility always being the original capacity, the healthy action, and the cultivation of the moral and intellectual faculties,—the measure of the former being in proportion to the degree in which the latter are possessed. In *legal* responsibility, the last element above mentioned is not admitted, and the first to a very limited extent only, the second alone being absolutely essential. The relation of original incapacity to legal responsibility has already been discussed, when treating of MENTAL DEFICIENCY; that of cerebral disease now comes up for consideration.

§ 167. The influence of this condition on responsibility will obviously be proportioned to its severity and the extent of its action, and though we cannot hope to become acquainted with all its grades, there is no reason why we may not be able to recognise and identify some of the more common and prominent.

If men had agreed to receive some particular analysis and arrangement of the affective and intellectual faculties, and to assign to each a particular portion of the brain as its material organ, we might then discuss the question how far disease of one cerebral organ affects the actions of the rest, with the prospect of arriving at something like definite results. But as no such unanimity exists, we can only consider the observations that have been made on the derangement of particular faculties, and thus form our opinions relative to their influence, by the general tenor of experience. Analogy would lead us to expect that this inquiry would result in establishing the principle ; first, that each and every kind and degree of mania does not equally diminish legal responsibility ; and secondly, that the effect of mania in this respect must be estimated not merely by the severity of its outward symptoms, but also in reference to the particular faculty affected. If now, these results are confirmed by the evidence of facts, we have only to keep them steadily in view, in order to avoid much of the difficulty usually complained of, in arriving at satisfactory conclusions on this much vexed and agitated subject.

Section I.

Legal Consequences of Intellectual Mania.

§ 168. The common law relating to insanity, as before intimated, is open to censure, not so much on account of the manner in which it modifies the civil and criminal responsibilities of the lunatic, as of the looseness, inconsistency, and incorrectness of the principles on which the fact of the existence of the disease is judicially established. The disabilities it imposes on this unfortunate class of our fellow-men are founded in the most humane and enlightened views, and have for their object the promotion of their highest welfare. To incapacitate a person from making contracts, bequeathing property, and performing other civil acts, who has lost his natural power of discerning and judging, who mistakes one thing for another, and misapprehends his relations to those around him, is the greatest mercy he could receive, instead of being an arbitrary restriction of his rights.

§ 169. In opposition to that principle of the common law, which makes the lunatic who commits a trespass on the persons or property of others, amenable in damages to be recovered by a civil action,[1] Hoffbauer declares, that if the patient is " so deranged that he is no longer master of his actions, he is under no responsibility, nor obliged to make reparation for injuries." [2] He gives no reason for this opinion, and we are unable to see how it can be even plausibly supported. To the maniac, who, when restored to his senses, discovers that during his derangement he has committed an injury to his neighbor's property, indemnity for which will strip him of his own possessions and reduce him to absolute beggary, his recovery must seem indeed

---

[1] Weaver r. Ward, Hobart's Reports, 134.

[2] Op. cit. § 131, p. 139.

like escaping from one evil only to encounter a
greater. Such a possible consequence of madness,
it is certainly painful to think of; but as the damage is produced and must be borne by one party
or the other, we cannot hesitate which it should
be ; for though it may be hard for a person thus
to suffer for actions committed while utterly unconscious of their nature, it would manifestly be
the height of injustice to make another suffer, who
was equally innocent and perhaps equally unconscious of the act.

§ 170. There is one operation of the common law,
however, which is justly a cause of complaint,
namely, that by which lunatics, even when under
guardianship, are subject to be imprisoned like
others, in default of satisfying a civil execution obtained against them ;[1] because, whether such imprisonment be considered as a penal or a merely
coercive measure, it is altogether inapplicable to the
insane. It cannot coerce one who has no control
over his own property, and whose mental condition
is supposed to be such that he is unable to see any
relation between the means and the end; and to
punish a person, for what he himself had no agency
whatever in doing, is a violation of the first principles of justice. To incarcerate some madmen in a
common jail would, in all probability, aggravate their
disorder, and if the confinement were protracted to
the extent which the law would allow, render it utterly incurable.

---

[1] Shelford on Lunacy, 407; *Ex parte* Leighton, 14 Mass. Rep. 207.

§ 171. The civil disabilities above-mentioned are not incurred by every one laboring under mental derangement ; the measure of insanity necessary to produce this effect, or in legal phrase, the fact of the party's being *compos*, or *non compos mentis*, is a question to be submitted to judicial investigation, the result of which will depend on the views of individuals relative to the effect of insanity on the mental operations, and to the respect due to opinions and decisions already promulgated.   General intellectual mania, as we have represented it, should be followed, to the fullest extent, by the legal consequences of insanity ; but partial intellectual mania does not necessarily render a person *non compos*, or so impaired in mind as to be no longer legally responsible for his acts, any more than every disease of the lungs or stomach prevents a patient from attending to his ordinary affairs, and enjoying a certain measure of health.   The question when mania invalidates a person's civil acts and annuls criminal responsibility, and when it does not affect his liability in these respects, has occasioned considerable discussion, and is certainly the most delicate and important that the whole range of this subject embraces.   No general principles concerning it are to be found in the common law, and cases seem to have been decided with but little reference to one another, according to the medical or legal views which happened at the time to possess the minds of the court and jury.   As insanity has become better known, decisions have occasionally been more correct, but as the prevalence of these improvements has not been universal this branch of jurisprudence has often retrograded, and thus the mind of the inquirer is confused by an array of opinions diametrically opposed. General principles on this subject, therefore, are yet to be established; and in furtherance of this object, we shall endeavor to lay down such legal consequences of partial intellectual mania, as seem to be warranted by correct medical knowledge of madness and by enlightened principles of justice.

§ 172. We see some persons managing their affairs with their ordinary shrewdness and discretion, evincing no extraordinary exaltation of feeling or fancy, and on all but one or a few points, in the perfect enjoyment of their reason. It has been elsewhere remarked, that strange as it may appear, it is no less true, that notwithstanding the serious derangement of the reasoning power which a person must have experienced, who entertains the strange fancies that sometimes find their way into the mind, it may be exercised on all other subjects, so far as we can see, with no diminution of its natural soundness. To deprive such a one of the management of his affairs, or to invalidate his contracts, under the show of affording him protection, would be to inflict a certain and a serious injury for the purpose of preventing a much smaller one that might never occur. The principle that we would inculcate is, that monomania invalidates a civil act only when such act comes within the circle of the diseased operations of the mind. The celebrated Pascal believed at times that he was sitting on the brink of a precipice over which he was momentarily in danger of falling, and a German professor of law, mentioned by Hoffbauer, thought the freemasons were leagued against him, while he discharged the duties of his chair with his usual ability, and numberless are the instances of worthy people who have imagined their heads turned round, or their limbs made of butter or glass, but who nevertheless manage their concerns with their ordinary shrewdness. No one, however, following the dictates of his own judgment, would seriously propose to invalidate such of these men's acts as manifestly have no reference to the crotchets they have imbibed.

§ 173. It is not to be understood however that in every case of partial mania we have only to ascertain the insane delusion and then decide whether or not the act in question could have come within the range of its influence. In many instances the delusion is frequently changing, in which case, it is not only difficult to determine how far it may have been connected with any particular act, but the mind, in respect to other operations, has lost its original soundness, to such a degree that it cannot be trusted in the transaction of important affairs. Still this is not a sufficient reason against applying the general principle, where it can be done without fear of mistake. In doubtful instances we must be governed by the circumstances of the case, and this course, with all its objections, seems far more rational than the practice of universal disqualification.

§ 174. The validity of a marriage contracted in a state of partial mania, is not to be determined exactly upon the above principles. Here it is not sufficient to consider merely the connexion of the hallucination with the idea of being married, nor should we form any conclusion in favor of the capacity of the deranged party, from the propriety with which he conducts himself during the ceremony. The mere joining of hands and uttering the usual responses are things not worth considering; it is the new relations which the married state creates, the new responsibilities which it imposes, that should fix our attention, as the only points in regard to which the question of capacity can be properly agitated. In other contracts, all the conditions and circumstances may be definite and brought into view at once, and the capacity of the mind to comprehend them determined with comparative facility. In the contract of marriage, on the contrary, there is nothing definite or certain ; the obligations which it imposes do not admit of being measured and discussed; they are of an abstract kind, and constantly varying with every new scene and condition of life. With these views we are obliged to dissent from the principle, laid down by the Supreme Judicial Court of Massachusetts, in a case of libel for divorce for insanity of the wife at the time of the marriage, that " the fact of the party's being able to go through the marriage ceremony with propriety, was *primâ facie* evidence of sufficient understanding to make the contract." [1] If by making the contract is meant merely the giving of consent and the execution of certain forms, then indeed the fact of the party's going through the ceremony with propriety may be some evidence of sufficient understanding to make it ; but if the expression includes the slightest idea of the

---

[1] 4 Pickering's Reports, 32.

nature of the relations and duties that follow, or
even of the bonds and settlements that sometimes
accompany it, then the fact here mentioned is no
evidence at all of sufficient capacity. Sir John
Nicholl, looking at the subject in a different light,
has very properly said, that " going through the
ceremony was not sufficient to establish the capacity
of the party ; and that foolish, crazy persons might
be instructed to go through the formality of the ceremony, though wholly incapable of understanding the
marriage contract." [1] In a similar case, Lord Stow-
ell, then Sir William Scott, had previously observed,
on the fact given in evidence, that the party " had
manifested perfect propriety of behavior " during the
ceremony, " that much stress was not to be laid on
that circumstance; as persons, in that state, will
nevertheless often pursue a favorite purpose, with
the composure and regularity of apparently sound
minds." [2]

§ 175. The principles that should regulate the
legal relations of the partially insane are few and
simple. While they should be left in possession of
every civil right that they are not clearly incapable of
exercising, they should be subjected to the performance of no duties involving the interests or comfort
of individuals, which may be equally well discharged
by others. In the former instance we continue the
enjoyment of a right that has never been abused;
in the latter, we refrain from imposing duties on

---

[1] Browning v. Reade, 2 Phillimore's Eccl. Rep. 69.
[2] Turner v. Meyers, 1 Hagg. Con. Rep. 414.

people who are not qualified to perform them. We cannot therefore agree with Hoffbauer, that a monomaniac should be allowed to manage the affairs of another, or be appointed to the office of guardian, however much we might be inclined to respect the validity of his civil acts. In some instances it is impossible to know or to conjecture, beforehand, how the predominant idea in his mind may be affected by his connexion with persons and things that have hitherto been foreign to his thought; while in others, it is far within the range of probability that the consequences will be ruinous to himself and others. Here for example, is a man who has long believed that he has an eel in his stomach, but on no other point has he manifested the slightest mental impairment. If a monomaniac is ever a suitable person to manage the affairs of another, it would seem, at first thought, that this one certainly is; yet nothing would be more injudicious than to entrust him with any such duty, for in all probability, though perfectly upright in his dealings, he would be irresistibly impelled to dissipate the property of others, as he always has his own earnings, in constant journeyings from one empiric to another, in purchasing medicines, and consulting physicians, for the purpose of getting relieved from his fancied tormenter. This exclusion, as Chambeyron the French translator of Hoffbauer, justly remarks, does the monomaniac no wrong, it frees him from a great responsibility, it prevents dangers, possible at least, either to the ward or to him.

§ 176. The above views, though not yet distinctly received in courts, are countenanced by many distinguished physicians and jurists. Hoffbauer supports them to the fullest extent, Esquirol sanctions them, by interposing no word of disapprobation, and Georget admits them in application to civil cases. Paris and Fonblanque have explicitly recognised their correctness in the following passage. "When a man suffers under a partial derangement of intellect, and on one point only, it would be unjust to invalidate acts which were totally distinct from, and uninfluenced by this so-limited insanity ; but if the act done bear a strict and evident reference to the existing mental delusion, we cannot see why the law should not also interpose a limited protection, and still less why courts of equity, which in their ordinary jurisdiction relieve against mistake, should deny their aid in such cases." [1]

§ 177. Mr. Evans, the translator of Pothier's Treatise on Obligations, expresses an opinion on this subject, no less positive and precise. "I cannot but think," he says, "that a mental disorder operating on partial subjects, should, with regard to those subjects, be attended with the same effects as a total deprivation of reason ; and that on the other hand, such a partial disorder operating only upon particular subjects, should not in its legal effects, have an influence more extensive than the subjects to which it applies ; and that every question should be reduced to the point, whether the act under consideration proceeded from a mind fully capable, in respect of that act, of exercising free, sound and

---

[1] Medical Jurisprudence, 302.

discriminating judgment ; but in case the infirmity is established to exist, the tendency of it to direct or fetter the operations of the mind should be in general regarded as sufficient presumptive evidence, without requiring a direct and positive proof of its actual operation." [1]

§ 178. It has been already remarked that the practice of the English courts in regard to partial insanity has been regulated by no settled principles. Of the truth of this remark we have a striking illustration in Greenwood's case, which has been so often cited. Mr. Greenwood was bred to the bar and acted as chairman at the quarter sessions, but becoming diseased, and receiving in a fever a draught from the hand of his brother, the delirium, taking its ground then, connected itself with that idea ; and he considered his brother as having given him a potion, with a view to destroy him. He recovered in all other respects, but that morbid image never departed ; and that idea appeared connected with the will by which he disinherited his brother. Nevertheless, it was considered so necessary to have some precise rule, that, though a verdict had been obtained in the common pleas against the will, the judge strongly advised the jury to find the other way, and they did accordingly find in favor of the will.

Farther proceedings took place afterwards and concluded in a compromise. [2] No one would be hardy enough to affirm that Greenwood's mind was per-

---

[1] 2 Pothier on Obligations, Appendix, 24.
[2] Lord Eldon, in White v. Wilson, 13 Vesey's Reports, 88.

fectly rational and sound, and as his insanity displayed itself on all topics relating to his brother,
every act involving this brother's interests, to go no
farther, ought consequently to have been invalidated.
A plainer case cannot well be imagined.

§ 179. More enlarged and correct views prevailed
in the able and elaborate judgment delivered by Sir
John Nicholl, in the case of Dew v. Clark,[1] where the
existence of partial mania is recognised, and the
necessity of bearing in mind the fact of its partial
operation on the understanding, while determining
its influence on the civil acts of the individual, is
strongly inculcated. The point at issue was the
validity of the will of one Stott (who left personal
property nearly amounting to £40,000), bequeathing
the complainant, who was his daughter and only
child, a life-interest in a small portion of his estate,
the most of which was devised to his nephews. The
object of inquiry was whether the extraordinary conduct and feelings of the deceased towards his daughter had any real cause, or was solely the offspring of
delusion in a disordered mind, and to this end an
unparalleled mass of evidence was offered by each
party. It was proved by the nephews that the testator
had considerable practice as a surgeon and medical
electrician from 1785 to 1820, and that at all times
down to the latter period when he had a paralytic
stroke, he managed the whole of his pecuniary
and professional affairs in a rational manner, and
rationally conducted all manner of business. They

---

[1] 3 Addams's Reports, 79.

admitted that he was a man of an irritable and violent temper; of great pride and conceit; very precise in all his domestic and other arrangements; very impatient of contradiction, and imbued with high notions of parental authority. They represented him to have entertained rigid notions of the total and absolute depravity of human nature and of the necessity of sensible conversion, and contended that all the singularities of his conduct could be attributed to his peculiar disposition and belief, without resorting to insanity for an explanation. By the daughter, it was shown by a body of evidence that placed the fact beyond the shadow of a reasonable doubt, that from an early period of her life, he manifested an insane aversion towards her. It appears that he was in the habit of describing her, even to persons with whom he was not intimately acquainted, as sullen, perverse, obstinate, and given to lying; as a fiend, a monster, a very devil, the special property of Satan; and charging her with vices, of which it was impossible that a girl of her age could be guilty. The peculiar and unequalled depravity of his child, her vices, obstinacy, and profligacy were topics on which he was constantly dwelling, and his general deportment towards her not only negatived all idea of natural affection, but betrayed a most fiend-like temper. His manner towards her was fiery and terrific; the instant she appeared, his eye flashed with rage and scorn, and he spurned her from him as he would a reptile. He compelled her to do the most menial offices, such as sweeping the rooms, scouring the grates, washing the linen and the dishes; to live in the kitchen and be sparingly fed.

He once stripped her naked, when ten or eleven years old, tied her to a bed-post, and after flogging her severely with a large rod intertwisted with brass wire, rubbed her back with brine. Repeatedly, and on the most trivial occasions, he struck her with his clenched fists, cut her flesh with a horsewhip, tore out her hair, and once aimed at her a blow with some weapon which made a dent in a mahogany table, and which must have killed her, had she not avoided it. Now it was abundantly proved that there existed no real cause whatever for this strange antipathy, but that the daughter was of an amiable, obliging, and docile disposition—that she had always shown a great filial affection for her father—that she conducted at home and abroad with the utmost propriety and decorum—that she was a person of strictly moral and religious habits, and was so considered and known to be by the friends of the deceased and others of high reputation and character. The court, in making up its decision, declared that the question at issue was, "not whether the deceased's insanity in certain *other* particulars, as proved by the daughter, should have the effect of defeating *a* will, *generally*, of the deceased, or even *this* identical will—but whether his insanity, on the subject of his daughter, should have the effect of defeating, not so much *any* will (*a* will *generally*) of the deceased, as this identical will." Accordingly, considering it proved that the will was the direct, unqualified offspring of that morbid delusion concerning the daughter, thus put into act and energy, it was pronounced to be *null* and *void* in law. In this decision we see the prevalence of those more correct and profound views of insanity, which have resulted from the inquiries of the last few years.

The same principle had been previously laid down in the following case which was adjudicated in Kentucky, in 1822. George Moore made his will in April 1822, and shortly after died. It was the validity of this will which was the point at issue. About twenty-four years previous to his death, he had a dangerous fever, during which he imbibed a strong antipathy towards his brothers, imagining that they intended to destroy or injure him, though they attended him throughout his illness, and never gave the slightest foundation for his belief. This antipathy continued to the day of his death, with a single exception, when he made a will in their favor, but afterwards cancelled it. When asked by one of the witnesses why he disinherited his brothers, he became violently excited, and declared that they had endeavored to get his estate before his death. The court, in its decision, observe, that, " he cannot be accounted a free agent in making his will, so far as his relatives are concerned, although free as to the rest of the world. But however free he may have been as to other objects, the conclusion is irresistible, that this peculiar defect of intellect did influence his acts in making his will, and for this cause it ought not to be sustained. It is not only this groundless hatred or malice to his brethren that ought to affect his will, but also his fears of them, which he expressed during his last illness, conceiving that they were attempting to get away his estate before his death, or that they were lying in wait to shoot him, while on other subjects he spoke rationally; all which are strong evidences of a derangement in one department of his mind, unaccountable indeed, but directly influencing and operating upon the act which is now claimed as the final disposition of the estate." [1]

Esquirol has related a case of a very similar kind, where a person conceived an antipathy against his brothers, sisters, and other relatives, who, he believed were seeking to destroy him. Under the influence of this delusion he made testamentary dispositions, and Esquirol being consulted respecting their validity, gave it as his opinion that the testator was laboring under insanity. [2]

§ 180. In criminal as well as civil cases, it is important to consider the operation of the predominant idea, and its influence on the act in question. There certainly is no reason why a person should be held responsible for a criminal act that springs from a delusion which would be sufficient to invalidate any civil act to which it might give rise. A monomaniac's sense of the *fitness of things* is not different when he signs a ruinous contract, from what it is when he commits a criminal deed; and if the inability to discern the true relations of things is the ground on which the former is invalidated, it ought equally to annul criminal responsibility ; unless it can be shown that the abstract conceptions of the nature and consequences of crime are never affected in insanity, or are compatible with a degree of mental soundness

---

[1] Johnson *v.* Moore's heirs, 1 Littel's Reports, 371.
[2] Annales d'Hygiène Publique, vol. 3, p. 370.

that would incapacitate a person from buying a house
or selling a piece of land.   It is yet a disputed point
however, whether partial mania should have the full
legal effect of insanity, in criminal cases.   By Hoffbauer, Foderè and some other writers, it is contended that the same principle which determines the
effect of mania in civil, should also determine its
effect in criminal cases ; that is, that criminal responsibility should be annulled only when the act comes
within the range of the diseased operations of the
mind.   In favor of this view, it may be urged, that
the connexion of the morbid delusion with the
criminal act is generally very direct, and not easily
mistaken.   A remote and circuitous association of
the predominant idea with the deed in question, presents fair ground for suspicion, because the farther
the thoughts of the monomaniac wander from the
object of his delusion, the less are they affected by
its influence.   If a man who imagines his legs are
made of glass, should see another approaching him
with a stick for the purpose of breaking them, he
could not help resisting even to bloodshed, in what
would be to him an act of self-defence, but it would
require a very peculiar concatenation of circumstances to warrant us in considering a rape or theft as
the offspring of this hallucination, because the idea
of these acts would carry the thoughts far beyond
the reach of its influence.

§ 181. Against these views it may be objected,
that it is not always easy to trace the connexion between the predominant idea and the criminal act.
The links that connect the thoughts which rise in
succession in the sound mind defy all our penetration,

and the few laws we have established are totally inapplicable to the associations of the insane mind.
No one will be bold enough to affirm that a certain
idea cannot possibly be connected with a certain
other idea in a healthy state of the mind, least of
all when it is disordered by disease, so that the existence of partial insanity once established, it is for
no human tribunal to arbitrarily circumscribe the
circle of its diseased operations.   We must remember also that sometimes the predominant idea is frequently changing, and at others, is obstinately concealed by the patient, and is not ascertained till after
his restoration to health.   The views here objected
to have also found a strong opponent in Georget
whose practical knowledge of the subject and acknowledged acuteness in observing the manners of
the insane, entitle his opinions to great consideration, if not to entire belief.   The following observations of his should never be forgotten in forming
conclusions on this disputed point.   "In conversing,"
says he, "with patients on topics foreign to their
morbid delusions, you will generally find no difference between them and other people.   They not
only deal in common-place notions, but are capable
of appreciating new facts and trains of reasoning.
Still more, they retain their sense of good and evil,
right and wrong, and of social usages, to such a
degree, that whenever they forget their moral sufferings and their delusions, they conduct, in their
meetings, as they otherwise would have done, inquiring with interest for one another's health, and
maintaining the ordinary observances of society.
They have special reasons even for regarding them-

selves with a degree of complacency ; for the most
part they believe that they are victims of arbitrary
measures, fraudulent contrivances, and projects of
vengeance or cupidity, and thus they sympathize
with one another in their common misfortunes. Accordingly the inmates of lunatic asylums are rarely
known to commit those reprehensible acts which are
regarded as crimes when dictated by sound reason,
though the most of them enjoy considerable freedom.
They often talk very sensibly of their interests, and
some even manage their property perfectly well."

"Those patients who are insane on one point only
more or less limited, may have experienced some
severe moral disorders which influence the conduct
and actions of the individual, without materially injuring his judgment. Those who conduct themselves so well in the asylum, in the midst of strangers with whom they have no relations, and against
whom they have conceived no prejudice nor cause
of complaint, and in quiet submission to the rule of
the house, are no sooner at liberty, in the bosom of
their families, than their conduct becomes insupport-
able; they are irritated by the slightest contradiction,
abusing and threatening those who address to them
the slightest observation, and working themselves up
to the most intolerable excesses. And whether the
reprehensible acts they then commit are really foreign
to the predominant idea or not, ought we to make a
being responsible for them whose *moral* nature is so
deeply affected ? " [1] These facts, it cannot be denied,

---

[1] Discussion medico-légale sur la Folie, pp. 10, 14.

furnish strong ground for the remark with which Georget closes his observations on this point, namely, that if, in following the rule that partial mania excludes the idea of culpability, " the moralist and the criminal judge run the risk of committing injustice by sparing a really guilty person, certainly, the opposite course would lead them into still greater errors."

§ 182. Hoffbauer has not only limited the exculpatory effects of partial mania to the acts which clearly come within its influence, but has laid down the principle that in the criminal jurisprudence of this condition, the predominant idea should be considered as true ; that is, that the acts of the patient should be judged as if he had really been in the circumstances he imagined himself to be when they were committed. It is based on the common, but erroneous notion, that insane people always reason correctly from wrong premises, and therefore it is inapplicable to the numerous instances where the premises and inferences are all equally wrong. If a person imagines he heard the voice of God commanding him to immolate his only child and he accordingly obeys, it may be said indeed that he is not responsible for the bloody deed, because it would have been perfectly proper, had he really heard the command ; but are we to be told, that if he had killed his neighbor for a fancied petty injury, he is not to be absolved from punishment, because, the act would have been highly criminal, even though he might have really received the injury ? It must not be overlooked that in cases like the latter, the insanity manifests itself, not only in the fancied injury, but in the disproportionate punishment which he inflicts upon the offender, and it is absurd to consider one manifestation as a delusion, and the other a crime.

§ 183. In the English courts there has been a great diversity of practice on this subject, according as it has been affected by the speculative opinions of the judge, the eloquence of counsel, the magnitude of the criminal act, and the ignorance or humanity of juries. If we carefully examine the cases tried within the last hundred years, as they are brought together in the various treatises on lunacy and on criminal law, the utmost respect for authority will not prevent us from observing the want of any definite principle as the ground of the difference of their results. Amid the mass of theoretical and discordant speculations on the psychological effects of insanity, and of crude and fanciful tests for detecting its presence, which these trials have elicited, the student who turns to them for the purpose of informing his mind on this branch of his profession, finds himself completely disheartened and bewildered. Instead of inquiring into the effect produced by the peculiar delusions of the accused on his ordinary conduct and conversation, and especially of their connexion with the criminal act in question, the courts in these cases, have been contented with laying down metaphysical dogmas on the consciousness of right and wrong, of good and evil, and the measure of understanding still possessed by the accused. Under the influence of the doctrines of lord Hale, partial insanity has seldom been considered as sufficient, *per se*, to annul responsibility for crime.

When received as an exculpatory plea, it has generally been in those cases where the principal delusions were of a religious nature, though the reason of this preference it might be difficult to assign.

§ 184. The practice of the American courts, judging from the few cases that have come to our knowledge, has been guided by more liberal doctrines. In the trial of Lawrence, at Washington, in 1835, for shooting at president Jackson, the jury were advised by the court to regulate their verdict by the principles laid down in the case of Hadfield, which had been stated to them by the district-attorney.[1] In the case of Theodore Wilson, tried in York county, Maine, in 1836, for the murder of his wife in a paroxysm of insanity, the court charged the jury that if they were satisfied the prisoner was not of *sound memory* and *discretion* at the time of committing the act, they were bound to return a verdict of acquittal. This is all that could be wished; and considering that two highly respectable physicians had given their opinion in evidence that the prisoner had some consciousness of right and wrong, and that the attorney-general, though he admitted the existence of insanity in some degree, denied that it was of sufficient extent to exempt him from punishment, supporting his assertion on the authority of the leading English cases relating to insanity, this decision

---

[1] Niles's Register, vol. 48, p. 119. The principle adopted in Hadfield's case was, that a person is not responsible for whatever criminal act is committed under the influence of delusion.

indicates an advance in the criminal jurisprudence
of insanity that does credit to the humanity and intelligence of that court.

Section II.

Legal Consequences of Moral Mania.

§ 185. General moral mania furnishes good ground
for invalidating civil acts, for notwithstanding the
apparent integrity of the intellectual powers, it is
probable that their operation is influenced to a
greater or less extent, by a derangement of the
moral powers. The mutual independence of these
two portions of our spiritual nature is not absolute
and unconditional, but is always liable to be affected
by the operation of the organic laws. The animal
economy is a whole ; no part of it can exist without
the rest, nor be injured or abstracted without marring
the energy or harmony of the whole system ; and
though each part is so far independent of the others
as to contribute its distinct share in the production
of the general result, even sometimes when surrounded by the ravages of disease, yet the general
law is, that disease in one part modifies more or
less the action of all the rest, and especially of those
connected with it by contiguity or by resemblance
of function. Nature has established a certain adaptation of the moral and intellectual faculties to one
another, leading to that harmony of action which
puts them in proper relation to external things, and

we can scarcely conceive of any disturbance of their equilibrium, that will not more or less impair the general result. Amid the chaos of the sentiments and passions produced by moral mania, the power of the intellect must necessarily suffer, and instead of accurately examining and weighing the suggestions of the moral powers, it is influenced by motives which may be rational enough, but which would never have been adopted in a perfectly healthy state. It is hard to conceive, indeed, that with an understanding technically sound, the relations of a person should be viewed in an entirely different light, the circle of his rights and duties broken and distorted, and his conduct turned into a course altogether foreign to his ordinary habits and pursuits. Notwithstanding the correctness of his conversation, and his plausible reasons for his singular conduct, a strict scrutiny of his actions, if not his words, will convince us that his notions of right and wrong are obscured and perverted, and that his own social position is viewed through a medium which gives a false coloring to its whole aspect. Now, though such a person may not be governed by any blind, irresistible impulse, yet to judge his acts by the standard of sanity and attribute to them the same legal consequences as to those of sane men, would be clearly unjust, because their real tendency is not and cannot be perceived by him. Not that his abstract notions of the nature of crime are at all altered, for they are not, but the real character of his acts being misconceived, he does not associate them with their ordinary moral relations. No fear of punishment restrains him from committing criminal acts, for he is

totally unconscious of violating any penal laws, and
therefore, the great end of punishment, the prevention of crime, is wholly lost in his case. If there
were no other reason for withholding punishment in
cases of moral mania, this alone would be sufficient,
that the fear of it, which with others is a powerful
preventive of crime, or at least is supposed to be, in
the most popular theories of criminal law, does not
and cannot exert its restraining influence on the
mind. No one would think of attributing moral
guilt to earl Ferrers for entertaining the insane idea
that his steward was a villain conspiring with the
earl's relatives against his comfort and interests
(§ 112); why then should it be charged to him as a
crime, that, amid the tumult of his passions disturbing the healthy exercise of his understanding, he
considered himself as the proper avenger of his own
wrongs ? Each delusion was alike the offspring of
the same derangement, and it is unjust and unphilosophical to regard one with indifference as the hallucination of a madman, and be moved with horror at
the other and visit it with the utmost terrors of the
law, as the act of a brutal murderer.

§ 186. Liberty of will and of action is absolutely
essential to criminal responsibility, unless the constraint upon either is the natural and well-known
result of immoral or illegal conduct. Culpability
supposes not only a clear perception of the consequences of criminal acts, but the liberty, unembar-
rassed by disease of the active powers which nature
has given us, of pursuing that course which is the result of the free choice of the intellectual faculties.
It is one of those wise provisions in the arrangement

of things, that the power of perceiving the good and
the evil, is never unassociated with that of obtaining
the one and avoiding the other.   When, therefore,
disease has brought upon an individual the very opposite condition, enlightened jurisprudence will hold
out to him its protection, instead of crushing him as
a sacrifice to violated justice.   That the subject of
homicidal insanity is not a free agent, in the proper
sense of the term, is a truth that must not be obscured by theoretical notions of the nature of insanity, nor by apprehensions of injurious consequences
from its admission.   Amid the rapid and tumultuous
succession of feelings that rush into his mind, the reflective powers are paralyzed, and his movements
are solely the result of a blind, automatic impulse
with which the reason has as little to do, as with the
movements of a new-born infant.   That the notions
of right and wrong continue unimpaired under these
circumstances, proves only the partial operation of
the disease ; but in the internal struggle that takes
place between the affective and intellectual powers,
the former have the advantage of being raised to
their maximum of energy by the excitement of disease, which, on the other hand, rather tends to diminish the activity of the latter.   We have seen that
generally after the fatal act has been accomplished,
and the violence of the paroxysm subsided, the monomaniac has gone and delivered himself into the
hands of justice, as if, overwhelmed with horror at
the enormity of his action, he either considered his
own life the only compensation he could offer in return ; or, it may be, felt that the presence of his fellow men, though it would seal his own fate, would

be a welcome relief from the crushing agony of his own spirit. It is not to be wondered at, however, if occasionally, the tide of feeling takes a different course, and the murderer is prompted to avoid what he cannot help thinking to be the just consequence of his act, by flying from the bloody scene, and even denying his agency in it altogether. Considering the diversity of habits, sentiments and education, uniformity in an unessential phenomenon like this is not to be expected. That flying from pursuit indicates a consciousness of having committed a reprehensible act, and also a fear of punishment, is not denied, but it has never been contended that the opposite course implies the absence of all ideas of this kind from the mind of the homicidal monomaniac. The real point at issue is, whether the fear of punishment or even the consciousness of wrong doing destroys the supposition of insanity, and this is settled by the well-known fact that the inmates of lunatic asylums, after having committed some reprehensible acts, will often persist in denying their agency in them, in order to avoid the reprimand or punishment which they know would follow their conviction. If insane persons have any rational ideas at all, and it is not denied that they have, it is not strange that they sometimes are conscious of the penal consequences of their acts and use the intelligence of a brute in order to avoid them. Besides, in moral insanity the intellectual faculties are supposed not to be impaired, and when the fury of the paroxysm which has borne him on in spite of every attempt at resistance has subsided, the homicidal monomaniac returns, in some degree at least, to his ordinary habit of thinking and feeling.

He regrets the havoc he has made, foresees its disgraceful consequences to himself, shudders at the
sight, and flies, like the most hardened criminal, to
avoid them.

§ 187. In medical science, it is dangerous to reason against facts. Now we have an immense mass
of cases related by men of unquestionable competence and veracity, where people are *irresistibly*
impelled to the commission of criminal acts while
fully conscious of their nature and consequences ;
and the force of these facts must be overcome by
something more than angry declamation against visionary theories and ill-judged humanity. They are
not fictions invented by medical men (as was rather
broadly charged upon them in some of the late trials
in France), for the purpose of puzzling juries and
defeating the ends of justice, but plain, unvarnished
facts as they occurred in nature ; and to set them
aside without a thorough investigation, as unworthy
of influencing our decisions, indicates any thing rather
than that spirit of sober and indefatigable inquiry
which should characterize the science of jurisprudence. We need have no fear that the truth on this
subject will not finally prevail, but the interests of
humanity require that this event should take place
speedily.

§ 188. The distinction between crimes and the
effects of homicidal monomania is too well-founded
to be set aside by mere declamation, or appeals to
popular prejudices, as has been repeatedly done in
courts of justice. On the trial of Papavoine for the
murder of two young children near Paris, in 1823,
the advocate-general, in reply to the counsel of the

prisoner who had pleaded homicidal insanity in his defence, declared that Papavoine committed the crime, in order "to gratify an inveterate hatred against his fellow-men, transformed at first, into a weariness of his own life, and subsequently into an instinct of ferocity and a thirst of blood. Embittered by his unhappy condition, excited by a sense of his sufferings and misfortunes, irritated by the happiness of others which awakened in him only ideas of fury, and drove him into seclusion which increased the perversity of his depraved propensities, he arrived at that pitch of brutal depravity where destruction became a necessity and the sight of blood a horrible delight. His hateful affections, after being long restrained, finally burst forth and raised in his bosom a necessity of killing, which, like a young tiger, he sought to gratify." [1] That beings in human shape have lived who delighted in the shedding of blood, and found a pastime in beholding the dying agonies of their victims, is a melancholy fact too well established by the Neros and Caligulas of history. For such we have no disposition to urge the plea of insanity, for though we are willing to believe them to have been unhappily constituted, we have no evidence that they labored under cerebral disease, and they certainly exhibited none of its phenomena. Motives, the very slightest no doubt, generally existed for even their most horrid atrocities, and even when they were entirely wanting, there was still a conformity of their bloody deeds with the whole tenor

---

[1] Georget: Examen des proces criminelles.

of their natural character. They followed the bent of their dispositions as manifested from childhood, glorying in their preëminent wickedness and rendered familiar by habit with crime ; and though conscience might have slumbered, or opposed but a feeble resistance to the force of their passions, yet it was not perverted by diseased action so as to be blind to the existence of moral distinctions. In homicidal insanity, on the contrary, every thing is different. The criminal act for which its subject is called to an account, is the result of a strong and sudden impulse, opposed to his natural habits and generally preceded or followed by some derangement of the healthy actions of the brain or other organ. The advocate-general himself represented Papavoine, "as having been noted for his unsocial disposition, for avoiding his fellow-laborers, for walking in retired, solitary places, appearing to be much absorbed in the vapors of a black melancholy." This is not a picture of those human fiends to whom he would assimilate Papavoine, but it is a faithful one of a mind over which the clouds of insanity are beginning to gather. Where is the similarity between this man, who, with a character for probity and in a fit of melancholy, is irresistibly hurried to the commission of a horrible deed, and those wretches who, hardened by a life of crime, commit their enormities with perfect deliberation and consciousness of their nature.

§ 189. It has been also urged that the subjects of homicidal insanity are, no less than criminals, injurious to society, the safety of which implicitly requires their extermination, upon the same principle that we do not hesitate to destroy a dog that has been so unfortunate as to go mad. Sane, or insane, criminal or not, such monsters should be cut off from the face of the earth, and it is a misplaced humanity to reserve them for a different fate. Such language might have been expected from people who are moved only by the feelings, that are immediately raised by the sight of appalling crimes, but it is an humiliating truth that the opinions of those who are in the habit of discriminating between various shades of guilt and of canvassing motives, are too often but an echo to the popular voice. If the old custom of smothering under a feather bed the miserable victims of hydrophobia be now considered as a specimen of the most revolting barbarity, we cannot see why the punishment of insane offenders should be regarded under a more favorable aspect.   Society has a right to protect itself against the aggressions of the dangerously insane, but unnecessary severity in its protective measures defeats the very purpose in view, and indicates a want of humanity and intellectual enlightenment. While confinement in prisons and mad-houses furnishes all the restraint which the necessity of their case requires, it is idle to urge the infliction of death as the only means by which society can be effectually shielded from a repetition of their terrible enormities.

§ 190. One of the principal objects of punishments should be to deter from the commission of crime, by impressing the mind with ideas of physical and moral suffering as its certain consequence ; and whenever it is found to produce a very different effect, it is the part of enlightened legislation to devise some other means of prevention. Nothing can be more absurd than to inflict the very punishment which the delusion

of the monomaniac often impels him to seek,—to put
him to death who voluntarily surrenders- himself and
imploringly beseeches it as the only object he had at
heart in perpetrating a horrid crime.   What is it but
converting a dreadful punishment into the dearest
boon that earth can offer ?   In religious monomania,
it is not uncommon for the patient to believe that the
joys of heaven are in store for him, and, under the
excitement of this insane idea, to murder a fellow-
creature, in order that he may the sooner enter on
their fruition.   To execute one of this class, is to per-
petuate an evil which needs only a change of penal
consequences to be effectually remedied.   A kind of
delusion has sometimes prevailed in certain parts of
Europe which persuades its unfortunate subjects that
eternal happiness can be gained by being executed
for the murder of some innocent person.   The idea
is that suicide being itself a sin will not be followed
by the happiness they seek, but that murder, though
a greater crime, can be repented of before the time
of execution.   This delusion prevailed epidemically
in Denmark, during the middle of the last century,
and to avoid sending an unprepared person out of
the world, the victim generally selected was a child.
Death, of course, was no punishment in this case,
and at last, the king issued an ordinance directing
that the guilty should be branded on the forehead
with a hot iron and whipped, and be imprisoned for
life with hard labor.   Every year, on the anniversary
of their crime, they were to be whipped.[1]   Lord

---

[1] London Quarterly Review, vol. 12, p. 219.

Dover, in his Life of Frederic, relates that such was the severity of discipline among the Prussian troops at Potsdam, that many wished for death to finish their intolerable sufferings, and murdered children, which they had enticed within their power, in order to obtain from justice the stroke they dared not inflict upon themselves.[1] Abolish capital punishment in such cases, and the delusion will disappear with it ; continue it, and no one can tell when the latter will end.

§ 191. Not only is the moral effect of punishment totally lost when inflicted on the subjects of homicidal insanity, since it does not deter other madmen from committing similar acts, but by a curious law of the morbid action, every publicity obtained for them by the trial and execution of the actors, leads to their repetition to an almost incredible extent. At a sitting of the Royal Academy of Medicine in Paris, August 8th, 1826, Esquirol stated that since the trial of Henriette Cornier, which occurred not two months before, he had become acquainted with six instances of a parallel nature. Among these was a Protestant minister who became affected with the desire of destroying a favorite child. He struggled against this terrible inclination for fifteen days, but was at last driven to the attempt on his child's life, in which he fortunately failed. Several other physicians, on the same occasion, bore similar testimony relative to the effect of that trial, and the newspa-

---

[1] Vol. 1, p. 321.

pers about that period teemed with cases of child-murder which had originated in the same way.

§ 192. It should not be forgotten, that well-grounded suspicion that the homicidal act was the result of physical disease, instead of moral depravity, is so horrid as to excite, in whatever mind it arises, feelings of distrust and jealousy towards the law and its ministers, infinitely more to be dreaded than the occasional acquittal of a supposititious maniac. When, on the contrary, the distinction is carefully made between the acts of a sound and those of an unsound mind, and a decision in doubtful cases is dispassionately and deliberately formed upon every species of evidence calculated to throw light upon it, the mind is impressed with a new sense of the wisdom and majesty of the laws and with a feeling of security under their discriminating operation.   The numerous trials for witchcraft in a former age, and the occasional condemnation of a maniac in the present, have done more to lessen men's respect for the laws, than all its overruled decisions have to weaken their confidence in its certainty.   Insanity is a disease, before the prospect of which the stoutest heart may quail, but how much more appalling is it made by the reflection, that in some wild paroxysm it may be followed by legal consequences, that will consign its unhappy subjects to an ignominious death.   In cases of simulated madness, the purposes of justice are more fully answered by receiving and examining all the evidence and patiently showing its value and bearings, and thus laying open the imposition to the conviction of all, than by repelling the plea with idle declamation on its injurious tendency.   Not only does the criminal obtain his deserts, by such a course, but the most cunning device of his ingenuity is seen to be baffled, and the plea that should ever shield innocence from destruction is ineffectually urged to protect the guilty. Every murmur at the injustice of the sentence is hushed, all scruples are removed and all fears are dissipated, that a fellow-being has been sacrificed, whose only crime was the misfortune of laboring under disease of the brain. Besides, what, if amid the obscurity in which a case may sometimes be involved, a guilty person do escape— though this event must be of very rare occurrence,— is it not a maxim in legal practice that it is better for ten guilty persons to escape punishment than for one innocent person to suffer ? But though he es- cape the sentence of the law, yet society is perfectly secure from the effects of mistake, because the very plea by which he obtains his acquittal, consigns him to confinement and surveillance.

§ 193. In those cases where there are some but not perfectly satisfactory indications of insanity,. the trial or sentence should be postponed, in order that opportunity may be afforded to those who are pro- perly qualified, for observing the state of the prison- er's mind. Where the moral powers have become so deranged as to lead to criminal acts, without, however, any perceptible impairment of the intel- lect, time only is necessary in the greater proportion of cases to furnish indubitable evidence of mental de- rangement. And whatever may be the result, the ends of justice are not defeated by waiting a few months, while the scruples of the over humane are removed, and the acquiescence of the ministers of the law in measures calculated to establish innocence rather than guilt, gains for them a confidence and respect that the conviction of guilt never can. Many instances might be mentioned where the accused, whose insanity was doubtful on trial, has, during the confinement subsequent to his acquittal on a criminal prosecution, become most manifestly insane. Hadfield, who was tried for shooting at the king and acquitted on the ground of insanity, though during the trial he displayed no indications of disordered mind, spent the remainder of his life in Bedlam hospital, and for thirty years showed scarcely any signs of mental alienation, except once, when suddenly and without any known cause, he became so furious that they were obliged to chain him in his cell. This paroxysm lasted but a short time, when he recovered his ordinary state of health.

§ 194. Another reason for delay is, that insanity is sometimes so completely veiled from observation, as never to be suspected even by the most intimate associates of the patient. An instructive case is related by Georget, in which the existence of insanity, though of several years duration, was not recognised till after the death of the subject. The circumstances were briefly these. Bertet, a revenue-officer, exercised the duties of his office for three years, in the manufactory of M. M. Ador and Bonnaire, at Vaugirard, where he was only noticed for his unaccommodating disposition, melancholic temperament and fondness for seclusion. One day while M. Ador was conversing with some of the workmen, he was requested by Bertet to affix his signature to certain papers. He proceeded to his room for this purpose,

and while in the act of writing, was shot dead by
Bertet, who immediately afterwards blew out his own
brains. Among his papers were found several addressed to the advocate-general, bearing the most
singular titles, such as *my last reflections, my last
sighs*, in which he declared that he had been
poisoned several years before, and gave a minute
account of the numerous remedies he had ineffectually used, insisting at the same time that his head
was not turned, that he acted deliberately, and
giving very coherent reasons to prove it. He announced that four victims were required, namely,
the two heads of the establishment, a woman
who was living in it, and his old housekeeper, and
that in case he should be contented with one, he
would leave to justice the charge of obtaining the
others. Some of these papers he finishes with saying, " To day my pains are less acute,—I feel better,
—my vengeance is retarded," or " my pains are
renewed—with them my thoughts of vengeance."
Among other wild fancies, he made a description of
the funeral monument to be raised to one of his victims, which was to be a gibbet covered with figures
of instruments of punishment. He also described
his own funeral procession. He wished the four
corners of the pall to be carried by the four persons
above-mentioned, in case he should not have sacrificed them ; that the advocate-general should follow
the cortege ; and that when it reached the cemetery,
the latter should prepare a large ditch in which they
should first cast him, Bertet, and then the four pall-
bearers. In another paper, he said he designed for
each of his victims two gilt balls, as an emblem of

their ambition and thirst of gold, and some pulverized cantharides, as an image of the torments which he suffered. Bertet had never shown any signs of mental alienation in his official letters and reports. He was sometimes abstracted and loved to be alone, but his disposition, in this respect, had been of long standing and seemed to be owing to the state of his health, of which he was constantly complaining, though judging from his exterior he seemed to be well enough. He had always discharged the duties of his office satisfactorily, and, by his own solicitation, had just before obtained a more profitable place. Had not Bertet recorded his insane fancies, but, failing in his suicidal attempt, had been brought to trial for the murder of M. Ador, the plea of insanity would have fallen on the most incredulous ears, and he would have paid the last penalty of the law. In a state of confinement and seclusion, however, nothing but time would have been necessary to reveal the true nature of his case.

§ 195. Homicidal monomania presents us with one of those remarkable phenomena, the existence of which men are slow to believe, long after the evidence in its favor has accumulated to such an extent as to render incredulity any thing but a virtue. The facts themselves cannot be denied, and the various methods of explaining them on the hypothesis of a sound understanding, though every phase of human character and every spring of human action has been resorted to for the purpose, are little calculated to diminish the confidence of impartial minds in the correctness of the above views. Strongly impressed as we are with their importance, we may have devoted more attention to the objections that have been urged against them, than they really deserve; we shall therefore say but little more on this part of the subject. Against Georget's proposition relative to the homicide committed by Henriette Cornier, that " an act so atrocious, so contrary to human nature, committed without interest, without passion, opposed to the natural character of the individual, is evidently an act of madness " ;[1] it has been seriously objected that though we may be unable to discover motives, yet this is not a positive proof that there actually are no motives. This objection depends upon a question of fact, and we shall content ourselves with putting it to every criminal lawyer to answer for himself, whether a criminal act, committed by a person whose motives defy all penetration or rational suspicion while his mind evinces no signs of impairment, is not one of the most uncommon occurrences in the world—so uncommon perhaps, as to have never fallen within their experience ?

§ 196. By those who delight not in metaphysical subtleties, a more summary, if not more philosophical, explanation of homicidal monomania has been furnished in the idea that it is to be attributed to an instinct of ferocity ; to unnatural depravity of character; to a radical perversity. That such qualities do exist as the too common result of a defective constitution, or a vicious education, is proved by the testimony of every day's experience, even if we had not the best authority for believing that the heart

---

[1] Discussion medico-légale sur la Folie, 126.

may be "desperately wicked." But even where they exist to the fullest extent, the actions to which they prompt have always some immediate motive, slight as it may be, of pleasure sought, or pain avoided; or if they can claim no higher title than that of *instinct*, it is one of no sudden, transitory character, but a constant and consistent portion of the constitution. It is an anomalous instinct that manifests itself but once or twice in a person's life; and therefore, we cannot, without indulging in the most unwarrantable use of language, apply this term to those uncontrollable, abnormal influences that lead to acts of fury and destruction. What resemblance can we detect between the Domitians and Neros of history, and the Papavoines and Corniers, whose terrible acts have been commemorated in the records of criminal jurisprudence? In the former, this instinct of ferocity appeared in their earliest youth; it imparted a zest to every amusement, and excited ingenuity to contrive new means for heightening the agonies of the wretched victims of their displeasure. In the latter, the character was mild and peaceable, and their days were spent in the quiet and creditable discharge of the duties belonging to their station, till a cloud of melancholy enveloped their minds and under its shadow they perpetrated a single deed, at the very thought of which they would have previously shuddered with horror. In short, all our knowledge of human nature, all our experience of the past, forces us to the conclusion, that "the presence of mental alienation should be admitted in him who commits a homicide without positive interest, without criminal motives, and without a reasonable passion."

§ 197. After what has been said on the subject of homicidal monomania, it will be scarcely necessary to enter into particulars relative to the legal consequences of the other forms of partial moral mania. Completely annulling, as we believe they do, all moral responsibility for acts committed under their influence, the law can rightfully inflict no punishment on their unfortunate subjects, though it should adopt every measure of precaution that the interests of society require. To punish the thief and the incendiary for acts which are the result of disease is not only unjust, but it serves to aggravate their disorder, and to prepare them, when their term of punishment has closed, for renewing their depredations on society with increased perseverance. The only proper course to pursue with this class of offenders when brought into courts of justice, is to place them, or obtain a guaranty from their friends that they shall be placed, where judicious medical treatment will be used for the purpose of restoring their moral powers to a sounder condition, and where they will be secluded from society until this end shall be accomplished.

If the doctrines here laid down relative to moral insanity and its legal consequences are correct, it would seem to follow as a matter of course, that they should exert their legitimate influence on judicial decisions. Nevertheless, it is contended—and that too by some who do not question the truth of these doctrines—that they ought not to have this practical effect, for the reason that insanity would thereby be made the ground of defence in criminal actions, to a most pernicious extent. This objection, stated in the plainest and strongest terms we presume to be this. If these doctrines should be recognised in our courts of justice, and suffered to influence their decisions, almost every criminal would resort to a defence, the tendency of which is invariably to puzzle and distract the minds of the jury, and to produce the acquittal of many a wretch, who would first hear the mention of his own derangement from the lips of ingenious counsel. Now, even if we were disposed to accord to this objection all the weight that is claimed for it, it would not seem to warrant the inference that is drawn from it. Are we to take from the maniac the defence which the law of nature secures to him, because it may be sometimes offered by those who use it as a means of deception? Are the innocent to be made to suffer for the devices of the guilty? To avoid this cruel injustice, therefore, without at the same time inflicting a positive evil on society, we would deduce from this objection an inference of a totally different kind. It is, to let the right of the accused party to make his defence be cumbered with no restrictions, expressed or implied; let the plea of insanity, if he choose to make it, be attentively listened to, the facts urged in its support closely scrutinized, the accused carefully and dispassionately examined, and his character and history investigated. If this duty be performed as it should be, and always may be, the case will seldom happen, when the truth will not be established to the satisfaction of every unprejudiced mind. If the accused be really insane, we have the satisfaction of reflecting, that an enlightened investigation of his case has saved an innocent person from an ignominious fate, while on the other hand, if he be simulating insanity, every doubt will be dissipated as to the justice of his sentence, and the conviction will be strengthened in the popular mind, that the law will prevail over every false pretence, and expose the guilty even in their most secret refuge.

CHAPTER IX.

DEMENTIA.

§ 198. THIS form of insanity is attended with a general enfeeblement of the moral and intellectual faculties which were originally sound and well-developed, in consequence of age or disease, and is characterized by forgetfulness of the past, indifference to the present and future, and a certain childishness of disposition. The apparent similarity of this state to that of imbecility or idiocy renders it necessary that they should be accurately distinguished ; for nothing could be more improper or unjust, than to view them merely as different shades of the same mental condition. Idiocy and the higher degrees of imbecility are congenital or nearly so, and consist in a destitution of powers that were never possessed. Little or nothing is remembered, because little or nothing has left any impression upon the mind, and no advance is made in knowledge, because the faculties necessary for obtaining it have never existed. The proprieties and decencies of life are unobserved, for the simple reason that their moral relations have never been discerned, and their indifference to the most pressing wants is to be attributed to the absence of the most common instincts of our nature. The idiot is restless, uneasy, and inattentive, because the faculties that direct the attention, and draw from its application valuable results, have been utterly denied. In idiocy and imbecility the manners and conversation strongly resemble those of childhood; in dementia they never lose the impress of manhood however disjointed and absurd they may be. The former appear at an early age of life ; the latter never takes place till after the age of puberty, and generally increases with time, from the slightest possible impairment of mental energy to the most complete fatuity. In dementia the past is forgotten, or but indistinctly and unconnectedly brought up to the mind; the attention wanders from one thing to another ; the affairs of the present possess no interest ; and the moral and social affections are inactive, because the faculties, in consequence of pathological changes in the brain, have fallen into a state of inertia that prevents their ordinary manifestations. The whole condition betrays the existence, not of physical imperfection, but of physical weakness (many of the bodily functions also frequently being enfeebled), and consequently it may sometimes be cured, or temporarily relieved. When once firmly seated, it is not incompatible with length of years; and after death, we may find, on examination, lesions of structure, or diminutions of size, which are accidental, the result of diseased action, and not original malconformations. The above comparison of mental deficiency with dementia shows, that they depend on two very different conditions of the brain, and consequently must display very different moral and intellectual manifestations ; from which we are warranted in inferring that in regard to their medico-legal relations, they cannot properly be placed on the same ground.

§ 199. Dementia is distinguished from mania, the only other affection with which it is liable to be confounded, by characters that will not mislead the least practised observer. The latter arises from an exaltation of vital power, from a morbid excess of activity, by which the cerebral functions are not only changed from their healthy condition, but are performed with unusual force and rapidity. The maniac is irrational from an inability to discern the ordinary characters and relations of things, amid the mass of ideas that crowd upon his mind in mingled confusion; while in dementia, the reasoning faculty is impaired by a loss of its original strength, whereby it not only mistakes the nature of things, but is unable, from want of power, to rise to the contemplation of general truths. The reasoning of the maniac does not so much fail in the force and logic of its arguments, as in the incorrectness of its assumptions; but in dementia the attempt to reason is prevented by the paucity of ideas, and that feebleness of the perceptive powers, in consequence of which they do not faithfully represent the impressions received from without. In mania, when the memory fails, it is because new ideas have crowded into the mind, and are mingled up and confounded with the past; in dementia the same effect is produced by an obliteration of past impressions as soon as they are made, from a want of sufficient power to retain them. In the former, the mental operations are characterized by hurry and confusion; in the latter, by extreme slowness and frequent apparent suspension of the thinking process. In the former, the habits and affections undergo a great change, the conduct becoming strange and inconsistent from the beginning, and the persons and things that once pleased and interested, viewed with indifference or aversion.   In the latter, the moral habits and natural feelings, so far as they are manifested at all, lose none of their ordinary character.   The temper may be more irritable, but the moral disposition evinces none of that perversity which characterizes mania.

§ 200. Dementia, it must be recollected, is something more than that mere loss of mental power which results from the natural decay of the faculties ; it is attended with those pathological changes also which are essential to the production of insanity. The mind is not only feeble, but it is deranged. Were it not so, every old man would labor under a certain degree of dementia.   The first symptom, which indicates the approach of this affection, is generally an impairment of the memory of recent occurrences.   The events of early life have lost none of their distinctness, while recent impressions are feebly made, and in a short time mostly forgotten. While the visits of his friends are forgotten beyond the day or the week they are made, the patient may talk of their former interviews, and relate the most trivial details concerning them.   From this weakness of memory seems to arise oftentimes the first appearance of mental alienation.   The patient forgetting the intermediate ideas, the connexion between those he does remember, and that order and filiation of them necessary to sound reasoning are destroyed ; and hence those gaps in his ideas and those inconsistencies of conduct which convey the impression of mental derangement.   Coincident with this failure of the memory, or very shortly afterwards, there is a diminution of the ordinary ability of recognising external objects, which arises not so much from a weakness of the organs of sensation, as of the organs of perception within. That is, the impressions of sound, light, touch, &c. are well enough received, but the qualities of form, size, weight, color, &c. are imperfectly discerned. Objects not very different are mistaken for one another, from an inability to perceive at first sight the qualities that distinguish them, though the individual may recognise his mistake when it is pointed out to him.

§ 201. Thus far there is nothing that can properly be called mental derangement; the pathological changes in the brain have only occasioned a diminution of the natural power and activity of the mind. The first symptom indicative of derangement (and it is the next which is observed), is a degree of incoherence in the ideas, like that of sleep. It may not appear for days or weeks together, or only on certain occasions; or it may be constant from the beginning and appear on all occasions. The above symptoms increase in intensity more or less rapidly till complete dementia is produced, when all the moral and intellectual powers are involved in this state of decay and derangement. The memory of recent impressions fades away as fast as they are formed, and the past is beheld with considerable indistinctness and confusion, though events and acquaintances of early life are not yet forgotten. The patient is often at a loss to know where he is, or thinks himself at home when in the house of another, and wonders why he is not engaged in his usual occupations. Places, times and circumstances are forgotten, or incorrectly remembered. His friends are not easily distinguished ; morning, noon, and evening, yesterday and to-morrow are being constantly blended together ; and he will get up in the night, mistake the light of candles for that of day, and persist in calling it morning. Objects the most dissimilar are mistaken for one another, and consequently his notions are often the most grotesque and absurd. The intellect gradually becomes incapable of discerning the relations of cause and effect, and of comparing ideas together ; in short any thing like an effort of reflection is beyond its powers. The person is unable to follow the conversation, unless it be of the simplest ideas, and particularly addressed to him. His thoughts, when left to follow their own course, succeed one another without connexion ; his language is equally incoherent ; and insulated words and phrases are repeated without any consciousness of their meaning. " It seems," says Esquirol, " as if they were listening to imaginary tales which they repeat, in obedience to an involuntary or automatic impulse excited by their old habits, or fortuitous associations with actual impressions." [1] Their mind is often occupied by hallucinations which continue a longer or a shorter time, and then disappear to be succeeded by others. The useful or ornamental arts which they may have practised with skill and followed with ardor, and the various other employments of life, seem to be utterly forgotten, as if they had never

---

[1] Dictionary of Medical Sciences, Art. Demence.

been thought of. Their time is spent either in moving about with restless activity, or passing days, weeks, or months in the same spot, in utter vacuity of thought or purpose; in setting their watches, or observing the changes of the wind; in pouring forth an incessant jargon of words at the top of their voice, or uttering low, muttering sounds consisting of scarcely articulated words and broken phrases; in singing, crying or laughing.

§ 202. Though often irascible and self-willed, their anger is momentary, and thus they readily yield to the direction of others. The moral powers, in fact, seem to be possessed of too little energy to maintain resolution, or cherish the passions. Their feebleness of purpose and passive obedience to the will of others, strikingly contrast with the pertinacity and savage fury often evinced by the maniac. With the remembrance of their friends and of their former employments, there also disappears all trace of the social and domestic affections. All interest in the concerns of others is lost, and family, friends and relations are viewed with the indifference of perfect strangers, and nothing is able to awaken an emotion of pleasure or pain.

§ 203. The derangement of the intellectual powers is generally indicated by remarkable changes of the countenance. The skin is pale and dry and wrinkled; the eyes sunken, dull and moistened with tears; the pupils dilated; the look uncertain and wandering; the cheeks hollow and emaciated; and the whole face destitute of expression and indicative of decay. The organic functions suffer but little; the appetite for food is so great that the patient seems to be constantly eating, and the quantity consumed is enormous.   Affections of the nervous system, however, particularly paralysis, are not unfrequent complications of dementia.

§ 204. Dementia appears under two different degrees of severity which are designated as *acute* and
chronic.   The former is a sequel of temporary errors
of regimen, of fevers, hemorrhages, metastases, suppression of customary evacuations, and the debilitating treatment of mania.   It differs from the latter in
being more rapid in its progress, and in its successive
stages not being so well distinguished from one
another.   It is readily cured by regimen, exercise,
bathing, tonics, anti-spasmodics, or simply by removing the exciting cause.   It sometimes terminates
in an explosion of acute mania, which then becomes
critical.

§ 205. Chronic dementia may succeed mania,
apoplexy, epilepsy, masturbation, and drunkenness,
but is generally that decay and derangement of mind
which occurs in old age.   It must be borne in mind,
however, that decay is not to be confounded with
derangement ; if it is, then almost every old man
may be pronounced to be demented.   It may be
difficult oftentimes to satisfy ourselves whether or
not the former is accompanied by the latter, but for
any practical purposes it may be seldom necessary.
The same decay which the bodily powers exhibit, as
they proceed to their natural termination in death, is
always participated by the mental ; but it sometimes
happens that the latter are irretrievably affected long
before the former have shown any symptoms of faltering in their course.   The causes of this inversion

of the natural order of decay, so far as they are external, are to be found probably in the great irregularity of exercise, both of kind and duration, to which the brain is subjected by the habits and wants of a highly civilized condition, whereby its healthy elasticity and vigor are so impaired, that it needs only the first touch of decay to lose for ever the nicely adjusted balance of its faculties. The transition from the greatest mental exertion to the most tedious inactivity, from the various phases of excitement to the irksome sameness of ennui, from the stimulus afforded by the performance of a thousand duties, and the glow that is constantly kindled by the hopes of the future, to the monotony too often occasioned by loss of business, friends, and the cares of long accustomed pursuits, is of such frequent occurrence, that every thing like regular and proper exercise, which is as indispensable to the health of the brain as it is to that of every other organ, is rarely enjoyed by men who are engaged in the active business of life.

§ 206. In the later periods of life—and particularly if the constitution is weakened by sickness or dissipation—any exertion of the mind far beyond its power to sustain is liable to be rapidly followed by a state of dementia. The same effect is produced when after many years of unremitting attention to certain pursuits, the mind is suddenly deprived of the objects on which it rested, and thrown upon itself to furnish the means of excitement in the declining years of life, when novelty presents no allurements, and the circle of earthly prospects is being constantly narrowed. Take an individual from the stir and bustle of a city residence ; from the unceasing strife of competition in the pursuit of wealth or honor ; throw down the goal on which for years his eye has rested, though ever receding from his grasp ; place him in the country, at a distance from familiar faces and scenes; and unless his mind be informed with various knowledge, or warmed by an interest in the moral concerns of his fellow-men around him, it will sink into that state of inactivity so favorable for the operation of the predisposing causes of this disease.

§ 207. It must not be supposed that old age is subject to no other kind of insanity than that of Dementia, for mania, even of the most furious description, is not uncommon at this period, and the importance of distinguishing between them, in a legal point of view, must be immediately obvious. Not only may the mind remain competent to the discharge of some of the civil duties of life, in mania, but there is always a prospect of its restoration to health. The characteristic symptoms, as well as the exciting causes that we have described above, if carefully observed, will generally prevent us from committing the serious mistake of confounding them together, as is too often done, with scarcely a thought of the impropriety of the practice.

CHAPTER X.

LEGAL CONSEQUENCES OF DEMENTIA.

§ 208. In its last stages, dementia does not differ of course, in respect to its legal relations, from general intellectual mania. It is only while the mind is in its transition-state, if we may use the expression, passing from its sound and natural condition to the enfeeblement and total extinction of its reflective powers—and the entire change may occupy months and years in its progress—that its legal incapacity is ever called in question. The successive steps of this disorder are so imperceptible and oftentimes affect the powers so unequally, that it is not strange that so much diversity of opinion should arise respecting the capacity of the mind which is the subject of it, or that groundless suspicions of improper influence should be so frequently excited. It must be considered too, as a circumstance calculated to favor this effect, that the judgment is debarred from forming an unbiassed decision by suggestions of interest or jealousy, which lead it to see lapses of the mind that would otherwise have appeared to be nothing more than that natural loss of energy, suffered by the mind as it "draws near to its eternal home." Most people too are so little accustomed to observe and analyze the mental phenomena, and so little acquainted with the physiologi-

cal laws that govern their manifestations, that circumstances are often adduced as indications of unequivocal insanity, which only evince some normal
peculiarities of the senile understanding. They need
only to be put in the proper bias, to confound the
natural decay of the mental faculties with that derangement which depends exclusively on pathological
affections; so strongly do they resemble each other
to the superficial observer. By how many would
Bichat's beautiful picture of the closing scenes of old
age be mistaken to represent the defaced and shat-
tered temple that has been prostrated by the touch
of disease. " Seated near the fire and concentrated
within himself, a stranger to every thing without
him, he passes his days there, deprived of desire,
of passion, and sensation; speaking little, because
he is determined by nothing to break his silence, yet
happy in feeling that he still exists, when almost
every other sentiment is gone." [1] Far greater then
must be the necessity of caution in distinguishing
between such degrees of capacity as exist in the
early and those of the latter stages of dementia, and
where too the causes of error are so much more
numerous. The deafness that generally accompanies the early stages, disables the individual from
participating in or listening to the conversation of
those around him, and thus gives to his countenance
an expression of dullness and stupidity that might
easily mislead one not particularly acquainted with
him, while in fact he needs only to be properly ad-

---

[1] Life and Death, p. 1, c. x.

dressed, to display a mind that has not yet ceased to think with some degree of accuracy and vigor. The latter fact, however, will be known only to his intimate friends, while the former is conveyed to that mass of common observers who are always ready to decide upon a person's mental capacity, from an occasional glimpse of his manner, or a few remarks on the most ordinary topics.

§ 209. A judge is seldom required to decide questions of more delicacy—questions that demand such nice and cautious balancing of evidence, such penetration into motives and biasses, such a profound knowledge of the mental manifestations as affected by disease,—than those of mental capacity in old age, where the mind is confessedly laboring under some kind or degree of impairment. The standard by which witnesses' opinions are formed in such cases is so different, and the pertinacity with which each one clings to his own conclusions,—in proportion generally to his ignorance of the subject—is so strong, that nothing but a great display of the above-mentioned qualities will enable the judge to perform his duty with credit to himself, and satisfaction to others. Unless he can state the grounds of his opinions, they are no better than surmises, and he fails of accomplishing one of the most desirable objects of the law—that of establishing and confirming the popular confidence in its ministers. Difficult as this duty is, it will be very much lightened by attending to some of those points which can always be ascertained, and which have an important bearing on the question at issue.

§ 210. Though some of the perceptive powers may preserve their wonted activity through the whole of the disease ; yet it is in these that the disorder is first manifested, and that long before the higher powers of the understanding have materially suffered. The memory of persons, things, and dates, and especially of recent impressions, is exceedingly treacherous : and so striking is this impairment to those unaccustomed to look beneath the surface of appearances, that when they find they are not recognised though once well-enough known ; that past events and the actors engaged in them, are either forgotten or singularly entangled and confused ; and that a certain listlessness and absence of mind takes the place of former animations and attentiveness ; they summarily conclude that for all business purposes, the patient is utterly incapacitated. The impressions produced by a single short interview have no chance of being corrected by subsequent opportunities, or by more philosophical observations, and the final opinion is adopted and authoritatively propounded, that the individual in question did not possess legal capacity. If he take no part in the conversation, and appear scarcely to know what is passing around him, we are not to draw unfavorable conclusions relative to his mental condition, until we ascertain, if possible, that there are no peculiar reasons why he should remain silent and alone, and that he is no. longer capable of pursuing a train of thought of some length and complexity. If he have forgotten the names and circumstances of those once familiar, but whom he has not been in the habit of seeing recently, it does not follow that he has also forgotten those whose relations to him have kept them within the sphere of his daily observation and made them the objects of his thoughts. An old servant or tenant whose countenance may not have been seen for weeks, or months, is not to be compared in this respect, with the near relative who is frequently in his company, and always regarded with feelings of interest and affection. However certain it may be that he has lost all sense of the ordinary proprieties of life, it needs farther evidence to prove that the persons and interests, which have been always nearest to his heart and connected with the great purposes of his life, have utterly faded from his mind. The evidence of those, therefore, who are qualified both by their habits of intimacy with the person whose mental capacity is in question, and by their intelligence and education, to appreciate the changes his mind may have undergone, is far more to be relied on than that of people of a different description, who make up their opinion hastily from a few casual and perhaps trivial circumstances. The great point to be determined is, not whether he was apt to forget the names of people in whom he felt no particular interest, nor the dates of events which concerned him little, but whether in conversation about his affairs, his friends and relatives, he evinced sufficient knowledge of both, to be able to dispose of the former with a sound and untrammeled judgment. It is a fact that many of those old men who appear so stupid, and who astonish the stranger by the singularities of their conduct, need only to have their attention fairly fixed on their property, their business, or their family, to understand them per-

fectly well, and to display their sagacity in the remarks they make. In the case of Kindleside v. Har-
rison,[1] which we shall briefly notice in illustration of
these remarks, the reader may obtain a better idea
than can otherwise be conveyed, of the kind of evidence generally produced in cases of senile dementia, and derive instruction and high intellectual
gratification from the clearness and ability with
which it is sifted and stamped with its proper value,
in the judgment of the court, Sir John Nicholl.

§ 211. The points contested in this case were four
codicils to the will of an old gentleman, on the
ground that at the time of making them, he was incapable, by reason of mental decay, of understanding their nature and effect. It was testified by some
of the servants of his brother, who lived at a little
distance from him, and by those of the lady with
whom he, the deceased, resided, that during the two
or three years within which the codicils were made,
he frequently did not know people with whom he had
previously been well acquainted, without being told
who they were ; that he would go about the house
and garden looking around, and appearing not to
know what he was about. On one occasion, he not
only did not recognise a certain person, but could
not be made to understand who he was, and it was
testified by a very different kind of witness, that the
deceased asked him how old was witness's father
(though he had been dead sixteen years and had
been his partner in business), and soon after, he

---

[1] 2 Phillimore's Reports, 449.

inquired of the witness after his health, as if he were addressing another person. Several other similar lapses of memory and various appearances of childishness in his conduct, were also revealed by the evidence, amply sufficient, no doubt, to induce superficial observers to believe that he was mentally incapacitated from disposing of property. It appeared however that he was in the habit of giving, in favor of his brother's butler, drafts accurately signed and filled up ; that at christmas-time, he gave the servants christmas boxes and the usual amount of money, and entered the sums in his account-book; that he received a farmer's bills for corn and paid them with drafts on his banker which he wrote himself, going through the whole business correctly, and that he docketed the bills and receipts on the back with the name of the person to whom paid, and the amount of the bill, making corresponding entries also in his private account-book ; that he signed twenty drafts at least one morning for payment of his brother's debts, without instruction or assistance, subscribing his own name as executor of his brother; that he would detect errors in the casting up of other people's accounts; that he discharged his physician's bills correctly; and in short that he managed his affairs, and that prudently and correctly, to the last. It was also testified that it was his practice to read aloud to the family the psalms and lessons of the day; that he was fond of a little fun and played at whist remarkably well. That a person might have done all this and yet been unsound in mind, is certainly not impossible ; but it was far beyond the power of a mind so broken up by old age and the invasion of disease as to be incapable of altering testamentary dispositions previously made. This consideration, and the fact that the circumstances of the case furnished abundant reasons for the alteration, induced the court to decide in favor of the capacity of the testator.

CHAPTER XI.

FEBRILE DELIRIUM.

§ 212. CEREBRAL affection of some kind or other, we have considered as essential to the existence of insanity—as constituting in fact the whole disease ; but there is another form of mental derangement of very common occurrence; in which the cerebral affection is only an accidental symptom of acute disease in the brain or some other organ. The functions of the brain are disturbed in each, but they differ so widely in their causes, progress, and termination, that the propriety of distinguishing them from each other for medico-legal, as well as therapeutical purposes, is universally recognised. Few diseases terminate in death without presenting at some period or other of their progress, but more particularly towards their close, more or less disturbance of the mental faculties; organic diseases of the brain, especially acute inflammation of its membranes and its periphery, are frequently accompanied with delirium ; and it is sometimes a symptom of acute disease in other organs, in consequence of the cerebral irritation which they sympathetically produce. It is seldom entirely absent in fevers of any severity, and is readily determined by inflammations of the mucous and serous membranes, particularly of the alimentary canal. In inflammation of the lungs, liver, spleen, and kidneys, it appears only towards the last period of the disease when it is approaching a fatal termination. Surgical operations too that prove fatal are ordinarily attended at last with delirium. In chronic diseases, such as cancer, dropsy, consumption, the mind is seldom impaired, except occasionally during the final struggle, it wanders over the mingled and broken images of the past. Delirium is also produced by intoxicating agents, when it simulates mania more perfectly than when it arises from other causes; but this form of the affection will be discussed in a different place.

§ 213. Delirium sometimes occurs suddenly, but generally comes on gradually, and is preceded by premonitory symptoms, such as pain or throbbing in the head, heat of the scalp, and flushing of the cheeks. Its first appearance is manifested by a propensity of the patient to talk during sleep, and a momentary forgetfulness of his situation, and of things about him, on waking from it. After being fully aroused, however, and his senses collected, the mind is comparatively clear and tranquil, till the next slumber, when the same scene is repeated. Gradually, the mental disorder becomes more intense, and the intervals between its returns, of shorter duration, until they are scarcely, or not at all perceptible. The patient lies on his back, his eyes, if open, presenting a dull and listless look, and is almost constantly talking to himself in a low, muttering tone. Regardless of persons or things around him, and scarcely capable of recognising them when aroused by his attendants, his mind retires within itself to dwell upon the scenes and events of the past which pass before it in wild and disorderly array, while the tongue feebly records the varying impressions, in the form of disjointed, incoherent discourse, or of senseless rhapsody. In the delirium which occurs towards the end of chronic diseases, the discourse is often more coherent and continuous, though the mind is no less absorbed in its own reveries. As the disorder advances, the voice becomes more indistinct, the fingers are constantly picking at the bed-clothes, the evacuations are passed insensibly, and the patient is incapable of being aroused to any farther effort of attention. In some cases, delirium is attended with a greater degree of nervous and vascular excitement which more or less modifies the above-mentioned symptoms. The eyes are open, dry, and bloodshot, intently gazing into vacancy, as if fixed on some object which is really present to the mind of the patient ; the skin is hotter and dryer ; and he is more restless and intractable. He talks more loudly, occasionally breaking out into cries and vociferations, and tosses about in bed, frequently endeavoring to get up, though without any particular object in view.

§ 214. While delirium thus shuts out all ideas and images connected with the present, it sometimes revives the impressions of the past which had seemed long before to have been consigned to utter oblivion, in a manner unknown in a state of health. A case once occurred in St. Thomas's hospital, of a patient who, when he became convalescent after a considerable injury of the head, spoke a language that nobody could understand, but which was, at last ascertained to be Welsh. It appeared that he was a Welshman, and had been from his native country about thirty years, during which period, he had entirely forgotten his native tongue, and acquired the English language. But when he recovered from the accident, he had forgotten the language he had been so long and recently in the habit of speaking, and acquired that which he had originally learned and lost.[1] Dr. Rush mentions, among many other similar instances, that the old Swedes of Philadelphia, when on their death-beds, would always pray in their native tongue, though they had not spoken it for fifty or sixty years, and had probably forgotten it before they were sick.[2]

§ 215. When delirium, or more properly speaking, the disease on which it depends, proves fatal, it usually passes into coma. Occasionally, however, it disappears, some days or hours before death, and leaves the mind in possession of its natural soundness. Though enfeebled by disease, and therefore incapable of much exertion of his faculties, the patient is rational and intelligent, recognises perfectly well his relations to others, and on familiar subjects, can arrange his ideas without dictation or guidance.

§ 216. So closely does delirium resemble mania to the casual observer, and so important is it that they should be distinguished from each other, that it may be well to indicate some of the most common and prominent features of each. In mania, the pa-

---

[1] Tupper's Inquiry into Gall's System.
[2] On Diseases of the Mind, p. 282.

tient recognises persons and things, and is perfectly
conscious of and remembers what is passing around
him.   In delirium, he can seldom distinguish one
person or thing from another, and, as if fully occupied
with the images that crowd upon his memory, gives
no attention to those that are presented from without.   In delirium, there is an entire abolition of the
reasoning power ; there is no attempt at reasoning
at all; the ideas are all and equally insane ; no single train of thought escapes the morbid influence,
nor does a single operation of the mind reveal a
glimpse of its natural vigor and acuteness.   In
mania, however false and absurd the ideas may be,
we are never at a loss to discover patches of cohe-
rence, and some semblance of logical sequence in
the discourse.   The patient still reasons, but he
reasons incorrectly. In mania, the muscular power is
not perceptibly diminished, and the individual moves
about with his ordinary ability.   Delirium is invariably attended with great muscular debility; the patient is confined to his bed, and is capable of only
a momentary effort of exertion.   In mania, sensation
is not necessarily impaired, and in most instances,
the maniac sees, hears, and feels with all his natural
acuteness.   In delirium, sensation is greatly impaired, and this avenue to the understanding seems
to be entirely closed.   In mania, many of the bodily
functions are undisturbed, and the appearance of the
patient might not, at first sight, convey the impression of disease.   In delirium, every function suffers,
and the whole aspect of the patient is indicative of
disease. Mania exists alone and independent of any
other disorder, while delirium is only an unessential

symptom of some other disease.   Being a symptom
only, the latter maintains certain relations with the
disease on which it depends ; it is relieved when
that is relieved, and is aggravated when that increases in severity.   Mania, though it undoubtedly
tends to shorten life, is not immediately dangerous,
whereas the disease on which delirium depends,
speedily terminates in death, or restoration to health.
Mania never occurs till after the age of puberty ;
delirium attacks all periods alike, from early childhood to extreme old age.

CHAPTER XII.

LEGAL CONSEQUENCES OF DELIRIUM.

§ 217. TESTAMENTARY dispositions made during the intervals of febrile delirium, are often contested on the ground of incapacity, especially where there is any suspicion, real, or pretended, of improper influence on the testator's mind. These cases are sometimes very embarrassing, and it is impossible to come to a conclusion upon the direct evidence respecting the state of mind; nothing more can be attained than an approximation to correctness, by a careful investigation of the attending circumstances When the delirium accompanies only the daily exacerbations of the fever, and disappears with them, there can be no doubt of the mind's being in a suitable condition, during the intervals, for devising property, but not for transacting other business of importance. The existence of delirium at any period of a disease will be sufficient to throw suspicion on any contracts entered into during such disease; and unless it can be shewn that the delirium was but an occasional symptom and of short duration when it occurred, and that the mind of the patient at other times was perfectly calm and rational, their validity is liable to be destroyed. When these two conditions are reversed, that of delirium being the habitual, and the lucid intervals the occasional state, the mind *may* have sufficient capacity to make a will, but certainly, no other civil act which it might perform ought to be held valid, for the same reason that the acts of imbeciles are avoided. Georget, however, does not hesitate to express his belief, that, under these circumstances, the reason is not so restored that the patient can be declared capable even of making a will, and we readily admit that it is often questionable whether the mind is sufficiently steady and collected to comprehend the relations of property, or appreciate the claims of kindred and friends. But we would not make the disqualification universal, for cases not unfrequently happen in which, after days of constant delirium, reason for a while resumes her dominion and the patient converses with his accustomed fluency and wisdom, describing his feelings, giving directions to his family, and alluding to the past with a clearness and accuracy that leave no doubt on the minds of those around of his perfect sanity. A safer practice probably would be, to be governed in our decision of this point by the circumstances that attend the making of the will, the previous intentions of the testator, and the nature of his disease.[1]

§ 218. The law requires that in this affection, as in mania, the occurrence of lucid intervals should be proved beyond a reasonable doubt, but as delirium is merely an adventitious symptom, and not, like

---

[1] It must be recollected that the question is, not whether the mind possesses its ordinary soundness and vigor, for we know it is always enfeebled, but whether it retains what may be called a testamentary capacity.

mania, the habitual state of the patient, it will be satisfied with much less proof in the former than in the latter affection. Sir John Nicholl has very justly observed, that " in cases of permanent, proper insanity, the proof of a lucid interval is matter of extreme difficulty, and for this among other reasons, namely; that the patient so affected is not unfrequently *rational* to all *outward* appearance, without any real abatement of his malady : so that in truth and substance, he is just as insane, in his apparently rational, as he is in his visible raving fits. But the *apparently* rational intervals of persons, merely delirious, for the most part, are *really* such. Delirium is a fluctuating state of mind, created by temporary excitement ; in the absence of which, to be ascertained by the *appearance* of the patient, the patient is, most commonly, *really* sane. Hence, as also indeed, from their greater presumed frequency in most instances in cases of delirium, the probabilities, *a priori*, in favor of a lucid interval, are infinitely stronger in a case of delirium, than in one of permanent proper insanity ; and the difficulty of proving a lucid interval is less, in the same exact proportion, in the former, than it is in the latter case, and has always been so held by this court." [1]

§ 219. In the case from which the above passage is taken, the testatrix, a widow lady, died of some

---

[1] Judgment in Brogden *v.* Brown, 2 Addams's Rep. 441. If the reader is desirous of extending his knowledge of this subject, he will be well rewarded for a careful perusal of this and the following cases, in which the luminous expositions of Sir J. Nicholl convey their usual pleasure and conviction : Evans *v.* Knight, 1 Addams, 229; Lemann *v.* Bonsall, ibid. 383.

acute disease after an illness of about ten days, during the two or three last of which she was more or
less delirious. Her will was made on the evening of
the day preceding her death, and its validity was
opposed on the ground, that she did not possess a
testamentary capacity at the time of its execution.
The evidence of the two consulting physicians who
visited her about four o'clock, which was but a few
hours prior to the execution of the will, was decidedly unfavorable to her testamentary capacity. One
considered it "doubtful whether she was capable of
making a will, or not ; his opinion rather was, that
she was not." He saw her once or twice afterwards,
when she was "quite delirious and clearly incapable." The other physicians who saw her at four
o'clock, conceived her "quite incapable of any complicated act; undoubtedly of any thing that required
fixed attention, or any exercise of mental faculty."
The attending physician, however, attributed the
delirium to the paroxysms of severe pain suffered by
the deceased, it being scarcely perceptible when
these were absent, and believed that in the intervals
she had perfect capacity. It appeared too that the
will, which had been prepared from instructions just
before received from her, was read over to the deceased, placed before her while she was sitting up in
bed, and subscribed by her in the usual form with a
dash below. The validity of the will was established.

§ 220. In another case, the testator who died on
Friday the 24th of April, of an attack of pneumonia,
during the latter stages of which he had considerable
delirium, made his testamentary dispositions on the

21st. One of the physicians deposed that when he saw the deceased on the 21st, " he was not in a state of sound mind, memory and understanding, or capable of doing any act requiring the exercise of thought, judgment and reflection." Another, who saw him for the first and only time on the 23d, thought it was extremely " improbable that the deceased should have been free from wandering and mental affection, on a day so shortly before he saw him, as the 21st." It appeared, on the other hand, that he gave instructions for a will without any suggestions whatever from the solicitor who reduced them to writing, and that after they were read to him, he approved and subscribed them. It was also deposed by other witnesses, that when the solicitor came and while giving him instructions, he appeared rational and conducted with propriety. The court pronounced in favor of the deceased's testamentary capacity.[1]

§ 221. In cases where the validity of testamentary dispositions is impugned on the ground of mental incapacity produced by delirium, or indeed by any other disorder, it is the practice of the English Ecclesiastical courts, not to confine their attention exclusively to the evidence directly relating to the mental condition of the testator, but to consider all the circumstances connected with the testamentary act ; for the object is not so much to settle the question of soundness or unsoundness in general, as it is in reference to that particular act. The principle is—and

---

[1] Evans v. Knight and Moore, 1 Addams, 229.

it is one that is well-grounded in the common experience of men—that a person may be capable of
testamentary acts, while technically and really unsound, and incapable of doing other acts requiring
much reflection and deliberation. Accordingly, his
testamentary capacity is to be determined, in a great
measure, by the nature of the act itself. If it be
agreeable to instructions or declarations previously
expressed, when unquestionably sound in mind ; if it
be consonant to the general tenor of his affections ;
if it be consistent and coherent, one part with another ; and if it have been obtained by the exercise of
no improper influence ; it will be established, even
though the medical evidence may throw strong doubts
on the capacity of the testator. On the contrary,
when these conditions are absent, or are replaced by
others of an opposite description, it will as generally
be annulled, however plain and positive may be the
evidence in favor of the testator's capacity.[1]

§ 222. In some affections of the head, and they
may be primary or sympathetic, the patient lies in a
comatose state, from which he may be aroused, when
he will recognise persons and answer questions correctly respecting his feelings, but drop asleep again
as soon as they cease to excite him. That the mind
is much embarrassed certainly cannot be doubted,
and it is well known that when the patient recovers,

---

[1] In illustration of these remarks the reader is referred to Cook v.
Goude and Bennet, 1 Haggard, 577 ; King and Thwaits v. Farley, ibid.
502 ; Waters v. Howlett, 3 Haggard, 790 ; Bird v. Bird, 2 Haggard,
142 ; Martin v. Wotton, 1 Lee's Eccl. Rep. 130 ; Bittleston by her guardian v. Clark, 2 Lee, 229 ; Marsh v. Tyrrel, 2 Haggard's Eccl. Rep.,
84.

he has, ordinarily, very little idea of what passed at those times ; indeed, he is generally unconscious of every thing he either said or did. It would be a bold assertion to say that the mind, under these circumstances, is legally capable of making testamentary dispositions, and they ought therefore to receive no favor from courts.[1] In case of injury to the head, it is not uncommon for the patient (after rallying from its immediate effects) to answer questions rationally, to appear collected and intelligent, in short to have fully recovered his senses, though he may subsequently declare that he is utterly unconscious of what were his acts, thoughts or feelings at that time. Few, even among medical men, who observe a person under such circumstances, would have any hesitation in expressing their belief in his testamentary capacity, though the event would show that they had labored under a serious error.

---

[1] Brydges *v.* King, 1 Haggard's Eccl. Rep. 256.

CHAPTER XIII.

DURATION AND CURABILITY OF MADNESS.

§ 223. With the exception of those cases of fatuity that occur at a period more or less remote from birth, mania is the only kind of insanity that admits of a cure ; and though its duration is various, the probability of this event is almost entirely destroyed within a comparatively short space of time. This is abundantly evident from the statistics of madness that have been published from time to time by the heads of various lunatic establishments. Esquirol concludes, on data furnished by the returns of the principal French and English hospitals, that the absolute number of recoveries from madness is about one in three ; and also that the number of recoveries varies from one in four, to one in two or two and a half of the whole number of persons affected. Pritchard regards this computation of recoveries as much below what really takes place under favorable circumstances, and undoubtedly if the cases that occur in private practice were included, the proportion of cases would be much greater, since patients are seldom sent to public establishments until private means, which are oftentimes successful, have been tried for a short time. It would seem indeed from some reports that in recent cases medical treatment is almost as successful, as in those of long standing it is unsuccessful. Dr. Burrowes states the proportion of recent cases cured under his care so high as ninety-one in one hundred, and in the Connecticut Retreat, according to capt. Hall,[1] no less than twenty-one out of twenty-three recent cases recovered.

§ 224. Next to the proportion of recoveries that take place in insanity, the most important question in this connexion is its comparative curability at different periods of the disease. Pinel, in a memoir presented to the Institute in 1800, was led to conclude from a selection of cases expressly chosen for this purpose, that a greater number of recoveries takes place in the first month than in any succeeding one, and that the mean time of the duration of the disease when cured is between five and six months. Esquirol, however, gives a table of recoveries at the Salpetrière during ten years, which shows a little longer term to insanity. Out of two thousand and five patients, twelve hundred and twenty-three were cured, viz., six hundred and four during the first year ; four hundred and ninety-seven in the second ; eighty-six in the third ; and forty-one in the seven succeeding years ; from which it appears that eleven twelfths of the number of cures is obtained within the first two years ; that the mean duration of cases cured is a little short of one year ; and that after the third year, the probability of a cure is scarcely more than one in thirty. M. Desportes states, from observations made at the Bicetre and

---

[1] Travels in North America, vol. 1, p. 316.

Salpetrière, that of the whole number of recoveries
in 1822, 1823, and 1824, seven hundred and forty-
six took place in the first year, and one hundred
and eighteen only from the second to the seventh
year.

§ 225. Recovery from insanity generally takes
place gradually, though occasionally the disease may
suddenly disappear on the occurrence of certain
moral or physical impressions. Pinel relates the
case of a literary gentleman, who, in a paroxysm of
suicidal mania resolved to go and jump into the river.
On arriving at the bridge, he was attacked by robbers, against whom he defended himself vigorously,
beat them off, forgot the purpose of his excursion,
and returned home cured. Dr. Rush relates that one
of his patients, for whom he had recommended gentle
exercise on horseback, was suddenly cured in consequence of the fright experienced from her horse
running away in one of her excursions. He was
stopped by a gate, and when her attendants came
up they found her entirely restored to reason. Several other cases of recovery are related, produced
by a similar cause. Esquirol speaks of having cured
a girl at once by the terror she experienced at the
sight of the actual cautery which he was about to
apply. He also mentions the case of a girl who
after being insane ten years, suddenly ran to her
mother's bed, exclaiming, as she embraced her,
" mother, mother, I am well." She had become
insane in consequence of a suppression of the menses,
which at last made their appearance on the evening
preceding her cure. Pritchard states that several
instances of sudden cure from the same cause have

occurred in some of the English hospitals. Insanity
has been sometimes cured by an attack of fever. A
number of maniacs were once cured, in the Pennsyl-
vania hospital, by a malignant fever which appeared
in that establishment. Direct appeals to the reasoning power have sometimes been followed by immediate recovery. Pinel relates the case of a watch-
maker who became deranged, and believed that he
had been guillotined, and that, in consequence of
the mixing of the heads of other victims, his own
had been replaced by another. When the miracle
of St. Denis was mentioned, who carried his head
under his arm and kissed it as he went, he contended for the possibility of the fact, by appealing
to his own case, when one of his companions burst
into a loud laugh, saying, "What a fool you are ;
how could St. Denis kiss his own head ? was it
with his heel ?" The absurdity of the idea struck
his mind and he never after spoke of the misplace-
ment. Dr. Cox speaks of a patient who believed
that he was the Holy Ghost. Another asked him
"Are there two Holy Ghosts ? how can you be
the Holy Ghost and I be so too ?" He appeared
surprised, and after pausing awhile said, "But
are you the Holy Ghost ?" and when the other
replied "Did you not know that I was ?" he answered, "I did not know it before ; then I cannot
be the Holy Ghost." It is probable that in nearly
if not quite all these cases of sudden recovery, by
means of mental impressions, the disease was declining, and that its termination was hastened only
by these impressions.

§ 226. Partial intellectual mania is said to be cured with much more difficulty than general mania, and the latter is more easily cured when the sequel of some violent cause, than when it has come on gradually from some steadily continued influence. Among the circumstances favorable to recovery may be mentioned a constitution not greatly debilitated by excesses of any kind, good moral and intellectual education, the absence of hereditary predisposition, and an early medical treatment.

227. The above facts and considerations will furnish the data, on which the physician is to form an opinion relative to the duration and curability of any given case of insanity. While in very many cases incurability is certain, and there can be no hesitation in certifying the same, there are none in regard to which we can predict a certain recovery. The utmost we can say in the most favorable cases is, that the patient will probably recover, and the physician cannot be too cautious how he commits his own reputation and the interests and happiness of others by the expression of hasty and positive opinions.[1] Idiocy, imbecility, and senile dementia admit neither of cure nor amelioration, and when mania is of more than two years standing, and especially if other circumstances are not favorable, it may be safely said there is but little hope of cure, but never that the case is

---

[1] If proof be required of the propriety of this warning, the reader will find a memorable one, in Wraxall's (Posthumous Memoirs) lively description of the contradictory statements and dogmatic assertions into which the medical attendants of George III. were betrayed by party zeal, and which resulted in the confusion and disgrace of some respectable physicians.

beyond all hope. When mania comes on in a violent, furious manner, it would be improper to procure the interdiction of the patient, until medical treatment, seclusion, &c. have been tried for a few months, and proved unsuccessful. Neither is this measure always justifiable when the disease is so slight as not to prevent him from going abroad and mingling in the affairs of the world. If the patient however is a merchant, for instance, and continues to engage in the management of his business, immediate interdiction would be required perhaps, to save him from the effects of ruinous contracts.

§ 228. An important feature of insanity in a medico-legal point of view, is its tendency to relapse during convalescence, and to recurrence after being perfectly cured. The general rule is, that a brain which has once been the seat of the maniacal action is far more liable to its recurrence, than one which has not. Many recover the full strength and activity of their mental faculties, but the majority, Pritchard thinks, are curable only to a certain extent. " They remain," says Esquirol, " in such a state of susceptibility that the slightest causes give rise to relapses, and they only preserve their sanity by continuing to live in a house where no mental agitation or inquietude, no unfortunate contingency is likely to fall to their lot, and throw them back to their former state. There are other individuals whose faculties have sustained such a shock, that they are never capable of returning to the sphere which they had held in society. They are perfectly rational, but have not sufficient mental capacity to become again military officers, to conduct commercial affairs, or to fulfil the duties belonging to their appointments." The proportion of cases in which insanity is recurrent, is estimated by different writers at from one tenth to one sixth. In those cases where the mind on recovery regains its usual capability, this disposition to recurrence is by no means so strong, as when it is left in a weak and irritable state, and it diminishes with the length of the interval since the recovery. This feature of insanity should ever be borne in mind by the physician, when required to give his opinion on the propriety of removing the interdiction of an insane patient, who is apparently restored to health. He should seriously consider the risk that he runs, by entering again on the busy scenes of life and enduring the anxiety and excitement attendant on the management of his affairs, of renewing that cerebral irritation which the quiet and repose of seclusion has temporarily subdued. In criminal cases also, it should lead to a thorough and candid investigation of the plea of insanity urged in defence of those who have previously suffered from it, and it should be satisfactorily settled whether or not the circumstances attending the criminal act were likely to reproduce that pathological condition on which insanity depends. If it should prove that they were of that nature, and that the individual had but *recently* recovered from an attack of insanity, then it would indicate a confidence that springs from some other source than a just appreciation of the phenomenon of insanity under consideration, to presume, nevertheless, the continuance of mental soundness and consequently of moral responsibility.

§ 229. It has been already remarked that in most instances, recovery takes place gradually and is completed only after a period, more or less long, of convalescence. Nothing therefore can be more chimerical than the idea of fixing on any precise moment when all disease has departed and perfect health is established ; and yet this is what we are called upon to do when required to determine, as we sometimes are in criminal cases, at what time the accused began to be responsible. To contend that a convalescent maniac may be irresponsible one day and responsible the next, would be no less absurd than to say to one recovering from inflammation of the lungs, that, as he valued his life, he must not leave his room to-day, though to-morrow he might safely expose himself to the severest inclemency of the weather ; and to believe that the former possessed a sound mind, because laboring under no hallucination and attacked by no fits of fury, would be as erroneous, as to consider the respiratory functions of the latter sound and vigorous, because we hear no cough and see no difficulty of breathing. The time that has elapsed since the unequivocal insanity of the accused, is therefore an important element in the determination of his mental soundness. Just as exposure to bad weather, a week after an attack of inflammation of lungs had begun to subside, would be more likely to reproduce the disease, than it would a month afterwards, so the longer the time since an attack of insanity has been apparently cured, the less likely is the cerebral irritation to be renewed by sudden provocations or other causes that tend to produce it. Ample time must be allowed to cover the period of convalescence, and if it be difficult to fix upon the exact duration of this state, so much greater the necessity of caution in determining the responsibility of the accused. Here it is often a merit to doubt, and justice requires that the accused should have the benefit of our doubts.

CHAPTER XIV.

LUCID INTERVALS.

§ 230. It is well known that many diseases—especially of the class called *nervous*—observe a law of periodicity which is not uncommon in the actions of the animal economy. One effect of this curious law consists in an intermission of the outward manifestations of the disease, so complete as to bear the appearance of a perfect cure, and this, in the present state of our knowledge, is all that we can, with certainty, say of it. As to the change that takes place in the organic condition of the part affected, during the intermission, we can at best hazard nothing more than a rude conjecture. We have no warrant for believing that the pathological affection itself entirely disappears with the symptoms that arise from it, and perhaps never shall have, until we are able to explain why, after such disappearance, the tendency of the disease to return at certain intervals should still remain ; or in other words, wherein the final, perfect cure differs from the temporary intermission. But in view of the established fact that organic disease often exists without producing its ordinary symptoms, or revealing itself by any appreciable signs, it seems the more probable supposition, that the pathological condition of the affected organs does not disappear entirely during the intermission, but continues with perhaps a modified intensity.

§ 231. The slightest examination will convince us, that in the most complete intermission of any disease, that affects the whole system to some extent, the patient is far from enjoying sound health, or free from every indication of morbid action. A greater contrast in the matter of health, can scarcely be presented in the same individual, than that between the paroxysm and the intermission of a quotidian fever; yet none will say, after the former has passed off and the patient is no longer shaking with cold nor parched with heat, but is able to arise and give some attention to his duties, that he is entirely well. Better, no doubt, he is; but his mind is weak, his stomach declines its once favorite food, a little exertion overcomes him, a certain *malaise* not easily described pervades his whole system, and which, though not excessively painful, is something very different from the buoyant sensation of health. We are therefore bound to believe, that the disease still exists, though its external aspect has changed. And here it may be as well to remark, that we must not be led by an abuse of language, to attribute *that* to the disease—to the pathological condition—which belongs only to one of its symptoms. When the epileptic, a few days after one of his frightful convulsions, appears to have regained his customary health, no intelligent physician imagines that the proximate cause of this disturbance has vanished with the fit, leaving the organ it affected as sound as ever. The fit itself, which is a mere symptom, is indeed of periodical occurrence, but the pathological condition on which it depends continues, slowly and surely though imperceptibly, to undermine the powers of the constitution. The general expression of all our knowledge on the subject of the intermission of diseases is, then, that certain pathological conditions give rise, among other phenomena, to some that disappear for a time only to recur after an interval of more or less duration.

§ 232. That insanity, or rather mania, is one of the diseases that are subject to this law of periodicity, in some respects, is universally admitted ; but to what extent the law operates, is a point on which there is much diversity of opinion. There are few cases in which we may not observe various periods in their course, when the severity of the symptoms is greatly alleviated ; when calmness takes the place of fury, and a quick and sober demeanor succeeds to noisy and restless agitation ; when reason, driven from her throne, seems to be retracing her steps and struggling for her lost dominion. In all this, however, there is nothing different from what occurs in many, if not the greater proportion of chronic diseases. That the intermissions of mania are ever so complete, that the mind is restored to its original integrity, would seem scarcely probable, from the fact, that the very seat of the pathological changes is the material organ on which the manifestations of the mental phenomena depend. For if the mind be rendered as sound as before the attack, it necessarily follows that the brain is equally restored, since in point of health they stand to each other in the relation of cause and effect. But as there is no proof that such is the case, and as the supposition is not supported by what we do know of pathological actions, we have no right, at present, to conclude that the physical condition on which mania depends is entirely removed during the intermission. We are thus led to scrutinize a little more closely these periodical restorations of the insane mind, or *lucid intervals* as they are called, in order to ascertain if possible, what is the actual state of the mind at these times. But before doing this, it will be proper to show what is understood in law by lucid intervals, as explained by eminent legal authorities.

§ 233. D'Aguesseau, in his pleading in the case of the Abbé d'Orleans, says, "It must not be a superficial tranquillity, a shadow of repose, but on the contrary a profound tranquillity, a real repose ; it must be, not a mere ray of reason, which only makes its absence more apparent when it is gone— not a flash of lightning, which pierces through the darkness only to render it more gloomy and dismal— not a glimmering, which joins the night to the day ; but a perfect light, a lively and continued lustre, a full and entire day interposed between the two separate nights, of the fury which precedes and follows it ; and, to use another image, it is not a deceitful and faithless stillness which follows or forebodes a storm, but a sure and steadfast tranquillity for a time, a real calm, a perfect serenity ; in fine, without looking for so many metaphors to represent our idea, it must be not a mere diminution, a remission of the complaint, but a kind of temporary cure, an intermission so clearly marked, as in every respect to resemble the restoration of health." [1]

---

[1] Pothier on Obligations, by Evans, Appendix, 579.

§ 234. Many years after, Lord Thurlow, in the court of chancery, thus stated his views of the condition of mind necessary to constitute a lucid interval. "By a perfect interval, I do not mean a cooler moment, an abatement of pain or violence, or of a higher state of torture—a mind relieved from excessive pressure; but an interval in which the mind, having thrown off the disease, had recovered its general habit."[1]

§ 235. Here then is the lucid interval as clearly and minutely described, as a profusion of words and metaphors could do it, and as such it was belived by these authorities, no doubt, to have a real existence. In the early periods of the English law, the doctrine of lucid intervals was universally admitted, and they seem to have been considered not a rare, but a very common phenomenon of mental derangement. Indeed, judging from the frequent mention made of them in all discussions on the subject, and from the fact that *idiocy* and *lunacy*—which latter was considered, as its name would lead us to suspect, to be of an intermittent nature—constituted, for a long time, the only division of mental diseases, it will not perhaps be too strong an expression to say, that they were viewed as an essential feature of mania. This, however, was in the infancy of medical science, before the phenomena of mania—which, until recently, has always been less understood than other diseases—were thoroughly and accurately observed, and the men whose ideas we have just

---

[1] Attorney General *v.* Parnther, 3 Brown's Ch. Cases, 234.

quoted had no practical acquaintance with the disorder whose phases they so vividly described. Before adopting their views, then, it will be proper to inquire how far they are supported by the investigations of modern medical science.

§ 236. While the doctrine of lucid intervals, as explained by the language above-quoted, is upheld by scarcely a single eminent name in the medical profession, we find that their existence is either denied altogether, or they are regarded as being only a remission, instead of an intermission of the disease; an abatement of the severity of the symptoms, not a temporary cure. Mr. Haslam, who is no mean authority on any question connected with insanity, emphatically declares, that, "as a constant observer of this disease for more than twenty-five years, I cannot affirm that the lunatics, with whom I have had daily intercourse, have manifested alternations of insanity and reason. They may at intervals become more tranquil, and less disposed to obtrude their distempered fancies into notice. For a time their minds may be less active, and the succession of their thoughts consequently more deliberate ; they may endeavor to effect some desirable purpose, and artfully conceal their real opinions, but they have not abandoned, nor renounced their distempered notions. It is as unnecessary to repeat that a few coherent sentences do not constitute the sanity of the intellect; as that the sounding of one or two notes of a keyed instrument could ascertain it to be in tune." [1]

---

[1] Medical Jurisprudence of Insanity, p. 224.

§ 237. Strong as this testimony is, and true, no doubt, as the result of an individual's experience, it cannot be denied that others, whose opportunities have not been less than Mr. Haslam's, have distinctly recognised the existence of intervals, when the patient not only becomes more tranquil and reserved, but is conscious of having been mad, and perceives the folly of the delusions that have engrossed his thoughts. But so far are they from attributing to the mind, during their occurrence, that degree of soundness which is contended for in the passages above quoted, that they have taken great care to inculcate a very different doctrine. " The mania, says Foderè, " which is accompanied by fury, is very often periodical; that is, as if granting an occasional truce to the patient, it appears only at certain epochs, between which he enjoys all his reason, and seems to conduct and judge in all respects like other men, if we except in regard to certain ideas, the thought of which may at any time occasion a fresh paroxysm." [1]

§ 238. Georget, while he speaks of lucid intervals " as returns to reason," is careful to add, that, " in this state, patients frequently experience some degree of *malaise*, of some disturbance of their ideas, and weakness of mind, which prevents them from fixing their attention, for any length of time, on a particular subject ; from engaging in reading, writing or attending to their affairs." [2]

---

[1] De Médecine Légale, t. i., p. 205, § 140.
[2] Des Maladies Mentales, p. 46.

§ 239. "There are few cases of mania or melancholy," says Dr. Reid, "where the light of reason does not now and then shine out between the clouds. In fevers of the mind, as well as those of the body, there occur frequent intermissions. But the mere interruption of a disorder is not to be mistaken for its cure, or its ultimate conclusion. Little stress ought to be laid upon those occasional and uncertain disentanglements of intellect, in which the patient is for a time only extricated from the labyrinth of his morbid hallucinations. Madmen may show, at starts, more sense than ordinary men." [1]

§ 240. Dr. Combe, in one of the most philosophical treatises on Insanity, which the present century has produced, expresses similar views in the most explicit and forcible language. "But however calm and rational the patient may appear to be, during the lucid intervals, as they are called, and while enjoying the quietude of domestic society, or the limited range of a well-regulated asylum, it must never be supposed, that he is in as perfect possession of his senses, as if he had never been ill. In ordinary circumstances and under ordinary excitement, his perceptions may be accurate, and his judgment perfectly sound ; but a degree of irritability of brain remains behind, which renders him unable to withstand any unusual emotion, any sudden provocation, or any unexpected and pressing emergency. Were not this the case, it is manifest that he would

---

[1] Essays on Hypochondriacal and other Nervous Affections: 21st Essay.

not be more liable to a fresh paroxysm, than if he had never been attacked. And the opposite is notoriously the fact; for relapses are always to be dreaded, not only after a lucid interval, but even after perfect recovery. And it is but just as well as proper to keep this in mind, as it has too often happened, that the lunatic has been visited with the heaviest responsibility, for acts committed during such an interval, which, previous to the first attack of the disease, he would have shrunk from with horror." [1]

§ 241. With the views of these distinguished observers before us, what are we to think of the doctrine, that in the lucid intervals the mind is restored to its natural strength and soundness; that it is capable of as great intellectual exertions, and of holding as tight a rein over the passions ; that it is as able to resist foreign influence and to act on its own determinations, with its ordinary prudence and forecast ; that having thrown off the disease, it has recovered its general habit," or that it has undergone a " temporary cure ? " Sounder pathology was never written, than is contained in the extract from Dr. Combe, and no physician, who has been much conversant with the insane, will be disposed to question its correctness. Foderè goes a step farther and hazards a theory which is plausible at least, to explain the pathological causes that produce this alternation of paroxysms and lucid intervals. The former state, he considers, is attended by an

---

[1] Observations on Mental Derangement, p. 241.

excessive plethora of the blood-vessels of the brain, and the latter by a relaxed, atonic condition of these vessels, which is an effect of their previous forcible distention. In this condition they are liable to be suddenly engorged by exciting causes, such as intemperance in eating or drinking, anger, violent exercise, insolation, &c. ; or in consequence of a certain predisposition of constitution.[1] Indeed, it is well known, that the return of the paroxysms is often retarded by regulated diet, bleeding, quiet, seclusion, kind treatment, and the absence of the above-named stimuli. It is thus shown, conclusively, that in every lucid interval, there remains some unsoundness of the material organ of the mind, which may be designated generally as a morbid irritability, which, on the application of the slightest exciting cause, may produce an outbreak of mania in all its original severity.

§ 242. The principle of law, which holds the civil responsibilities of the insane to be unimpaired during the lucid interval, we are willing to admit, is generally correct. It should be the duty of courts, however, to view their acts done at such times with the most watchful jealousy, because their minds, though left free from all delusion, are nevertheless weak and irritable, and they are easily induced by the arts of unprincipled men to enter into transactions, the folly of which would have been obvious enough to them before they began to be insane. It is proper too that the proof of the lucid interval should come up

---

[1] De Médecine Légale, t. i., p. 208, § 140.

to the requirements of distinguished legal authorities—of those, to go no farther—to whom we have
already referred. D'Aguesseau, in continuation of
the remarks above quoted, declares, that, "as it is
impossible to judge in a moment of the quality of
an interval, it is requisite that there should be a
sufficient length of time for giving a perfect assur-
rance of the temporary re-establishment of reason,
which it is not possible to define in general, and
which depends upon the different kinds of fury, but
it is certain there must be a time and a considerable
time." Lord Thurlow also, on the same occasion,
which elicited his views of the nature of the lucid
interval, says, that "the evidence in support of the
allegation of a lucid interval, after derangement at
any period has been established, should be as strong
and demonstrative of such fact, as where the object
of the proof is to establish derangement.[1] The evi-

---

[1] It appears from a note in 1 Beck's Med. Juris. 586, that Lord Eldon
dissented from this proposition and thus stated his objections to it to
Lord Thurlow himself. "I have seen you exercising the duties of
lord chancellor with ample sufficiency of mind and understanding,
and with the greatest ability. Now if providence should afflict you
with a fever, which should have the effect of taking away that sanity
of mind for a considerable time (for it does not signify whether it is
the disease insanity, or a fever that makes you insane), would any one
say, that it required such very strong evidence to show that your mind
was restored to the power of performing such an act as making a will—
an act, to the performance of which a person of ordinary intelligence
is competent?" We are not informed how this objection struck Lord
Thurlow, but we trust that no reader of the present work will be at a
loss to perceive its weakness for a moment. It does signify every thing,
whether it is the disease insanity or a fever that makes one insane, for
the delirium of fever is but a casual symptom of that disease, and,
together with the pathological condition that gave rise to it, is presumed to disappear with the main disorder on which it depends. This

dence in such a case, applying to stated intervals, ought to go to the state and habit of the person, and not to the accidental interview of any individual, or to the degree of self-possession in any particular act." We shall presently see how far the practice of the courts has accorded with these views.

§ 243. In cases of wills, the English ecclesiastical courts, in a commendable respect for the sacred character of testamentary acts, have assumed considerable latitude, and, no doubt, very properly, in their construction of lucid intervals; but occasionally they have gone farther than even the truths of pathology will warrant.

In Cartwright v. Cartwright,[2] the deceased, a single woman, made her will on the 14th of August, 1775, which will was contested on the ground of the insanity of the testator. " It was proved in general, says the court, that her habit and condition of body, and her manner, for several months before the date

---

is the ordinary course of nature. On the contrary, mental alienation is the essential, the pathognomonic, and oftentimes, the only clearly discernible symptom of mania, and its disappearance furnishes the only intimation perhaps that we have, of the cure of this disease. Thus, our means of deciding this point being so small, we are necessarily led to require stronger evidence of their certainty, than of the restoration of the mind in fever, because the latter is confirmed by a multitude of symptoms. Recovery from an attack of fever is a phenomenon that any one can see, but not such is recovery from an attack of mania; because, though the insane delusions or conduct by which it was manifested may disappear, it remains to be determined in every case, whether they are not purposely concealed from observation, or proper opportunity has been offered to the patient to bring them forward. Just as the existence of mania requires stronger proof than that of the delirium of fever, so does recovery from the former require stronger proof than recovery from the latter.

[2] 1 Phillimore's Reports, 90.

of the will, was that of a person afflicted with many
of the worst symptoms of that dreadful disease, and
continued so certainly after making the will." It
appears from the evidence, that for some time previous to the date of the will, she was very importu-
nate for the use of pen, ink, and paper, which however were withheld from her by the direction of her
physician, Dr. Battie, who was eminent for his
knowledge and treatment of mental disorders. Her
importunity continuing, he at length consented, in
order to quiet and pacify her, that she might have
them, observing that it did not signify what she might
write, as she was not fit to make a proper use of
pen, ink, and paper. These being carried to her,
her hands which had been constantly tied were
loosed, and she sat down to a bureau to write. Her
attendants, who were watching her outside the door,
saw her write on several pieces of paper in succession, which she tore up and threw into the grate,
walking up and down the room in a wild and furious
manner, and muttering to herself. After one or
two hours spent in this manner, she finally succeeded
in writing a will that suited her, though it occupied
but a few lines. Such are the facts that have any
bearing on the point at issue. It was decided by the
court, Sir William Wynne, that she had a lucid interval, while making the will, the validity of which
was consequently established. The grounds of this
decision were, that the will made a natural and consistent distribution of her property, and, in short,
that it was "a rational act rationally done;" hence
it was to be inferred, that her mind was visited by a
lucid interval, at the moment of making it. For,

says the court, "I think the strongest and best proof, that can arise as to a lucid interval, is that which arises from the act itself; that I look upon as the thing to be first examined, and if it can be proved and established, that it is a rational act rationally done, the whole case is proved." It seems to have occurred to the court, that some catenation must be made out between such an act and a lucid interval; and it being in evidence, that, at times, she would converse rationally, we have the following deductions therefrom. "If she could converse rationally, that is a lucid interval; and that she did so and had lucid intervals, I think is completely established." The fact is, that the court, throughout its whole judgment, confounded testamentary capacity with a lucid interval, without once seeming to be aware that though the will might be a rational act, and therefore perhaps valid,[1] it by no means followed, that a lucid interval had taken place. What it considered as such here scarcely amounted to the kind of re-

---

[1] This is in accordance with the law as laid down by Swinburne. "If a lunatic person, or one that is beside himself at sometimes but not continually, make his testament, and it is not known whether the same were made while he was of sound mind and memory or no, then, in case the testament be so conceived as thereby no argument of phrensy or folly can be gathered, it is to be presumed that the same was made during the time of his calm and clear intermissions, and so the testament shall be adjudged good, yea although it cannot be proved that the testator useth to have any clear and quiet intermissions at all, yet nevertheless, I suppose that if the testament be wisely and orderly framed, the same ought to be accepted for a lawful instrument." Part ii. sec. 3. So on the other hand, he adds, "if there be in it a mixture of wisdom and folly, it is to be presumed that the same was made during the testator's phrensy, even if there be but one word sounding to folly."

mission described by Mr. Haslam (§ 236), for not a single fact appears in the evidence, from which we can infer any alteration whatever in the state of her disease. True, the court thought, that her reason had returned, because, though released from the confinement of a straight-waistcoat, and trusted with a candle, she did no mischief and did not abuse her liberty ; but such things would have little weight with medical men, especially at the present day. Nothing indeed can be more chimerical, because so utterly contradicted by all that we know of insanity, than this idea of a lucid interval of a few minutes duration suddenly interposed amid years of mania, and as suddenly disappearing.[1] The point particularly insisted upon by the judge is, that she would sometimes converse rationally, as indeed most insane people do. " If," he says, " she had particular subjects or topics in her mind, and at such times would converse rationally upon them, and when those topics were out of her mind would fly into outrages of phrensy and extravagance, does that all show that at the former time she was deprived of rational capacity ? " He does not seem to be aware, that it would not be surprising if wills should sometimes be found among the number.

---

[1] Its consequences seem to render it as pernicious as it is absurd. In the trial of Hadfield for shooting at the king, Lord Kenyon, after admitting that he was insane both before and after the act, and that it was improbable he had recovered his senses in the interim, declared, that " were they to run into nicety, proof might be demanded of his insanity, at the precise moment when the act was committed ! " as if such proof were not utterly beyond the reach of human means.

§ 244. We have no fault to find with the principle of law, which makes these wills valid, but we would have the ground on which such validity is established, distinctly understood to be the character of the act, not the condition of the testator's mind ; and if, in the above case, the court had been contented with proving the will to be a rational act and thence inferring testamentary capacity, there would have been nothing to complain of. It is important that on subjects like medical jurisprudence, language should be used with strict adherence to its original and proper signification ; and therefore when a *lucid interval* is defined by competent authority to be a "temporary cure" of the disease, a recovery of the mind's general habit, the occurrence of which must be proved by the "state and habit," of the person, observed during a sufficient length of time, we have to complain, that the term is applied to a mere remission in the violence of the symptoms, which lasts but a few minutes and is proved by a single coherent act.

§ 245. The construction here put upon the lucid interval, not only conflicts with the opinions of the eminent authorities we have quoted, but has not been countenanced by subsequent decisions even in the ecclesiastical courts. In a recent case, where the testamentary acts of an insane person were propounded by the executors, who endeavored to prove the occurrence of a lucid interval at the time of their execution, the court, Sir John Nicholl, decided that the proof was not sufficient, though it was unquestionably stronger than in the case of Cartwright *v.* Cartwright. The surgeon of the testator who saw him once within the period,—a little more than ten

months—that included the two wills in question, and
commenced a frequent attendance on him between
two and three months afterwards, deposed, that on
none of these occasions did he exhibit any symptoms
of insanity, but "conducted himself, and talked and
discoursed in a rational manner, and was in the full
possession of his mental faculties." The solicitor
who took the instructions for the last will, considered him of sound mind, and deposed that neither
of the witnesses treated him as a person of deranged
intellect or of unsound mind. In the testamentary
dispositions themselves, there was nothing to negative the idea of the most perfect soundness of mind.
In view of the fact, however, that the testator was
so deranged that he was attended by a keeper from
a lunatic asylum, till within a few months of the
date of the first will, and frequently manifested absurd delusions during the period including both wills,
the above proof was not considered as sufficient for
the purpose, reasoning upon the general principles
of insanity. "It is clear," said the court, "that
persons essentially insane may be calm, may do acts,
hold conversations, and even pass in general society
as perfectly sane. It often requires close examination by persons skilled in the disorder, to discover
and ascertain whether or not the mental derangement is removed, and the mind again become perfectly sound. When there is calmness, when there
is rationality on ordinary subjects, those who see the
party usually conclude that his recovery is perfect.
. . . . . Where there is not actual recovery, and a
return to the management of himself and his con-

cerns by the unfortunate individual, the proof of a lucid interval is extremely difficult."[1]

§ 246. It has been admitted, that, with certain reservations, the civil responsibilities of the insane are unimpaired during the lucid interval, because the mind is sufficiently restored to enable the individual to act with tolerable discretion in his civil relations. In respect to crime, however, the matter is altogether different, for reasons that will not be without their force, we trust, to those who have attentively considered the preceding remarks. These reasons are, that the crimes which are alleged to have been committed in a lucid interval, are generally the result of the momentary excitement produced by sudden provocations; that these provocations put an end to the temporary cure, by immediately reproducing that pathological condition of the brain called *irritation*, and that this irritation is the essential cause of mental derangement, which absolves from all the legal consequences of crime. The conclusion is, therefore, that we ought never perhaps to convict for a crime committed during the lucid interval, because there is every probability, that the individual was under the influence of that cerebral irritation, which makes a man insane. The difference between a person in the lucid interval and one who has never been insane, on which we particularly

---

[1] Groom and Thomas *v.* Thomas and Thomas, 2 Hagg. Eccl. Rep. 433: In White *v.* Driver, 1 Phillimore, 84, however, a lucid interval was held to be established, on much less proof than was offered in the above case, though far more certainly than was admitted in Cartwright *v.* Cartwright.

insist, is, that, while in the latter, provocations stimu-
late the passions to the highest degree of which they
are capable in a state of health, though still more or
less under his control, they produce in the former
a pathological change which deprives him of every
thing like moral liberty. It is scarcely necessary to
do more than barely state these views, since their
correctness seems to have been universally recognised in practice, not a single case having occurred,
so far as can be ascertained, where a person has
been convicted of crime committed during a lucid
interval. Burdened as the criminal law is with false
principles on the subject of insanity, the time has
gone by when juries will return a verdict of *guilty*
against one who is admitted to have been insane,
within a short period of time before the criminal act
with which he is charged.

CHAPTER XV.

SIMULATED INSANITY.

§ 247. The supposed insurmountable difficulty of distinguishing between feigned and real insanity has conduced, probably more than all other causes together, to bind the legal profession to the most rigid construction and application of the common law relative to this disease, and is always put forward in objection to the more humane doctrines that have been inculcated in the present work. That such difficulty has been experienced, and given rise to much perplexity and mistake, cannot be denied ; but it is to be considered, whether it has not arisen, less from the obscurity of the subject, than from the imperfect means that have been generally applied to its elucidation. The opinions of physicians, which are ordinarily taken in doubtful cases, have been received with a deference, that was warranted more by general professional reputation, than by superior knowledge of this particular disease. The treatment of insanity is now so much confined to the heads of extensive establishments in which its subjects are congregated, that opportunities for studying it are comparatively limited in ordinary practice, so that a physician may be justly celebrated in the knowledge and treatment of other diseases, and at the same time be poorly qualified to decide upon questions relative to insanity, in which every effort is made to perplex and mystify his mind. This truth cannot be disguised, and though physicians are frequently reluctant to recognise what indeed cannot be very discreditable to themselves, and are disposed to act on the popular notion that all medical subjects are equally familiar to them, this is no reason why courts and juries should ever forget it. Nothing indeed requires a severer exercise of a physician's knowledge and tact, than a case of simulated insanity, but the same might be said with quite as much truth, of other diseases that men have been led to feign, but which, nevertheless, are every day investigated and understood.

§ 248. The workings of an insane mind—such as attract the popular notice—are apparently so confused and discordant, so wild and unnatural, as to have given rise to the notion as prevalent as it is unfounded, that insanity may be easily imitated. The method that is in madness, the constant and consistent reference to the predominant idea, which the practised observer detects amid the greatest irregularity of conduct and language, is one of those essential features in the disease, which is generally overlooked, or at least very unsuccessfully imitated. Those who have been longest acquainted with the manners of the insane, and whose practical acquaintance with the disease furnishes the most satisfactory guaranty of the correctness of their opinions, assure us that insanity is not easily feigned, and consequently that no attempt at imposition can long escape the efforts of one properly qualified to expose it. Georget does not believe, "that a person who has not made the insane a subject of study, can simulate madness so as to deceive a physician well acquainted with the disease."[1]   Mr. Haslam declares, that, "to sustain the character of a paroxysm of active insanity, would require a continuity of exertion beyond the power of a sane person."[2]   Dr. Conolly affirms, "that he can hardly imagine a case which would be proof against an efficient system of observation."[3]   Another writer, while admitting that attempts to deceive are sometimes successful, on account of the imperfect knowledge of the operations of the mind in health and disease possessed by medical men in general, observes, however, that when we consider the "very peculiar complex phenomena which characterize true madness, and reflect on the general ignorance of those who attempt to imitate them, we have no right to expect such a finished picture as could impose on persons well acquainted with the real disease."[4]   With such authority before us, to urge as an objection against the free admission of insanity in excuse for crime, the extreme difficulty of detecting attempts to feign it, can no longer be any thing more than the plea of ignorance or indolence. The only effect such difficulty should have on the minds of those, who are to form their opinions by the evidence they hear, should be to impress them with a stronger sense of the necessity of an intimate, practical acquaintance with insanity on the part of

---

[1] Des Maladies Mentales, p. 60.
[2] Medical Jurisprudence of Insanity, p. 322.
[3] Inquiry concerning the indications of Insanity, 467.
[4] Cyclopædia of Practical Medicine: Article, Feigned Diseases, p. 146.

the medical witness, and convince them that without this qualification, the testimony of the physician is but little better than that of any one else. We shall now notice those features of insanity the knowledge of which, either from their not being generally obvious, or not easily simulated, will enable us to distinguish the reality from the imitation ; and as general mania is oftener chosen than the other form of mental derangement, for the purpose of deception, we shall begin with that.

§ 249. The grand fault committed by impostors is, that in their anxiety to produce an imitation that shall deceive, they overdo the character they assume, and present nothing but a clumsy caricature. The representations of mania put forth in the works of novelists and poets, with a few such admirable exceptions as the Lear and Hamlet of Shakspeare, are, of all their attempts to copy nature, the least like their model. If then men of education, who may have had some opportunities for observing the disease, have after all so imperfect a picture of its phenomena in their mind, what success could be expected from the attempts of persons who, for the most part, assume their task upon the spur of the occasion with little preparation, and who have derived all their ideas of madness from a casual visit to an insane hospital, or from observing the manœuvres of some roving maniac? With such, insanity is but another name for wildness, fury, and unlimited irregularity, and consequently, under the thin disguise they assume, there can readily be detected a constant effort to impress on the beholder the conviction they are anxious to produce by the mere force of noise and disorder. The really

mad are, generally speaking, not readily recognised
as such by a stranger, and they retain so much of
the rational as to require an effort to detect the impairment of their faculties.   In feigned cases, all this
is very different ; the person is determined that his
derangement shall not be overlooked for want of
numerous and obvious manifestations of its existence.
Under this impression, the impostor is constantly
guilty of some word or act grossly inconsistent with
real insanity, and affording an easy clew to the truth
of the case.

§ 250. Generally speaking, a maniac has no difficulty in remembering his friends and acquaintances,
the places he has been accustomed to frequent,
names, dates, and events, and the occurrences of
his life. The ordinary relations of things are, with
some exceptions, as easily and clearly perceived as
ever, and his discrimination of characters seems to be
marked by his usual shrewdness. His replies to
questions, though they may sometimes indicate delusion or extravagant notions, generally have some
relation to the subject, and show that it has occupied
his attention. Now, a person simulating mania will
frequently deny all knowledge of men or things, with
whom he has always been familiar, especially whenever he imagines that such ignorance, if believed,
may be considered as a proof of his innocence. The
very names, dates and transactions, with which he
has been most lately and intimately conversant, he
will, for the same reason, refuse to remember, while
the real madman will, seldom, if ever, forget them,
in whatever shapes they may appear to his mind, or
with whatever delusions they may be connected. His

distorted perceptions may transform his humble dwelling into a princely castle, and the people about him
into generals and courtiers ready to execute his slightest orders, but he will never deny that he has an
abode, nor forget the existence or names of those
whose station and duties he has so entirely mistaken.
Grant his premises, and oftentimes nothing can be
urged against the conclusions of the madman's reasoning; but in simulated madness, the common error
is to imagine that nothing must be remembered correctly, and that the more inconsistent and absurd the
discourse, the better is the attempt at deception sustained. In partial mania, the subject of delusion,
though it may frequently change, completely occupies the mind for a longer or shorter period, and the
patient's discourse will always have some kind of
relation to it. When this form of the disease is
simulated, the hallucinations are not only frequently
changing, but when questioned concerning them, the
person is more likely than not to shape his answer
without any reference to the subject, and embrace
the opportunity to introduce a new insane idea. In
simulated madness there is also a certain hesitation
and appearance of premeditation in the succession of
ideas, however incoherent, very different from the
abruptness and rapidity, with which in real madness,
the train of thought is changed. This, of itself, is
sufficient, in the majority of cases, to reveal the
deception to the practised observer of insanity. In
simulated mania, the impostor, when requested to
repeat his disordered ideas, will generally do it correctly, as if anxious that none of his ravings should
escape attention, or be forgotten ; while the genuine

patient will be apt to wander from the track, or introduce ideas that had not presented themselves before. The following case, which we find in one of Georget's works, will furnish an appropriate illustration of the foregoing remarks, and give an insight into the devices of imposture, to be obtained only from examples.

§ 251. "Jean-Pierre, aged forty-three years, formerly a notary, was brought before the court of assizes of Paris, on the 21st February, 1824, accused of crimes and misconduct, in which cunning and bad faith had been prominently conspicuous. He had already been condemned for forgery ; and was now accused of forgery, swindling, and incendiarism. When examined after his arrest, he answered with precision every question that was put to him. But about a month after, he would no longer explain himself, talked incoherently, and finally gave way to acts of fury, breaking and destroying every thing that came in his way, and throwing the furniture out of the window. At the suggestion of the medical men who were called to examine him, Jean-Pierre was sent to the Bicêtre, to be more closely observed. There he became acquainted with another pretended lunatic, accused also of forgery and swindling, and retained in that house for the same purpose—that of being observed by the physicians. One night a violent fire broke out at the Bicêtre, in three different places at once, in one of the buildings occupied by the insane, which circumstance led to the suspicion that the fire was the effect of malice. The next day it was discovered that the two supposed madmen had disappeared. Jean-Pierre hid himself in Paris in a

house where his wife was employed and where he
was again arrested. Immediately on his escape from
the Bicêtre, he wrote a very sensible letter to one of
his friends ; but scarcely had he been taken when he
again assumed the character of a madman. From
the indictment, it appears that the person who ran
away at the same time with Jean-Pierre, confessed
that they had formed the plan of escaping in company, and that they had profited by the occurrence
of the fire to put it into execution. He also said that
Jean-Pierre had made him swear to reveal nothing ;
and he seems to have told as a secret to one of the
officers of La Force, that the fire was the work of
Jean-Pierre.

All the witnesses, who had had any transactions
with or known any thing of the accused before his
arrest, deposed that he always seemed to them rational enough, and even very intelligent in business.
One of the prisoners in La Force, who occasionally
met and talked with Jean-Pierre, declared that his
conversation was often very incoherent, and that in
some of the phases of the moon, his mind was much
excited. But these observations were made *after*
the arrest of the accused. It was his conduct at the
trial, however, which, more than any thing else,
proved that the madness of Jean-Pierre was only
assumed ; for there is perhaps not one of his answers
that would have been given by a madman. The following are a few of them.

Q. How old are you ?—A. Twenty-six years, (he
was forty-three).

Q. Have you ever had any business with Messrs.
Pellene and Desgranges (two of his dupes) ?—A. I
don't know them.

Q. Do you acknowledge the pretended notarial deed which you gave this witness?—*A.* I do not understand this.

Q. You have acknowledged this deed before the commissary of police?—*A.* It is possible.

Q. Why, the day of your arrest, did you tear up the bill for three thousand eight hundred francs?—*A.* I don't recollect.

Q. You stated in your previous examinations, that it was because the bill had been paid.—*A.* It is possible.

To many other of his own depositions the accused answered, in like manner, that he did not recollect any thing about them.

Q. Do you know this witness (the portress of the house he lived in)?—*A.* I don't know that woman.

Q. Can you point out any person who was confined in La Force with you and who can give any account of your then state of mind?—*A.* I don't understand this.

Q. You made your escape from the Bicêtre?—*A.* Was you there?

Q. At what hour did you escape?—*A.* At midnight—one o'clock—three o'clock.

Q. What road did you take?—*A.* That of Meaux en Brie. (He took that of Normandy).

Q. Can you tell us who set the Bicêtre on fire?—*A.* I do not know what you mean.

Q. You wrote a letter to captain Froyoff the day after your escape from the Bicêtre?—*A.* I did not write that letter. (It was his own handwriting).

When charged with setting fire to the Bicêtre, Jean-Pierre uttered the most horrid imprecations, and incessantly interrupted his counsel and the advocate-general in their pleadings, with contradictions, ridiculous remarks, and curses.

§ 252. In commenting on this case, Georget observes, that "among those madmen who have not entirely lost their senses, and Jean-Pierre is not one of this kind, probably not one will be found who would mistake the persons with whom he has been connected,—who would not understand what a notarial act is,—who would have forgotten his actions,— who would not know what was meant when a memorable event was recalled to him, and who would make such singular answers as those we have quoted. The latter appear as so many contradictions to those who are accustomed to observe the insane. When people have completely lost their reason, they either do not reply to questions at all, or branch off to subjects that have no relation to the questions addressed to them. I have seen patients whose understanding was reduced to a few isolated sensations, and who recognised their parents and friends, and called them by name. Some, it is true, can recognise nobody, but they certainly would not have returned all the answers above-mentioned, and their mental disorder would have been otherwise characterized." [1]

§ 253. The change that takes place in the moral character of the insane, in their affections and desires, furnishes an excellent test of the genuineness of any particular case, inasmuch as this fact hardly enters

---

[1] **Des Maladies Mentales, p. 61.**

into the popular notions of this disease. Perhaps no character of mania, general or partial, is more common than that inversion of feeling, which is manifested in reference to every person or thing, that comes within the circle of the domestic and friendly relations. The feelings of the parent, child, and spouse, seem to be completely eradicated, while family loses its ties, home its endearments, and friends their kind and soothing influence. Suspicion takes the place of confiding trust ; jealousy, of love; and fierce and hostile demeanor, of grace and suavity of manner. As the severity of the disease abates, the current of the affections begins to resume its ordinary direction, and no indication of improvement is more to be relied on, than manifestations of regard for those to whom they are bound by ties of intimacy or relationship. The impostor is seldom aware of these facts, and generally evinces no settled diminution of his attachment to his family or friends. He does not scruple to show his ordinary fondness for his children or parents, or if he happen to be aware of the trait of insanity here described, and has suppressed all such displays, the first menace of injury to these objects of his regard, is sufficient to tear away his disguise and disclose the rational and affectionate man. In the conspiracies and hostile plans that constantly perplex the madman's brain, his intimate friends bear the most prominent part, while the impostor always pitches upon those as the disturbers of his peace, with whom he has had some previous disagreement, or at least, no particular intimacy.

§ 254. In real mania there is generally more or less insensibility to the ordinary proprieties and decencies of life, insomuch that those who were formerly noted for the purity of their manners, freely indulge in obscene language and filthy practices. Indeed, it seldom happens that in general mania the patient preserves the natural propriety of his conversation and manners, and this departure from the ordinary character will go far to distinguish the real from the simulated disease.

§ 255. If, as we have endeavored to prove elsewhere, mania arises from cerebral disorder, we might reasonably expect to find it giving rise to physical disturbances of more or less moment, and accordingly, in most cases, it actually is manifested by various pathological symptoms which no device of imposture can ever imitate. To say nothing of the wildness of the eye, and a certain strangeness of expression, as easily recognised when once impressed on the mind, as it is difficult to describe, there is some degree of febrile action which it requires no very labored examination to discover. The pulse will be found more frequent than in health, and when this increased frequency is observed in doubtful cases, it will furnish a strong collateral proof of the genuineness of the mental disorder. In the case of a criminal condemned to be executed who was suspected of feigning madness, the opinion of the late Dr. Rush was requested, and when that critical observer of disease found the pulse twenty beats more frequent than in the natural state, he decided, chiefly on the strength of this fact, that the prisoner was really mad.[1] Of course, it is not to be understood

---

[1] Introductory Lectures, p. 369.

that whenever the pulse remains at the natural standard, the plea of madness is fictitious, nor vice versa;
it is mentioned merely as a valuable means in connexion with others, of arriving at correct conclusions in doubtful cases.

§ 256. Sleeplessness, which is so common in mania,
is another of those symptoms, the presence of which
would furnish conclusive proof of real insanity, and
though its absence would hardly warrant the contrary conclusion, it would certainly produce strong
suspicions, and thus give additional weight to less
prominent symptoms. In real mania, the patient
will be days and even weeks without sleep, while
the simulator, if aware of this feature of the disease,
will be observed, when faithfully watched, not to
protract his sleeplessness to any thing like the period
which it commonly remains in the real disease. In
fact, in spite of all his efforts, sound sleep will invariably overtake him before the second or third day.
Impostors almost always attempt to imitate the nocturnal restlessness and disorder of maniacs, but the
imitation is as different from the reality, as the occasional disturbance by sound slumbers can make it,—
a difference which it would require but little watching to establish.

§ 257. Perhaps there is nothing which of itself
furnishes a better test in doubtful cases, than the
manner of their invasion. Well-marked, real mania
almost never occurs suddenly, but is preceded, as
has been elsewhere noticed, by a course of preliminary symptoms which occupy a period of more or
less duration, and which, though they do not always
suggest to the beholder the suspicion of derange-

ment, will, when the disease has become indubita-.
bly established, be recollected as having appeared
strange and unaccountable. In simulated insanity,
on the contrary, the invasion is as sudden as is most
frequently the occasion that leads to it. The simulator being unaware of the progressive nature of the
invasion, suddenly, in the midst of health, startles
his attendants by an outbreak of the most extravagantly wild and furious conduct, while the minutest
inquiries will fail to establish the previous existence
of any precursory symptoms. No instance of strange,
or eccentric conduct or language, not the slightest
departure from the individual's natural thoughts and
affections, or manner of manifesting them, nor any
indication of bodily derangement, will have been
observed by those who were about his person.
When, therefore, the disease has come on in this
manner, it may be safely concluded, if there be any
other the least ground of suspicion, that the case
is one of simulation.

§ 258. When other tests fail, the habits and constitutional peculiarities of the individual may sometimes furnish us with valuable information. If, for
instance, the person have indulged in intemperate
drinking, the occurrence of mental derangement
would be no unnatural sequel to the sudden abstinence from intoxicating drinks to which prisoners
are generally subjected. If insanity have been a
disease of his family, more especially if it have been
manifested in former periods of his life, when there
existed no motive for deception, there must be additional evidence strong enough to counterbalance the
presumption drawn from this fact, to induce the be-

lief that the case is one of simulation. When too the person is well known to possess an irritable, nervous temperament, inordinately excited by moral or physical causes, this fact will very justly raise a bias in his favor, and lead us to require so much additional weight in the proofs of deception, and its force will be strengthened by the consideration, that the circumstances in which he has been recently placed, are of the very kind most calculated to produce the effect to which he is thus predisposed.

§ 259. In real mania there is always an extreme irritability of temper which makes the person impatient of the least contradiction, and is constantly breaking out into furious gusts of passion, as sudden as the apparent causes are inadequate to account for them. This feature of mania is not easily imitated, and nothing less than long personal observation of the insane, joined with no inconsiderable powers of mimicry, would enable the simulator to arrive at even an approximation to the reality. When therefore, the pretended madman maintains his temper under various little annoyances and contradictions, or only displays a clumsily-enacted passion, it may be pretty safely concluded that he is feigning the disease.

Persons feigning mania lack the bold, unflinching look of real maniacs; they never look the physician steadily in the face, nor allow him to fix their eye, and on being accused, their change of countenance plainly betrays that they are conscious of the nature of the charge. Dr. Hennen speaks of an instance, where a person feigning madness confessed that he

could not support the inquiring glance of the physician who examined him.[1]

§ 260. It is a well-known fact that in real madness, the system becomes singularly insensible to the
power of certain medicines—particularly emetics,
drastic purgatives, and opium. A dose of the last
article, which would not procure a moment's sleep to
a real maniac, would completely overpower the simulator, and in doubtful cases the result of this experi-
ment should be entitled to considerable weight. The
same may also be said of experiments on the effect of
tartar emetic.

§ 261. Partial insanity, in consequence of the
superior difficulty of the attempt, is much less frequently simulated, and with a much smaller degree
of success, than the general form of the disease.
Those who undertake it "are deficient," says Haslam, "in the presiding principle, the ruling delusion, the unfounded aversions, and causeless attach-
ments which characterize insanity—they are unable
to mimic the solemn dignity of characteristic madness, nor recur to those associations which mark this
disorder ; and they will want the peculiarity of look
which so strongly impresses an experienced observer."[2]   The mental and physical peculiarities of
partial mania are of a kind that do not obtrude themselves on the observation, and instead of loudly pro-
claiming the presence of a crazed condition and soli-
citing the attention of the beholder, some investigation
is required before they are discovered.   All this is

---

[1] Principles of Military Surgery, p. 364.
[2] Medical Jurisprudence of Insanity, p. 323.

contrary to the purposes of the simulator, which
require that an immediate and powerful impression
should be made on those in whose charge he is placed.
If however, in consequence of ignorance or presumption, these difficulties are unknown or under-estimat-
ed, and the task of simulating partial madness is
assumed, we have only to bear in mind the characteristic features of the affection, to detect the coun-
terfeit almost at a glance.   In real monomania the
patient never troubles himself to make the subject
of his delusion square with other notions with which
it has more or less relation, and the spectator wonders
that he can possibly help observing the inconsistency
of his ideas, and that when pointed out to him, he
should seem to be indifferent to or unaware of this
fact.   In the simulator, on the contrary, the experienced physician will detect an unceasing endeavor
to soften down the palpable absurdity of his delusions, or reconcile them with correct and rational
notions.   This too obvious anxiety to produce an
impression, strongly contrasts with the reserve and
indifference of the real disorder, and will, of itself,
furnish almost conclusive proof of simulation.   "A
real monomaniac," says Marc, "is strongly prejudiced in favor of his opinions, the slightest contradiction excites his temper, while the simulator readily
overlooks this essential point in his part, if the contradiction be skilfully managed.   The taciturnity
peculiar to the real subjects of monomania, frequently
leaves simulators at fault, since the complaints of the
latter when sure of being seen or heard, and their
repugnance at dwelling in solitude are not met with,

or at least, not in the same degree, in the others." [1]
In addition to these characteristics of this form of
mental derangement, it may be remarked that many
of the peculiarities diagnostic of general mania, are
no less so of partial mania, such as sleeplessness,
insensibility to opium, and irritability of temper.

§ 262. Idiocy and imbecility are sometimes simulated, and the imitation would be very likely to deceive those not practically acquainted with these mental affections ; but the history of the individual and
his physical constitution furnish such conclusive proof
of the imposture, that the attempt is less successful
than when the other forms of insanity are selected
for simulation.   In genuine cases, if the affection be
congenital, the history of the patient or form of the
head will establish this fact.   If it have occurred at
an after period of life, the circumstances that have
occasioned it may be learned from the acquaintances
of the patient.   If the form of the head present
nothing unnatural, it is to be supposed that the mental deficiency, if there be any in reality, is of the
acquired kind, so that if the person pretends to have
been from birth in his present condition, this of itself
would be sufficient proof of imposition.   If however,
he is capable of referring his mental deficiency to
the influence of any particular adventitious causes,
the practitioner can determine for himself, in a certain measure, how far these alleged causes could
have contributed to produce the condition in question.   If they appear to be plainly and palpably

---

[1] Dictionnaire de Medicine: Article, Alienès.

inadequate, he has a right to conclude that the person is acting the part of an impostor. It sometimes happens that the simulator has had frequent opportunities of observing the manners of an idiot or imbecile, and possessing some powers of mimicry, is able to give a pretty faithful copy of the example he has studied. But there is a stupid vacant cast of countenance in these affections, which it is difficult, if not impossible to imitate well enough to deceive one much conversant with this class of beings. Full as difficult is it to imitate the unfixed, uncertain, expressionless look, and the frequently and abruptly fluctuating train of their ideas. Zacchias offers as a test of idiocy the pusillanimous and submissive character of its subjects, but it is now well known that most idiots are liable, on provocation, to gusts of furious, brutal passion, as transient as they are sudden. Imbecility presents such a diversity of mental deficiency both in kind and degree, that the simulation of it will baffle the scrutiny of the observer, who is not prepared for his task by a considerable acquaintance with the phenomena of the imbecile mind. In the first degree of real imbecility there is a singular mixture of stupidity and shrewdness, in the fraudulent imitation of which, the vigilant observer may discover proofs of simulation. He will find that on points directly involving the interest of the simulator, he will display the full endowment of the shrewdness compatible with this condition, while he reserves his stupidity for occasions where his own interests are not particularly concerned. In replying to the questions put to him, he will be careful, amid all his display of imbecility, to say nothing likely to favor a belief of his guilt in the matter which has led him to assume the part of an impostor. What he says is intended to leave an impression favorable to his innocence, and this effect he will endeavor to produce as far as he dares. When therefore, the person replies to inquiries in such a manner as to criminate himself, it may be pretty safely concluded that the imbecility is genuine ; and though the converse of this rule may not be equally true, yet if the whole tenor of his replies has an exculpatory turn, strong ground of suspicion at least is afforded, that all is not right. Imbecility in the first degree will seldom be counterfeited however, from the simple fact, that the real affection seldom annuls the criminal responsibilities of those who are acknowledged to be its subjects.

§ 263. Senile dementia may be simulated by aged persons, but it is so imperfectly known as a distinct form of insanity, that its peculiar features would probably be mingled with those of general and partial mania, and thus lead to an easy detection. If the physician will steadily bear in mind that senile dementia is essentially characterized by deficiency of mental excitement, he will not be long in arriving at the truth in doubtful cases, for the simulator will inevitably indulge in hallucinations, and perform physical movements indicative of excessive mental excitement. The principal points that distinguish this affection from mania may be briefly recapitulated. In senile dementia, the delusions are based on some previous event of life, and though irrational, are not always absurd. The memory decays, first, relative to recent events, and finally, to every thing it had previously stored up. The senses lose their acuteness ; the power of recognising persons, places and things, fails at last, and has gone for ever ; and one looks in vain for the least exertion of thought. The whole conduct and language are indicative of complete childishness; and in this second childhood, the necessity of vigilance to prevent the miserable patient from injuring himself or others, is no less imperative than in the first. In mania the delusions are generally absurd as well as irrational ; the memory manifests no decay, unless we except on subjects that relate to the predominant idea ; the strength and accuracy of the senses are unimpaired ; persons and things are as readily recognised as ever ; and occasionally the mind flashes forth with more than its usual power and vividness. At times the character assumes its natural manliness and dignity, and the individual conducts with a propriety and discretion scarcely to be distinguished from those of perfect soundness of mind. Bearing in mind these characteristic differences which are so little known to any but medical men, we cannot be easily deceived by the best managed attempt at simulating senile dementia.

§ 264. Homicidal insanity, when the fact of its existence shall be generally recognised, will undoubtedly, be often falsely pleaded in excuse for crime, and the task imposed on the physician in such cases, will be sometimes a difficult and a delicate one. The characteristic and distinctive features of this affection have been elsewhere stated (§ 162), and it is to a knowledge of them we are to look for the means of detecting its counterfeits ; and though our investigation may occasionally result only in doubt and uncertainty, yet generally speaking, when rightly conducted, it will lead us to the truth.

§ 265. Besides a knowledge of the symptoms of insanity, which will enable the physician to detect its simulation, his own ingenuity may often contrive some plan for outwitting the pretender, and entrapping him in his own toils. To perform the part of an insane person, carrying through its numerous and complicated phases, requires an endowment of the imitative powers, seldom bestowed on any, least of all, on those who would have occasion to use it for such purposes, so that the measure of ingenuity by which it is maintained, is scarcely ever a match for the devices which a shrewd and vigilant physican has always at hand. In the case of a girl feigning mania, Foderè informed the keeper in her presence, that if she were not better the next day, he should apply a hot iron between her shoulders. This immediately produced a decided amendment. In the Cyclopædia of Practical Medicine, is related the case of a sailor, whose simulated madness was manifested by a vehement desire to throw himself overboard, which, after being prevented for some time, he was at last permitted to do ; immediately on reaching the water, however, he swam vigorously and called loudly for a boat.[1] A device frequently resorted to, is to mention in the hearing of the person some symptom of madness which is easily imitated, as not being present ; at a subsequent examination, if the disease is

---

[1] Article, Feigned Diseases.

feigned, this symptom will certainly be observed, whether it is or is not a symptom of madness. In the English naval and military service, where the medical officer is often called on to deal with feigned insanity, punishment is much resorted to, on the principle that if the affection be counterfeited, it will be more efficacious than any thing else in restoring the impostor to his right mind ; and if real, it will do good by acting as a powerful derivative. If the latter part of the alternative were true, nothing certainly could be more proper than sound flagellation ; but if any thing, more surely than another, will push a case of mental derangement beyond the reach of curative means, it is corporeal punishment. The misery thus produced is poorly compensated by the few cases of imposture which it may be the means of detecting. In the following case, however, where this kind of treatment was used, it would undoubtedly have been very proper had the disorder actually existed ; and as it may serve as a guide to the practitioner in similar instances, a brief notice of it may not be out of place in this connexion.

Jean Gerard, a bold villain, murdered a woman at Lyons in 1829. Immediately after being arrested, he ceased to speak altogether, and appeared to be in a state of fatuity. He laid nearly motionless in his bed, and when food was brought, his attendants raised him up and it was given to him in that position. His hearing also seemed to be affected. The physicians who were directed to examine him, concluded that if this were actually what it appeared to be, a paralysis of the nerves of the tongue and ear, the actual cautery applied to the soles of the feet, would be a proper remedy. It being used however, for several days, without any success, it was agreed to apply it to the neck. For two days, no effect was produced, but on the third, while preparations were making for its application, Gerard evinced some signs of repugnance to it, and after some urging, he spoke, declaring his innocence of the crime of which he was charged. His simulation was thus exposed.[1]

§ 266. When required to examine and report upon cases of suspected simulation, the medical man cannot be too cautious in arriving at his final decision. The judgment is not to be determined by any single symptom however striking, but every pathological indication, every possible motive to action, in short the whole moral, intellectual and physical history of the individual should be faithfully studied, before we venture to make up our definite opinion. Ample time should be demanded for this purpose, and unless it be granted, the physician would be justified in declining altogether the duty assigned him. Opportunities must be provided of observing the simulator, when, thinking himself not watched, he throws off the guise he has assumed (which he will do at such times), and returns to his own proper character. The physician should never forget, however, the extreme perseverance and vigilance with which these people manage their impositions, and not be too easily induced to regard them favorably in consequence of the results which such opportunities may sometimes furnish. For they will often suppose they

---

[1] Annales D'Hygiène Publique, vol. ii. p. 392.

are watched at times when they have no means of knowing whether they are so or not. Foderè speaks of a girl, undoubtedly a simulator, who committed every kind of indecency in her cell; and another case is related of some French prisoners of war, who carried " their simulation to so exquisite a height, as to eat their own excrement, even when shut up in their cells, suspecting that they might be overlooked." [1] In suspected cases, therefore, the persons should be strictly, and as far as possible, secretly watched, in order that in their moments of forgetfulness or sense of security, they may be seen laying aside their false colors, and suddenly assuming their natural manners. That this will happen sooner or later in every case, there cannot be a doubt, for the mind will instinctively seek relief from the painful exertion and sense of restraint, rendered necessary by an elaborate attempt at deception, by throwing off the disguise that has been adopted, and again returning to its natural condition. Again we caution the practitioner not to be in haste to form his opinion, but to wait long and patiently, for opportunities that may shed new light on the difficulties before him.

---

[1] Cyclopædia of Practical Medicine; Article, Feigned Diseases.

CHAPTER XVI.

CONCEALED INSANITY.

§ 267. It sometimes happens, that when maniacs have learned what notions of theirs are accounted insane by others, and have understanding enough left to appreciate the consequences of their mental condition, they endeavor to conceal it, for the purpose of avoiding the effect of those measures which the law prescribes. If the address and ingenuity which they then manifest have occasionally succeeded in baffling the scrutiny of the most practised experts, it is not strange that common observers should have been frequently deceived, and that some of the medical profession even, with a knowledge of this fact before their eyes, should have been outwitted by their manœuvres. When it is considered, that the insanity of many consists in a few insane notions, which do not to all appearance affect their general conduct and conversation, the difficulty of concealing it, by professing to have renounced their belief in these notions, is perhaps not greater than that which attends the accomplishment of most of their designs. Their task too is materially lessened, it is to be recollected, by the prevalent error, that madness is inseparable from boisterous behavior and complete disorder of the ideas. At the commencement of the French Revolution, when the mob broke into the lunatic hospitals, for the purpose of liberating those among their inmates whom they supposed to be unjustly confined, many recounted their wrongs so clearly and connectedly, that they were deemed at once to be victims of oppression, and ordered to be released. Their conduct, on being set free, soon convinced these enlightened champions of their race, that those who had put them in confinement, had, what they themselves had not, some reason for their measures. Lord Eldon once related that after repeated conferences and much conversation with a lunatic, he was persuaded of the soundness of his understanding, and prevailed on Lord Thurlow to supersede the commission. The lunatic, calling immediately afterwards on his counsel to thank him for his exertions, convinced him in five minutes, that the worst thing he could have done for his client, was to get rid of the commission.[1] In another place (§ 21), will be found a case which well illustrates the adroitness and perseverance, with which maniacs will sometimes conceal their mental derangement.

§ 268. In England and in this country, the choice of the means for establishing the existence of insanity when concealed, is left to individual sagacity. This, no doubt, is sufficient, where great practical acquaintance with insanity readily suggests the course best adapted to each particular case, but the great majority of medical men will feel the need of some system or order of proceeding, that will sim-

---

[1] *Ex parte* Holyland, 11 Vesey's Reports, 11.

plify their inquiries and render them more efficient. The French arrange their means into three general divisions or classes, which are made use of, each in succession, when the preceding class has failed of its object. They are called the *interrogatory*, the *continued observation*, and the *inquest*, and as no better arrangement has ever been offered, it may be well to describe it ; and it may be added in passing, that it would materially conduce to our success in inquiries of this kind, if they were always pursued in the course here indicated.

§ 269. *Interrogatory.*—The interrogatory embraces only those means of information, which are applicable in a personal interview with the patient. After learning generally his moral and intellectual character, his education and habits of living, the duration and nature of his mental delusion (if it can be ascertained from his acquaintances), and the state of his relations to others, and after observing the expression of his countenance, his demeanor and general appearance, we may proceed to a direct examination of his case. In the first place, it is necessary to lull his suspicions and remove his distrust, as far as possible, by a free and courteous deportment, and an air of kindness and unaffected interest in his welfare. He should then be engaged in conversation, which should lead him by easy and imperceptible transitions to the particular subject on which his mind is deranged ; and the manner in which he treats it should be carefully observed, for if he is really insane on that point, he will probably avow it ; while if he is not so, he will take the opportunity to declare his disbelief in the notions imputed to him, and bring forward various considerations to support the truth of his assertions. He should be led to speak of his relatives and friends, especially if they have taken any part in provoking his interdiction, or otherwise interfered in his affairs, and here he will need all his self-control to restrain himself from the angry and revengeful feelings which he entertains towards them. When confined in hospitals or other lunatic establishments, we should not fail to ask how they like their situation, and what they think of their companions; for Georget observes that many even of those the least deranged, are such poor observers, or have so little penetration, that they are ignorant of the nature of their abode, and the character of those around them. When the mental disorder is that of imbecility or dementia, we must not confine our questions to the simple topics of their present condition or feelings, for they may be able to answer them clearly and rationally, when subjects requiring a little more reflection or exertion of memory, may be far beyond their comprehension. It not unfrequently happens that the mental deficiency affects the faculties of the mind unequally, degrading some to the scale of idiocy and leaving others in a state of tolerable strength and developement. When, therefore, the capacity of the mind is in question, whether for interdiction or any other purpose, we must not fail to test the soundness of all the faculties, by inquiries relative to the objects with which they are respectively concerned, since, if satisfied with a partial examination, we may grossly deceive ourselves and injure the interests of others. True, this requires a knowledge of the mental constitution not possessed by every one charged with this kind of investigation ; but the deficiency, common as it is, proves nothing against the importance of this knowledge.

§ 270. The importance of the above suggestions is strikingly shown by the case of a young man, B——, noticed by Dr. Abercrombie,[1] and Dr. Combe,[2] which occasioned much trouble and litigation to the parties concerned. This person was educated for the church, and had made such proficiency in the study of Latin and Greek, that, for several years, he acted as a tutor in these languages. He also displayed great keenness and adroitness in driving a bargain. When, however, his mind was directed to those studies and topics, which require the exercise of the higher powers of the intellect, he was found so deficient that he utterly failed in his second examination before the presbytery, in which his reasoning powers were tasked, though the first, which was in the languages, he passed successfully and creditably. It was found, too, that he was incapable of comprehending the relations of business, or even performing the ordinary duties of life. Accordingly, it appeared in the course of the law-proceedings, that those witnesses who knew him only as a linguist or a purchaser, did not hesitate to pronounce him an able, clever man ; while those who had business transactions with him that called his reflective powers into action, had no doubt whatever of his imbecility.

---

[1] On the Intellectual Powers.
[2] On Mental Derangement, p. 244.

§ 271. The interrogatory is sometimes sufficient of itself, to establish the existence of madness; but it oftener fails of accomplishing its purpose, and we are obliged to resort to other means. General moral mania will inevitably elude its scrutiny, this kind of derangement being exclusively manifested in the conduct, for the folly and extravagance of which clear and plausible reasons are always at hand. No definite conclusion in favor of the mental soundness of the individual in question, can be drawn from the result of the interrogatory, unless confirmed by those of the subsequent measures. The correctness of this rule was strongly contended for, even in the time of D'Aguesseau, who declares that however wise and rational under the interrogatory, yet if the fact of insanity is proved by a multitude of particular *acts* and the general tenor of conduct, interdiction must be pronounced.[1]

§ 272. *Continued observation.*—A systematic course of observations continued for some time, may establish the fact of insanity in doubtful cases, after several personal interviews have completely failed. Opportunities, therefore, should be demanded for visiting the patient freely and frequently; for watching him at times when he supposes himself unobserved; and for exercising a general surveillance over his conduct and conversation. Those about him should be enjoined to watch his movements, and he should often, but cautiously, be led to speak of the motives of those who are anxious to prove his insanity. It

---

[1] Oeuvres Completes, t. iii. p. 592.

often happens too, that those who are most successful in concealing every indication of disordered mind,
in their conversation, will betray themselves the moment they commit their thoughts to paper. They
should be induced, therefore, to write letters to their
friends describing their present situation, and to prepare statements of their wrongs and grievances, and
thus we may be readily furnished with instances of
incoherence and folly, which the patient had self-
command enough to withhold, when put on his guard
by questions which he knows well enough are designed to entrap him. " The rapid transitions and
odd unions of discordant subjects, the relations of
things which have not happened, and could not have
happened, are in many cases very remarkable ; and
a forgetfulness of common modes of spelling, or of
the arrangement of the letters of words well-known,
will be evinced by maniacs who have been well
educated, and who would commit no such mistakes
but for their malady." [1]

§ 273. *Inquest.*—When the above means fail, our
inquiries must take a wider range and be directed
to the previous history of the patient, as made known
to us by the testimony of friends and relatives, and
those who have been connected with him in business,
or had any other good opportunity of becoming acquainted with his mental condition. " The *Inquest*,"
says Georget, "consists in collecting information
respecting the patient's condition before and after
the presumed disease, and the causes suspected to

---

[1] Conolly : Inquiry concerning the Indications of Insanity, p. 469.

have impaired his mind. For this purpose, we consult his writings, and recur to the testimony of those who have been about him and conversed with him; who have been able to observe him closely and to witness his insane actions and irrational discourse. We should be particularly careful however to require of witnesses, facts rather than opinions.[1] We should ascertain if madness be a disease of the family ; if he have already evinced a degree of singularity in his moral and intellectual character, or exaltation of any kind ; if he have been exposed to the influence of powerful causes, such as chagrins, severe and repeated crosses, reverses of fortune, &c. ; if, without any real motive, he has manifested any change of his habits, tastes, or affections ; in short, we should inquire into all those circumstances which so frequently precede the developement."[2] We are to look into his business transactions, his management of family affairs, his conduct in the domestic and social relations, and the part he has taken in public scenes and duties. His letters and written communications should be closely scrutinized, especially those that have any reference to the state of his health, or to the legal measures that have been taken against him, for here we may meet with incoherent and foolish ideas, that we have found nowhere else. In short, no source of information likely to enlighten us on the subject of the patient's mental condition, should be suffered to go unexplored. If the means thus

---

[1] See Hathorn *v.* King, 8 Mass. Reports, 371.
Des Maladies Mentales, p. 57.

indicated are faithfully used—if the whole life of the individual have passed in review before us, and after all, we are unable to prove the patient's insanity beyond a doubt, we are bound to conclude that his mind is sound, or at least, *that he is not a proper subject of legal interference.* This conclusion will be no less proper, even though we still entertain some doubt of his mental soundness, for if he have sufficient self-control and penetration to enable him to conceal his mental impairments and conduct himself rationally, but little harm will probably arise from leaving him at present to his own discretion.

CHAPTER XVII.

SUICIDE.

§ 274. At the present day the subject of suicide is deprived of much of the medico-legal importance which it once possessed. Still, however, as questions occasionally come up in which dispositions of property are made to depend on the judicial views which are formed respecting its relations to mental derangement, it is highly proper that mistakes should not be committed from a want of correct notions of its nature. With all the light on the subject which the researches of modern inquirers have elicited, many probably are yet unable to answer understandingly the question so often started, whether suicide is always or ever the result of insanity. It may be proper, therefore, to lay before the reader the present state of our knowledge on this subject, in order that he may have the materials for forming correct and well-grounded opinions respecting it.

§ 275. To the healthy and well-balanced mind, suicide appears so strange and unaccountable a phenomenon, that many distinguished writers have inconsiderately regarded it as in all cases, the effect of mental derangement; while, by many others, it has, with still less reason, been viewed as always the act of a sound, rational mind. Neither of these views can be supported by an impartial consideration of all the facts, and the truth probably lies between the two extremes. Suicides may be divided into two classes founded upon the different causes or circumstances by which they are actuated. The first includes those who have deliberately committed the act from the force of moral motives alone ; the second, those who have been affected with some pathological condition of the brain, excited or not by moral motives.

§ 276. If it be considered that life is not the only nor perhaps the best gift we have received from the author of our being, it ought not to appear strange that men should sometimes be willing to relinquish it for the sake of securing a good, or avoiding an evil. We know well enough that life is not so dear that it will not be readily sacrificed, when all that makes it worth retaining is taken away. The intrepid Roman chose rather to fall on his own sword, than survive the liberties of his country or live an ignominious life ; and reverses of fortune which hurl men from the pinnacles of wealth or power, or the certain prospect of infamy and the world's scorn, are no very inadequate motives for terminating one's existence. In these cases, the person, no doubt, may act from error of judgment, and thus be guilty of foolish and stupid conduct, but we have no right to confound such error with unsoundness of mind. Inasmuch as the prospect before him may be such that it will appear to his mind more painful to live than to die, it is not to be wondered at, if, for want of courage to bear up against the ills that threaten to overwhelm him, and battle it to the last, he should prefer the latter ; for, after all, the choice might indicate less folly than that which often characterizes the conduct of men.   True, the motive may seem sometimes totally inadequate to lead to such a determination, when in reality it may be the only and sufficient motive ; and, this, probably, must always continue to be one of the mysterious facts in our constitution, that the termination of our existence, from which we instinctively shrink with feelings of horror, should so often be voluntarily hastened from the most trivial and insignificant motives.   No doubt the mental disturbance is always great, but the same may be affirmed of all cases where crime is committed under the excitement of strong passions, and therefore is in itself no proof of insanity.   It cannot be denied, however, that the cases are comparatively few in regard to which it would be safe to affirm, that the excitement of the organic action of the brain and nervous system, which accompanies this perturbation of mind, had not transcended the limits of health and passed into real pathological irritation. Among these few we can have no hesitation in placing the case of the pair of youths noticed by Mrs. Trollope, who, after dining sumptuously at a fashionable restaurant at the expense of their entertainer, went to their lodgings, and suffocated themselves together in the same bed ;[1] or that of suicidal clubs, the members of which bind themselves to die by their own hands within an appointed time.   Men, who, with cultivated intellects and refined passions, entertain only the meanest conceptions of the great moral

---

[1] Paris and the Parisians.

purposes of life, are ready to terminate their existence the moment it ceases to impart its usual zest to
sensual gratification. Here, self-destruction is obviously, not the effect of physical disease, but of moral
depravity. But how are we to account for those instances of *juvenile* suicide so often recorded, where
the dreadful propensity is excited by the most trivial
causes ? Burrows speaks of a girl, but little over
ten years of age, who, on being reproved for some
trifling indiscretion, cried and sobbed bitterly, went
up stairs and hung herself in a pair of cotton braces;
and of another, eleven years old, who drowned herself for fear of a simple correction.[1] A French
journal has lately reported the case of a boy twelve
years old, who hung himself by fastening his hand-
kerchief to a nail in the wall, and passing a loop of
it around his neck, for no other reason, than because
he had been shut up in his room and allowed only
dry bread, as a punishment for breaking his father's
watch. The same journal gives another case of
suicide committed by a boy eleven years old, for
being reproved by his father; and several more of a
similar description are also recorded.[2] In these
cases, the moral causes seem altogether inadequate
to excite the suicidal propensity, without first producing some serious physical disturbance, for here
are none of those motives for self-destruction which
have just beeen mentioned, as influencing the adult
mind.

---

[1] Commentaries on Insanity, p. 440.
[2] Medico-Chirurgical Review, N. S. vol. xxvii. p. 212.

§ 277. That suicide is often committed under the impulse of mental derangement, even when mental derangement would not otherwise have been suspected, is a doctrine that was long since taught by some medical writers, and has been confirmed beyond the shadow of a doubt, by the researches of recent inquirers. The propensity to suicide connected with an obviously melancholic disposition, is now universally recognised as a form of monomania, for its symptoms are plainly indicative of cerebral derangement. These patients labor under a constant melancholy, conjuring up the darkest prospects, and presaging nothing but evil fortune. They have been guilty of some sin, real or imaginary, which they believe to be of the most heinous nature, and thenceforth there is no more happiness nor comfort in the world for them. They imagine their friends are constantly watching their movements and engaged in machinations against them, or silently neglecting and despising them. At one time, morose and taciturn; at another, uttering the most bitter complaints, weeping and traversing the room, as if in extreme mental anguish. If their thoughts take a religious turn, they imagine they have committed the unpardonable sin, that their prayers are rejected, that the Saviour turns away his face from their sight, and that the miseries of the damned are to be their everlasting portion. This unquiet and melancholic mood will occasionally give way to short periods of comparative cheerfulness, when the clouds seem to be breaking away, and the individual approximating to his natural character. Their nervous system is weak and irritable, the circulation is quickened, the digestion more or less impaired, the secretions, especially the biliary, more or less deficient, or vitiated, and the mind is incapable of continued exertion. After this state has continued for some time, the mental derangement becomes more prominent, and the wretched victim begins to see visions and hear strange voices, and believes that he has communications from superior beings. All this time the idea of self-destruction is frequently, if not constantly before the mind, and unless the patient be narrowly watched, he will finally succeed, after various attempts, in accomplishing his purpose.

§ 278. The suicidal propensity here described is universally attributed to pathological causes; but there is, besides, a large class of cases, in which no insanity of mind or body has been observed or suspected, though we have good reason to believe its existence. That one may be so harassed with the ills of life, as to deem it best to rid himself at once of both, is not perhaps very strange; but when a person apparently in good health, and surrounded with every thing that can make life dear to him, deliberately destroys himself without any visible cause, no balancing of motives, or scrutiny of private circumstances, can satisfactorily explain it, and we are obliged to consider it as a form of partial moral mania. Within a few years past, the attention of the medical profession has been directed to this subject, and their researches have abundantly established the fact, that the efficient cause is some pathological change, or physical peculiarity, not in every case easily defined or understood, but none the less certain on that account.

§ 279. Sometimes this monomania is attended apparently by no physical or moral disorder, the individual being driven by mere impulse to self-destruction, without being able to assign any reason therefor, real or imaginary. He feels that he is urged on by an impulse he can neither account for nor resist, deplores his sad condition, and beseeches his friends to protect him from himself. In another class of cases, some powerful physical or moral impression only is needed, to call the suicidal propensity into fatal activity. The wonderful effect of mental influences on diseases of the bodily organs, is so common a fact, that we have no rational ground for disbelieving a similar kind of agency in the production of this phenomenon. The distinguished accoucheur, who attended the princess Charlotte in her fatal confinement, observed a pair of pistols in the room to which he had retired for repose,—the sight of which was sufficient, to a mind harassed by long and anxious attendance, and overwhelmed, as it were, by the responsibilities of his situation, to provoke a desire—which he may never have felt before—to die by his own hands. The case of Sir Samuel Romilly, who committed suicide immediately after sustaining a severe domestic bereavement, strongly shows how far the propensity to commit this act is beyond the control of moral principle or christian virtue, even when, as it was with him, previously contemplated and conditionally determined upon.

§ 280. Among the features which ally the propensity to suicide with ordinary mania, is that of its hereditary disposition. Dr. Gall knew several families in which the suicidal propensity prevailed through several generations. Among the cases he mentions, is the following very remarkable one. "The Sieur Ganthier, the owner of various houses built without the barriers of Paris, to be used as entrepôts of goods, left seven children and a fortune of about two millions of francs to be divided among them. All remained at Paris or in the neighborhood, and preserved their patrimony; some even increased it by commercial speculations. None of them met with any real misfortunes, but all enjoyed good health, a competency, and general esteem. All however, were possessed with a rage for suicide, and all seven succumbed to it within the space of thirty or forty years. Some hanged, some drowned themselves, and others blew out their brains. One of the first two had invited sixteen persons to dine with him one Sunday. The company collected, the dinner was served, and the guests were at the table. The master of the house was called, but did not answer,—he was found hanging in the garret. Scarcely an hour before, he was quietly giving orders to the servants, and chatting with his friends. The last, the owner of a house in the rue de Richelieu, having raised his house two stories, became frightened at the expense, imagined himself ruined, and was anxious to kill himself. Thrice they prevented him, but soon after he was found dead, shot by a pistol. The estate, after all the debts were paid, amounted to three hundred thousand francs, and he might have been forty-five years old at the time of his death.

"In the family of M. N. * * *, the great-grandfather, the grandfather, and the father committed suicide." [1]

§ 281. Fabret, whose researches have thrown much light on this affection, believes that it is more disposed to be hereditary than any other kind of insanity. He saw a mother and her daughter attacked with the suicidal melancholy, and the grandmother of the latter was at Charenton for the same cause. An individual, he says, committed suicide in Paris ; his brother who came to attend the funeral, cried out on seeing the body—" What fatality ! My father and uncle both destroyed themselves ; my brother has imitated their example ; and twenty times during my journey hither, I thought of throwing myself into the Seine." [2]

§ 282. Gall also relates the case of a dyer of a very taciturn humor, who had five sons and a daughter. The eldest son, after being settled in a prosperous business with a family around him, succeeded, after many attempts, in killing himself by jumping from the third story of his house. The second son, who was rather taciturn, had some domestic troubles, lost part of his fortune at play, and strangled himself at the age of thirty-five. The third threw himself from the window into his garden, but did not hurt himself ; he pretended he was trying to fly. The fourth tried one day to fire a pistol down his throat, but was prevented. The fifth was of a bilious, melancholic temperament, quiet, and devoted to business ; he and his sister shew no signs of being

---

[1] Functions of the brain, vol. iv. p. 213.
[2] Sur la Hypochondria et Suicide.

affected with their brother's malady.   One of their cousins committed suicide.[1]

§ 283. Like other kinds of mental derangement, the suicidal propensity undergoes occasional exacerbations, from the influence of the seasons, periodical congestions, &c.   The patient, perhaps, may have thrown off some of the gloom which overshadowed his mind, resumed a portion of his ordinary cheerfulness and interest in his affairs, courted the company of his friends, and thus excited strong expectations of a perfect cure, when suddenly his malady breaks out afresh ; the sentiments are again perverted, the judgment disturbed, his breast torn with anguish and despair, and the utmost watchfulness is necessary to prevent him from accomplishing his fatal designs.

§ 284. Another trait which the suicidal propensity possesses in common with some nervous diseases, though not insanity, is its disposition to prevail epidemically, as it were, in consequence of that law of our constitution, not well understood, called sympathy.   It is a matter of common observation, that the occurrence of one case of suicide is followed, oftener than not, by one or more in the same community.   In a sitting of the Academy of Medicine at Paris a few years since, it was mentioned by M. Costel that a soldier at the Hotel des Invalids having hanged himself on a post, his example was followed in a short time, by twelve other invalids, and that by removing this fatal post, the suicidal epidemic was arrested.

---

[1] Op. cit. sup. vol. iv. p. 216.

It is related that thirteen hundred people destroyed themselves in Versailles in 1793 ; and that in one year, 1506, sixty perished by their own hands in Rouen.[1]

§ 285. The analogies, thus presented between the suicidal propensity and insanity or other nervous diseases in its symptoms, are also strengthened by the pathological changes observed after death. In the larger proportion of instances where examination is made, the brain or abdominal viscera are found to have suffered organic lesions, more or less extensive, which, when confined to the latter, have affected the mind by sympathetic irritation. Even in those cases where the fatal act was preceded by no indications of disease, or other symptoms that excited suspicions that the individual was tired of life, dissection has often revealed the most serious disease, which must have existed for some time previous to death. True, the most careful dissection will sometimes fail of revealing the slightest deviation from the healthy structure, and it is not necessary to the support of the above views of the nature of this affection, that it always should. For here, as in mania, sometimes the pathological change may not have gone beyond its primary stage, that of simple irritation, which is not appreciable to the senses, but the existence of which we are bound to believe on the strength of the symptoms.

---

[1] Burrows's Commentaries on Insanity, p. 438.

CHAPTER XVIII.

LEGAL CONSEQUENCES OF SUICIDE.

§ 286. By the common law of England, a *felo de se* forfeited all chattels, real or personal, which he had in his own right, and various other property, and his will became void as to personal property.[1] Such severity has been generally avoided by the almost universal practice of coroners' juries returning an inquest of insanity. At present, the fact of suicide has no other importance, than what it derives from its connexion with the mental derangement, which may be supposed to have given rise to it. Courts would very justly refuse to consider it as sufficient proof of insanity, in the absence of other proofs, because it might have been the act of a rational mind, and because too if it really did spring from insanity, the delusion might have been so circumscribed, as not to have perverted the judgment in regard to testamentary dispositions and other civil acts. The principle adopted in the ecclesiastical courts is, that in cases of doubtful sanity—among which those of suicide must always be ranged—the validity of the individual's testament must be determined solely by the character of that instrument itself. Here is an inherent difficulty, that courts will

---

[1] Blackstone's Commentaries, vol. iv. p. 190.

never be very anxious to encounter, and, that is, to
determine the exact connexion of suicide with insanity—supposing the latter to be admitted—in point
of time.   When this act is the only proof we have
of mental derangement, we are left without the
means of ascertaining when this condition began to
exist or to disappear, and consequently nothing can
be more difficult than to decide within what time,
either before or after the suicidal attempt, the individual can be pronounced insane. It not uncommonly
happens that a person kills himself, or makes the
attempt, shortly after making his will, when the
question requires a judicial decision, whether or not
the insanity which led to the fatal act, existed at the
time of making the will.   The practice has usually
been, if there were no other evidence of unsound
mind, either in his conduct or conversation, or in the
testamentary dispositions themselves, not to impeach
the testator's sanity.   In Burrows v. Burrows, it was
held by Sir John Nicholl, that where there was no
evidence of insanity at the time of giving instructions for a will, the commission of suicide three days
afterwards, did not invalidate the will, by raising an
inference of previous derangement.[1]   Chief justice
Parker also held that suicide, committed fifteen days
after the date of the person's will, was not sufficient,
in the absence of other evidence, to prove him insane
and thus invalidate the will, on account of the difficulty we have just mentioned.[2]

---

[1] Burrows v. Burrows, 1 Haggard's Eccl. Reports, 109.
[2] His language was, that, " even if the act itself [suicide], should be
considered as proof demonstrative that the reasoning faculty was dis-

§ 287. Where, however, the unreasonableness of the will itself raises a suspicion of the testator's sanity, the act of suicide within a short time will always be strongly confirmatory of it, and, in connexion with attending circumstances, may, in some instances, turn suspicion into conviction. There will be little danger of going wrong in any cases of this kind, if we are willing to be governed in our decisions by the principles of equity and common sense, rather than by technical distinctions and antiquated maxims. If the will be a rational act rationally done, a suicidal act or attempt ought not to invalidate it, because the presumption is, either, that the will was made before the mind became impaired, or that the derangement was of a kind that did not prevent the judgment from using its ordinary discretion in the final disposition of property. If, on the contrary, it be an unreasonable act, and especially if it be contrary to the previously expressed intentions of the testator, then the act of suicide will be in itself strong proof, that the mind was impaired at the time of making the will.

---

turbed at the time of its commission, the difficulty of ascertaining with precision the very inception of derangement, weakens its force in relation to any antecedent act." Brooks and others *v.* Barrett and others, 7 Pickering's Reports, 94.

CHAPTER XIX.

SOMNAMBULISM.

§ 288. WHETHER this condition is really any thing more than a coöperation of the voluntary muscles with the thoughts which occupy the mind during sleep, is a point very far from being settled among physiologists. While to some, the exercise of the natural faculties alone seems to be sufficient to explain its phenomena, others have deemed it necessary to suppose, that some new and extraordinary powers of sensation are concerned in its production, though unable to convey a very clear idea of their nature or mode of operation. Without discussing this question here, our purpose will be answered, by inquiring how far the natural faculties are exercised during its continuance, and thus ascertaining, as well as may be, in what respect it differs from the sleeping and the waking states.

§ 289. Not only is locomotion enjoyed, as the etymology of the term signifies, but the voluntary muscles are capable of executing motions of the most delicate kind. Thus the somnambulist will walk securely on the edge of a precipice, saddle his horse and ride off at a gallop, walk on stilts over a swollen torrent, practise airs on a musical instrument ; in short, he may read, write, run, leap, climb, and swim, as well as, and sometimes, even better than when fully awake.

§ 290. The extent, to which vision is exercised, differs in different cases. In one class of cases, it is very certain that the somnambulist does not use his eyes in the various operations which he performs. Negretti, an Italian servant, whose celebrated history is related by two different physicians, would rise in his sleep, go into the dining-room, spread a table for dinner, and place himself behind a chair with a plate in his hand, as if waiting on his master. When in a place with which he was not perfectly acquainted, he was embarrassed in his proceedings, and felt about him with his hands; and sometimes he struck himself against the wall and was severely injured. He sometimes carried about with him a candle as if to give him light, but when it was taken away and a bottle put in its place, he failed to perceive the difference.[1] Galen says of himself, that he once walked about a whole night in his sleep, till awakened by stumbling against a stone which laid in his way. Here, it appears that the long-continued habit of performing certain operations enabled the individual, with the aid of feeling alone, to repeat them in his sleep.

At other times, objects are clearly discerned, but the imagination transforms them into those with which the mind happens, at the moment, to be engaged. Thus, a somnambulist described by Hoffman, who dreamed he was about going on a journey,

---

[1] Muratori: della forza della Fantazia Umana.

strided across the sill of an open window, kicking with his heels, and exerting his voice, as if he supposed himself riding on his horse.

In other instances again, things are done, in which vision, or an analogous power, is unquestionably exercised. Castelli, whose case which is one of the most remarkable, is related by Francesco Soave,[1] was, one night, found translating Italian into French, and observed to look for the words in a dictionary. His light having gone out, he found himself in the dark, groped about for a candle, and went into the kitchen to light it. He would also get up, and go into his master's shop, and weigh out medicines for supposed customers. When some one had altered the marks which he had placed in a book he was reading, he noticed the change and was puzzled, saying, " Bel piacere di sempre togliermi i segni." Another somnambulist, a priest whose case was published in the French Encyclopedie, would arise from his bed and compose sermons, reading over each page when finished, and erasing and correcting with the utmost accuracy. On one occasion, after writing " ce divine enfant," he erased the word " divine," and wrote " adorable " over it. Perceiving that ce could not stand before the last word, he altered it to cet, by inserting after it a t. He would also write music with the greatest accuracy.

It appears that the eyes of somnambulists are sometimes closed while walking about, and perhaps always so when they first get up, though by one

---

[1] Riflessioni sopra il Somnambolismo.

writer they are described as being sometimes half
open. In some of the cases which have been alluded to, the eyes were observed to be open and
staring.

§ 291. The senses of hearing and of taste present as many different modifications as that of sight.
The sound of persons' voices talking loud in his
presence is unperceived by the somnambulist, and
that of a trumpet is no better heard, unless put close
to his ears. At other times, very faint sounds are
heard at considerable distances. Negretti did not
distinguish between strongly seasoned cabbage, and
some salad he had prepared. He drank water instead of wine which he had asked for, and snuffed
ground coffee instead of snuff. By other somnambulists, however, such deceptions have been instantly
detected. All that can be offered, by way of explanation of these diversities in the power of sensation
in the same individual, is, that those impressions only
are recognised, which have some reference to or bond
of association with the thoughts that are passing
through the mind,—a fact strictly analogous to what
sometimes occurs in dreaming. It is well known
that a person, who will hear and reply to questions
addressed to him relative to the subject he is dreaming about, may not notice nor be aware of loud
sounds made near him. The difference in the senso-
rial powers of different somnambulists, probably indicates merely a difference in the degree to which
this peculiar condition is carried. Where it is but
little removed from that of ordinary dreaming, the
sense of feeling alone, in a limited measure, is added
to the locomotive power ; when still farther removed,

the senses of sight and hearing come into play,
though but partially exercised ; and when displayed
to its utmost extent, they enjoy a range and nicety
of perception, not witnessed in the ordinary state,
and hardly explicable in the present state of our
knowledge.

§ 292. There is another form of this affection,
called *ecstasis* or cataleptic somnambulism, from its
being conjoined with a kind of catalepsy, in which
the walking and other ,active employments are replaced by what appears to be a deep quiet sleep, the
patient conversing with fluency and spirit, and exercising the mental faculties with activity and acuteness.   Both in this and the former kind, the person
generally loses all recollection of whatever transpires
during the paroxysms, though it may be revived in
a subsequent paroxysm.   In some cases that have
been related, the memory during the paroxysms
embraced only the thoughts and occurrences of those
periods ; those of the lucid intervals being as entirely
forgotten, as those of the paroxysms were, after they
had subsided.

§ 293. It now scarcely admits of a doubt, that
somnambulism results from some morbid condition
in the system, involving, primarily or secondarily,
the cerebral organism.   We see that its lighter forms
are but a slight modification of dreaming, which is
universally admitted to be very much influenced by
the state of the corporeal functions, and which, in
certain disorders, is produced in a very troublesome
degree.   The analogy of ecstasis to hysteria and
epilepsy with which it is often conjoined, is too strong
to escape the most cursory observation, and not

merely in its phenomena, but in its curability by the use of remedial means. Indeed, these affections are known to pass into each other by frequent and rapid transitions, and to possess a strong common relation to insanity. The attacks of cataleptic somnambulism are invariably preceded by derangements of the general health—in females, of the uterine functions especially, and their recurrence is prevented by the methods of treatment, which are found most successful in those affections with which it is pathologically related. The more active forms of sleep-walking, seldom, if ever, exist, except in connexion with those habits or conditions, that deteriorate the general health. Intemperate drinking is said to be among the causes that produce it ; and an observer of Negretti's case attributed the disorder to his immoderate fondness of wine. A plethoric condition of the vessels of the head is also a strong predisposing cause of it; and in proof of this, Muratori relates that he was assured by a physician, that nothing but having his hair cut off once in a couple of months, saved him from being a somnambulist. Its hereditary character, which, like the same trait in insanity, we may fairly conclude depends on morbid conditions, also indicates its physical origin ; and the same inference may be drawn from the influence of age and sex in its production. The cataleptic form of the disorder chiefly appears in females before the last critical period ; while the other is as much confined to males, in whom it mostly appears in childhood and the early periods of manhood,—seldom in old age.

§ 294. In the somnambulist, either the perceptive organs are inordinately excited, and thus he is led to mistake inward for outward sensations; or the perceptions, if correct, are misapprehended by some obliquity of the reflective powers; in some instances probably, both these events take place. He talks, moves, and acts, unconscious of his real condition, and of nearly all his external relations. The ideal images that are brought before the mind are mingled up and confounded with the real objects of sense, and the conduct is regulated accordingly. Psychologically considered, then, somnambulism appears to be not very remote from mania, the difference consisting in some circumstances connected with the causes that give rise to the derangement of the faculties. In the latter, the pathological affection of the brain is continuous; in the former, it appears only during sleep, by which its effects are greatly modified. When the maniac finds himself restored to health, he looks on the period of his derangement as on a dream crowded with grotesque images, heterogeneous associations, and ever-changing scenes. So the somnambulist, on awaking, is conscious only of having been in a dream, the events of which have left a more or less vivid impression on his memory.

§ 295. Like the maniac, too, the sleep-walker's sentiments and propensities are often included in the same circle of morbid action, in which the operations of the understanding are involved. The case of a Carthusian monk is related, who, while awake, was remarkable for his simplicity, candor, and probity; but unfortunately, almost every night, walked in his sleep, and like the fabled Penelope, undid all the good actions for which he was celebrated by day. On such occasions, he was a thief, a robber, and a plunderer of the dead. A case of a pious clergyman is somewhere described, who in his fits of somnambulism would steal and secrete whatever he could lay his hands upon, and on one occasion, he even plundered his own church. In a case of somnambulism which occurred a few years since in Maine, there was a strong disposition to commit suicide. The paroxysms appeared every night, and watchers were required, as if the somnambulist had been laboring under an acute disease. He always attempted to escape from his keepers, and having succeeded one night, an outcry was heard from a neighboring pasture, and he was found suspended by a rope from the limb of a high tree. Fortunately, he had attached the rope to his feet instead of his neck, and consequently was but little injured.

CHAPTER XX.

LEGAL CONSEQUENCES OF SOMNAMBULISM.

§ 296. SOMNAMBULISM may sometimes incapacitate a person from the proper performance of the duties and engagements of his situation, and then unquestionably it may impair the validity of contracts and other civil acts to which he is a party. By rendering him troublesome, mischievous, and even dangerous, it furnishes good ground for annulling contracts of service, whether it existed previously and was concealed, or had made its appearance at a later date. Whether it should be considered a sufficient defence of breach of promise of marriage, or a valid reason for divorce when concealed from one of the parties previous to the marriage, are questions which do not properly admit of a general answer. Since its evils may be in some, of the lightest, in others, of the most serious description, each particular case ought, in justice, to be decided solely on its own merits, reference being had to the amount of injury as compared with the magnitude of the obligation sought to be avoided. If it be studiously concealed or denied, when its avowal would undoubtedly prevent the other party from entering into a contract, the latter ought to be enabled to set aside his own obligations on the ground of fraud.

§ 297. As the somnambulist does not enjoy the free and rational exercise of his understanding, and is unconscious of his outward relations, during the paroxysms, none of his acts can rightfully be imputed to him as crimes. Hoffbauer places him on the same footing with one who labors under *erreur de sentiment*, or erroneous perceptions, a form of monomania, except that the former is not fully excused, if, knowing his infirmity, he has not taken every possible means to prevent injurious consequences to others. Both law and equity too would undoubtedly hold him liable, with the maniac, in an action of trespass, for injury committed to the property of others, though as to what extent this power would be exercised, we have no means of forming an opinion. Hoffbauer suggests as a reason for not regarding the criminal actions of the somnambulist with too much indulgence, that they have probably originated, if not in premeditation, at least in the deep and deliberate attention which the mind has given to the subject when awake. This is, no doubt, the case in many instances, and if men were to be punished for their meditations, the suggestion would be not without its weight ; but as such is not the law, it is not very obvious how this fact can affect the legal consequences of somnambulism. Foderè too, by a somewhat similar kind of logic, comes to the conclusion that the acts of a somnambulist, instead of resulting from mental delusion, are more independent than any others, because they are the free and unconstrained expression of his waking thoughts and designs, and therefore that they are not altogether excusable. He seems to have forgotten that by no human law are men responsible for their

secret thoughts, but only for their words and acts.
To these only does it look, and if they are found to
have proceeded from a mind not in the full possession
of its powers, they must be excused without the
slightest reference to the former.   And as it cannot
be denied that they are sometimes excited by unfounded delusions, that have no affinity with the natural character and purposes of the individual, every
sentiment of justice cries out against ever regarding
them like criminal acts.   Georget quotes from an
anonymous work a curious instance of somnambulism
in a monk, which was related to the author by the
prior of the convent who witnessed it himself.   Late
one evening, this somnambulist entered the room of
the prior, his eyes open but fixed, his features contracted into a frown, and with a knife in his hand.
He walked straight up to the bed, as if to ascertain
if the prior were there, and then gave three stabs
which penetrated the bed-clothes and a mat which
served the purpose of a mattress.   He then returned, his features relaxed, and an air of satisfaction
on his countenance.   The next day, the prior asked him what he had dreamed about the preceding
night.   The monk confessed that having dreamed
that his mother had been murdered by the prior,
and that her spirit had appeared to him and cried
for vengeance, he was transported with fury at
the sight, and ran directly to stab her assassin.
Shortly after, he awoke covered with perspiration,
and rejoiced to find that it was only a dream.[1]   A

---

[1] Des Maladies Mentales, p. 127.

similar case is also related of two individuals, who, finding themselves out over night in a place infested with robbers, one engaged to watch while the other slept, but the former falling asleep and dreaming of being pursued shot his friend through the heart.

CHAPTER XXI.

SIMULATED SOMNAMBULISM.

§ 298. This disorder may be simulated, first, by those who have, at other times, really experienced its attacks ; secondly, by those who have not at any time. The motive may be, either to do something which the individual would not otherwise dare to attempt, or to avoid the punishment of an action, which is alleged to have been committed in one of its paroxysms. The difference, however, in the difficulty of proof, is not so great, as at first sight might be apprehended; for, since the mind is generally unconscious of what passes during the paroxysm, the somnambulist possesses but little advantage over others, from his experience, in feigning this affection. He will be no less at fault in respect to those little traits, which mark the difference between the real and feigned attacks, as well as the more important phenomena. When, however, it is admitted that the person has been subject to its attacks, this fact certainly furnishes a presumption of its reality in doubtful cases, which diminishes the strength of the evidence which the alleged case requires.

§ 299. When the feigned paroxysm is witnessed by others who are capable of describing minutely what they saw, a comparison of his conversation and acts with those observed in the real paroxysms, may

furnish us with a clew to the real nature of the act
imputed to him ; for it is scarcely possible that, if
feigning, he will not be caught tripping in some of
his manœuvres. A curious case is quoted by Hoffbauer
from an old writer, where nothing was wanting but a
tolerable knowledge of the state of the mental faculties in somnambulism, to expose the deception.   An
old ropemaker frequently fell into a profound sleep
in the midst of his occupation, whether sitting, or
standing, or walking in the street, when he would
begin to repeat, by means of words and gestures,
every thing he had been doing during the day, from
his prayer in the morning till the very moment of
his falling asleep.   If taken while walking abroad,
he would pursue his course just as if he had been
awake, avoiding persons and things which might
harm him.   The story was related as one of genuine
somnambulism, though there were two circumstances
in it sufficient to have exposed the deception.   In the
first place, to repeat the transactions of the day in
this manner, is contrary to what we know of somnambulists, who do only what they have premeditated, or what has strongly engaged their attention.
Secondly, this man acted a double part,—those of
the sleeping and of the waking states,—without
making the proper distinction.   He first repeated
what he had done during the day, and then went on
with what he was in the act of doing when the paroxysm took him.   The ruse was finally discovered.
The man professed himself cured, as soon as a physician charged with examining his case proposed to
bandage his eyes, to see if he would then be able to
perform those actions, which had excited so much

surprise. No doubt can remain of the genuineness of the attack, if the person performs feats which he would not dare to do when awake, unless—which would hardly be possible—he has systematically concealed his skill and abilities ; the converse of the proposition, however, cannot be equally true. It will also be a strong confirmation of the evidence in favor of its reality, if the physical symptoms, we have mentioned as sometimes attending the somnambulic disposition (§ 293), are shown to have been present. But it generally happens that the somnambulist walks unwitnessed, and must rest the proof of his mental condition on his own testimony and the circumstances of the case. The full burden of proof manifestly devolves on him, and if he fail of establishing it satisfactorily, he must suffer the consequence. There can be no other rule, for once acquit a criminal on the score of somnambulism, which is imperfectly or at best but plausibly proved, and it will soon become a favorite excuse for crime, whenever the offender possesses the requisite address for maintaining the deception. Among the proofs, however, necessary to establish this defence, a prominent place should be claimed for those drawn from the nature of the criminal act itself. If this be manifestly contrary to the known character and disposition of the accused, and especially if it can be shown that he could have entertained no motive for injuring the other party, but little else beyond a straight story and an air of sincerity ought to be required to establish the truth of his own assertions.

CHAPTER XXII.

EFFECT OF INSANITY ON EVIDENCE.

§ 300. THE insane are disqualified by law [1] from
appearing as witnesses in courts of justice, their incompetence being *inferred* from their mental unsoundness. The fact of incompetence to testify, however,
is not necessarily connected with that of insanity,
and it would be far more correct to consider the
former an independent fact to be established by a
distinct order of proofs. The truth is, an analogy,
in a medico-legal sense, has been too hastily assumed,
between the act of testifying, and that of performing
business-contracts, or other civil acts, and in consequence, has shared with them in the same sentence
of disqualification, without an attempt to ascertain
the kind and degree of intellectual power which they
respectively require. The practice of including them
in the same category, is certainly not favored by the
present state of our knowledge of insanity, nor does
it approve itself to the common sense of mankind.
To see what foundation in nature this rule of law
really has, we shall proceed to inquire how far the
competency of a witness is actually impaired by the
different forms of insanity.

---

[1] 3 Thomas's Coke's Littleton, 489 ; Livingston *v.* Kiersted, 10
Johnson's Reports, 362.

§ 301. According to Hoffbauer, before a witness
can be deemed competent, it is necessary that his
senses should be sufficiently sound to take cognizance
of the facts to which he testifies ; that their impressions should have been really what he believes they
were ; that his testimony should coincide with his
belief ; and lastly, that he should be able to convey
to others his own ideas without fear of being misin-
terpreted.   These conditions, it may be added, constitute the capacity of a witness, and wherever they
are present, his evidence should be received without
agitating the question of his mental unsoundness,
which is not absolutely incompatible with their existence.[1]

§ 302. The higher degrees of imbecility must of
course disqualify a witness, but its less aggravated
forms may not, under all circumstances, have this
effect.   His senses may be acute enough to see and
to hear what he deposes to ; no illusions may obtrude and mingle with their impressions ; and his
memory may be retentive enough, provided too long
a space of time do not intervene between the occurrence of the facts and his deposition concerning them,
to bear them in mind till relieved by judicial investigation.   The facts to which he testifies must be of
the simplest kind, requiring the smallest perceptive
effort to seize and appreciate, and so intelligible to

---

[1] The third condition above-mentioned, may not at first sight appear
to be connected with capacity ; but if the reader will refer to the observations (§ 122) on a class of people, who, in consequence of some natural defect, or organic disease, are incapable of telling the truth, even
when most conducive to their own interests, he will be convinced of
the propriety of placing it in this connexion.

the meanest understanding, that the memory can easily retain them. If the details are too numerous and complicated, and especially if they include words or actions not familiar with or analogous to his own ordinary experience, or if they happened at too remote a period, they become confused and entangled in his mind, and many of them fade from it altogether, while some important members of the series may not have been attended to at all. Hence the evidence of imbeciles may present many a contradiction and hiatus, of which they may be perfectly unconscious themselves, and which it would be wrong to attribute to intentional omissions, or a wish to deceive. If we bear in mind too that these persons are easily embarrassed, it might naturally be expected that the presence of spectators, the perplexing questions of counsel, and the formalities of a trial, would so disorder their ideas as to make their testimony appear, to those unacquainted with their mental deficiency, like the most impudent trifling, or downright mendacity. The more, however, the witness is permitted to tell his story in his own way, and finds encouragement in the looks of those around him, the less of this will be observed. The class described in § 52, are competent to testify in matters of a more complicated kind, requiring a larger grasp of the reflective faculties to embrace, and more tenacity of memory to retain them, but like the others, they are very liable to be disconcerted by the questions of strangers, and in consequence, betrayed into numerous contradictions of their own testimony. Since then the competency of these imbeciles is well established, nothing can be clearer than the propriety of admitting their evidence, and leaving it for the jury to decide upon its credibility.

§ 303. In partial intellectual mania the capacity of testifying under certain circumstances and with certain reservations, is still preserved, though considerable knowledge of the case and extreme caution are requisite to measure the witness's credibility. In regard to the greater proportion of cases, the only doubt is respecting the second and third conditions of capacity (§ 301), no question being raised as to the presence of the others ; that is, whether the witness has really seen, heard, &c., what he believes he saw and heard, and whether his testimony coincides with his belief. That he may offer in evidence the offspring of a disordered imagination, sincerely believing it to have come under the cognizance of his own senses, is undoubtedly true ; but no less so however, that he may testify solely to what has come under his own observation. Which of these events does actually take place, is a question to be settled by reference to the nature of the evidence and the character of the witness's insanity. When the matter on which he testifies, is remote from the insane delusion which he entertains, and cannot very obviously come within the circle of its influence, it would be wrong to reject his testimony on the score of incompetency. When we see these monomaniacs rational on every topic but that which constitutes their derangement, shrewd and methodical in the transaction of business, quick to perceive and able to profit by whatever appears conducive to their interests, trusted and respected by their neighbors, it seems more difficult to disprove than to prove their competency. The power of remembering and telling correctly what they have seen or heard, requires no more strength or soundness of mind, than numberless other duties that nobody doubts their ability to perform, and the burden of proving their incompetency should rest on those who urge it. Even on topics connected with their insane belief, their capacity is not necessarily destroyed, and in doubtful cases it would seem better to receive their evidence, and leave it for the court or counsel to disprove its credibility. While the predominant idea is highly false and absurd, they may, and very often do reason upon it with force and correctness, their deductions being sound and their reflections appropriate. Indeed, this mixture of the rational and the irrational, this inability to discern the relations of congruity between the true and the false, constitutes one of the most characteristic features of madness. Hence, it would not be unnatural for them to see things in some way connected with the delusion, in most of their relations, in their true light, and of this fact we should certainly avail ourselves in deciding on the admission of their evidence. The man who believes that he is charged by government with the regulation of the weather, may, notwithstanding, observe meteorological changes, and testify accurately concerning the state of the weather at a particular time, perhaps no one more so ; and he who believes that he has made an immense fortune by a commercial speculation, may talk sensibly on mercantile interests, and be perfect master of the price current, and thus be competent to testify on any matter connected with the same that has come under his observation. The credibility of such witnesses, however, depends very much on the importance of the subject on which they testify, and on the relations of their evidence to that of other witnesses. When they corroborate the statements of other witnesses, they may justly challenge our belief, while we should very properly hesitate to decide upon any great interests of person or property, solely upon the ground of their testimony.

§ 304. The reported cases, where the competence of witnesses is destroyed by reason of insanity, are too few, to render it very apparent how far the following represents the ordinary practice of American courts. It strikingly illustrates the effect of a rigid adherence to the common-law maxim, that the insane are incapable of testifying, and therefore, may be properly introduced in this place. Jacob Schwartz was tried on an indictment for assaulting, with intent to kill, Jonathan Jones, at a term of the Supreme Court for the county of Lincoln, in Maine, in May 1833. Jones himself was the principal witness, and he stated that he went into Schwartz's house, for the purpose of conversing on religious subjects with his wife, who was also Jones's sister ; that Schwartz, who had often forbidden him to do so, followed him into the house, drove him out, seized his gun, and threatened to shoot him ; that he then ran several rods, occasionally looking back at Schwartz, who stood in his door-way presenting his gun, as if in the act of firing ; that Schwartz finally fired and hit him, several shot lodging in his hat and coat, and a few penetrating into the skin of his back, from which they were taken out by some persons in a house to which he immediately ran. The transaction was witnessed by no one, besides Jones. By other witnesses it was testified, that Jones ran into the house where they were, exclaiming that Schwartz had shot him, and that they assisted in taking the shot out of the skin. Thus far his testimony was rational and consistent, and his manner calm and composed. On being cross-examined by the defendant's counsel who had some knowledge of his case, he testified, that he used to work on a piece of land which he owned, but that feeling himself called to exhort sinners to repentance, he went about, in imitation of Christ and the apostles, preaching the gospel and exhorting sinners to forsake their evil ways. He declared himself to be an apostle, and inspired by the holy ghost ; also, that he was one of the saints who are to judge the world, and that he should bear a part in the judgment of the great day. On this subject he dilated largely and incoherently, his countenance being animated, and his language and manner ardent and impassioned. Other witnesses having testified, that in his domiciliary visits, he had sometimes represented himself to be the Lord Jesus Christ, he was examined on this point. Here he was not very explicit, and did not seem disposed to make a full disclosure, as, he said, he could not perceive its connexion with the question at issue. He did not expressly deny, however, that he so considered himself, but seemed disposed to leave it to be inferred from particular things in which he resembled Jesus Christ, as in his poverty, in his going about to do good, and in the persecution he suffered. The jury, not thinking it safe to convict the defendant on

Jones's testimony, acquitted him, and the court signified its approval of the verdict.

§ 305. If the testimony of Jones had stood alone, unsupported by confirmatory circumstances, no fault could have been reasonably found with this verdict. It would have been sufficient for the jury, to know that he was laboring under extensive hallucinations, with which the alleged criminal act was not very remotely connected in his mind, to be justified in shrinking from the responsibility of depriving another on his testimony, of his good name, and subjecting him to legal punishment. Of the two evils, that of convicting on insufficient evidence, and that of suffering a guilty person to escape a few years' imprisonment, they would not have been liable to blame, for choosing to incur the risk of that which they considered the least. The circumstances of this case, however, being very different from what is here supposed, might we not have reasonably expected a different verdict ? That Jones was assaulted at, or very near the time alleged, could not be doubted for a moment, and his exclamation, as he entered the house with the appearance of sudden fright, that Schwartz had shot him, and his coming in the direction from Schwartz's house, strongly authenticated his statement, that the assault was committed by Schwartz,—so strongly indeed, that in the absence of any conflicting evidence on the part of the defendant, it was entitled to implicit belief. Such a scene might, no doubt, have been got up by a sane person, for the purpose of gratifying some malignant feelings, but men, affected with the kind of insanity under which Jones was laboring, rarely, if ever, contrive such schemes. It was a circumstance too, which should have had its weight, that in relating the facts of the assault, he was calm and consistent, and that it was only when touching on the subject of his delusions, that he was excited and incoherent. His insanity was not of the kind which would deprive him of the second condition of capacity to testify (§ 301), and it is the third only, in regard to which there could have existed any reasonable doubts ; and these obviated more or less satisfactorily, by the above-mentioned circumstances.[1]

§ 306. The view here taken of the competence of some monomaniacs, as witnesses, is not without some support in the legal profession.   " Of an insane person," says Mr. Evans, " it might for defect of other evidence, merit to be considered, whether in civil cases at least, the testimony of such might not be admissible, upon points where his understanding did not appear to be subject to disturbance ; it being well known that in many of these melancholy instances, especially when the result of some violent passion, the party affected is entirely cool, clear, and collected in his ideas, and as free as other persons, from the delusions of a perverted imagination, in every thing not connected with the cause of his insanity ; with regard to persons who have only temporary fits of madness (those usually termed lunacy), and at other times are in all respects sound of reason,

---

[1] For the facts of the above case, the author is indebted to the kindness of J. G. Reed, Esq. of Waldoborough, Me., who was the defendant's counsel.

these are then considered as capable of testimony as of any other legal act." [1]

§ 307. If the evidence of the monomaniacs in question be rejected, it must be from a fear of deception ; and probably most of the distrust manifested towards such witnesses arises from a lurking suspicion, that their mental impairment is necessarily accompanied with impaired veracity. It cannot be denied that there is some ground for this suspicion, and though it should not have the effect of totally invalidating their testimony, it is proper to bear it in mind whenever their credibility is in question. It is well known how prone the inmates of lunatic asylums are to complain of the servants, the overseers, and one another, and prefer against them special charges that are without any foundation whatever ; whether from an involuntary propensity to lying and mischief, or from a morbidly exalted imagination which distorts and discolors its perceptions, it is not easy to decide. Some, however, will relate very accurately what they see and hear, and their statements are received with implicit credit. On the whole, we may conclude with Georget, "that it is necessary to know the patient, the character of his madness, his customary relations to surrounding objects, before we can know what degree of confidence to place in his assertions." It should not be forgotten also, that in the greater proportion of cases of mental derangement, there is a weakness of memory that prevents it from retaining impressions so long

---

[1] 2 Pothier on Obligations, Appendix, 259.

and so faithfully, as when in its sound condition ; and therefore, the facts to which a monomaniac testifies should always be of recent occurrence, to render his testimony at all credible.

§ 308. In the subjects of general mania, all competence to testify is lost, except during what is called the lucid interval, when they may testify in regard to transactions that occurred during a lucid interval, or at a time previous to their illness. Their evidence should be implicitly received only when it relates to simple facts easily perceived, for their intellect may be hardly strong enough to bring to mind and expose in order, a complicated mass of details.

§ 309. In partial moral mania, there is nothing to incapacitate one from testifying, unless we except in that kind of it where the individual labors under an uncontrollable propensity for lying. Of all the forms of mania, this really diminishes competence more than any other, but it will be long, probably, before it will be considered in this light, in courts of justice.

§ 310. In general moral mania, as illustrated before (§§ 110, 112), it has been seen that the intellectual powers are not perceptibly impaired, and that the patient loses none of his interest in what passes around him, nor of his power to observe and remember them with ordinary distinctness. Under such circumstances, there would be little reason for rejecting his evidence on the score of incapacity. Considering, however, the great derangement of the affective powers under which he labors, and the unfounded likes and dislikes which it produces, his veracity may be justly suspected, and his evidence should be entitled to little weight, except when limited to facts in regard to which it can be shown that his feelings are not interested.

§ 311. The competence of old men in the early stages of dementia to testify, is a point frequently discussed in courts of justice, and the want is severely felt, of some fixed principles that shall serve as a guide to correct decisions. In every stage of this affection, the impairment of the memory is more perceptible in regard to recent than remote impressions, and it often happens that a person may have a distinct recollection of things that occurred in his youth, while those of a month's or a year's date, are but imperfectly remembered, if at all. To test the strength of his memory respecting certain things, it is only necessary to ascertain if he remembers various other transactions of about the same date in which he is known to have been engaged. If he can do this, it is a strong presumption in favor of his competency ; if not, it is incumbent on the party offering his testimony to show why his memory should have been more faithful in the one case than in the other. This is rendered still more necessary by the fact, that the weakness of mind incident to this condition makes its subjects more easily swayed by the suggestions of others, and leads them to believe that they remember what they are told they ought to remember, or what they are assured they actually did remember till within a recent period. The slightest examination will show how much dependence can be placed on their recollections of recent events.

CHAPTER XXIII.

DRUNKENNESS.

§ 312. BEFORE we can properly appreciate the legal consequences of drunkenness, it is necessary to understand its immediate and remote effects on the mind, and the organism with which it is connected. Correct information of this kind will enable us to avoid many of the prevalent errors that have arisen from vague and imperfect notions respecting the nature of drunkenness. We shall first consider the symptoms, or immediate effects, of free indulgence in intoxicating drinks ; for the following account of which we are chiefly indebted to Hoffbauer and Macnish.[1]

§ 313. The first effect of alcoholic liquors is to exalt the general sentiment of self-satisfaction, and diffuse an unusual serenity over the mind. The intellectual as well as physical powers act with a little increase of vigor and activity, the thoughts flow with more facility and accuracy, and the individual becomes perfectly well pleased with himself and others. He feels an exhilaration of spirits, a sense of warmth and gayety, and his imagination is crowded with delightful images. The sight and hearing are very

---

[1] Anatomy of Drunkenness.

slightly affected ; a low, humming sound is heard in the pauses of the conversation, and objects are enveloped in a slight mist which prevents them from being seen distinctly. Thus far there is no appearance of drunkenness. Soon the torrent of his ideas becomes more rapid and violent, and he can scarcely repress them. This is the moment of his happiest sallies, and he pours forth his thoughts with a force of expression and a richness of conception unknown in his sober hours, and now he feels the ecstatic pleasures of getting drunk. As yet the brain is in tolerable order, but a great effort is necessary to relate a story or transaction at all complicated in its details, for the thoughts succeed one another too rapidly, to allow sufficient time to arrange them in the order that the recital requires. This is the first well-marked symptom of intoxication. Now his ideas succeed one another with constantly increasing force and rapidity ; his sensations lose their ordinary delicacy ; and his imagination gains as fast as they lose. His language is, in some respects, more oratorical and poetical, though he now feels an irresistible propensity to talk nonsense, but is perfectly conscious, all the while, that it is nonsense. His voice is louder, because he hears less acutely, and judges of the hearing of others by his own. Now the organic activity of the brain is at its height. His imagination is filled by strange and queer images, and he is conscious, if so it may be called, of a sense of oppression and giddiness in his head. His perceptions of colors, forms, distance, and numbers become utterly confused ; he confounds one person with another ; the candles burn all colors in succession, and are multiplied fourfold; and in stretching forth his glass to set it on the table, he lets it go before reaching its edge. He is apt to imagine, either that he has offended some one, and shows a ludicrous anxiety to apologize, or that he has been offended, and fixes upon some one as the object of his maledictions, perhaps his blows. Judging from his discourse, his ideas begin to want connexion, notwithstanding their vivacity, but this vivacity and rapidity of his ideas give to his passions an insurmountable power against which reason has nothing to oppose, and unless some accident turn him from their object, he is hurried on wherever they impel him. Soon his tongue stammers and his voice gets thick ; his legs falter, he falls from his seat, and is plunged into a profound sleep, in which the manifestation of his physical and intellectual powers is completely extinguished. In this condition, he is said to be dead drunk. Such is the ordinary course of a fit of drunkenness, but it sometimes varies more or less, with the temperament or habits of the individual, and the attending circumstances.

§ 314. Such is the immediate effect of drunkenness on the mind ; we have now to show how the long-continued use of alcoholic liquors affects the moral and intellectual powers. Except in some happily-organized natures, the original delicacy and acuteness of the moral perceptions are invariably blunted ; the relations of neighbor, citizen, father, spouse, have lost their accustomed place in his thoughts ; great moral interests no longer obtain a strong hold on his attention ; the voice of distress is apt to fall on his ear like an unmeaning sound ; and the finer emotions of the soul, which will occasionally be felt by the least cultivated minds, have entirely deserted his nature. The injury sustained by the intellect is more obvious, if not more deplorable. The course of the ideas is sluggish, and they want their former force and brilliancy ; the mind has lost its comprehensiveness of grasp, and experiences a difficulty in seizing the relations of one idea to another ; it is incapable of the long-continued efforts which were once easy, and of concentrating the whole force of its faculties on the subjects submitted to its examination. The consequence is, that the brain having been so much accustomed to artificial stimulus, according to a well-known law of the animal economy, becomes incapable of an effort without the aid of this stimulus, which is necessary to the performance of even its most ordinary exercise. Drinking is thus made an indispensable habit, and by this means, the tame, cold, and lifeless being, as if touched by a spark of Promethean fire, is converted into the animated, sociable, and efficient man of his better days. Sheridan never spoke in the house of commons without the inspiration of half a pint of brandy, and numberless are the heroes of the buskin and the sock, who require to be wound up, as it were, to a certain pitch, by artificial stimulus, before they venture to undertake the labors of the night.

§ 315. This account of the pathological effects of drunkenness would be incomplete, without some mention of that curious disease to which it often leads, called *delirium tremens*, or *mania a potu*. It may be the immediate effect of an excess, or series of excesses, in those who are not habitually intemperate, as well as in those who are; but it most commonly occurs in habitual drinkers, after a few days of total abstinence from spirituous liquors. It is also very liable to occur in this latter class when laboring under other diseases, or severe external injuries that give rise to any degree of constitutional disturbance. The approach of the disease is generally indicated by a slight tremor and faltering of the hands and lower extremities, a tremulousness of the voice, a certain restlessness and sense of anxiety which the patient knows not how to describe or account for, disturbed sleep, and impaired appetite. These symptoms having continued two or three days, at the end of which time they have obviously increased in severity, the patient ceases to sleep altogether, and soon becomes delirious. At first, the delirium is not constant, the mind wandering during the night, but, during the day when its attention is fixed, capable of rational discourse. It is not long, however, before it becomes constant, and constitutes the most prominent feature of the disease. This state of watchfulness and delirium continues three or four days, when, if the patient recover, it is succeeded by sleep, which, at first, appears in uneasy and irregular naps, and lastly in long, sound, and refreshing slumbers. When sleep does not supervene about this period, the disease is fatal; and whether subjected to medical treatment, or left to itself, neither its symptoms nor duration are materially modified.

§ 316. The character of the delirium in this disease is peculiar, bearing a stronger resemblance to dreaming, than any other form of mental derangement. It would seem as if the dreams which disturb and harass the mind during the imperfect sleep that precedes the explosion of the disease, continue to occupy it when awake, being then viewed as realities, instead of dreams. The patient imagines himself, for instance, to be in some particular situation, or engaged in certain occupations, according to each individual's habits and profession, and his discourse and conduct will be conformed to this delusion, with this striking peculiarity, however, that he is thwarted at every step, and is constantly meeting with obstacles that defy his utmost efforts to remove. Almost invariably, the patient manifests, more or less, feelings of suspicion and fear, laboring under continual apprehension of being made the victim of sinister designs and practices. He imagines that certain people have conspired to rob or murder him, and insists that he can hear them in an adjoining apartment, arranging their plans and preparing to rush into his room; or that he is in a strange place where he is forcibly detained and prevented from going to his own home. One of the most common hallucinations, is, to be constantly seeing devils, snakes, vermin, and all manner of unclean things around him and about him, and peopling every nook and corner of his apartment with these loathsome objects. The extreme terror which these delusions often inspire, produces in the countenance, an unutterable expression of anguish, and, in the hope of escaping from his fancied tormentors, the wretched patient endeavors to cut his throat, or jump from the window. Under the influence of these terrible apprehensions, he sometimes murders his wife or attendant, whom his disordered imagination identifies with his enemies, though he is generally tractable and not inclined to be mischievous. After perpetrating an act of this kind, he generally gives some illusive reason for his conduct, rejoices in his success, and expresses his regret at not having done it before. So complete and obvious is the mental derangement in this disease, so entirely are the thoughts and actions governed by the most unfounded and absurd delusions, that if any form of insanity absolves from criminal responsibility, this certainly must have that effect.

§ 317. Before being able to decide the question understandingly, of the relation of drunkenness to moral agency, it is necessary to proceed one step farther in this investigation, and inquire into the pathological, or as it is technically called, the *proximate* cause of drunkenness. No impressions, whether from within or without, can affect the mind, but through the brain. In drunkenness, therefore, it is this organ which is principally affected, and that portion of it more particularly which is connected with the manifestation of the moral and intellectual powers. The vital actions of which it is the seat, receive an increased share of activity, so that every process that goes on, is conducted with fresh energy and speed. Drunkenness, however, depends on something more than mere increase of cerebral action, because it varies, in some degree, with the nature of the intoxicating agent, but what this specific action is exactly, it is impossible for us to know. As the fit proceeds, this increase of action continues, until it arrives at such a pitch, that the organ is unable to perform its functions properly ; hence, the disorder and tumult of mind that attends the last stages of the fit. The torpor and exhaustion that follow, are the natural consequence of the previous excessive stimulation, and the one is generally proportioned to the other. This increased action that takes place in drunkenness, degenerates, after frequent repetition, into a permanent state of irritation which, at last, becomes real inflammation. The coats of the vessels are thickened and less transparent than usual, and in some places, they assume a varicose appearance. The cerebral texture is less delicate and elastic, becoming either unnaturally hard, or soft. Slight effusions of water are not uncommon. These appearances, to a more or less extent, are found in the brains of nearly all confirmed drunkards, and it may be now considered a well-established fact that the habitual drunkard has always more or less of cerebral disease.

§ 318. Obviously as these pathological changes are the effect of a long-continued voluntary habit, there is strong evidence in favor of the idea that they, in turn, become efficient causes, and act powerfully in maintaining this habit, even in spite of the resistance of the will. So deplorably common has drunkenness been in this country, that there are few who have not seen the melancholy spectacle of the most powerful motives, the most solemn promises and resolutions, a constant sense of shame and danger, bodily pain and chastisements, the prayers and supplications of friendship, of as little avail in reforming the drunkard, as they would have in averting an attack of fever, or consumption. With a full knowledge of the dreadful consequences to fortune,

character and family, he plunges on in his mad
career, deploring, it may be, with unutterable agony
of spirit, the resistless impulse by which he is mastered.   Macnish relates the case of a young man of
fortune, twenty-six years old, which presents an
impressive illustration of this truth. "Every morning
before breakfast," he says, "he drank a bottle of
brandy; another he consumed between breakfast and
dinner, and a third, shortly before going to bed.
Independently of this, he indulged in wine and whatever liquor came within his reach.   Even during the
hours usually appropriated to sleep, the same system
was pursued—brandy being placed at the bed-side
for his use in the night-time.   To this destructive
vice he had been addicted since his sixteenth year;
and it had gone on increasing from day to day till it
had acquired its then alarming and incredible magnitude.   In vain did he try to resist the insidious
poison.   With the perfect consciousness that he was
destroying himself, and with every desire to struggle
against the insatiable cravings of his diseased appetite, he found it utterly impossible to offer the
slightest opposition to them."[1] Another, whose case
he quotes, replied to the remonstrances of his friend
who painted the distresses of his family, the loss of
his business and character, and the ruin of his health,
"my good friend, your remarks are just; they are
indeed too true; but I can no longer resist temptation.
If a bottle of brandy stood at one hand, and the pit
of hell yawned at the other, and I were convinced

---

[1] Anatomy of Drunkenness, 163.

that I would be pushed in as sure as I took one glass, I could not refrain. You are very kind, I ought to be grateful for so many kind, good friends, but you may spare yourselves the trouble of trying to reform me; the thing is out of the question." [1]

§ 319. These phenomena strongly remind us of some of the manifestations of moral mania, and if farther evidence is necessary to convince us that they are both connected with similar pathological conditions, it is abundantly furnished in some other phenomena of drunkenness. It is now well understood that this vice sometimes assumes a *periodical* character, persons indulging in the greatest excesses periodically, who are perfectly sober during the intervals, which may be from the space of a month to that of a year. From a state of complete sobriety, they suddenly lapse into the most unbounded indulgence in stimulating drinks, and nothing but absolute confinement can restrain them. Macnish, who saw several cases, says that they "seemed to be quite aware of the uncontrollable nature of their passion, and proceeded systematically, confining themselves to their room, and procuring a large quantity of ardent spirits. As soon as this was done, they commenced and drank to excess till vomiting ensued, and the stomach absolutely refused to receive another drop of liquor. This state may last a few days or a few weeks, according to constitutional strength, or the rapidity with which the libations are poured down. So soon as the stomach rejects every thing

---

[1] Idem, 162.

that is swallowed, and severe sickness comes on, the fit ceases. From that moment recovery takes place, and his former fondness for liquor is succeeded by aversion or disgust. This gains such an ascend- ency over him, that he abstains religiously from it for weeks, or months, or even for a year, as the case may be. During this interval he leads a life of the most exemplary temperance, drinking nothing but cold water and probably shunning every society where he is likely to be exposed to indulgence." [1]

§ 320. Esquirol has distinctly recognised this dis- order,[2] and attributing it to the influence of patho- logical changes, considers its unhappy victims as not morally responsible. This distinguished observer of mental affections affirms, that "sometimes the abuse of intoxicating drinks and drunkenness are the first symptoms, or rather the most prominent symptoms, of the first stage of madness;" that "the stomach being in that peculiar condition which produces an extremely painful, moral, and physical depression, craves strong drink;" that "this craving is imperi- ous and irresistible;" that "it continues as long as the paroxysm, after which the patient becomes sober and assumes all the habits of a temperate life." He also says, that these people "obey an impulse which they have not the power of resisting;" that they are "true monomaniacs;" and that if carefully observed we shall find in them "all the characteristic features of partial madness." In illustration of his views he relates the following case. "M. N., a merchant,

---

[1] Op. cit. 36.   [2] Note in Hoffbauer, § 195.

aged about forty, of a robust but nervous constitution, became, six years before, towards the beginning of autumn, gloomy and disquieted, in consequence, apparently, of some reverses in his affairs. After a few weeks, he neglected his business, and became irritable and ill-tempered in his family. His taste and habits changed, he took to drinking, and seriously endangered the safety of his fortune and his family. The prayers and tears of his wife and children, the authority of his father, and the inroads upon his property, were equally unavailing in checking his career. Thus passed the winter ; at the approach of spring, the craving for drink ceased. M. N. resumed his regular and sober habits, and by his application to business and increased tenderness towards his family, he endeavored to forget the occurrences of the past winter. In the following autumn there appeared the same phenomenon, the same disorders, and the same spontaneous cure in the spring. It was the same for the two following years except that the symptoms were so aggravated, that his property suffered severely, and his wife's life was sometimes endangered. At the end of his fourth paroxysm, in 1817, M. N. came to Paris to consult me and submit to my directions, conjuring me to deliver him from a disease that rendered him the most miserable of men.'' Esquirol subjected him to a course of medical treatment, and in August sent him off on a journey into Italy. That year he escaped, except that in December he manifested a slight desire to drink, but found himself able to resist, and never afterwards had a return of his complaint. He also relates the case of a lady, who, after being melancholic for six weeks, with weakness of the stomach and indisposition to take the least exercise, was suddenly seized with the strongest craving for spirituous drinks, together with sleeplessness, agitation, disturbance of mind and perversion of the affections. For six years, these symptoms made their appearance annually, and continued two months.

§ 321. A case is related in the *Journal des Progres, &c.* vol. xi., of a Parisian bookbinder, sixty years old, who for fifteen years was afflicted with periodical drunkenness, having previously been a model of sobriety and virtue. The paroxysm lasted two or three months with an interval of equal duration. M. Pierquin, the narrator of the case, observed him closely for the space of two years, and found that his daily habit was, to rise at five or six o'clock in the morning, take some money out of the till, and hasten to the nearest cabaret, where he would drink incessantly, until ten or eleven o'clock. He would then stagger home, go down into his cellar, bring up some large bottles of wine, and drink night and day, seldom sleeping and very rarely eating. During the early period of the attack, he would go to the cabaret, forenoon and afternoon ; but during the last eighteen or twenty days, he never went from home. Then he became reserved, passionate, avoiding the light, and seeking the darkest corner of the kitchen. He was never observed to be delirious, nor deranged in mind, but would answer questions correctly, and follow the train of conversation. The paroxysm ended in a profound sleep from which he would awake in his sober senses, and resume his avocations as if he had just quitted them the preceding evening, being unconscious, or pretending to be so, of any thing that had occurred.

§ 322. It can scarcely be doubted that the above cases originated in pathological changes ; and there is also another class of cases which strongly point to the same origin, and present a close affinity, both in this respect, and in that of their symptoms. In the cases referred to, the persons who are habitually sober, are irresistibly impelled to indulge in the reckless, unlimited use of intoxicating drinks, whenever agitated by strong moral emotions. The author was once acquainted with a very amiable, intelligent, and virtuous young seaman, who, by means of strict attention to his duties, his staid deportment, and his knowledge of navigation, rose to the command of a ship, at a very early age. During his second voyage as captain, while in a foreign port, in a hot climate, some circumstances occurred, which subjected him to considerable fatigue and exposure and great anxiety of mind, and seriously affected his health. By this and some other things which took place on the passage home, his mind was so disturbed, that this young man, who hardly knew the taste of ardent spirits, suddenly abandoned himself to the wildest excesses. The fit continued till within a few days of their arrival in port, during which time he was totally unconscious of what was going on, and the first officer took charge of the vessel. The same scenes again occurred the next voyage, and he lost his employment ; but with these two exceptions, no man living practised more rigid abstinence from every kind of intoxicating drink. Nothing could tempt him to the slightest indulgence, and he evinced the strongest repugnance to all spirituous liquors of whatever kind. The author also knew another young man of similar character, who rose in a similar manner to the command of a ship ; but no sooner did he reach this reward of his merits, than he began to drink with all the recklessness of an old toper. As soon as he was degraded to an inferior station, no man could be more temperate, and this appearance of reform each time encouraging his friends with the hope, that he had abandoned his bad habits altogether, they would restore him to the station he had lost, to be again and again forfeited by his mad propensity. In these cases, it seems as if the anxiety arising from a sense of heavy responsibility, and from adverse circumstances, produced an irritation, if not inflammation of some portion of the brain—of that which, if phrenology be true, is connected with the appetite of hunger and thirst.

§ 323. Esquirol mentions the case of a servant-girl in the Salpétrière, who, upon the slightest cross or contradiction, began and continued to drink until prevented by strict seclusion. If not prevented in time, she got drunk, became furious, and attempted suicide.

CHAPTER XXIV.

LEGAL CONSEQUENCES OF DRUNKENNESS.

§ 324. BEFORE we undertake to estimate the legal responsibilities of drunkards, it will be necessary to retrace our steps for a moment, in order to ascertain what is the exact state of the mind, while under the immediate influence of intoxicating drinks, and for this purpose we shall distinguish, with Hoffbauer, three degrees, or periods of drunkenness. In the first degree, to use in some measure the language of this writer, the ideas are only uncommonly vivacious ; consequently the empire of the understanding over the actions is so little weakened, that the individual perfectly retains the consciousness of his external condition, and in fact may be said to be in complete possession of his senses. Still, this rapid flow of ideas is unfavorable to reflection, and there also accompanies it great irritability and activity of the moral emotions. It must be remembered however, that anger is more rare in this degree of drunkenness, in consequence of the self-satisfaction which the person enjoys, and which renders him more patient ; but, on the other hand, some previous circumstances that may have increased his susceptibility, even the sallies of a wild gayety, or a simple dispute of words, though conducted with courtesy, strongly dispose him to transports of passion. Still, as long as drunkenness does not exceed the first degree, the passions can be repressed. In the second degree of drunkenness a man has still the use of his senses, though they are remarkably enfeebled ; but he is entirely beside himself ; memory and judgment have abandoned him. He acts as if he lived only for the present, with no idea of the consequences of his actions, nor their relations to one another. The past has gone from his mind, and he cannot be influenced by considerations which he no longer remembers. He conducts himself as if no control over his actions were necessary. The slightest provocation is sufficient to awaken the most unbounded rage. He is therefore not unlike the maniac, and can be responsible for his actions, only so far as he is for his drunkenness. In the last degree, he not only loses the possession of his reason, but his senses are so enfeebled, that he is no longer conscious of his external relations. In this condition he is more dangerous to himself than to others.

§ 325. In the first stage of drunkenness, it is obvious that the legal relations of the individual cannot be affected, inasmuch as he has lost none of the ordinary soundness of his judgment. In the second and third stages, so much is the soundness of his understanding and clearness of his perceptions impaired, and his passions excited, that he acts more or less unconsciously and without deliberation. But since drunkenness is itself a sin, it becomes a question how far a person's liability for the consequences of his acts in that state can be affected, by a condition which is itself utterly inexcusable. A remarkable diversity of views has prevailed on this point at different times and among different nations, and it would certainly be a curious, if not useful inquiry, to investigate the peculiar circumstances that have given rise to it. In ancient Greece, he who committed a crime when drunk, received a double punishment ; one for the crime itself ; another for the drunkenness that prompted him to commit it ; and in a magistrate it was made a capital offence. The Romans, on the contrary, admitted drunkenness as a plea in defence of any misdeeds committed under its influence, except when it occurred in a woman ; then it was punished with death. In the Austrian law under Joseph II. drunkenness is made a sufficient excuse for crime, whenever it is not accompanied with an intention relative to the criminal act. In the French penal code, no mention is made of drunkenness, either as a ground of defence for crimes and offences, or as impairing the validity of civil acts.

In 1807, the court of cassation[1] decided that drunkenness, being a voluntary and reprehensible state, could never constitute a legal or moral excuse, and the practice in France has subsequently been in accordance with this decision. Georget, however, has quoted a case,[2] where this principle seems to have been avoided by the jury by means of a technicality in their verdict. J. M. Erion was tried on a charge of assault and battery upon his mother, and it appeared on the trial that at the moment of com-

---

[1] This is the highest court in the kingdom, and receives appeals from all the other courts.
[2] Discussion medico-legale, p. 23.

mitting the assault, he was in a fit of intoxication. The verdict of the jury was, that he was guilty, but acted *involuntarily;* and consequently, he was discharged in virtue of the 364th art. of the code of criminal instruction, viz. : " The court will acquit the accused if the act for which he is indicted is not prohibited by any penal law." [1]

§ 326. The common law of England has shown but little disposition to afford relief from any of the immediate consequences of drunkenness, either in civil or criminal cases. It has never considered mere drunkenness alone, a sufficient reason for invalidating a deed or agreement, except when carried to that excessive degree which deprives the party of all consciousness of what he is doing.[2] Courts of equity also have strenuously refused their relief, unless the drunkenness were procured by the fraud or imposition of the other party, for the purpose of obtaining some unfair advantage.[3] Writers on natural and public law, however, have regarded drunkenness under any circumstances, as a sufficient cause

---

[1] The apparent want of connexion between the discharge of the accused and the provisions of this article, is to be explained by the difference of procedure in French and English courts. The former, unlike the latter, permit the jury, in criminal cases, as well as civil, to render a *special* verdict, and accordingly they found Erion guilty of the assault, but that having "acted involuntarily," he was guilty of no *crime,* and was entitled to a discharge from the court, as much as if he had been found by the same verdict, guilty of the assault, but *deranged,* and not acting voluntarily. The law makes no man responsible for an involuntary act, and drunkenness is not recognised as a circumstance that deprives acts of this quality which are committed under its influence.

[2] Cole *v.* Robbins, Buller's Nisi Prius.

[3] Cooke *v.* Clayworth, 18 Vesey's Rep. 12.

for avoiding any acts that may have been executed under its influence, upon the principle, that the free and deliberate consent of the understanding is essential to the validity of such acts.[1]

§ 327. The general doctrine to be derived from the above principles, is, first, that moderate drunkenness does not deprive the understanding of the power of rational consent, is not very apparent to others, and therefore ought not to be allowed to avoid any deed or contract ; secondly, that, inasmuch as excessive drunkenness deprives a person of all consciousness of what he is doing, and is perfectly obvious to every one, all acts executed while in that condition are strongly exposed to the suspicion of fraud, and may be avoided on that ground. Nothing, certainly, can be fairer than this, since it equally guards the interests of the drunken party, and of those who deal with him.

§ 328. In regard to the effect of drunkenness in criminal cases, it has been declared by a learned expounder of the common law, that, "a drunkard, who is *voluntarius demon*, hath no privilege thereby ; whatever ill or hurt he doeth, his drunkenness doth aggravate it." [2] Drunkenness itself has never been regarded as a crime, and, in the practice of the present time at least, it is not literally true, that it is an aggravating circumstance when attending the commission of real offences.   It may be said more correctly, that it has no legal effect whatever, on any

---

[1] Puffendorf's Law of Nature and Nations, B. 1, ch. 4, § 8; Pothier, Traité des Obligations, n. 49.
[2] Thomas's Coke's Littleton, 46.

offence which it accompanies ; it neither modifies its nature, nor increases, nor mitigates its penalties. Drunkenness gives rise, however, directly or indirectly, to various pathological conditions affecting the operations of the mind, and it has become a question of considerable delicacy in some cases, to decide how far legal responsibility is diminished by their presence. Different cases have been decided on different grounds, and to make any remarks on the subject perfectly intelligible, it will be necessary to select a few in which the circumstances and grounds of decision are fully reported. In the three following, the condition, under the influence of which the crime was committed, was *Delirium tremens*, or *Mania à potu*.

§ 329. I. At the May term, in 1828, of the circuit court of the United States, Alexander Drew, commander of the whaling ship John Jay, was tried for the murder of his second mate, Charles F. Clark. It appeared in evidence, that previously to the voyage during which this fatal act occurred, Drew had sustained a fair character, and was a man of humane and benevolent disposition, though addicted to the excessive use of ardent spirits. After recovering from a drunken debauch, in the latter part of August, 1827, he resolved to drink no more, and all the liquor on board the ship was thrown overboard. In two or three days after, he lost his appetite, was unable to sleep, and manifested various hallucinations. He thought the crew had conspired to kill him, and expressed great fear of an Indian belonging to the ship, calling him by name when not present, and promising that he would drink no more rum, if he would not kill him. Sometimes he would sing obscene songs, and sometimes, hymns, and would pray and swear alternately. In the night of the 31st of August, he went on deck, and attempted to throw himself overboard, but was restrained by the witness. At seven o'clock in the forenoon, September 1st, while the witness, Drew, and Clark were at breakfast, Drew suddenly left the table, and appeared to conceal something under his jacket which was on the transom in another part of the cabin. He immediately turned round to Clark and requested him to go upon deck. The latter replied that he would when he should have finished his breakfast. Drew then exclaimed, "Go upon deck, or I will help you," and immediately took a knife that had been covered over by his jacket, and before another word was spoken by either, he plunged it into the right side of Clark's breast. Clark fell instantly, but soon afterwards, rose and went upon deck. As the witness left the cabin, Drew cocked his pistol, pointed it at him and snapped it, but it missed fire. Drew followed them upon deck, and addressing the chief mate, said, "Mr. Coffin, in twenty-four hours, the ship shall go ashore." He was then seized and confined. His whole demeanor, for some weeks after, was that of an insane person. When he first appeared to be in his right mind, he was informed of Clark's death and its cause, he replied that he knew nothing about it, that when he awoke, he found himself handcuffed, and that it appeared to him like a dream. It also appeared that there had not been for months any quarrel between Clark or Drew.

§ 330. After hearing the witness who testified the

above facts, the court interposed, and through Mr. Justice Story, delivered its opinion, that on these admitted facts, the indictment could not be maintained, because the prisoner was unquestionably insane at the time of committing the offence. "The question made at the bar," continued the court, "is whether insanity, whose remote cause is habitual drunkenness, is or is not an excuse in a court of law for a homicide committed by the party while so insane, but not at the time intoxicated or under the influence of liquor. We are clearly of opinion that insanity is a competent excuse in such a case. In general, insanity is an excuse for the commission of any crime, because the party has not the possession of his reason, which includes responsibility. An exception is when the crime is committed while the party is in a fit of intoxication, and while it lasts, and not as in this case a remote consequence, superinduced by the antecedent exhaustion of the party, arising from gross and habitual drunkenness. However criminal, in a moral point of view, such an indulgence is, and however justly a party may be responsible for his acts arising from it to Almighty God, human tribunals are generally restricted from punishing them, since they are not the acts of a reasonable being. Had the crime been committed while Drew was in a fit of intoxication, he would have been liable to be convicted of murder. As he was not then intoxicated, but merely insane from an abstinence from liquor, he cannot be pronounced guilty of the offence. The law looks to the immediate and not to the remote cause, to the actual state of the party and not to the cause which remotely produced it. Many species of insanity arise remotely from what, in a moral point of view, is a criminal neglect or fault of the party, as from religious melancholy, undue exposure, extravagant pride, ambition, &c., yet such insanity has always been deemed a sufficient excuse for any crime done under its influence." The jury returned a verdict of not guilty.[1]

§ 331. II. At a term of the supreme court in York county, Me., April, 1836, Theodore Wilson was tried for the murder of his wife in June, 1835, at Kittery. It appeared in evidence, that for several years, Wilson had been addicted to intemperate drinking; that on the Saturday previous to the murder, he brought some rum from Portsmouth, N. H., and that on the next day he had drunk it all. It did not appear that he drank any more after this, and circumstances render it probable that he did not. There was nothing strange or unusual in his conduct till Wednesday morning, when he arose early and went to the house of a neighbor to get some barley and procure a person to sow it for him. He returned home about six o'clock, and then complained of being sick. His wife assisted him to undress, and he laid down, saying that he was dying. In the meantime he complained that his wife would do nothing for him; that she had often set traps for him, and once put fire and wood into the oven to burn him up. He ate some porridge only for his breakfast, was constantly talking, and among other things, spoke of his having been fishing when he was four years old.

---

[1] 3 American Jurist, 7—9 ; 5 Mason's Reports, 28.

While the family were at dinner, he arose from bed and walked about in great agitation, striking the walls with his fists, and beating in the door with the tongs. As he became more furious, a woman who resided with him at this time, left the house, he and his wife then being the only persons in it. A short time after, he was seen coming out of the house stark naked, and in this condition he walked rapidly down the road, throwing up his arms, and making a wild, howling noise, and finally laid down by a fence. It appeared that after he left the house, his wife went to one of the neighbors to ask his aid in getting her husband back, but this person declining to interfere, she went alone. As she approached him still lying by the fence, she asked him why he was lying there and making such a noise. He immediately sprung up, put his hands upon her shoulders, threw her down, and beat out her brains with a stone. He then left the body, and on reaching a house near by, broke in the windows with his fists, and also struck at the doors and side of the house, to seal it, as he said, with his wife's blood. Here he proclaimed that he had killed his wife and meant to kill two more; he was then arrested. To those who watched with him during the night, he declared he was not sorry for what he had done, but was glad of it, and intended to have done it before. He continued furious, talking wildly and incoherently, making unnatural noises, sleeping none, and apparently anxious to kill himself, till the next Saturday morning, when he became, and remained rational. It further appeared, that in 1830, he went on a fishing voyage, and that being deprived of spirits, he became deranged three days after sailing, and had to be confined. He then began to tear his clothes, and try to tear the clothes of others. He complained of being sick, said, he should die, and requested the captain to tell his sons to take care of their mother. He was afterwards set ashore, and did not go on the voyage.

His counsel set up the plea of insanity in his defence, and the court, in charging the jury, observed that it was not material for them to determine what *species* of insanity it was under which the prisoner had been suffering, if satisfied with the fact of its existence. He was acquitted.[1]

§ 332. III. John Birdsell was tried in 1829 by the supreme court of Ohio, on an indictment for the murder of his wife, on Thursday, 5th of March, 1829. It appeared in evidence, that for several years the prisoner had indulged in fits of intoxication, which, in the latter part of the time, had been followed by delirium tremens, which generally lasted for several days, and went off spontaneously. In these paroxysms, he had the physical and moral symptoms that usually characterize the disease. Among many hallucinations under which he labored, the prevailing one was, that his wife was in a combination with three of his neighbors, one of whom was his son by a former wife, and that they had conspired to take his life. He imagined that his wife had a criminal intimacy with these persons, and even

---

[1] For the facts in this case, the author acknowledges his obligations to Nathan Dane Appleton, Esq., one of the defendant's counsel.

threatened to kill her if she did not desist. On the Sunday before the murder, he drank freely and was intoxicated, in which condition, he was quiet, dull, and disposed to lie in bed. Monday, Tuesday, and Wednesday, presented nothing special. On Wednesday evening he complained to a neighbor, of feeling unwell, and asked his son's assistance in the performance of some necessary manual labor for his family. He seemed to the witness to be rational. During the night, he slept none, and complained of cramp in the stomach. The next morning, his family thought him crazy, but were not alarmed, as they were accustomed to such attacks. In the course of the day, he took an axe and walked rapidly to the house of a neighbor whom he desired to go home with him, saying that they wanted to kill him; and about the same time he told another of the supposed conspirators, that he had overheard his wife and him, that morning, whispering about taking his (the witness's) life. He spent the day at home in the midst of his family, apparently in agitation and terror, but said he would not hurt any one and did not wish to be hurt. He also placed a scythe with the axe under the bed, where the latter was often kept. He manifested jealousy of his wife, and told her to act better, for she had already caused the death of thirty thousand men. He fancied that the persons of whom he was jealous, were in the loft manufacturing ropes to hang him, and going up, returned, saying that he had cut the ropes in pieces and brought down the fragments in his hands, though he had nothing in them. In the course of the afternoon, he fastened both the doors of his house. At the usual time, the wife went out to milk, and he barred the door after her. On her return, he fastened it again. She was seated near the fire, and he was walking the room. At length, he took the axe from under the bed, and gave the fatal blow, following it up with two others on the face. His oldest daughter caught the axe which he yielded up, and then he seized the scythe, with which he attempted to strike her. She defended herself with a chair, till the smaller children having opened the door, she escaped. He took the youngest child in his arms, and sat down by the window. The child exclaimed, "mamma bleeds!" which, he said, made him feel badly. When his neighbors arrived immediately afterwards, he gave himself up, acknowledged what he had done, said he knew he should be hanged for it, but that he ought to have done it nine months sooner ; that if he had to do it again, he would strike two blows where he only struck one. It was testified that he talked so rationally, that many of the witnesses could not believe him deranged ; that he evinced no dread of punishment for his crime, but was still in great apprehension from the persons, who, he had believed, intended to kill him ; and that he was glad he had defeated their calculations. On his way to jail, he talked rationally and composedly about his affairs, and various other subjects, but frequently asked the guard if they did not hear sweet sounds of different kinds, and on being answered in the negative, insisted that he could not be mistaken. After his committal, he became rational and expressed his regret, at what he had done.

§ 333. The point submitted to the jury for their determination, was, whether the prisoner was capable of discriminating between right and wrong. They concluded that he was, and returned a verdict of *guilty*. In consequence of a petition from quite a number of persons who had no doubts of Birdsell's insanity, the punishment was commuted by the governor, to that of imprisonment. Previous to the commutation, he again became insane, and continued so permanently.[1]

§ 334. The essential features of the above cases being alike in every thing relative to their pathological nature, we are left without any satisfactory reason to account for the issue of the last. It is probable that the court adhered to the antiquated maxims of the common law on the subject of insanity, and that the jury were governed by the opinions of the court, or relied, with that confidence which ignorance usually inspires, on their own crude and erroneous notions. The verdict of the jury in Birdsell's case, furnishes another instance of the deplorable consequences of obliging a body of men, the most of whom are utterly unacquainted with the phenomena of insanity, to decide the question of its existence in a given example, and with it the fate of an unfortunate fellow-being, for weal or for woe, here and hereafter. They concluded that the accused was *capable of distinguishing right from wrong*, probably, because others who knew as little of insanity as themselves testified, that immediately after committing the murder,

---

[1] This case was reported, and the medico-legal questions growing out of it were discussed at considerable length, by Dr. Drake, in the Western Journal of the Medical and Physical Sciences, vol. iii. Extracts from his papers may be found in the American Jurist, vol. iii. p. 10—16.

" he talked so rationally that they could not believe him deranged," and on such a conclusion they founded their fatal verdict. Of course, it would have been too violent a contradiction in terms, to have denied the existence of any insanity at all in a disease whose very name is delirium, but it appeared that the prisoner was not altogether bereft of his senses, not quite reduced to the condition of a brute or an idiot. Now without resting upon the general fact that the mind is always and unequivocally deranged in delirium tremens, there is proof enough that various hallucinations took possession of Birdsell's mind and prompted him to the bloody deed for which he was condemned—that he was under the influence of manifest, unequivocal, strong delusion, that test of insanity, which, when present, never deceives. If any one, on being made acquainted with the particulars of Birdsell's case, can pronounce it not to be insanity, he must have derived his notions of this disease from some other source than the wards of the hospital and asylum.

§ 335. In the first two cases, the directions of the court to the jury were, substantially, that if they were satisfied the accused was insane when he committed the criminal act, they were not to go back and inquire into the causes of the insanity, but, on this fact being established in their minds, the prisoner was entitled to an acquittal. In the first case, the court examined the question, whether the legal consequences of insanity are affected by the character of the cause which produces it, and so clear and satisfactory is its opinion, that any thing further on this point is rendered unnecessary here.

In Birdsell's case, there was presented a new feature of no little interest to the medico-legal student, which, though it was suffered to have no influence on the verdict, might, if the court had chosen to urge its opinion respecting it upon the jury, have prevented an acquittal, even if they had satisfied themselves beyond a doubt, that the party was incapable of distinguishing between right and wrong. In replying to the arguments of counsel for a new trial, the court observed in the course of its remarks, " that they were not called upon to give an opinion whether *Mania à potu* would, under any circumstances, be an excuse for the commission of a crime, but they felt no unwillingness to express their opinion, that if the insanity were the offspring of intemperance and the prisoner *knew* that intoxication would produce it, he could not plead it as an apology." Birdsell, it has been seen, had experienced several fits of delirium tremens following his drunken debauches, previous to that in which he destroyed his wife, and consequently *knew* that intoxication would *be likely* to produce insanity. How far this fact changes the attitude of the case, is a point which deserves a careful examination, before being allowed to have a bearing on judicial decisions. If the party had known, that in his previous attacks of delirium tremens, he had attempted the life of his wife, then indeed, this opinion would not have been without some foundation, for in that case, perhaps, he might have been justly held responsible for whatever criminal acts he committed while in a state of insanity, just so far as he was responsible for the intoxication that produced it. All that Birdsell *knew* on this subject, however,

was, that indulgence in drinking, having frequently
occasioned delirium tremens, would be liable to produce a renewal of its attacks.   As to what acts he
might commit while under their influence, he knew
absolutely nothing.   It is not very clear how delirium
tremens can have a different effect on legal responsibility, from that which would follow any other form
of mental derangement resulting from habits of intemperance.   If Birdsell's habits had led to attacks of
common mania instead of delirium tremens, his
guilt, in a moral point of view, would certainly have
been no less; nor, on the hypothesis of the court
that insanity is no apology for crime, if the party
knew that intoxication would produce it, would his
legal responsibility have been diminished.   It does
not appear however, that, in ordinary cases where
insanity is pleaded in excuse for crime, the question
is ever raised whether the insanity be a consequence
of intemperate drinking, and, in the event of its being so, whether the party *knew* that such a result
might be expected.   It is not easy to resist the impression, that the opinion of the court, against the
exculpatory effects of Birdsell's insanity, was determined, in some measure, by the reprehensible character of its cause.   If his insanity had been produced
by mingling in scenes of religious excitement, by
indulging in schemes of commercial speculation, or
a more criminal species of gambling, would the
court have said it furnished no apology for crime,
because he had suffered previous attacks in consequence of exposure to the action of these same
causes ?   Probably not ; and yet if guilt is made to
consist in disregarding the lessons of experience

relative to the manner in which the insanity is produced, then the nature of its exciting causes is clearly
an immaterial circumstance. In short the opinion of
the court of Ohio conflicts with the principles laid
down by Mr. Justice Story (§ 330), and if the latter
be admitted, as they must be, undoubtedly, by every
one, so far as they relate to the causes of insanity,
the former is untenable for a moment, and therefore
it is scarcely necessary to pursue this train of reflections any farther.

§ 336. In persons who have recovered from attacks
of disease or injury of the head, drunkenness sometimes produces a temporary madness which continues
only during the drunken fit, and leaves the mind in
the possession of its habitual sanity. Is insanity a
valid excuse for criminal acts committed while under
the influence of this condition, and while liquor is
exerting its immediate effects upon the brain?
"There are many men, soldiers, who have been
severely wounded, in the head especially, who well
know that excess makes them mad ; but if such persons wilfully deprive themselves of reason, they
ought not to be excused one crime by the voluntary
perpetration of another." [1] In the opinion of Mr.
Justice Story above quoted, it is also said, that insanity is not a competent excuse for crime, if it be committed "while the party is in a fit of intoxication
and while it lasts," and the following case furnishes
an instance of the practical application of this principle.

---

[1] Paris and Fonblanque: Medical Jurisprudence, vol. iii.

§ 337. IV. William McDonough was tried and convicted, on an indictment for the murder of his wife,
before the supreme court of Massachusetts in November, 1817. It appeared in evidence, that many
years previous, the defendant had received a severe
injury of the head, in consequence of which he had
suffered occasional paroxysms of insanity, though the
general habit of his mind was sound and clear. It
appeared that they were often produced by intoxication, and there was some evidence to prove that they
sometimes occurred unconnected with any apparent
exciting cause. In one of these fits of insanity induced by drinking, and while actually under the influence of liquor, he murdered his wife. The court,
in its charge to the jury, observed, that, "if they
believed the prisoner was in a fit of lunacy when he
committed the act, he should be acquitted ; but if
they believed he was of sound mind, or, if his reason
were impaired, that it was caused by intoxication
only, the fact being proved, and no palliating circumstances existing he must be convicted."[1] If, in
using this language, the court had in view any circumstance that might be deemed to be of a palliating
character, it is not easy to see what it was, unless it
were the pathological condition resulting from the
injury of the head which rendered him peculiarly
susceptible to the effects of ardent spirits. If the
court actually did consider this a palliating circumstance, it is to be regretted that its language was not
more explicit on this point. It is very probable, that,

---

[1] Trial of William McDonough for the murder of his wife, p. 65.

in this case also, the jury were considerably influenced by the character of the exciting cause of McDonough's insanity. If it had been testified that instead of getting drunk, he was in the habit of attending religious meetings where warm and pungent appeals were addressed to his feelings ; that the excitement thus produced, occasionally degenerated into a fit of madness, in one of which he killed his wife, the jury would have acquitted him without leaving their seats. Yet the essential condition of guilt would have been the same as in the case that actually happened. "The voluntary use of a stimulus," as it is expressed by Dr. Beck, "which he was well aware would disorder his mind, fully placed him under the purview of the law."[1] It is not a satisfactory reply to this objection, that in the one case, the exciting cause is, in itself, of a commendable character, while in the other, it is in the highest degree, sinful and pernicious. Drunkenness in itself, is not by law, a crime ; and, though the moral sense of the community at the present day condemns even the moderate use of intoxicating drinks, it must be recollected that twenty years ago, and especially in the class to which McDonough belonged, such use was generally considered not only harmless but absolutely necessary to the bodily health. Had he not labored under this peculiar irritability of the brain, it is not supposed that the bloody act would have been com-

---

[1] Medical Jurisprudence, 627. In a subsequent edition of his work, however, the Doctor observes, that, in using the language above-quoted, he has "probably expressed himself too strongly," and seems inclined to retract his approval of the verdict of the jury.

mitted or even thought of, so that McDonough was virtually convicted for the consequences of a bodily infirmity.

§ 338. V. The following case related by Georget presents us with another striking illustration of mental disorder excited by the use of spirituous liquors. Vatelot, a gendarme, while passing the Place Louis Quinze, suddenly struck the sieur Chardon with his sabre. The latter turned round, and seeing a stranger brandishing a sabre over his head, asked if he knew him and what he meant. "I know you," replied Vatelot, "you are my enemy, and I will give it to you." At the same moment he aimed at him another blow, and after pursuing him a while with his drawn sword, left him. He soon met the sieur Bellon whom he struck on the head, and aimed two blows at the sieur Avenel who accompanied Bellon. The sieur Beaupied who ran to their assistance, and another person who never injured him, he also threatened; and finally, observing a young lady standing at her door, he struck her over the head with his sabre, and then fled. On trial before the court of assizes at Paris, he denied the facts, and admitted that he had been drinking, but was not drunk. He was convicted of homicide committed voluntarily, but without premeditation, and condemned to hard labor for life.[1]

§ 339. The homicidal acts of Vatelot obviously have all the characteristics, that distinguish those committed by furious maniacs. "He attacked indiscrimi-

---

[1] Discussion Medico-Legale, p. 159.

nately all whom he met," said the court, "and made four successive attempts at homicide without being moved by any of the passions characteristic of crime, but, in consequence of a fatal frenzy which impelled him to the shedding of blood whenever an opportunity offered." One of the elements of guilt in McDonough's case is wanting in this, for it does not appear that strong drink had ever produced a fit of insanity before, and thus it could not be urged that Vatelot sinned against the light of his own experience. If he had not drank enough to intoxicate him under ordinary circumstances, he had done nothing which the law or public opinion recognised to be wrong, and there was not a shadow of justice in rejecting his plea of insanity. Even if he had, are we to make no distinction, as Georget forcibly inquires, between a drunken person who commits a crime from motives of interest, such as theft, or to gratify a criminal passion existing before the intoxication, and one who, like Vatelot, becomes a murderer without interest, without motive, without any rational cause for his conduct?

§ 340. The following passage from a recent writer on criminal law, indicates, it is to be hoped, the dawn of more correct and humane sentiments on this point of medical jurisprudence. "If, either the insanity has supervened from drinking," says Mr. Alison, "without the panel's having been aware that such an indulgence in his case leads to such a consequence; or if it has arisen from the combination of drinking with a half crazy or infirm state of mind, or a previous wound or illness which rendered spirits fatal to his intellect, to a degree unusual in other men, or which could not have been anticipated, it seems inhuman to visit him with the extreme punishment which was suitable in the other case. In such a case, the proper course is to convict ; but in consideration of the degree of infirmity proved, recommend to the royal mercy." [1]

§ 341. In the present state of public opinion, it would be difficult, perhaps, to convince a jury that the wretched victims of periodical drunkenness, or of that other form of the disorder which we have illustrated (§ 329), ought not to be held responsible for their criminal acts. It would be objected probably, that these conditions are the result of habitual indulgence, and that at the utmost, the only difference between these and other drunkards is, that they are impelled to the gratification of their insatiable cravings by different degrees of violence—a circumstance which it would be mischievous to recognise in estimating the degree of criminal responsibility. The truth would be overlooked or disputed, that this irresistible propensity to excessive drinking is manifested as often, if not oftener, in temperate men, as in habitual drunkards, and that it is either a symptom of the first stage of madness, or of a temporary impairment of the mind produced by some disturbance of the cerebral circulation. The drunkenness being thus an accidental, involuntary, consequence of a maniacal state of the mind, it cannot impart the character of criminality to any action to which it may give rise. If the merchant or servant-girl whose

---

[1] Principles of the Criminal Law of Scotland, 654.

cases we have quoted from Esquirol (§§ 320, 323), had committed murder in one of their paroxysms, we should, no doubt, have had the testimony of that distinguished physician, as he has already recorded it in his writings, that they were "true monomaniacs," "not morally responsible." The other cases we have related, though differing a little from these, in some of their accidental symptoms, evidently proceeded from the same pathological causes, and if moral responsibility ceases in the former, it must equally cease in the latter.

CHAPTER XXV.

INTERDICTION.

§ 342. With respect to the kind and degree of mental impairment that warrants interdiction, there prevails the utmost diversity of opinion, and such must continue to be the case, till sounder views are entertained of the true purposes of this measure. The radical fault of speculations on this subject is, that the attention has been directed to general rules and abstract distinctions, rather than to a thorough and discriminating examination of the particular circumstances of each individual case. In the following paragraphs will be found abundant illustrations of the truth of this remark.

343. Imbeciles in the first degree cannot be justly deprived of the management of their property, on the ground of mental deficiency alone. If they have shown no disposition to squander their money on trifles, nor suffered their affairs to be grossly neglected, there can be no reasonable pretence for taking it altogether from their control and enjoyment. Neither should we be too rigid in our scrutiny of these cases. If a whole life of extravagance, or hazardous speculation, is not enough to produce the interdiction of a sound person, why should an occasional act of either in one of feeble intellect, provoke that measure ? Of course there can be no

question of its propriety when it is perfectly obvious that he is dissipating his fortune, to the great detriment of himself and of those who are dependent on him.

§ 344. Much discussion and tedious litigation have arisen from the difficulty of determining the exact measure of intellectual capacity requisite to the undisturbed enjoyment of civil rights and privileges, chiefly in consequence of losing sight of the real object before us, and pursuing a shadow of our own creating. It is a question of capacity in reference to certain ends and duties, and we are not called on to go beyond the consideration of these, in our endeavors to settle this question. The speculative opinions of the imbecile person, the little peculiarities of his conduct, his style of living and talking, and his general deportment in society, are points that require but little attention in this inquiry. Our business is with the manner in which he has conducted his affairs, and from this chiefly, we are to draw our inferences respecting his probable future conduct and capacity. And here we are not bound to institute a rigid comparison between his habits and those of people enjoying ordinary soundness and vigor of intellect. We are not warranted in stripping him of all his possessions and leaving him at the mercy of others, the moment we can fix upon a single instance in the course of his life, where he has neglected to profit by a happy turn of fortune, or has rewarded a service, or bestowed his bounties, in a manner altogether opposed to our ideas of forethought and economy. Has the individual indulged in repeated acts of extravagance, or of profitless expenditure? Has he engaged in the execution of visionary projects with reckless indifference as to the extent of his means and appliances ? Has he squandered his money on favorites, or become an instrument in the hands of designing and profligate associates for advancing their own selfish projects ? These are among the most prominent questions that require a satisfactory answer, and if they are kept steadily before us, there will be little fear of losing ourselves in the maze of perplexities which the judicial investigation of cases of imbecility frequently creates.

§ 345. These views, it will be seen, afford no countenance to the usual practice of canvassing the whole history of the imbecile person, arraying act against act, and speech against speech, and drawing from each an inference for or against his capacity of managing his own affairs in his own way. Few of those whose interests become involved in protracted litigation, are so destitute of intellect as never to conduct like persons of well-developed minds under similar circumstances. They may write sensible letters, make shrewd bargains, and converse on ordinary topics without betraying any mental deficiency, while yielding implicitly to the will of others, and committing acts of folly that can arise from nothing short of unequivocal imbecility. The popular error that imbecility is only an inferior endowment of mind considered in regard to its absolute quantity, has led people to forget that in this condition, the mental faculties may be very unequally defective ; and, therefore, that very different conclusions would be formed respecting an individual's capacity, according as the attention is exclusively directed to the manifestation of this or that faculty. Many also, who, while surrounded by their usual circle of associations, manage their slender means with the utmost prudence and economy, would prove themselves totally inadequate to the management of a large property, and be easily led, by the influence of new associates and the excitement of new desires, into habits of extravagance and dissipation.

§ 346. The little success that has attended every attempt to fix upon certain criteria as tests of that degree of imbecility which is incompatible with the management of property, and to run the line between this mental condition and that of legal capacity, is another circumstance in favor of the course here indicated. "In order to arrive at the true meaning of ' imbecility of mind,' " says Sir John Nicholl, " we may resort to what the law describes as perfect capacity, which is most correctly found in the form of pleadings used in the ecclesiastical courts, in the averment in support of a will, that the testator was of ' sound mind, memory, and understanding—talked and discoursed rationally and sensibly, and was fully capable of any rational act requiring thought, judgment, and reflection.' Here is the legal standard." [1] It may be doubted if this definition can ever be of much practical service, for no definition can be so which embraces either more or less than is strictly warranted by the exact nature of the thing defined. Many an imbecile who could not be safely trusted with the control of property for a single week, may nevertheless " talk and discourse rationally and sen-

---

[1] Ingram v. Wyatt, 1 Haggard's Eccl. Reports, 401.

sibly," so long as the conversation is confined to simple subjects that have long been familiar to the mind ; and many a man of legal capacity may be found, of whom it cannot be said that he is "fully capable of any rational act" whatever, "requiring thought, judgment and reflection." The very point to be decided is, whether the person in question, who talks and discourses so rationally and sensibly, and does so many rational acts, is or is not capable of managing his affairs ; and however much we may scrutinize the character of his intellect, the only just and accurate test of such capacity is the manner in which he has already managed his affairs. The tests of legal capacity so much sought after in imbecility, cannot be obtained, from the nature of things, because the general strength of mind is but an uncertain index of its ability when exercised on particular subjects. The ministers of the law therefore should be extremely cautious how they are moved by theoretical considerations, instead of particular facts bearing on the point at issue, in examining requests for interdiction on the ground of imbecility.

§ 347. General intellectual and general moral mania are always a sufficient cause of interdiction; for the reflective faculties are too much deranged in those disorders to discern the relations of property, or to provide the necessary arrangements for preserving and improving it. The only question is, how soon after the manifestation of the disease, are we warranted in taking this measure. Since its publicity serves to expose the patient and his family to the popular and not unfounded prejudice against insanity, and since mania, when early attended to, is cured, in the larger proportion of cases, within the first or second year, this step should be delayed, unless extraordinary reasons require immediate action, till the effect of judicious treatment has been observed. The restraint and seclusion which curative measures necessarily require, prevent the patient from engaging in business, and indeed place him in the same condition as would sickness of any other kind. No harm is done by a little delay, but the practice of taking property from its lawful possessors to place it in the control of others, who may have no other object than that of enriching themselves by their trust, the first moment the presence of madness is satisfactorily established, must lead to positive and considerable evils. So jealous is the French law of this hasty interference, that it permits nothing less than *habitual* insanity to procure interdiction. [1]

§ 348. In partial mania, Hoffbauer [2] thinks we should be governed by the nature of the predominant idea, not considering it a sufficient ground of interdiction, unless connected with the subject of property, in a manner likely to lead to its wasteful and improvident management. Such too was the opinion of Dr. Rush, [3] and a late writer [4] has contended against the opposite practice with signal ability and skill. "Mental derangement, to be a sufficient reason for interdiction," says a French jurist, [5] "should have reference to the ordinary affairs of civil life, and to

---

[1] Code civil, Art. 489.   [2] Op. cit. § 110.
[3] Lecture on Medical Jurisprudence, Philadelphia, 1811.
[4] Conolly's Indications of Insanity.
[5] Toullier, le Droit civil Français, &c., 1811.

the government of the person and property of the
individual; a man who is merely visionary, or entertains speculative notions that are palpably false,
should not be interdicted, if he manage his affairs
well enough in other respects." [1]   Georget, however, thinks that monomaniacs are not to be trusted,
and that we can never be sure that the predominant
idea may not, by means of some mental associations,
lead to the dissipation of their fortunes. Accordingly, he is dissatisfied with the decision of the
tribunal of La Seine, who rejected a petition for the
interdiction of M. Selves, a celebrated advocate,
although admitted to be a "meddler in his family,
litigious in society, impertinent towards the magistrates, vainly profuse in his expenditures, and subject
to some illusions." [2]   This distrust of the insane of
whatever description, is nowhere more strongly implied than in the habitual practice of Great Britain
at the present day.   One finds it difficult to believe
on what slight grounds, interdiction is there every
day procured,—a measure, that with the ostensible
purpose of protecting the interests of the insane
party, is too often, in reality, designed to promote
the selfish views of relatives and friends.   A kind
and degree of mental impairment that has never
obscured the patient's knowledge of his relative situation, never altered his disposition to be kind and
useful to those around him, never weakened his
enjoyment of social pleasures, and never affected

---

[1] Toullier, le Droit civil Français, &c. 1811.
[2] Des Maladies Mentales, p. 108.

his capacity to manage his concerns with his usual prudence, has been repeatedly deemed a sufficient reason for depriving him of the use and enjoyment of his own property, and subjecting him to all the disabilities the law can impose. Dr. Conolly speaks of a gentleman on whose account his family applied for a commission of lunacy, because he had become possessed with the idea, that the queen of England was in love with him. Yet this person conducted himself very well in most of the offices of life, and on one occasion after this application was made, while dining with a party of friends in company with the lord chancellor, he contributed so remarkably to the enjoyment of the day by his polite, agreeable and amusing manner, that this functionary could not help expressing to him how much he had been gratified by his introduction to him, and how utterly absurd it now appeared to him, to have ever given credit to the story of his delusion. This was enough to produce its avowal from the patient, and the issuing of the commission from the lord chancellor. The sequel furnished a striking comment on the injustice of this act ; for the insane gentleman gave so much assistance to those entrusted with the management of his affairs, that he was the means of their getting over difficulties which, without his aid, would have been insurmountable ; and in the end, he was actually, if not formally, constituted the steward of his own estate. It is well known that a monomaniac in England, who fancied himself duke of Hexham and was accordingly interdicted, became the agent of his own committee for the management of his own estate, and did the duties of the office, for a time at least, not incorrectly.

§ 349. The case of Mr. Edward Davies, which engrossed the attention of the English public, a few years since, being, says Dr. Gooch, "by far the most important lunatic cause which has been tried in our time," furnishes a striking illustration of the manner in which these things are managed in England. Mr. Edward Davies was born of humble parents, and though particularly shy and reserved among his school-fellows, he was generally considered sharp and intelligent. On leaving school, he commenced the business of a tea-dealer in London, and by indefatigable industry and cautious management, rapidly became rich. It appears that his health, at best, was delicate, and that he suffered much from dyspepsia and nervous excitement. He was fond of reading medical books; and, like most persons who indulge in such a taste, was fanciful about his complaints and subject to false alarms. The defects of his early education, he endeavored to remedy, by reading what he took to be the best authors, and was often guilty of making a ridiculous display of his acquirements, by making long quotations which he would spout with a theatrical air. He was of a remarkably timid and yielding disposition, to such a degree as to be completely subjected to the authority of his mother. Though he was twenty-seven years of age, and managing an extensive and lucrative business, she would not allow him to carry any money in his pocket, nor to spend the most trifling sum without her permission. He dared not go to the play, nor leave the house for a few hours, without asking her leave. She was particularly at great pains to prevent his meeting young women, lest, in the event of

his marriage, she might be displaced from the control
of his conduct, and the command of his purse; and
she took various opportunities of inducing him to give
considerable sums of money to different branches of
her family. At the age of twenty-seven, he grew
restive under the maternal restraints, and made many
attempts to emancipate himself. He offered to leave
the shop to his mother and take his own property
away; or to give her seven thousand pounds, on her
consenting to leave the concern; but she was not to
be got rid of at that price. The incessant state of
contention at last seriously impaired his health and
his mental tranquillity, and on the first of July, 1829,
he applied to Mr. Lawrence, the surgeon. He told
this gentleman a long story about his health and his
tea-trade; and at another interview, he recited
poetry and expressed a strong antipathy to his
mother and several relations. Mr. Lawrence considered him of unsound mind, but thought that if he
could be reconciled to his mother and family, the
disease would be at an end—that his antipathy to his
mother was his chief delusion.

§ 350. About this time, he applied to Dr. Latham,
claiming his protection. His discourse was wild and
rambling, and his manner strange and excited. He
told the doctor in a sort of whisper, that he had a
tale to relate of the greatest horror, and then flung
himself away and stalked into the middle of the room.
He appeared very apprehensive lest he might be
overheard, and begged that he might lock the doors
and close the windows. He spoke of his wealth and
his trade, and quoted poetry largely, using great
gesticulation and throwing his arms about. Several

times he asked if he looked insane, and on leaving the house, he said; "If you fail (in his promise to call on him) dread the vengeance of a madman; for I carry a loaded pistol." Dr. Latham thought him insane, though not prepared to recommend that he should be shut up as an acknowledged lunatic.

Shortly after this, he left his own house and went to spend the night at Furnival Inn, on the third of August. About one o'clock in the night, he rang the bell, and told the waiter that there were thieves in the house; that he heard them snapping off pistols, and striking a light. On being remonstrated with by the waiter, on the impropriety of his ringing the bell, and thus disturbing the lodgers, he said he was sorry for it, went upon his knees, and humbly begged his pardon.

§ 351. It must be borne in mind, that on the same days on which Dr. Latham, Mr. Lawrence, and others, saw him in his most explosive state, his friends who had known him long, passed hours with him; and though he was ill and terrified, he appeared to them quite himself, and as equal as ever he had been to give directions about his shop affairs.

Indeed, the very persons who were trying to confine him as unfit to take care of his business, were themselves consulting him about the management of that business.

§ 352. Mr. Davies was shortly after this removed to a private mad-house, where he remained till the end of December, when he was liberated by the verdict of the jury. Here his agitation subsided, his incoherence diminished almost to nothing; and the only remaining grounds for believing him a lunatic, were his antipathy to his mother, and certain suspicions that were considered to be delirious. Nevertheless, a commission of lunacy was granted by the lord chancellor, which finally resulted in restoring him to liberty, and the management of his property. The evidence of the physicians, who were sent expressly for the purpose of examining Mr. Davies, at various interviews, and who pronounced him to be mad, is worthy of a little notice, inasmuch, as they present the grounds on which, in the year 1829, the most eminent physicians for diseases of the mind shut up patients in mad-houses, among the English.

§ 353. Sir George Tuthill testified, that he was of unsound mind, at the period of his last visit; principally, because he spoke indignantly of the manner in which he had been treated by his family. His additional reasons for thinking him insane, and unable to manage his affairs, were his learning to box, his purchasing a fowl for ten shillings, and his saying that he could weep over his little rabbits, which he had not seen for six weeks.

Dr. Algernon Frampton testified, that he could not consider him sane on the seventh of December, because he would not admit himself to have been insane on the eighth of August. He thought there was a delusion in his mind as to his mother's conduct, though he admitted there would be no delusion, if his mother had interfered as Davies described, and as other witnesses testified. He thought that the purchase of a certain estate for 6000 guineas was in itself an act of insanity, considering his circumstances, though he admitted that he knew nothing of his circumstances. A man of business, he thought, ought not to lock up so much of his capital. He never inquired how Mr. Davies managed his business, though he declared that he was incapable of managing it.

Mr. Haslam testified, that he was induced to consider him insane, from his manner of complaining of the dirty habits of the keepers of the establishment where he was confined. He said decidedly, that as long as his morbid hostility remained against his mother, it was not safe for him to go at large.

§ 354. In opposition to this evidence—and it is but a small portion of what might be given—it may be well to exhibit a specimen or two of that given by Mr. Davies's medical witnesses. Dr. Macmichael who had been sent down by the lord chancellor to examine into the state of his mind, satisfactorily showed that Mr. Davies's peculiar notions and views, which had been considered by many as delusions, either did not exist at all, or proved upon examination, to be perfectly rational and proper. In attributing his prosperity to the favor of providence, which had been mentioned as one of his delusions, he said he did not mean immediate or special interference, but that general providence which regulates human affairs. His boast of having improved the revenue by his biddings, which had also been imputed to him as a delusion, he explained by saying that there was a certain kind of tea that was now almost given away; that if he bid higher than others, the duty would be increased, and that thus he should put money into the pocket of government. He showed, that instead of sacrificing his property by this course, he realized a large sum of money in a very short time. Dr. Macmichael was not willing to admit that his learning pugilism, or carrying pistols, was any evidence of unsoundness of mind, for he might have had good reason for doing both.

§ 355. Dr. Mackinnon, who was connected by marriage with the family of Mr. Davies, and had visited him several times during his confinement, thought him, from the first interview to the last, capable of managing himself and his affairs. He showed that many of his peculiar habits and manners, which had given rise to the idea of insanity, he had always manifested when in good health. His letters, which, from being full of quotations and puns, were thought to indicate disordered mind, he showed were not different, in that respect, from those he wrote long before insanity was imputed to him. He conversed with him freely on the affairs of his family, and his remarks upon his mother's interference were rational, just, and free from excitement. His inquiry into the imputed delusions, ended in the same result as Dr. Macmichael's. In particular, he did not consider his hostility to his mother as a delusion, for, from the son's account, there was good reason for it. On a variety of other subjects, his discourse was calm and rational.

§ 356. It certainly would not be strange, if this case should induce every one to adopt the conclusion of Dr. Gooch, that "it ought to be made punishable, by heavy fine and imprisonment, to deprive a man of his liberty for any cause excepting mischievousness to others and to himself, and the parties who commit such outrages ought to be prosecuted at the public expense." [1]

§ 357. This case is not calculated to recommend the opinion of those, who look on the slightest mental aberration as a sufficient ground of interdiction. The principle to be followed here is precisely that, which we have indicated as applicable to cases of imbecility. Instead of puzzling ourselves with vain attempts to guage the depth and breadth of the absolute capacity of the mind, our duty is simply to ascertain if the individual has been guilty of any instances of gross improvidence, of expenditure beyond his means, or for objects unsuited to his station and pursuits. If it be found that he has, then interdiction is implicitly required by a regard to his own and the interests of those who are dependent on him for support, or entertain rational expectations of being benefited by his wealth. If he has not, it is not very clear how his property can be taken from his control, without deeply violating the first principles of civil liberty. If no one doubts that the mental operations in monomania may be perfectly sound, except within a certain very narrow circle, why should it be a matter of surprise, that ideas of property should sometimes be among those which are unaffected by the influence of the disorder ? To deprive a person, laboring under a partial mania that does not involve his notions of property, of the natural right of controlling and disposing of his own for-

---

[1] The facts of the above case are taken from an article written, it is said, by the late Dr. Gooch, in the London Quarterly Review, vol. xlii.

tune, is as unjust and irrational, as it would be to inflict upon a felon convicted of theft, the penalties attached to the violation of every article in the criminal code. If, too, we interdict one monomaniac, whose derangement is limited to a single subject, we are bound in consistency to proceed till we have included all, from him who believes he has lost his rational soul, to the poor hypochondriac who imagines his legs are made of glass, or that a fish has taken up its abode in his stomach. The mischief that would arise from such a course of disqualification, may be easily enough conceived, without the aid of any more particular description. Even when the hallucination has reference to property, as the idea for instance, that the individual possesses immense wealth, or that every ship which enters the harbor is his and freighted with his goods, we are not too hastily to strip him of what is really his own, for he might, nevertheless, in the management of it, evince the most commendable prudence and economy. It is a remarkable, but not an uncommon fact, that monomaniacs often make no practical application of their insane notions to their own conduct or concerns, but continue to manage both, as if no such delusion existed.

§ 358. In the progress of dementia, there always comes a period sooner or later, when interdiction is required, wherever the patient has much property, or conflicting interests are involved in its disposition. To decide when this period has actually arrived, is generally a difficult and responsible duty. To avoid the disagreeable alternative of favoring the designs of selfish relatives, which would be promoted by the interdiction and seclusion of the old man, by premature interference, or of delaying proper measures, for fear of being thought accessory to schemes of fraud and oppression, until too late to be of any service, is to gain the happy medium which all should seek, but which few perhaps are successful enough to obtain. The difficulties which medical men have to encounter, who are consulted in such cases, are graphically described by Dr. Conolly. "An old gentleman," he says, "whose intellects are so impaired that he does not know whether he has received his rents or not, or who is unable to arrange his own dress decently, and requires, when up stairs, all the attention of a child, is seen by the medical practitioner, for the purpose of its being ascertained how far interference with his property is justifiable. The very servant who is hourly robbing him, takes care to send him down very carefully drest. The mere effect of habit is to cause the patient himself to be more guarded and exact in his manner and words in the presence of a stranger ; he feels under a temporary and a wholesome restraint ; asks and answers common questions as well as most other old men, and is perfectly correct in his deportment. Two very serious evils may ensue. If the practitioner is unacquainted with the varieties of the mind and their tendencies ; and imagines that insanity and sanity cannot be mixed up together in the mind as they are in the body ; he feels a degree of conscientious horror concerning any interference with an old gentleman who may be a little weak, but who, he is quite convinced, is no more mad than any of those about him. He turns his thoughts to the probable motives of interest, in the children or the friends, and, determining not to warrant any kind of restraint, inwardly applauds his own sagacity and incorruptibility. The friends, now more afraid to interfere than before, allow the old man to do as he likes, and he sets off, and gets married to a worthless and designing woman, or he alters his will in favor of some unprincipled person, or finds his way to some neighboring town, where he becomes a disgraceful spectacle, and gets robbed of his money and illtreated ; or perhaps he falls into the pond, and is drowned ; all the world then exclaiming against the heartlessness and inattention of those about him, and the unaccountable supineness of those who were consulted about the case. Thus, the view of a very plain and easy duty is, not unfrequently, obscured by prevalent opinions respecting the nature of insanity, and respecting the measures which insanity is supposed to render indispensable. If the patient whom I have described, as conducting himself so satisfactorily in a short and common conversation, is left to his own thought for a little time, and his attention is not excited by those about him, his state will become evident enough. He will be seen to be wandering, and lost in his reflections, and will perhaps rise up, and endeavor to make his way out of the room, but without seeming to remember the situation of the door. Or he will declare his intention to set off on a long journey, or by many slight indications show that his mind is reduced to imbecility. In some, the effects of the recent restraint of a stranger's presence may be more permanent than in others ; but half an hour or a few hours at the utmost, will suffice to show the state of the case. The decision is important, and due time must be allowed for it. If one visit is not sufficient, the visit should be repeated, until the practitioner can give a clear and decided opinion.

" But now comes the other danger. A sanguine practitioner sees the undoubted signs of folly and weakness in the old man, and forgetting that they are as much the effects of age as are the unsteadiness of his limbs, and the dullness of his hearing, pronounces the patient to be mad ; and to gratify persons of no feeling or compunction, consigns the poor patient to strange hands, and causes him to spend the little remnant of his days away from his own house, and unseen by any of those whom his former care perhaps preserved, and whom his wealth will enrich." [1]

§ 359. The principles we have indicated, as proper to guide us in deciding questions of interdiction in the various forms of imbecility and mania, are not to be so implicitly relied on here, because the unfitness of the patient to manage his own concerns is often proved, not so much by specific acts of extravagance or folly, as by his subjection to the will of those who are deliberately and cautiously preying upon his substance. We may also bear in mind, that although we take from him the control of his property, even while his faculties are sound enough to make him capable of performing the duty himself, yet we are only prematurely taking a measure which a few weeks or months will generally render absolutely necessary.

---

[1] Indications of Insanity, 440.

§ 360. It is to be regretted that in cases of insanity, where the mental disorder does not seem sufficient to warrant so extreme a measure as complete interdiction, while it occasions reasonable doubts of the ability to manage property with ordinary prudence, our laws have established no inferior grades of restraint. The civil code of France ordains that "in rejecting a demand for interdiction, the court may nevertheless, if circumstances require it, debar the defendant from appearing in suits, making contracts, borrowing, receiving payment for debts or giving a discharge, alienating or pledging his property, without the aid of a council which shall be appointed in the same judgment."[1] It would be well, if something of this kind always found a place in the legal regulations of the insane.

§ 361. Restraint is a measure entirely distinct from that of interdiction, and neither should be considered, as they sometimes are, necessarily dependent on the other. On no point in the whole range of the subject under consideration, is it more necessary that we entertain clear and definite notions, than on that of the restraint of the insane, because, while often essential to the restoration or comfort of the patient, and to the safety of the community, it is, at the same time, liable to the most serious and shameful abuses. In this country, it is true, the public attention has scarcely been attracted to this subject, but either human nature is very different here from what it is in other countries, or we shall, at some

---

[1] Code Civil, Art., 499.

time or other, have to deplore the abuses which they are now anxiously seeking to remedy, unless, admonished by the lesson there set before us, we prevent them altogether by suitable and seasonable legislation.

§ 362. In confining the insane, we have in view one or more of the following objects; first, their own restoration to health; secondly, their comfort and well-being merely, with little expectation of their cure; thirdly, the security of society. When the restoration of the patient is the object sought for, as it always is or should be, in recent cases, no unnecessary restrictions should be imposed on this measure. The simple fact of the recency of the case should be sufficient, when properly attested, to warrant his seclusion, if it be deemed necessary to his cure. It is in that large class of patients, whose disorder is of too long standing to admit of any rational expectations of cure, that restraint is most in danger of being abused. Among the reasons generally offered for taking this measure, we hear, perhaps, that the patient is destroying the peace of his family by constant ill-temper, or by overbearing or furious deportment, or that he cannot receive in his own house the attentions which his situation requires. The idea of depriving a person of his liberty, merely because certain other persons who would be benefited by such a step, say that he is mad, is of so monstrous a nature, that one finds it difficult to believe that it has ever been actually carried into practice. Perhaps, in this country, it never has; if so, however, it is not because it has been prevented by the salutary restraints of the law,

which, in many states, at least, is utterly silent respecting it. It may not have entered into the minds
of grasping and ill-natured relatives, that removal
and confinement present a readier means of obtaining the control of property on which their affections
are placed, than the slow and uncertain effects of
disease or old age ; but it would be unwise to act as
if this state of innocence were to continue always.
In Great Britain, where the confinement of the insane
has been the subject of much parliamentary inquiry,
and various acts and amendments to acts have been
passed, for the purpose of preventing the abuses that
from time to time have been brought to light, this
measure has in consequence become so hedged round
with checks and precautions, that it would seem
difficult, if not impossible, that it should become a
means of injustice and cruelty. How far the object
proposed has been obtained, may be sufficiently understood from the testimony of one whose ample experience rendered him well qualified to give it. " It
is a miserable thing to come away from a lunatic
house, as I have many times done, with a conviction
that there were individuals in it, whose liberation
and a proper superintendence would turn wretched-
ness into comfort, without endangering the interests
of any human being ; persons unfit, perhaps, to return to their families, or even to see them every
day; but yet alive to warm affections, never more
to be indulged ; longing, as parents long, to see the
faces of their children ; but, in consequence of an
infirmity of temper, doubtless of a morbid kind, and
requiring superintendence, subjected to live and die
in a place which was to them a prison, without a

friend with whom they could unreservedly converse." [1]

§ 363. It would be out of place here to detail the provisions of such a legislative act, as would place the restraint of the insane as far as possible beyond the reach of abuse, but its general features may be stated in a few words. The right of keeping the insane in confinement should be obtained by license from the government, which should impose such conditions as will best promote their welfare. It should appoint a board of commissioners, two or more of whom should be medical men of some practical knowledge of insanity, whose duty it should be to visit, from time to time, houses licensed for the reception of the insane, examine their accommodations, the moral and medical treatment made use of, and every other point in which the welfare of the inmates is deeply concerned, and submit their report to some branch of the government. They should have the power of discharging any patient whom they may consider unjustly confined, or capable of enjoying himself more at his own home. No patient should be admitted without a certificate of two or more physicians, one of whom should be an *expert*, countersigned by the selectmen of the town or mayor of the city in which the patient resides, that the individual is insane, and is unable to receive at home that care or attention which is necessary to his restoration, or to his temporary comfort and final welfare. The superintendents of these houses should be re-

---

[1] Conolly: Indications of Insanity, 438.

quired to keep a register, in which should be noted
the names of the patients, the date of their admission, the character of their insanity, by whom their
certificates are signed, and such other particulars as
may be deemed necessary by the commissioners.

§ 364. The third object above-mentioned, as
sought by the confinement of the insane, is the
security of society. By the laws of Maine, any two
justices of the peace are authorized to commit to the
house of correction any person within their county,
who, they are convinced, is lunatic, and so furiously
mad, as to render it dangerous to the peace or the
safety of the good people, for him to go at large,
there to be detained till he or she shall be restored
to his or her mind, or otherwise delivered by due
course of law.[1] It may naturally excite some surprise that so grave a question, as that of the perpetual imprisonment of a person, should not have
been entrusted to the decision of a higher set of

---

[1] The same was the law of Massachusetts, until quite recently ; but
by the laws now in force in that state, all lunatics, " so furiously mad
as to render it manifestly dangerous to the peace and safety of the community, that they should be at large," are, upon complaint made to the
Judges of Probate in the several counties, to be committed to the State
Lunatic Hospital at Worcester; and, " whenever request for that purpose shall be made by the person complained against," the Judge is
obliged to order a jury to be summoned, to try the question of insanity.
By a law passed April 13, 1836, two justices, one of the quorum, are
authorized to commit to the house of correction, any " idiot or lunatic
or insane " person, "not being furiously mad; " and, at this date,
March 20, 1838, a bill is pending before the Legislature, giving the
right of trial by jury, upon request of the person complained against, in
those cases also. After the passing of this law, no person in Massachusetts can be confined by process of law, as an idiot, lunatic or insane person, without the right of a trial by jury.

functionaries than a couple of justices of the peace. When, in addition to this, it is considered that no plan of inquiry is laid down for them to pursue, nor a single hint to guide them in their examination ; that they are left to summon only what witnesses they please, and with as much or as little publicity as they please, we are forced to believe that it is not in human nature, that such power should escape frequent and flagrant abuses.[1] Temporary confinement is all that the immediate security of society requires, and therefore the term of imprisonment, for which justices should have the power to commit, should be limited to a few weeks or months. If it be deemed necessary that this term should be protracted, it should be only by order of the judge of probate or one of the justices of the courts of law, whose duty it should be to examine the circumstances of the case, and if he decide in favor of farther imprisonment for another term which should be fixed by law, to ascertain by proper inquiries from time to time, whether any change in the mental condition of the patient will warrant his release before the end of such term.

---

[1] It is stated in the first annual report of the Trustees of the State Lunatic Hospital of Massachusetts, that under a similar provision of law then in force in that state, an idiot had been committed who could neither stand nor walk, who was unable to extend the lower limbs from the closest possible contraction towards the body, and who had but little muscular strength even in his arms. *Reports and other documents relative to the State Lunatic Hospital*, p. 42.

INDEX.